Educational Assessment for the Elementary and Middle School Classroom

Second Edition

Gary D. Borich
University of Texas at Austin

Martin L. Tombari
University of Denver

PEARSON

Merrill
Prentice Hall

Upper Saddle River, New Jersey
Columbus, Ohio

Library of Congress Cataloging-in-Publication Data

Borich, Gary D.
   Educational assessment for the elementary and middle school classroom /
   Gary D. Borich and Martin L. Tombari.—2nd ed.
     p. cm.
   Rev. ed. of: Authentic assessment in the classroom / Martin L. Tombari,
   Gary D. Borich. © 1999.
   Includes bibliographical references (p.) and index.
   ISBN 0-13-094789-X
   1. Educational tests and measurements. 2. Examinations—Design and
   construction. 3. Examinations—Validity. 4. Motivation in education. I. Tombari,
   Martin L. II. Tombari, Martin L. Authentic assessment in the classroom.
   III. Title.
   LB3051.T595 2004
   372.126—dc21   2003011224

Vice President and Executive Publisher: Jeffery W. Johnston
Publisher: Kevin M. Davis
Editorial Assistant: Autumn Crisp
Production Editor: Mary Harlan
Production Coordinator: Karen Ettinger, The GTS Companies/York, PA Campus
Design Coordinator: Diane C. Lorenzo
Text Design and Illustrations: The GTS Companies/York, PA Campus
Cover Design: Mark Shumaker
Cover Image: Getty One
Production Manager: Laura Messerly
Director of Marketing: Ann Castel Davis
Marketing Manager: Amy June
Marketing Coordinator: Tyra Poole

This book was set in Garamond by The GTS Companies/York, PA Campus. It was printed and bound by R. R. Donnelley & Sons Company. The cover was printed by The Lehigh Press, Inc.

Pearson Prentice Hall™ is a trademark of Pearson Education, Inc.
Pearson® is a registered trademark of Pearson plc
Prentice Hall® is a registered trademark of Pearson Education, Inc.
Merrill® is a registered trademark of Pearson Education, Inc.

Pearson Education Ltd.
Pearson Education Singapore, Pte. Ltd.
Pearson Education Canada, Ltd.
Pearson Education—Japan

Pearson Education Australia Pty. Limited
Pearson Education North Asia Ltd
Pearson Educación de Mexico, S.A. de C.V.
Pearson Education Malaysia, Pte. Ltd.

10 9 8 7 6 5 4 3 2 1
ISBN 0-13-094789-X

Preface

Two decades ago the National Commission on Excellence in Education published a report critical of American schools titled *A Nation at Risk* (National Commission on Excellence in Education, 1983). That report cataloged some of our schools' failures, one of which was an inability to teach children how to think critically and apply what they have learned. Other reports followed, providing the impetus for educational reform that continues today.

The essence of these reform movements has been an attempt to have teachers teach based on the way the learner's mind works rather than on traditional views of learning that reflect solely a "mechanical" or behavioral view of human competence. In the last two decades teaching and learning have changed considerably, replacing a more mechanistic "drill and practice" view of learning with one that could embrace the excitement, thirst, and motivation for learning that all children start out with in life. These changes have led to a new view of learning and assessment in which learners are provided the opportunity to construct their own sense of what is being learned by building connections or relationships among the ideas and facts being taught.

Philosophy of This Text

This new view of learning and assessment (Bruer, 1993) derives from nearly three decades of research by cognitive scientists. From studies of how the mind works, these scientists have accumulated a wealth of information about how learners become proficient in knowledge domains such as reading, language arts, social studies, science, and mathematics.

Today learning is seen as an active process by which learners construct "knowledge structures" or "mental representations." They not only construct these structures when teachers teach subject matter content, but they also construct the strategies needed for thinking about information and ways to become consciously aware of and improve the use of these strategies.

When teachers assess learning today, they can no longer simply test for knowledge with objective-type formats. Those tests, when taken alone, support a model of knowledge as collections of bits of information demanding fast responses in which the task is to find the correct answer rather than to engage in interpretation, critical thinking, and problem solving. Today, teachers must have a broader menu of tools to assess how a learner organizes new information, the strategies that a learner employs while doing this, and the metacognitive skills that a learner uses while consciously employing learning strategies.

Thus, a new technology of classroom assessment has arisen alongside traditional assessment methods. This book is an attempt to give the elementary and middle school teacher a comprehensive menu of assessment techniques for assessing not only what learners know, but also how they think, perform, and apply what they know in authentic, real-world contexts. This text is a gateway—a bridge between the old and the new. It provides the beginning teacher with a foundation of not only how to assess a learner's knowledge base with traditional objective-type tests and essays, but also how to assess a learner's declarative and procedural knowledge, cognitive and metacognitive strategies, skill in transferring knowledge to new contexts, and habits of mind by observing and recording what their learners actually can do when performing in authentic ways within the natural ongoing context of the classroom.

Organization of This Text

With this goal in mind, we have woven a number of themes throughout the fabric of this book, making it unique and timely to new instructional methods and assessment techniques. These themes are

- Motivation for learning and doing well in school occurs when assessments are learning experiences.
- The skills that are assessed should be the skills that are practiced in class and required in subsequent learning.
- Students become more engaged in learning when assessments represent challenging tasks encountered in real-world contexts.
- A good assessment measures not only the products of learning but also the cognitive—or thinking—processes the learner uses to create them.
- Assessments of specific subject matter should occur over time, during which the role of the teacher is to help the learner improve.

The first four chapters set the framework for these assessment practices. We call this framework "authentic learning assessment" because it attempts as much as possible to capture learner performance in natural classroom settings and with meaningful tasks that are steppingstones to subsequent learning.

In chapter 1 we present the highlights of recent advances in how learners learn, establishing the need for authentic learning assessment and its link with students' motivation to learn. The theme of this chapter is that learners will become more motivated to learn the more assessment practices measure their ability to perform and apply what was taught with tasks and activities that are meaningful to subsequent learning and to their world outside the classroom. In this chapter we show that how you engage your learners' memory—either as a static storehouse of facts or as a dynamic and fluid experience that can be stimulated into action by your assessment—will be important to your interpretation of what your students have learned. In this chapter we show you how your assessments can unleash the constructive and intuitive nature of your learners' own contribution to the learning process, and that your learners' motivation to learn is linked as much to how you assess as it is to how you teach.

Motivation to learn comes from a connection between teaching and assessment. The term *authenticity* characterizes this unbroken bond. In chapter 2 we review the importance of this bond by describing the science of cognitive learning and its principal findings aimed at teaching learners how to think and how they should be assessed. It demonstrates that thinking, especially higher order thinking, is best taught and assessed in your classroom in the context of real-world activities and tasks that your learners will be expected to perform outside the classroom.

Chapter 3 shows you how to select assessment goals and determine the learning outcomes you will measure. Establishing an assessment goal involves choosing the proper balance among norm-referenced, criterion-referenced, and growth-referenced assessments and establishing how you will set expectations, make a diagnosis, monitor learning, and assign grades. This chapter introduces the *Taxonomy of Educational Objectives* by Bloom and colleagues and Gagné's *Learning Hierarchies* to help you plan assessments. And, since standardized tests will continue to be an important feature of the school landscape, we discuss their strengths and limitations. In chapter 11, we return to this topic to show you how to accurately interpret standardized tests for students and parents and use them with your teacher-made assessments to guide what and how you will teach.

Your classroom assessments will accomplish their mission if they meet standards of validity and reliability. Chapter 4 presents both traditional and emerging definitions of reliability and validity. These will help you address two related questions: (a) How do you know that your assessments of student learning are measuring what you want? and (b) how do you know that your assessments of student learning are dependable?

Chapters 5 through 10 demonstrate how you can assess important learning outcomes using a variety of student tasks, including oral performances, problem-solving activities, products, and portfolios. Chapters 5 and 6 cover how to assess your learners' knowledge base with selected-response (objective) and constructed-response (short-answer and essay) tests. You will learn in chapter 5 how to construct measures that reliably and validly assess factual knowledge, simple understanding, and knowledge organization using objective-type formats. And, in chapter 6 you will learn how to measure these behaviors with short-answer, essay, and open-book questions, dialectical journals, and concept maps. Chapter 7 describes how your learners acquire procedural knowledge (knowledge about how to do things) and the most appropriate ways to assess this type of learning. Chapters 8, 9, and 10 explain how to authentically measure higher order learning outcomes within the natural context of your class activities. Specifically, chapter 8 shows how to assess problem-solving strategies with observational tools; chapter 9 demonstrates how to assess deep understanding with performance assessments; and chapter 10 details how to plan and assess genuine achievement using portfolios.

Because standardized assessments play such an important role at the national, state, and school district level, in chapter 11 we present examples of their reporting formats and interpretation. Most important, however, this chapter is about how the results from standardized tests can work in harmony with the information provided by your classroom assessments to monitor student performance, inform your instructional decisions, and identify learning problems. We also show in this chapter what you can do to prepare your students for standardized tests. Finally, because grading is an important goal of classroom assessment, in chapter 12 we explain and illustrate how to construct an overall grading plan and illustrate various types of reporting methods.

Applications to Practice in This Text

Embedded within each chapter of this text are classroom applications in which students are asked to stop, reflect, and apply what they have just read to a lesson or unit that they will be teaching. To help the reader make these transitions from text to classroom, real-life examples, often conveyed through the words and deeds of an experienced teacher, appear in boxes adjacent to the application. Then, at the end of each chapter students will find additional activities and questions for practice and discussion that review chapter content and make further applications to the elementary and middle school curriculum.

This book is written specifically for the elementary and middle school teacher. Its goal is to avoid "pie-in-the-sky" theorizing and to get straight to the heart of what elementary and middle school teachers actually do every day to assess learners in their K through 8 classrooms. To further accomplish this goal, this text illustrates each method of assessment with subject-matter content taken from state and national curriculum standards for Grades K through 2, 3 through 5, and 6 through 8 in the areas of reading/language arts, social studies, science, mathematics, and health. These Lesson Contexts, 180 in total, placed at the conclusion of each chapter, represent examples of actual lesson content and assessment questions that illustrate and apply each of the assessment practices discussed in the preceding chapter for assessing basic knowledge (chapters 5 and 6), procedural knowledge (chapter 7), problem solving (chapter 8), deep understanding (chapter 9), and portfolios (chapter 10). These content examples demonstrate each method of assessment in the context of subjects, themes, and topics that are actually taught in the K to 2, 3 to 5, and 6 to 8 curriculum.

In this manner, each chapter links assessment with the content children are actually taught at each grade. Our intent is to ground assessment with practical examples of what is actually taught and how it can be assessed in authentic classroom contexts. We strive to excite teachers about the possibilities for teaching and assessing knowledge, understanding, and performance at their specific grade levels. We want to help teachers articulately communicate what has been learned to parents, learners, and school administrators.

Acknowledgments

We would like to thank the reviewers who provided invaluable comments and suggestions. They are Paula J. Arvedson, California State University, Los Angeles; Cecelia Benelli, Western Illinois University; Carol S. Christy, Columbia College; John R. Criswell, Edinboro University; Craig Mertler, Bowling Green State University; Ruth Struyk, Northern Illinois University; and Robert A. Wiggins, Oakland University.

Gary Borich
Marty Tombari

Educator Learning Center: An Invaluable Online Resource

Merrill Education and the Association for Supervision and Curriculum Development (ASCD) invite you to take advantage of a new online resource, one that provides access to the top research and proven strategies associated with ASCD and Merrill—the Educator Learning Center. At **www.EducatorLearningCenter.com** you will find resources that will enhance your students' understanding of course topics and of current educational issues, in addition to being invaluable for further research.

HOW THE EDUCATOR LEARNING CENTER WILL HELP YOUR STUDENTS BECOME BETTER TEACHERS

With the combined resources of Merrill Education and ASCD, you and your students will find a wealth of tools and materials to better prepare them for the classroom.

RESEARCH

- More than 600 articles from the ASCD journal *Educational Leadership* discuss everyday issues faced by practicing teachers.
- A direct link on the site to Research Navigator™ gives students access to many of the leading education journals, as well as extensive content detailing the research process.
- Excerpts from Merrill Education texts give your students insights on important topics of instructional methods, diverse populations, assessment, classroom management, technology, and refining classroom practice.

CLASSROOM PRACTICE

- Hundreds of lesson plans and teaching strategies are categorized by content area and age range.
- Case studies and classroom video footage provide virtual field experience for student reflection.
- Computer simulations and other electronic tools keep your students abreast of today's classrooms and current technologies.

LOOK INTO THE VALUE OF EDUCATOR LEARNING CENTER YOURSELF

Preview the value of this educational environment by visiting **www.EducatorLearningCenter.com** and clicking on "Demo." For a free 4-month subscription to the Educator Learning Center in conjunction with this text, simply contact your Merrill/Prentice Hall sales representative.

Brief Contents

Contents

NOTE: Every effort has been made to provide accurate and current Internet information in this book. However, the Internet and information posted on it are constantly changing; therefore; it is inevitable that some of the Internet addresses listed in this textbook will change.

The Purpose of Classroom Assessment

Promoting Learning

Classroom assessment should promote learning. Medical tests promote health. The diagnostics that your local auto mechanic runs help your car run smoothly. Likewise your neighborhood electrician and plumber have testing tools that help to keep your home in working order. Similarly, because learning is what classrooms are all about, it stands to reason that classroom assessments should promote learning also.

But this isn't always the case, for two reasons. For one, teachers often assess more to assign grades than to help them determine what to teach. In other words, classroom assessments may be used more for summative than for formative purposes. **Summative assessment**[1] is conducted for the purpose of assigning a grade or rank to classroom learners. Many classroom assessments do this well. **Formative assessment**, on the other hand, is conducted to help diagnose classroom learning problems and to suggest ways to overcome them. Why aren't formative assessments used more frequently in the classroom? The answer brings us to another reason why classroom assessments don't always promote learning.

Formative assessments improve learning only if they are based on valid information about how learning takes place. Until recently, there has been an absence of models of how higher order thinking and learning takes place in the minds of your learners that could serve as a roadmap for formative assessments that promote classroom learning. The models of learning that have influenced formative assessments until recently have been models that view learning as the accumulation of facts. We now know that the problem solving, decision making, and critical thinking we want to promote in classrooms require far more than the accumulation of facts.

The formative assessments that we describe in this book promote learning in two ways. First, they provide evidence to teachers about the progress their learners

---

[1]Bold-faced terms appear in the Glossary at the end of the text for review and study.

are making toward becoming mature thinkers and learners. As you will see in this chapter, good thinking involves not only knowing a lot, but also being able to organize knowledge, being aware of oneself as a learner, and being able to transfer new learning to new situations. Once teachers are aware of how well their learners are developing good thinking habits, they can better make day-to-day and month-to-month decisions about what and how to teach.

In addition to providing evidence to teachers about their learners' development as good thinkers, formative assessments promote learning in another important way. They provide evidence to learners about their own progress as learners and thinkers. It is this feedback that motivates them to higher levels of achievement. The last section of this chapter discusses the important link between assessment and motivation, particularly as it relates to your students' development as a self-determined and self-regulated learner.

The Assessment Triangle

Formative classroom assessments promote good thinking when they inform your learners how well they can perform the skills and competences you have taught, and provide you information to make informed instructional decisions. Another way to think of formative classroom assessment is as a process of gathering evidence of your learners' thinking from a variety of assessments that can inform and alter what and how you teach. But precisely how does a teacher go about making decisions from the evidence provided by these assessments?

Figure 1.1 illustrates a process for reasoning from evidence that is called the **Assessment Triangle**. This process was developed by the Committee on the

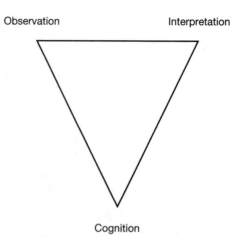

Figure 1.1
The assessment triangle

Foundations of Assessment (National Research Council, 2001) comprised of scholars in the fields of cognitive science and measurement working under the sponsorship of the National Science Foundation.

The corners of the triangle represent key components of the process of reasoning from the evidence provided by classroom assessments. **Cognition** refers to a model or set of beliefs about how learners develop cognitive competence within the subject areas taught in school. Without such a model of how cognitive competence develops, teachers have no framework or context from which to make sense of the data gathered from their assessments. Since this cognitive model is the core of the Assessment Triangle, we will describe this model here and in chapter 2.

Observation encompasses the variety of tools that teachers use to gather information about their learners. These tools include teacher-made and standardized tests, formal and informal observations, the results of class work and homework, and products and performances such as portfolios, science projects, and cooperative learning tasks. Teachers whose thinking about assessment is guided by a cognitive model know how to arrange classroom situations and tasks that provide valid assessments about how their learners' thought processes are developing. For example, one component of cognitive competence is the ability to transfer new learning to novel situations. Knowing this, the skilled teacher arranges for assessment situations and tasks that inform her about how well learners transfer acquired knowledge and skill learned from classroom examples to increasingly real-world authentic environments.

Interpretation is the way the teacher makes sense of the information from these observations to make judgments about learners and decisions about what to teach. When interpreting observations for what they say about a learner's cognition, the teacher is aware that any single observation may be fallible. Therefore, a wide assortment of evidence is observed and interpreted, from formal classroom tests to portfolios, exhibits, and cooperative activities, before a valid and reliable judgment can be made. She must also be acutely aware of the standards for evidence for making reliable and valid judgments. These standards will be covered in chapter 4.

As you can see, the three components of the Assessment Triangle are intricately related with each supporting the other to provide valid inferences about a learner's competence within an area of instruction. A *cognitive model* of how learners become competent informs the teacher about what assessment situations and tasks to arrange so that reliable and valid *observations* of learners can be made. Moreover, this model helps the teacher *interpret* or make sense of the evidence provided by the observations. We will illustrate throughout this text how to use the Assessment Triangle to build reliable and valid assessments for monitoring student performance, guiding your instructional decisions, and uncovering learning problems.

Application 1.1 asks you to recall a particularly stressful or unpleasant assessment situation in which you were not able to show your true ability. Let's begin by seeing if your responses and the Assessment Triangle can help you understand why this assessment context was so unpleasant.

APPLICATION 1.1

Think of a personal testing or assessment situation in which you were convinced that nothing could be done to make things better. Looking back, what were some assessment conditions that, if changed, might have prevented you from feeling helpless? Were any of these conditions related to (a) how the teacher viewed the way people think (cognition), (b) the observations or data collected to report your competence (observations), or (c) the judgments made from the data collected (interpretations)?

Circumstances promoting a feeling of helplessness:

Assessment conditions that might have been changed:

Were any of these conditions related to cognition, observation, or interpretations?

What Is a Model of Good Thinking?

Our perspective on cognition is that it involves good thinking. Good thinking has two dimensions. One involves the processes that the mind follows to attribute meaning to the information taken in from the senses. The other dimension deals with the information itself. Just as good car manufacturing involves raw materials and a production process, good thinking involves raw materials like sensory information (e.g., auditory, visual, etc.) and a way to process it, or make sense out of it. The notion of the brain as an information processor is one of the dominant metaphors explaining how the mind works (Neath, 1998).

It is now believed that good thinking takes place in the memory system. So when we talk of the processes of thinking we are really talking about the processes of memory. Memory is often pictured as a place in the brain where information is kept. Figure 1.2 shows the most common way to represent the memory or information processing system.

Such models seek to describe what happens to information when it is taken in by the senses of your learners, for example, the first time seventh grade earth science students see a picture of the solar system, touch a plastic model of it, and hear an explanation of how this system works. What happens to all the visual, tactile, and

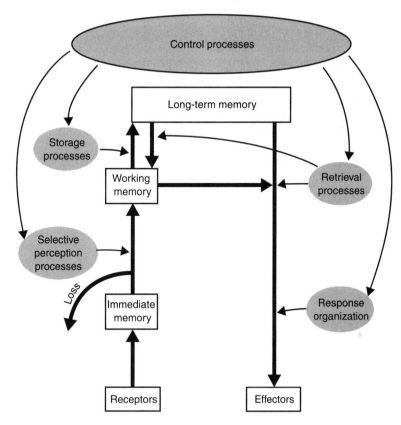

Figure 1.2
Basic elements of the human information processing system
Source: From Ellen Gagné, Carol Walker Yekovich, and Frank R. Yekovich. *The Cognitive Psychology of School Learning,* 2/e. Published by Allyn and Bacon, Boston, MA. Copyright © 1993 by Pearson Education. Reprinted by permission of the publisher.

auditory information their senses are absorbing? How is all this information processed?

The model you see in Figure 1.2 is a general metaphor for information flow that applies to any situation where the brain receives new information. In this figure we see five rectangles labeled receptors, effectors, immediate memory, working memory, and long-term memory. These boxes represent different functions or processes that are activated as information is being processed. Arrows in the model represent an hypothesized sequence in which these functions occur, whereas ovals stand for executive processes that govern or regulate the information flow. These processes include goal setting, strategy selection, expectations, and the monitoring of progress toward a goal.

With respect to classroom assessment, the most important components of this model are working and long-term memory. But before we explain the implications of these memory components for how you assess your learners, we want to emphasize one important point—the distinction between memory as a structure in the mind and memory as a process. Models such as the one above give the impression that memory is a place in which information is stored, sort of like the storeroom in your school or closet in your classroom. This is called the **structuralist view** of memory. But the most recent research and theory about memory conceptualizes memory as a process. This view is sometimes referred to as the **proceduralist view**. It emphasizes the fluid processes involved in continually creating and recreating new memories. This will be an important distinction for how you assess your learners. The following quote by David Wechsler (1963) explains the proceduralist position:

> Memories, like perceptions and eventually sensations, have no separate existences. The memory of what you saw yesterday has no more existence until revived than the pain you felt in your arm before it was pinched.... In short, for the experiencing individual, memories do not exist before they are revived or recalled. Memories are not like filed letters stored in cabinets or unhung paintings in the basement of a museum. Rather, they are like melodies realized by striking the keys on a piano. Memories are no more stored in the brain than melodies in the keys of the piano. (pp. 150–151)

We know that memories exist, and so at some level they must be kept somewhere. The structuralist view leads us to believe that a memory occupies a static place in an individual brain cell. Your memory of your high school prom, then, is kept in a cell or several cells and can be lost if that place is destroyed.

Within the past two decades a more constructive, creative, and dynamic view of memory is evolving, which holds not that memory resides in a single place but within the fluid assemblies of brain cells that processed the original event (Schacter, 1996, 2001). Think back to one of your fondest childhood memories. The features of this memory are distributed over those brain cells that originally processed the sights, sounds, smells, tactile sensations, and even tastes you experienced at that time. Right now, as you are attempting to revive that memory, cell assemblies all over your cortex are lighting up.

Your recall of this event is even more complicated than you think. This is because some of the information you are reviving is coming from sources that were not part of the original event, and this is the important part for how you unleash your learners' memories and call them into action. You may have blended that memory with some other, perhaps, similar memories. Would anyone else recognize it as one of your fondest childhood memories? Maybe, but you might be unsure about this because you have added to its personal meaning for you by blending it with many other similar childhood memories. Clearly then you have no single place where memories are stored. Your learners' memories are constantly growing and changing with their experiences both inside and outside of the classroom. So, when your learners' memories are being called into action, what should be assessed is almost always something larger than the original event in order for it to be meaningful and sometimes even recognizable to the learner.

For purposes of assessment of good thinking, why does it matter whether you adopt a structuralist or proceduralist view of the memory system of your students? The structuralist view, by presenting memory as a place, brings with it the implication that memory can be good or bad, weak or strong. Standardized tests that assess memory span may contribute to this view. Teachers often receive reports of the results of such tests that describe a child as having a weak or strong short-term memory. The evidence for such a conclusion usually comes from a test of a child's immediate memory for a sequence of numbers read to him or pictures displayed on cards. After reading such a report, a teacher inevitably expects the child to have difficulty following a sequence of directions, remembering information about a science lesson presented that morning, or perhaps recalling number facts or names of colors or the events in a movie.

In contrast, the proceduralist view is that we cannot make general statements about a child's memory because there is no one place where memories are kept. Memories for numbers, pictures, melodies, science knowledge, writing conventions, dance routines, or directions about how to get from one place to another are distributed throughout the brain in the cell assemblies that processed the information at the original time it was perceived. Moreover, these memories are continually being created and re-created as the child experiences similar events or hears others tell about these events. In other words your memory of even a single event is continually expanding, growing richer with new experiences of increasingly larger expanse. Thus, the proceduralist view of memory cautions teachers to be wary of making general interpretations of memory strengths or weaknesses from evidence gathered in a particular context. In other words, the memory and learning potential of your learners is a process that can be highly situation specific or context bound, that is, the result of not only *when* but also *how* a specific lesson is taught (Neath, 1998). Therefore, how your assessments engage your learners' memory—either as a static storehouse of facts or as a dynamic and fluid experience that can be stimulated into action by your assessment—is important to your interpretation of what students have learned. In this text we will show you how your assessments can unleash the constructive and intuitive nature of your learners' own contribution to the learning process, called constructivism. **Constructivism** is an approach to teaching and learning in which learners are provided the opportunity to construct their own sense of what is being learned by building internal connections or relationships among the ideas and facts being taught.

How Does Memory Work?

Because memory and the learning potential of your learners are so closely bound, it is important for you to know how your learners' memories work. For most of the 20th century, the dominant model of memory was the one shown in Figure 1.2. According to this view, the memory system follows a sequence of stages that involves: taking information in through sensory receptors, storing it briefly in a way station called immediate or sensory memory where the mind attempts to make sense of it, and transferring the information that has not been forgotten to a short-term store for further processing and understanding, following which meaningful information is stored in long-term memory. Long-term memory is viewed as a vast, almost inexhaustible warehouse of information that resides in the memory system permanently.

Alan Baddely and his colleagues believe that this model (Figure 1.2) with its boxes and organized sequential stages fails to capture the dynamic, creative, and constructive nature of memory (Baddely, 1986, 1998). Instead, Baddely adds to the notion of a memory warehouse, an interactively linked workshop into which flows new information from the senses and stored information from the warehouse. As we will see, the idea of a workshop operating in the heads of your learners which can mold, form, and access even distant memories will be particularly relevant to your classroom assessment.

Baddely appropriately names this workshop "working memory." You may think of it as a place (the structuralist view) or a process (the proceduralist view), but it is working memory that is responsible for our memories of people, places, events, skills, and emotions. What happens during working memory is very much under the control of you or your learners. Baddely refers to this control feature of working memory when he uses the expression "executive function." This executive function is what keeps the learner's attention focused as she constructs memories. It is also responsible for the student's expectations about learning, goal setting, the selection of strategies to achieve goals, and the learner's monitoring of progress toward her goal attainment.

It is in working memory that we solve math word problems, design an experiment, figure out a creative way to express a thought, or make a map of how to go from one place to another. Another way to think of the memory system is to picture a vast factory with floor space to fashion an infinite variety of products and where, continually, new raw materials are coming in, new products are being fashioned and stored, and old products are being updated or replaced. Working memory is the section of the factory that is the focus of attention at any particular time. If we could somehow see a picture of the mind as it solves a math problem, or record the expenditure of nutrients in the activated neurons that solve math problems, working memory would be those portions of the brain's cortex that are lit up or burning lots of glucose.

A clear example of how working and long-term memory work in dynamic interaction is when a learner attempts to solve balance-scale problems. Figure 1.3 shows a picture of the type of balance scale presented to children to study how they develop an understanding of the principle of torque. The balance scale contains a fulcrum and an arm that rotates around it like a seesaw. Depending on which side has the most weight, the arm tips left or right on either side of the fulcrum. Weights can be placed on the pegs on either side of the arm. A lever (not shown) is set to hold the arm motionless while placing weights.

When weights are placed on the pegs, the child is asked to predict the direction of arm rotation when the lever is released. In order to make correct predictions as to what side will go up, the child must attend to and reflect on two things at once: the amount of weight on each side of the fulcrum and the distance of the weight

Figure 1.3
A type of balance scale presented to children to study how they develop an understanding of the principle of torque. Working memory is the place where children construct new information and solve such problems

from the fulcrum. It is during working memory that this type of thinking is done, but long-term memory also plays a crucial role. Into working memory the child must bring two pieces of information stored in long-term memory: the rule relating distance from the center and weight and the multiplication facts. When the same amount of weight is on both sides of the fulcrum but at different distances, the child must multiply the weight times the distance, compare the products, and predict that the arm will tilt to the side with the higher value. Conversely, when different weights are at unequal distances from the fulcrum, the child must also use the multiplicative rule, recall multiplication facts, compare products, and predict arm rotation.

With this example we see that working memory is the place where we solve problems with the help of information retrieved from long-term memory. Still, there is also a back and forth flow: Working memory also helps construct new information that is then transferred to long-term memory. An example of this would be a discovery learning lesson where learners are conducting science experiments that lead to the production of a rule for gravity, electrical conductivity, magnetism, and so forth. Once this rule is constructed, it becomes a part of the child's long-term memory in the domain of physical science, which may change the nature of some other related long-term memories. In each of these instances, we see memory becoming most energized for problem solving and thinking when the learning event and assessment engages its fluid and dynamic nature.

Where in the Mind Is Information?

The structuralist position leads us to view long-term memory as a place where different types of information are stored. According to this view, information has a particular location in this storage place and it occupies this place relatively permanently. The problem with this view is it never clearly explains how the information gets to the storage area, in what form it is stored, how it is retrieved, and why it is forgotten. These are all obvious issues that one who viewed long-term memory as a place would raise.

The proceduralist view suggests that what distinguishes information relatively impervious to loss from information that is quickly forgotten is not where the information is placed but how it is processed or thought about to begin with. Consider this example. Look at the two lists of words below.

ankle	apple
arrow	barrel
butter	candy
cabin	elbow
cellar	hammer
cottage	meadow
engine	message
flower	oven
lemon	slipper
sugar	salad

Read the list on the left and notice whether the words contain an *e* or a *g*. Now read the second list of words and just think about whether the words are pleasant or unpleasant. Then try and recall the words in the lists. Most people who do this experiment invariably recall more words in the second list. Why? The proceduralist view says that more words were recalled from the second list because you processed these words at a deeper level of thought than the first list, accessing previous experiences and memories. Reflect back on your thinking when you were reading these two lists. Would you agree that you thought about the words in the first list at a more superficial or surface level than you did with the words in the second list?

Now imagine a student reading an assignment in history or biology. What will determine this student's level of recall of the information that she absorbs. The proceduralist view would say the student will remember more if she spends time relating the information to previous information already learned, and reads the information with a purpose such as to find an answer to a particular question or to validate a particular prediction. But just reading and re-reading the assignment while processing at a superficial level (maybe just reading to get the assignment done), even though a lot of time is spent on it, will result in little recall of the information.

This could also account for how two different assessments, one a structuralist test and the other a proceduralist test, could yield two different interpretations of what had been learned. Because the structuralist version holds that memory is a place in which specific content has been stored, the structuralist version might ask the learner to bring it out of storage by regurgitating what was presented in the assignment. Because the proceduralist version holds that memory is fluid and dynamic and rests in no single place, the proceduralist version might ask the learner to relate what was being recalled to previous information that had been learned for the purpose of

---

APPLICATION 1.2

Think of an assignment a teacher might give that would embrace the view that learners' memories are static places in the mind that hold discrete facts and information. What might that assignment be and how would you assess whether or not your learners could remember what they had stored in memory?

Now think of another assignment a teacher might give that would embrace the view that learners' memories are fluid and ever changing, always being updated with more recent memories and experiences. What might your assignment be that would assess whether or not your learners could remember what they had been taught but in a context that might create associations with more recent events and experiences that could stimulate their recall?

finding an answer to a particular question or making a prediction meaningful to the learner. Only the proceduralist version might be expected to be sufficiently engaging to unleash the dynamic relationship between working and long-term memory and apply *experience* and *interest* to the recall of information.

Thus, the proceduralist view of memory holds that the most important factor explaining recall of information is not *where* the information is stored (i.e., the long- or short-term memory bank) but *how* the information is processed or thought about when the learner is listening, studying, or being assessed.

In Application 1.2, try applying your knowledge of the structuralist and proceduralist views of memory by composing a classroom assignment that would represent each view.

What Makes Up the Content of Memory?

Modern memory theorists describe the contents of memory in different ways (Neath, 1998; Kandel, 1991; Schacter, 2001). What does memory contain? A simple way to answer this question is that memory contains what we have learned. We have learned information both informally in our homes and communities and formally in school. Some of this information takes the form of facts, concepts, and principles of history, biology, reading, or geography.

As we have stated above, this information is probably stored in those areas of the brain that processed it at the time of initial learning and remembering. Thus information is likely organized in domains specific to the features of particular types of knowledge. Information about rocks, planets, animals, transportation, geometry rules, physics principles, or writing conventions can be found in domain-specific networks representing specific areas of content. We use this information in working memory to think and problem-solve. This information is sometimes called **declarative knowledge** or knowledge gained from explicit learning. Explicit knowledge is knowledge of which we are aware as we are learning it and can talk about it.

Memory experts like Eric Kandel (1999) use the expression "nondeclarative" knowledge to describe those contents of memory that were learned more unconsciously or implicitly or without explicit awareness. Other terms for this type of knowledge are implicit knowledge or **procedural knowledge**. It includes emotional knowledge (fears, anxieties, attitudes) and such learning as how to ride a bike, tie a shoelace, fix a flat tire, compute a square root, design a simple experiment, or write a short story. We will discuss ways you can assess different types of declarative and procedural knowledge in chapters 5, 6, and 7.

What Are Some Implications of Your Learners' Memory for Classroom Assessment?

We have stated above that your learners engage in different memory processes and use different memory contents to accomplish different educational goals. It stands to reason that assessments of how well learners think address different memory processes and contents. If a learner is having difficulty grasping the workings of the solar system, for example, a teacher would, initially, want estimates of what the learner knows in that domain and how well it is organized. Thus the teacher of this earth science learner should also assess these aspects of the learner's memory system when trying to make decisions about how to help him think and reason better about the solar system. In chapter 6 we will discuss how to create classroom assessments for determining the knowledge organization of your learners.

When might assessments of working memory processes be called for and how is this done? After repeated attempts to adapt and adjust instruction to a learner based on the above assessments have failed, one might begin to question the capacity of this learner to deal with new information and relate this to already learned knowledge. We stated above that problem solving takes place in working memory. Thus, estimates of this learner's working memory capacity would be helpful to further understand learning difficulties and adapt to them. Standardized tests administered by trained school psychologists can be useful for making these types of decisions. We discuss the use of standardized tests and how they can be used to supplement information from classroom assessments in chapter 11.

Another implication that memory models hold for assessing and understanding good thinking has to do with the distinction between declarative and procedural learning. There is sufficient evidence from cognitive science that declarative learning (knowledge of facts, concepts, rules, and generalizations) and procedural learning (knowledge of how to do things) may engage different memory systems (Kandel, 1999). Thus, if you have concerns about a learner's capacity for declarative knowledge learning your school psychologist might give the learner an aptitude test, but such tests may tell us little about a learner's capacity for procedural or implicit and unconscious learning. There is evidence to suggest a learner may be strong in procedural learning yet weak in declarative learning (Jensen, 1998; Macintosh, 1998). Assessments of the procedural learning system may help you adapt instruction to a learner who has deficits in the declarative learning system.

What Do Good Thinkers Know and Do?

Good thinking is largely domain specific. In other words, there are good thinkers with expertise in history, chess, writing, geometry, or military strategy, but rarely do we find general good thinkers. Cognitive psychologists focus on two principal features of subject expertise: organization and metacognition. Good thinkers in any field have extensive, organized knowledge bases, and can think about what they have learned and how they learned it. Conscious thinking of and control by the learner of what and how they have learned is called **metacognition** (Bransford, Brown, & Cocking, 1999).

A common method for examining and analyzing the knowledge base of experts in a particular domain is called the novice–expert study. In these studies, cognitive scientists compare the extent of factual knowledge of experts in fields like psychology or physics with that of newcomers such as undergraduate majors or beginning graduate students. These comparisons show that, although experts have more information, the key feature distinguishing their knowledge from that of novices is its organization. As we will see in chapter 3, an organized knowledge base is hierarchically arranged with sets of principles and rules (sometimes referred to as schemata) at the apex connected to increasingly more specific concepts, facts, and discriminations, as shown in Figure 1.4.

There are two advantages to this type of organization: it is more usable and generalizable than a list of discrete facts, and it is more accessible when working memory processes demand readily available information for problem solving. For example, when a behavior specialist observes a student's disruptive classroom behavior to give the teacher some helpful suggestions about what to do, the specialist's knowledge about classroom management is more than a list of facts about adolescent development, social behavior, seating arrangements, and definitions of terms like positive and negative reinforcement. Instead she relates her observations of the child's behavior to general principles of behavioral learning, group dynamics, and peer culture. The

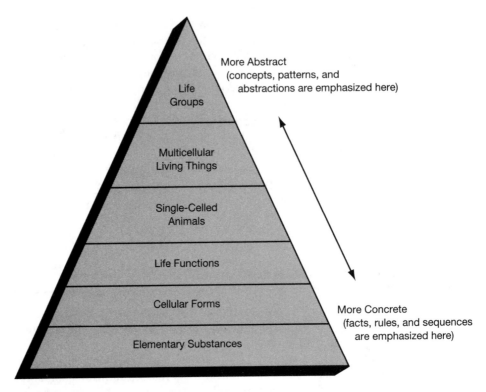

Figure 1.4
A hierarchy of possible topics in a science curriculum showing how knowledge is organized
Source: Effective Teaching Methods, 5th edition (p. 206), by Gary Borich, 2004, Upper Saddle River, NJ: Merrill/Prentice Hall.

specialist can make sense of the child's behavior in terms of patterns and principles of classroom management. She can quickly and efficiently problem-solve and make helpful, on-the-spot recommendations to the classroom teacher.

In addition to having organized, readily accessible knowledge bases, experts in particular domains do things like question their knowledge and assumptions, remind themselves to think and problem-solve in certain ways, reflect on using particular strategies for solving problems, and evaluate if the strategies worked. They know their mental strengths and can observe or monitor themselves while problem solving to evaluate success. In other words, they are metacognitive. We will see the importance of these behaviors in the classroom in chapter 2.

How does such expertise develop? What characteristics of educational settings and learners impact the development of extensive, organized knowledge bases and metacognitive skills? In the next section we will point out important aspects of school instruction and learner motivation that play significant roles on the development of good thinking.

How Do Novice Learners Develop into Good Thinkers?

Classroom instruction contributes to the development of good thinking principally in four ways: by (a) linking new knowledge to old or prior knowledge, (b) providing practice and giving feedback, (c) teaching for transfer, and (d) taking into consideration the social context of learning.

In this chapter we have discussed the fluid and ever-increasing expanse of the memory of your learners. In chapter 8, we discuss that one of the hallmarks of cognitive science approaches to learning is the assumption that novice learners construct their knowledge bases when they link new information acquired in school with the old information they have acquired formally in earlier grades and informally from their culture. Classroom teachers play a vital role in the knowledge construction process when they use assessment tools to measure prior knowledge, detect misinformation, teach new knowledge to add to the depth and breadth of learners' knowledge base, and monitor its transformation in terms of elaboration and organization.

It takes a long time to become an expert. Studies of eminent scientists, artists, and athletes describe years of daily practice mastering their craft always under the watchful eyes of master tutors who provided extensive feedback on the learners' progress (Pressley, 1995). Scores of studies that explore the factors responsible for the long-term recall of declarative and procedural knowledge highlight the critical role played by practice and feedback. In particular, these studies emphasize the importance of periods of practice interspersed with rest periods (called distributed practice) for memories to become consolidated and organized for efficient recall.

Knowledge and skills acquired in one context do not necessarily transfer to a different context unless such transfer is an explicit goal of instruction (Bransford et al., 1999). Because the ability to take the knowledge and skills learned in one setting and use it in another is something we expect of experts, we should expect teachers to plan for, teach, and assess for such transfer. Research carried out over the past two decades has begun to clarify what teachers can do to ensure that what they teach can be used in new and unfamiliar settings.

For example, a strategy that reading teachers teach to learners to improve their reading comprehension includes previewing titles and pictures before reading and making predictions about what they are going to read. Learners who master this strategy in a language arts class, use it, and improve their understanding and memory of literature, may not use this strategy to help them when they study history or earth science. Experts transfer strategies learned in one context to another. How do learners acquire this capability?

Studies of how to promote transfer on the part of learners have shown that awareness of themselves as learners who actively monitor their learning and improvement promotes the use of newly learned skills in different contexts (Pressley, 1984, 1985; Zimmerman & Schunk, 2001). Thus, teachers should view transfer as a capability that can be taught and prompted rather than as an ability the learner has or does not have.

Learning develops in a social context. Reading skills and strategies, methods for carrying out science projects, procedures for constructing maps, and knowledge of history facts and concepts are usually learned through conversations, interactions, and collaboration with classmates. Social learning processes not only teach knowledge, skills, and strategies but also affect certain motivational characteristics of learners related to goal expectations and goal setting, beliefs about one's ability to attain goals, the persistence with which goals are pursued, and the methods of pursuit.

Assessing Good Thinking

Our knowledge about the content and development of good thinking suggests directions for classroom assessment. If one of the distinguishing traits of experts and novices is the knowledge organization of the former group, then teachers should know something about the knowledge organization of their learners and its assessment. We suggest ways to do this in chapter 6. Moreover, when teachers observe that certain learners are taking inordinate amounts of time to complete certain subject area tasks, they might want to assess how these learners are organizing information in order to account for this delay.

As discussed in the previous section, experts not only use strategies when they solve problems, they choose to use them and keep track of the benefits that ensue from using the strategy. We called this capability metacognition. It is important for teachers to assess for metacognition, and we suggest ways to do this in chapter 8.

Finally, because prior knowledge, opportunities for practice and feedback, transferring knowledge and skills to new contexts, and social learning processes are critical for the development of subject matter expertise, assessment practices should pay close attention to these components. In chapter 9 we describe how to assess the misconceptions of learners. These assessments will suggest the practice and feedback some learners may need to attain an errorless performance and to achieve mastery.

Because learners acquire knowledge and skills around particular people, using particular materials, activities, examples, and kinds of practice, new knowledge does not transfer to new situations as easily as we would like. Teachers, as a routine aspect of assessment practice, must design tests and observations that allow the learner to demonstrate increasingly greater degrees of transfer and generalization of knowledge. Chapters 8 and 10 present useful techniques that allow learners to demonstrate transfer.

Finally, as we pointed out above, children learn new information in a social learning milieu. Thus, individual displays of achievement may not allow for valid inferences about learning in comparison to collaborative or cooperative assessment contexts. Performance assessments, which are discussed in chapter 9, lend themselves to assessing the results of social learning.

Becoming a Self-Regulated Learner

In the final analysis, learning is an activity that learners must do for themselves rather than having it done for them. Assessments therefore should include your learners transferring and applying material on their own. For most of the 20th century educational reforms were built on the assumption that the origins of a student's learning and motivation came primarily from the outside, that is, from the ways educators arranged the classroom instructional and learning environment. The assumption was that improved achievement would come about when clearer standards were set, more flexible scheduling and curricular requirements were instituted, or testing was required that demanded certain levels of proficiency before a learner moved to another grade or graduated.

Toward the latter part of the 20th century, a view of learners as active agents in their own learning and motivation had asserted itself. This viewpoint emphasized the particular processes learners acquire to take charge of their learning. They set performance goals for themselves, believe they can achieve, acquire the strategies that help them achieve, are aware of their accomplishments as they gradually acquire or fail to acquire expertise, adapt their learning strategies as they encounter difficulties, and persist.

Although, there are many theories about how learners acquire the capacity for self-regulation, the principal mental processes used by learners who take charge of their learning are self-observation, self-judgment, and self-reaction. **Social Cognitive Theory** is the name applied to the system of assumptions and beliefs about learning that encompasses the notion of learners as self-regulated individuals (Schunk, 2001; Zimmerman & Schunk, 2001). This theory starts from the fact that most learning, and especially classroom learning, occurs around other learners, that is, in a social context. In social settings, learners observe what others say and do and make comparisons to what they themselves say and do. This process of self-observation is one of the key elements of becoming a learner who self-regulates.

Self-observation informs learners about their achievement of personal goals and motivations. Self-recording or keeping records of one's own performance enhances self-observation. Self-observation works best when it goes on continually and when it occurs in the immediate environment where learning takes place. Meeting these two criteria give the learner a continuous record of information that aids in her judgments about progress.

Self-judgment, therefore, is the second principal mental process that self-regulated learners use to learn. When learners self-judge, they compare their present performance in a subject area with their goal. These goals may be of different types. Some learners set goals to surpass others. These are often referred to as norm-referenced goals. Other learners set what are called performance goals—goals that involve attaining certain levels of mastery. Research over the past 30 years demonstrates the superiority of performance goals over norm-referenced goals for bringing about higher levels of motivation and achievement.

The goals self-regulated learners set for themselves are influenced by the goals they see others set, in particular, their peers and teachers. Thus, what teachers do in classrooms has a pronounced influence on the goals set by learners and on their self-judgments of goal progress. Specific goals (e.g., to be able to read at the rate of 300 words per minute) influence learning to a greater extent than general goals (to become a good reader). Goals that are immediate (accomplish something this week) are more effective than more distant goals (accomplish something by the end of the grading period), and difficult goals result in higher levels of self-regulation than do easy goals.

Finally, based on their self-observations and self-judgments about the attainment of personal goals, self-regulated learners will feel good about their progress and work and study harder if they feel they are the principal agents of their own learning. This process of learners is called **self-reaction**.

These three self-regulatory processes—self-observation, self-judgment, and self-reaction—are linked to a perspective on motivation called **self-efficacy motivational theory**. Social cognitive theorists maintain that beliefs about one's self-efficacy provide the impetus to self-regulate one's learning. Self-efficacy theorists hold that self-regulated learning leading to high levels of achievement hinges on a learner's beliefs that they can succeed at specific academic tasks (Bandura, 1977, 1997). In other words students are more likely to self-observe, self-judge, self-react, and master tasks of which they think they can excel. This judgment that they are proficient at a task is the meaning of self-efficacy.

Social-cognitive theorists have identified several sources of information with which learners make judgments about self-efficacy and that have implications of how learners may be assessed (Schunk, 2001). One source of information is verbal persuasion through which the teacher expresses faith and confidence to learners that they can be successful. Another source is seeing peers be successful at particular tasks. If a learner sees someone who they like and admire receive high ratings or praise from a teacher for solving a difficult science problem or writing a creative story, she is more likely to believe that she can do likewise.

Perhaps the most important piece of information used by learners when making self-efficacy judgments is past experience of success or failure with a particular task. The learner who has received high ratings for her three previous essays will have higher self-efficacy for the next writing project than the learner who consistently does poorly. Thus, a learner weighs a variety of information when coming to a judgment of self-efficacy about a particular task. Once made, the judgment directly affects the learner's self-regulated learning processes and the level at which further achievement is obtained.

Teachers can play an important role in a learner's self-efficacy for a specific subject area or task. This is because they control the difficulty level of the task, the nature of the instruction that teaches the task, and the assessment techniques that provide learners with information on the basis of which they self-observe, self-judge, and self-react.

Classroom assessments provide the critical information by which learners make judgments of self-efficacy and acquire the motivation to be self-regulated learners. One important thing to remember is that the more assessments used, and the greater the variety of these assessments, the more information the learner has to continually self-observe, self-judge, and self-react. Equally important for the development

APPLICATION 1.3

After each summary below provide a specific example in which your motivation to learn was influenced in a manner consistent with the particular theory.

Social Cognitive Theory:

A theory about learning that starts from the fact that most learning and especially classroom learning occurs around other learners, that is, in a social context. In social settings, learners observe what others say and do and make comparisons to what they themselves say and do.

Self-Efficacy Motivational Theory:

A motivational theory that stresses the importance of learners' beliefs that they can succeed at school tasks, especially when they begin with, persist at, and master tasks on which they think they can excel.

of self-regulation is the validity of the assessment, and the most important factor affecting the validity of classroom assessment is how closely it is linked with instruction. In the ensuing chapters we will see how all of these considerations can be an important adjunct to how and when you assess your learners.

In Application 1.3 see if you can explain a personally motivating learning experience that you have had using social cognitive theory and self-efficacy motivational theory.

Summary

We have emphasized in this chapter that classroom assessments should promote good thinking. Assessments can do this only if they have two principal qualities: they derive from a theory of cognitive learning and they are closely linked to your instruction. As we have seen in this chapter, assessments built from a model of good thinking can provide continuous formative information to you about the complexity of your learners' thinking and expertise in a domain of knowledge. In addition to these goals we have emphasized that assessments should motivate learners to develop self-regulated learning processes. If the key process underlying self-regulation is a positive judgment of one's own capacity to learn, then classroom assessments should promote learner beliefs that they can do well in school. Guided by these principles, the remaining chapters will show you how to develop assessments that provide the information you need to make decisions about your students' achievement and your teaching, and provide to students the feedback they will need to become life-long, self-regulated learners.

Activities

1. This chapter introduced several purposes for assessment in your classroom. Identify two of these purposes that apply to your students and one that applies to you, as teacher.
2. Provide a specific example from your experience in which you were motivated to learn. In your opinion, to what extent were positive self-perceptions and expectations of success responsible for your motivation?
3. Using what you know from this chapter about social-cognitive theory and self-efficacy motivational theory, describe how each theory could account for a student's good performance in a subject you will be teaching. Identify a learner characteristic relevant to each theory that could impede good performance.

Suggested Reading

Anderman, E. M., & Maehr, M. L. (1994). Motivation and schooling in the middle grades. *Review of Educational Research, 64,* 287–310.
    This article reviews some of the most important and most thoroughly researched perspectives on academic motivation. It emphasizes how these research findings apply to students in the middle grades.

2

The New Cognitive Science
of Learning and Assessment

We have seen from chapter 1 that your learners' cognitions may be linked as much to how you assess as they are to how you teach. This approach to assessment is the result of research that has provided new insights on how children learn. In this chapter we begin to link this research on teaching and testing to assessment practices that can motivate your learners to higher degrees of effort.

Cognitive science approaches to learning are concerned with how everyday experiences are transformed, processed, or represented as mental images or sounds and stored for later use. In other words, they are concerned with how information is processed in the minds of your learners. Let's look at some of the ways information is processed and, then, the significance of this understanding for classroom assessment and motivation.

Basic Knowledge

The importance of basic knowledge is highlighted in studies of the differences between how experts in reading, writing, mathematics, social studies, or science think, remember, and learn in comparison with novices. Thinking, whether in reading, language arts, social studies, science, mathematics, music, or art springs from a well-organized and easily accessible knowledge base.

As we saw in chapter 1, this knowledge base takes two forms: declarative knowledge and procedural knowledge. **Declarative knowledge** contains the facts, concepts, rules, and generalizations pertaining to a specific area or topic. Learners who can recite the battles of the Civil War, perform addition and subtraction, complete a writing assignment, play chess, or predict gravitational forces know a lot about these domains. Learners who know little cannot think as effectively when faced with problems to solve in these areas regardless of their motivation or aptitude, because they have not acquired the facts, concepts, rules, and generalizations with which to build higher forms of learning (Ceci & Liker, 1986).

Good thinkers in any area also possess **procedural knowledge**. They know how to quickly and automatically perform the *actions* required for effective writing, typing, weighing, focusing a microscope, setting up lab equipment, booting a floppy disk, or doing triple-column subtraction with regrouping. Procedural knowledge is knowledge of how to do things. If you can tell someone the names of the parts of a shoe, for example, lace, eyelet, tongue, and knot, you have declarative knowledge. If you know how to use this knowledge to actually tie a shoe, you have procedural knowledge.

Novice thinkers lack the declarative knowledge and procedural knowledge necessary to move to higher levels of performance, such as problem solving, critical thinking, decision making, and valuing. When a problem is presented to them, they lack the facts, concepts, or other information necessary to understand or make sense of the task and to perform the action sequences needed to actually complete the task. Making sense of the task involves the learner constructing a mental idea or representation of the problem, such as a simple number line for learning to add, as shown in Figure 2.1. Performing the task involves completing the sequence of actions that puts the mental idea or representation into practice. Both are prerequisite for effective thinking and problem solving.

The notion of mental representation is crucial for understanding. Representations are the ideas, images, or words you construct in your head to think about what you see or hear. When you ask first graders to add the numbers 4 and 2, successful learners use a mental number line to help them compare and count. They hear or read the words "What is four plus two?", visualize a number line in their heads (which allows them to see that 4 is greater than 2), and then they "count up." In other words, they say to themselves or speak out loud, "four (pause), five, six."

This mental number line is part of the declarative knowledge that expert adders possess, whereas the counting strategy is part of their procedural or "how-to" knowledge. Cognitive scientists have learned that unsuccessful adders do not yet

Figure 2.1
Making sense of a task involves the learner constructing a mental idea or representation of the problem

possess the ability to represent the addition problem in terms of a mental number line. Only when they acquire this knowledge do they become successful at simple addition.

Thus, learners who have little prior knowledge (whether declarative or procedural) when first learning will have difficulty learning anything new. Middle school children studying science who lack knowledge about friction and gravity will have a difficult time later correctly representing force and motion problems in high school physics, and, those elementary school children who have little knowledge about plant life will understand little of what they might read on photosynthesis in the middle school.

Cognitive psychologists believe that learners, even at the earliest grade levels, have some knowledge about nearly every topic they study. This information may be in the form of ideas, unconnected facts, implicit rules, or images, and often the information may be wrong—what cognitive psychologists call misconceptions. These misconceptions can be found in declarative knowledge (e.g., a first-grade learner believes that small objects like sand or sugar have no weight). Most middle school learners accept the faulty rule that when two objects of different weight are dropped, or thrown horizontally, the heavier one always hits the ground first. Such misconceptions will affect how these students represent problems of force and motion.

A learner's procedural knowledge can also be faulty. In the 1970s Brown and his colleagues found that many children approach multidigit subtraction with a set of procedures that render them virtually helpless (Brown & Burton, 1978). They identified eighty simple flaws in students' procedures, such as switching to addition if the minuend is smaller than the subtrahend in a subtraction column. When faced with a 0 to borrow from, the students change the 0 to a 9 but forget to do anything else. The problem looks right but gives the wrong answer.

Sometimes misconceptions are so entrenched in the learners' minds that they continue to use mistaken ways of thinking and behaving, even when alternative methods have been taught (Roth, 1990, 1991). Sometimes prior beliefs are so strong that learners ignore statements that they disagree with or they choose not to believe what they see.

The implications of this research for teaching and assessment are clear:

1. Before teaching something new, know what important facts, concepts, principles, generalizations, and procedures are needed.
2. Assess the extent of both correct and incorrect prior knowledge.
3. Teach correct ways for learners to represent what is taught.
4. Assess both correct learning and the processes used to get there.

In Box 2.1 we asked Mr. Choe to describe how each of these steps applies to a lesson he was planning on the basics of expository writing in his eighth-grade classroom. Notice how Mr. Choe blends each of these steps seamlessly into his lesson.

BOX 2.1 Mr. Choe's Lesson on Expository Writing

Step 1. Before teaching something new, know what important facts, concepts, principles, generalizations, and procedures are needed.

I begin by analyzing the task I am about to give my students. I want them to write a short essay that has an introductory paragraph, two or more paragraphs that represent the body of the essay, and a concluding paragraph. In their introductory paragraph I want them to write an eye-catching first sentence followed by a topic statement. In the body of the essay I want them to write at least two paragraphs, each representing a major idea. I want one of the main ideas to make a generalization that is backed up in succeeding sentences with documentation or an illustration. Finally, I want the concluding paragraph to summarize the main points and end with a thought-provoking idea. To help my students recall all of these components of the task, I will place the following diagram on the board.

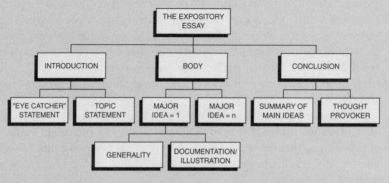

Step 2. Assess the extent of both correct and incorrect prior knowledge.

I will begin my lesson by reading to my students some examples of introductory, main, and concluding paragraphs written by former students. I will question and correct students on their understanding of an eye-catching topic and thought-provoking statement, emphasizing the distinctions among them.

Step 3. Teach correct ways for learners to represent what is taught.

I then will read an example of a paragraph that makes a generalization followed by documentation from a local newspaper supporting the truth of the generalization. I will show various ways to document or illustrate the truth of a generalization through facts, personal experience, and the word of experts.

Step 4. Assess both correct learning and the processes used to get there.

I then will ask the class to work on writing their essays for the rest of the period. They will be told to complete them at home using any resources available, including dictionaries for correct spelling and word usage, encyclopedias, magazines, and newspapers for documentation, and their computer for word processing. I will ask my students the next day to share parts of their essay with the class from which various approaches they have taken to the assignment will be discussed. They will be allowed to improve their essay from what is learned from the discussion and hand it in the following day.

Cognitive Strategies

Extensive, well-organized, and easily accessible declarative or procedural knowledge is a necessary but insufficient condition for good thinking and learning. We know this from studying how expert writers, readers, chess players, or historians go about doing their business. They plan, model, draw analogies, search memories, underline, take notes, ask themselves questions, elaborate on what they hear or read, and monitor their understanding as they are listening or reading, practicing, and rehearsing.

Cognitive learning specialists use a variety of expressions to refer to these types of thinking skills: learning-to-learn skills, general thinking skills, reasoning skills, or problem-solving skills. These terms all refer to general methods of thinking that improve learning across a variety of subject areas, called **cognitive strategies**. When learners use cognitive strategies, they are engaged in mental activities that go beyond the processes that are naturally required for carrying out a task.

For example, as you read this paragraph you are engaged in decoding processes (eye movements, sounding out phonemes, searching memory for meaning, etc.). Decoding is not a cognitive strategy because it is naturally required for reading. However, if before you began to read this chapter you scanned the headings and asked yourself questions about the chapter's content, and if as you were reading you regularly paused and asked yourself if you understood what you were reading, then you would be using cognitive strategies to help your reading comprehension.

Similarly, students are not using a cognitive strategy when they regroup and borrow to solve a subtraction problem—they are doing what is naturally required to perform the task. However, if before solving the problem and during the act of problem solving learners prompted themselves with statements such as, "What am I supposed to do? What information am I given? First, I'll draw a picture of what the problem is asking," they would be using a cognitive strategy. There are cognitive strategies to improve memory (e.g., mnemonics), reading comprehension, writing, math problem solving, and spelling.

Throughout most of the 1970s and early 1980s, cognitive learning specialists believed that general skills and reasoning abilities, such as generating ideas, analyzing arguments, reasoning by analogy, problem solving, and decision making, etc., would improve a learner's performance across all areas of the school curriculum. Because these strategies could be used in any area or subject domain, they are referred to as **domain-general skills**. Domain-general skills, once learned, were believed to transfer to learning in any academic field (Sternberg, 1989). **Domain-specific knowledge**, on the other hand, applies to a specific content area, subject or topic.

Research carried out in the 1980s, however, convinced cognitive researchers that extensive experience and knowledge in a specific domain, such as reading, history, chess, or biology, was more important for learning than general thinking or cognitive strategies (Gardner, 1993; Pressley, 1995; Wineburg, 1998). The most recent research (Bruer, 1993; Sternberg, 1996) suggests that schools should teach both domain-specific knowledge as well as domain-general skills, and that the development of subject matter expertise requires both types of instruction. This new synthesis draws one other important conclusion: Learners must learn to control and monitor their own thinking and learning—a process called **metacognition**.

Metacognition

Knowing how to use a cognitive strategy to improve learning in math, writing, or reading is no guarantee that a learner will use it (Pressley, 1995). Learners must also be aware of when to use the strategy and to monitor how it is working. When students engage in mental processes called metacognition, they think about how they think. They are consciously aware of themselves as thinkers, are aware of the thinking strategies they use, and ask themselves if these strategies are helping them learn. Teachers usually control the learning of cognitive strategies, but learners must control their use. Metacognition is the conscious control by learners of the use of cognitive strategies (White & Frederickson, 1998).

Metacognitive strategies include:

Planning.   The learner analyzes the problem, compares the problem to problems encountered previously, and identifies strategies to solve the problem.

Draft and tryout.   The learner makes several attempts to solve the problem.

Monitor and revise.   The learner makes preliminary checks on whether goals are achieved and strategies are working.

Evaluate and reflect.   The learner examines the adequacy of the problem solution and the effectiveness of strategies used to reach a solution.

This knowledge, awareness, and control of thinking processes develops with age. Researchers have shown that children in early elementary school can engage in metacognition (Pressley, Borkowski, & O'Sullivan, 1984, 1985). However, their ability to do so is not learned automatically. For example, although using one method for improving spelling works better for one group of learners than another, the learners are not aware that one strategy is better than another unless this is explicitly pointed out.

Along with extensive exposure to declarative and procedural knowledge and the teaching of cognitive strategies, the new science of cognitive learning tells us that learners must be taught metacognition. Thus, if you want your learners to use cognitive strategies to improve their reading, you must teach them four things: the declarative knowledge that comprises the basics of reading (e.g., vowels and consonants), the procedures one follows while actually reading (e.g., go from left to right, pause at periods), the cognitive strategies used for learning to read (e.g., scan headings to get an idea of the story), and the metacognitive skills that tell you which cognitive strategies are working (e.g., ask yourself if scanning the headings beforehand helped). This latter process involves teaching learners to (a) attend to the effectiveness of strategies, (b) attribute differences to the relative effectiveness of a particular strategy, and (c) make a commitment to use the more effective strategy in future decision making. Otherwise, learners may not use a given strategy, not notice whether it is effective, or fail to use it when they should.

In Box 2.2, we asked Mr. Choe to identify from his lesson on expository writing an example of declarative and procedural knowledge, a cognitive strategy, and a metacognitive behavior that he expects his students to learn. Using his responses as a guide, in Application 2.1 identify an example of declarative and procedural knowledge, a cognitive strategy, and a metacognitive behavior for a lesson or unit you will be teaching.

BOX 2.2 An Example of Declarative and Procedural Knowledge, Cognitive Strategies, and Metacognition from Mr. Choe's Lesson on Expository Writing

Declarative Knowledge: Knowledge that tells learner facts, concepts, rules, and generalizations:

I will teach my learners the definition of an eye-catching first sentence, a topic statement, a major idea, and a concluding thought and show them examples so they see the distinctions among them.

Procedural Knowledge: Knowledge that tells learners how to quickly and automatically perform required actions.

I will read a paragraph that makes a generalization followed by documentation from a local newspaper supporting the truth of the generalization. Then, I will demonstrate various ways to document or illustrate the truth of a generalization through facts, personal experience, and the word of experts so that they can repeat the procedure in their own essays.

Cognitive Strategies: Thinking skills and processes that include learning-to-learn skills, general thinking skills, reasoning skills, and problem-solving skills.

I will show my students how to distinguish effective eye-catching sentences, topic statements, major ideas, and concluding thoughts from less effective ones from the reading assignments of former students.

Metacognition: Conscious recognition of and control by the learner of the cognitive strategies being used.

I will ask students to think about the distinctions they have made to correctly classify an effective eye-catching sentence, topic statement, major idea, and concluding statement from an ineffective one. Then, I will ask them to remember to use those distinctions when writing their essay.

APPLICATION 2.1

Identify examples of the following learning outcomes for a lesson or unit you would like to teach.

Declarative Knowledge: Knowledge that tells learner facts, concepts, rules, and generalizations.

Procedural Knowledge: Knowledge that tells learners how to quickly and automatically perform required actions.

Cognitive Strategies: Thinking skills and processes that include learning-to-learn skills, general thinking skills, reasoning skills, and problem-solving skills.

Metacognition: Conscious recognition of and control by the learner of the cognitive strategies being used.

The Development of Good Thinking

Expert thinkers in any area use general thinking or cognitive strategies to solve important problems. They plan, practice, model, draw analogies, evaluate, and rehearse. They are also consciously in control of these processes. They are aware of themselves as thinkers, monitor how their thinking is going, and evaluate how they are improving or learning. They apply these cognitive strategies and control their use on a foundation of an extensive, well-organized, and deeply understood declarative and procedural knowledge base.

Your learners will be novice thinkers who are in the process of becoming expert thinkers—or at least more competent ones. They will pass through four overlapping but distinguishable stages of learning during this journey to mastery (Anderson, 1983; Bransford et al., 1999).

Stage 1. The initial stages of learning in any subject area are characterized by vague ideas, misconceptions, and rudimentary knowledge. As you give your students information, they gradually transform their prior knowledge into new facts, concepts, and generalizations.

Stage 2. During a second phase of learning, your students' knowledge accrues and becomes better organized, and their know-how, or procedural knowledge, allows them to perform more fluently.

Stage 3. In the third phase of learning, students gradually get better at controlling the use of cognitive strategies. With these strategies they begin to learn how to problem-solve, think critically, and make decisions.

Stage 4. Finally, in the fourth phase learning is characterized by the efficient use of declarative and procedural knowledge, the flexible use of cognitive strategies, and especially metacognition or the ability to think about their own thinking and ways to improve it.

Classrooms which produce high levels of learner effort monitor and assess the development of these building blocks of good thinking as conscientiously and systematically as a swimming coach monitors the development of lung capacity, swimming stroke, and kicking and turning techniques. The challenge for your assessment is the development of instruments and observational records that allow you to track the growth of your learners' thinking as they move from the initial states of learning facts (declarative knowledge); to learning how to use and apply the facts (procedural knowledge); to learning how to reason and solve problems (cognitive strategies); to the final stage of expertise, competence, and mastery, in which they consciously apply cognitive strategies, monitor their effectiveness, and revise how they are used (metacognition). In subsequent chapters we will show you how you can assess each of these stages of learning in your classroom.

Your Lesson as the Test: The Seamless Link between Teaching and Assessing

Now that we have given you what cognitive science says is important for the development of good thinking in any subject area, let's look at some examples of this new perspective on learning for teaching, motivation, and assessment. We begin by examining the work of two researchers who provide an example of this perspective on learning.

Griffin and Case (1975) set out to create a program to develop successful math learners. They were particularly interested in readiness for first-grade math instruction. Such instruction usually begins with teaching learners rudimentary addition and subtraction skills. Griffin and Case concluded that the knowledge about numbers that learners bring to the first grade is a principal determinant of whether they master first-grade math skills or experience problems learning math throughout the early elementary school years. Griffin and Case's research focused on how to identify or assess correct or incorrect prior number knowledge (prior to learning how to add), identify the new knowledge and thinking strategies required for the successful learning of addition, develop ways to teach new knowledge and thinking skills, and then assess the extent of learning.

Griffin and Case (1975) began their work with children living in economically deprived inner-city communities in the United States. They administered tests of conceptual knowledge of math and found that these children entered kindergarten and first grade significantly behind their middle-class peers in the conceptual understanding and knowledge of facts and procedures that are minimally necessary for success in early addition and subtraction. Moreover, they found that much of the children's prior knowledge was nonadaptive; that is, it prevented the learning and development of strategies that would make them successful at basic computation. Griffin and Case developed the **Rightstart Program** to remedy this.

The Rightstart Program began with a comprehensive analysis of the knowledge and skills required for correctly solving addition and subtraction problems. Successful kindergarten and first-grade math students can count, know which of two numbers is larger or smaller, which numbers come before or after others, and which numbers are closer or farther away from a given number; but most important, they think about or represent simple addition or subtraction problems in terms of a mental number line. Children who conceptualize quantities on a number line can think about numbers in a continuous fashion. Those without such a representation see numbers in a global or polar fashion. Their quantitative thinking is restricted to ideas (e.g., big things are worth more than small things), and they do not perceive a continuous stream of numbers.

From this task analysis, Griffin and Case (1975) developed a test to assess the number knowledge and strategies of novice math learners. They next developed a curriculum to teach learners to think in terms of a mental number line and to use adaptive strategies to solve simple computation problems. They created a series of thirty interactive games that involved hands-on activities for learners to acquire necessary number knowledge.

Learners were regularly tested on their development of this knowledge. At the end of the program, low socioeconomic status (SES) learners who experienced Rightstart far surpassed control groups. More significantly, at the end of first grade the math skills of these low SES learners equaled those of their middle-class peers.

The Rightstart Program illustrates a seamless link between teaching and testing. Testing informed teaching: It identified the knowledge and skills learners needed to be successful at computation. Teaching flowed from testing: It focused on developing the knowledge and skills that tests showed learners lacked. Testing was conducted to help develop a learner's skill and not simply to label a learner as deficient and assign a grade. It provided *diagnostic information* to teachers to help them better focus their instruction.

Moreover, children learned to try to produce results. Each test produced concrete evidence of students' learning and development. Each lesson was linked with the test. In most cases the lesson was the test—the teacher taught, coached, provided practice, and observed and recorded improvement. The procedures involved in such assessment helped convince learners that they were in control of their learning; that if they tried, they would improve. Rightstart is one of many educational programs in which teaching flowed from testing, focusing, and developing the knowledge and skills that tests showed learners lacked.

Other educational programs employing some of the Rightstart instructional and assessment practices have had similar successes. One of these, ThinkerTools, is a physical science curriculum used in middle schools to change some of the misrepresentations or naive ways of thinking about ideas such as force, motion, and gravity. It was developed by Barbara White, a cognitive psychologist, and Paul Horwitz, a physicist (White & Horwitz, 1988). It combines innovative assessment and instructional techniques that have been shown to motivate learners and help them acquire scientific thinking skills. Similarly, grade school writing (Scardamalia & Bereiter, 1986), middle school social studies (McKeown & Beck, 1990), middle school reading comprehension (Campione & Brown, 1990), and high school geometry (Wertheimer, 1990) programs have been shown to benefit from the close bond between teaching and assessment.

The cognitive science of learning has provided new purposes for classroom teaching and assessment. Cognitive science has reasons for why some learners think and learn better than others. Rather than attribute such differences to intelligence, cognitive science tells us that good thinkers in any subject possess declarative and procedural knowledge, cognitive strategies, and metacognitive skills. Differences in these four areas underlie learners' performance differences. Students who have a good grasp of declarative and procedural knowledge within a subject and cognitive strategies and metacognitive skills that apply across subjects far exceed the school performance of those students who do not. Therefore, your instruction and assessment should focus on these areas as goals for student learning.

Thus, cognitive science proposes a new purpose for classroom assessment: Classroom tests should assess learners' *performance changes* in what they know and how they think about specific subjects. These results should allow teachers to track the growth of learners' knowledge and thought processes. They should provide diagnostic information to teachers about what needs to be learned and how it should be taught. Cognitive scientists have a new term for such testing that distinguishes it from traditional measurement practices: They call it **authentic learning assessment** (Glaser, Lesgold, & Lajoie, 1987).

The most important steps in the authentic learning assessment process are

1. *Identifying the important knowledge and thinking skills necessary for good thinking in your particular subject areas.*   This is what Griffin and Case did as part of Rightstart.

2. *Developing a variety of ways to measure the knowledge and thinking skills identified in item 1.*   These can involve observation checklists of actual behaviors, oral questioning, paper-and-pencil tests, writing assignments, attitude scales, collaborative projects, and investigations. The information from these

instruments and activities should affect your daily and weekly instructional planning.

3. *Interpreting this information.*   To what extent is the learner acquiring the knowledge and thinking skills that are the focus of instruction? How automatic is the learner's use of declarative and procedural knowledge, cognitive strategies, and metacognitive skills? You do not assign a number or grade at this point. Rather, you develop brief descriptions of your learner's performance that serve to identify learning problems and inform subsequent teaching.

4. *Using this information to guide further teaching.*   Based on your interpretation of the learner's performance on tasks developed in item 2, you provide more practice and/or more feedback or gradually fade your involvement, giving the learner more independence.

5. *Writing some type of summative description of learning.*   This description can represent the overall development of the student's learning from the beginning or novice stages to the competence stage.

As you can see, authentic learning assessment requires more than testing. It involves diagnosing, interpreting, giving feedback, and grading as part of the instructional process.

Summary

Motivation to learn comes from a connection between teaching and assessment. The term "authenticity" characterizes this unbroken bond. In this chapter we reviewed the importance of such a bond by describing the science of cognitive learning and its relevant findings for assessment. This science of learning and assessment provides a theoretical and research base not only for new approaches to teaching but also for new approaches to classroom assessment. The term "authentic learning assessment" refers to these new approaches. In chapter 3 we will begin the process of applying authentic learning assessment in your classroom.

Activities

1. Drawing on your own experience and your responses to Application 2.1, how would you describe the differences among declarative and procedural knowledge and between cognitive and metacognitive strategies?
2. Recall Griffin and Case's Rightstart Program to develop successful math learners. What principles of cognitive science did their program include that helped make it a success?
3. In your own words, describe the differences among the terms *testing* and *assessment*. What do these concepts have in common?

Suggested Readings

Bransford, J., Brown, A., & Cocking, R. (1999). *How people learn: Brain, mind, experience, and school.* Washington, DC: The National Academy of Sciences.
This text presents the state of the art results of a two-year project evaluating new developments in the science of learning.

Bruer, J. T. (1993). *Schools for thought: A science of learning in the classroom.* Cambridge, MA: MIT Press.
This is a highly readable and substantive presentation of the contributions of cognitive science to our understanding of classroom learning.

CHAPTER

3

Developing a Framework for Assessment

Why develop an assessment? What is the purpose of spending significant amounts of time developing a variety of assessment tools, administering them, and then collecting, organizing, and communicating the information they provide? Although the result of these activities will usually be a report card grade, your purpose for assessment should go far beyond grading. Formulating such a purpose involves articulating your unique educational philosophy, an understanding of community and school values, and your own thoughts on how learning occurs from an understanding of cognitive science. To help you formulate a coherent purpose for your assessment, we will raise two important questions:

1. What frame of reference will you use to interpret what you measure?
2. What are the purposes your assessments should serve?

As we will see, how you answer one question will influence how you answer the other. So, let's consider each question in turn.

Frames of Reference

Your assessment techniques will generate a lot of information about students. How do you want this information to be interpreted? In other words, what will be your **frame of reference** for making sense out of the numbers, scores, percentages, and descriptions of performance that your tests or observations produce? Teachers can employ three types of interpretations—or comparisons—when making sense out of assessment information: norm-referenced, criterion-referenced, and growth-referenced.

Norm-Referenced Interpretations

One type of information tells you where a student stands in comparison to other students. In other words, it helps you determine a student's place or rank among other students. This is accomplished by comparing a student's performance to a norm or the average performance of other, similar students. A test that provides this type of information is called a norm-referenced test, or NRT. When these tests are administered according to strict guidelines and time limits, they are referred to as *standardized* tests.

Standardized test developers create their tests to fit a normal—or bell-shaped—distribution of scores with the assumption that the behavior being measured is distributed in this manner in the population from which the test-takers come. When you grade on the curve in your classroom you are also making the assumption that your learners' performance is also distributed in the form of a normal or bell-shaped curve. A normal distribution illustrating percentages of students falling within each interval of the curve appears in Figure 3.1. This curve allows standardized test users to compare a student's score with how others performed on the same assessment. If you were to use an NRT to measure your students' achievement, the percentages in Figure 3.1 might be used to distribute their grades from A to F, because every student's performance must be ranked or compared to other students.

You probably have heard many criticisms about the relevance of standardized tests. You are already familiar with this type of test, because you have taken some during your high school years and for entry to college. Let's look at three often heard questions about standardized tests that can help your understanding of the NRT frame of reference. These questions are

- How much of classroom learning is measured by a standardized achievement test?
- Are these tests fair to learners from diverse cultures and ethnic backgrounds?

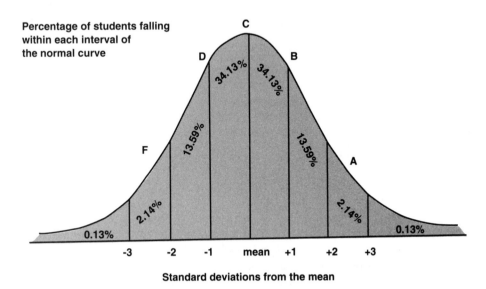

Figure 3.1
A normal curve, illustrating examples of percentages for distributing grades on an NRT

- Do such tests provide information useful for making instructional decisions in the classroom, such as was demonstrated by the Rightstart program in the previous chapter?

1. *How much classroom learning is measured by a standardized achievement test?* Think of school learning as a pie and a portion of that learning is measured by standardized tests. If we conceptualize school learning in this manner, we can ask the question: How large a piece of classroom learning is represented by a learner's standardized achievement score? Another way to ask this same question is this: Of all the factors that make a learner successful in your classroom, how important is her standardized achievement? Many factors besides your learners' standardized achievement score will come to mind to represent success in your classroom. Some things that come to mind may be their problem-solving strategies, their abilities to apply what you have taught, the products and performances they have created, the cognitive and metacognitive strategies they have acquired for learning, their motivation, and their collaborative skills that help them become active participants in learning. Add to this their specific talents which have made some of their contributions to your class unique, and we have quite a list of important outcomes that are not measured by a standardized test.

2. *Are standardized tests fair to learners from diverse cultures and ethnic backgrounds?* It is sometimes assumed in our culture that standardized tests are unfair to certain minority groups (Cole, 1981; Haney, 1981; Jensen, 1998). You have probably said at some point in your education that "standardized tests are biased." Do you mean biased because they contain information or words that favor one racial, ethnic, or gender group over another? Or, do you mean they are biased because they contain pictures or refer to specialized topics of greater significance to one racial, ethnic, or gender group than to others? Test developers today screen test questions scrupulously for racial, ethnic, and gender insensitivity, making this source of bias much less a problem than in the past (Thorndike, Cunningham, Thorndike, & Hagen, 1997). Let's look at several other related sources of test bias that may, to varying degrees, be present in a standardized test.

Bias in Group Differences.   Test bias can also mean that certain groups, on the average, score higher than other groups on these tests. For example, on average Asian Americans score higher than Caucasian Americans, who score higher than African Americans. These differences are cited as evidence of bias because of the assumption that all cultural groups should have the same average scores and distributions of scores (Reschly, 1981).

Also, opponents of standardized tests would say standardized achievement tests do not measure achievement only. They also measure certain processes such as memory, quickness, and test-taking skills, which may apply to only a limited type of school learning, and which may not be relevant to one's ability to adapt to and succeed outside the test-taking situation. In other words, a test can be biased by favoring those who happened to have or have acquired skills that may make them good test-takers, but who are unable to apply the knowledge they have in situations and contexts beyond the prescribed content and format of the test.

Sample Bias.   Some say that standardized achievement tests are biased because certain cultural groups are not represented in the norm—or comparison—group to which they are being compared to the extent that these groups are represented in the general population. Test publishers would have difficulty marketing, and therefore do not develop, tests of which norms are based on unrepresentative groups. However, this does not preclude inappropriately administering a standardized achievement test to learners who do not match those on which the test was normed. Some standardized test publishers provide norms for special populations, for example, low-income (chapter 1) schools, English as a Second Language learners, and learners receiving special education services. In this manner special populations can be compared to a norm group with the same characteristics and level of opportunities and resources as those to whom the test is administered. But, the composition of students in your classroom in any given year, to varying degrees, may not be representative of the norm group to whom they are being compared on the standardized test used by your school district or state.

Examiner and Language Bias.   Most psychologists are Anglo American and speak standard English. Psychologists, educators, and parents concerned about test bias sometimes attribute the lower standardized achievement scores of minority learners to this fact. Some suggest that minority learners in the early elementary grades would obtain higher scores on standardized tests if they were tested by members of their own culture using language more typical of that culture. Also, the tests themselves are written and their directions spoken in "Standard American English" to which all test-takers may not be equally familiar due to disparities in opportunity to learn and to practice English in the home. Adding to this possible source of bias is the increasing number of school-age learners in America who speak English only as their second language, placing some students at a disadvantage to their native-speaking peers with whom they are being compared on a standardized test of achievement.

Bias in Test Use.   Reschly (1981) had a unique perspective on bias in test use. He believed that even when the scores themselves may be unbiased and reflect valid and reliable achievements, the use to which they have been put may have been to the disadvantage of minority children. Rather than used to design educational environments that promote learning and development, standardized test scores may have been used to place some learners in lower track classrooms, in low-ability reading groups, and in special education programs of unknown instructional effectiveness. Reschly cites statistics that demonstrate that some minority learners as well as economically disadvantaged learners are overrepresented in special education programs. At the same time, these groups are underrepresented in programs for the gifted. Orfield and Kornhaber (2001) concur that our social values should encourage the development of tests that enhance opportunities for all individuals. They argue that standardized tests used in grade schools perform a gate-keeping function. They may admit members of some groups to the best educational programs while denying these programs to other groups.

    3. *Do Standardized Tests Provide Information Useful for Instructional Decision Making?* Elliott and Shapiro (1990) and Ysseldyke and Marston (1990) advocate that it is not enough for a standardized achievement test to measure past learning; it must also show the way to attain higher achievement. These and other researchers believe that tests should be required to demonstrate **instructional validity**. That is, they must be valid for improving instruction and learning. Researchers show that many standardized tests lack two fundamental properties required for improving instruction and learning: (a) behavioral definitions of the cognitive processes that are measured and (b) specification of how the skill being measured was chosen or sampled from all the possible skills that could measure that ability. While we will see in chapter 11 how standardized tests are striving to attain these properties, let's look at these two arguments.

Argument 1: Behavioral Definition. If you read the individual performance profile of a fourth grader on a standardized achievement test, you are likely to see subject-matter areas such as reading comprehension, spelling, capitalization, usage and expression, social studies, science, and math computation. These are the categories in which performance data, usually in the form of percentage correct for a student, the class average percentage correct, and the national average percentage correct, are given.

    Test manuals typically list these subject areas, identify test questions that require them, and present evidence that these topics are adequately being measured. For these tests to have day-to-day value for planning instruction in the classroom, they must describe in observable terms the precise cognitive processes or mental operations that make up the skills being tested. That way the classroom teacher would know what cognitive processes to teach in order to improve their students' performance. Some standardized tests fail to behaviorally define the cognitive processes required by their test items. They identify the topic being measured, but may not describe precisely what observable functions the learner must perform to exhibit the declarative and procedural knowledge, cognitive strategies, and metacognitive behavior that may be required for a correct response.

Argument 2: Sampling Specificity. One of the consequences of not having a precise behavioral definition for the competencies being measured is the lack of sampling specificity. Sampling specificity refers to the clarity with which a test developer describes the test sampling plan or blueprint for test question development and selection (Kubiszyn & Borich, 2003). For example, pretend that a classroom teacher is preparing an assessment for her learners to measure the following math skills:

- Recall of multiplication facts
- Multiplication of two-digit multiplicand by a one- or two-digit multiplier without regrouping
- Multiplication of two-digit multiplicand by a one-digit multiplier requiring regrouping

Many test items could be devised to assess these skills, but due to limitations in testing time, a standardized test might contain only a small sample of test items. These can provide an inadequate basis for making diagnostic decisions about a student's performance.

Figure 3.2 shows a classroom assessment developed by a classroom teacher for analyzing her learners' multiplication errors and remediating the needed skills. By noting the commonality among wrong answers (circled), the teacher learns that this learner needs more practice on multiplication problems that require "carrying." Not all standardized achievement tests intend their tests to specifically target cognitive processes as specific as these for purposes of remediation, and thus may not have this level of instructional validity.

In chapter 11 we will show how standardized test results can be used together with the results of your classroom assessments to identify learning difficulties such as these, and help you make instructional decisions about what and how to teach in your classroom,

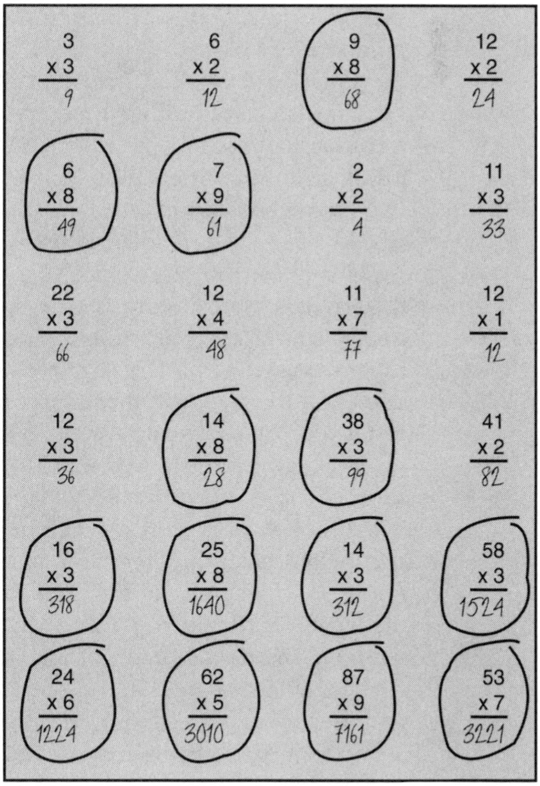

Figure 3.2
Diagnostic math assessment.
Results of a multiplication test
derived from a test plan
indicating specific skills to be
remediated.

Criterion-Referenced Interpretations

Standardized test developers create tests with the assumption that the behavior being measured is normally distributed. This allows you to compare a student's score with how others performed on the same assessment. How your learners perform in comparison with others is only one facet of what they can do with what you have taught and may not measure at all what they can do best. Not all tests need or should assume your learners' performance will be normally distributed in a bell curve. For example, when you teach a lesson well and give a test over what you have just taught, you expect most of your students to get most of the questions correct. Here you would expect your classroom test to measure the effects of your teaching more sensitively than a standardized test, because you used a standard or criterion of learning established by you (e.g., 90 percent correct) and taught to that standard. This is another standard to which you can compare student performance.

A criterion-referenced interpretation is a second frame of reference from which you can view your learners' performance. Criterion-referenced interpretations are like those given to members of the track team: "You ran the mile in 5 minutes and 32 seconds"; or to a journalism student: "Your first draft contained two grammatical errors"; or to a typing student: "You typed 45 words a minute with two errors." **Criterion-referenced** interpretations require that a teacher specify various criteria of mastery for a particular area. After students take the "assessment," their performance is described in terms of how well they met the criteria specified—not how far above or below the class average they are.

Criterion-referenced grading occurs when various categories or grades (A, B+, etc.) are associated with different degrees of student mastery. For example, a grade of A means a student can type better than 60 words a minute with no more than one error, a B is given to learners who type from 50 to 60 words a minute with no more than two errors, and so forth.

As you can see, criterion-referenced interpretations of test scores tell learners what they can do. They have the potential for fostering student effort and task-focused goals because the teacher knows precisely what must be taught or retaught for the learner to get each item correct . The challenge for the teacher is determining the degree of mastery required. For norm-referenced interpretations, the benchmark of success is in comparison to the average performance of a larger sample of test-takers, called the norm group. For a criterion-referenced assessment, a standard *external* to the test is not required for assigning scores and making interpretations. Instead, the standard comes from the teacher's judgment as to what constitutes mastery.

Although judgments for the purpose of assigning grades must be made for both norm- and criterion-referenced interpretations, criterion-referenced interpretations require a judgment as to the standard (usually percentage correct) below which students will be considered not to have acquired a sufficient degree of knowledge or mastery. The identification of this standard or criterion, however, can be problematic for the criterion-referenced test (CRT) developer. When the standard for a CRT is chosen arbitrarily without the benefit of knowing what level of mastery constitutes a sufficient basis to perform needed functions in subsequent learning activities, the

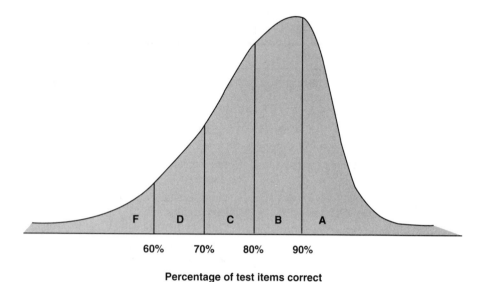

Figure 3.3
A negatively skewed curve, illustrating the distribution of test scores and grades on a
CRT

next grade, or authentic real-world contexts, they can provide no better measure of
student mastery than an NRT. Figure 3.3 illustrates a typical distribution of grades using a criterion-referenced assessment. In contrast to our norm-referenced distribution, notice that a large number of students can reach the criterion if the instruction
is effective. This is because test items are chosen to reflect exactly what was taught,
not to report performances relative to one another. Table 3.1 summarizes and compares NRT and CRTs.

Growth-Referenced Interpretations

A growth-referenced interpretation is a third frame of reference from which you can
view your learners' performance. Most teachers would like to acknowledge not only
learning but also growth or improvement in learning through **growth-referenced**
interpretations. When grading the six-week exam, they would like to distinguish between the learner who started third grade knowing no multiplication facts and has
now mastered most of them and the learner who scored just as well but who knew
the multiplication tables at the start of the third grade. The former student warrants
additional recognition for improvement.

Typically, however, growth-referenced interpretations are conveyed informally
to learners and their parents in conversations or comments made on report cards.
They rarely are presented as a grade. Consequently, improvement in learning,

Table 3.1
Comparing NRTs and CRTs

Dimension	NRT	CRT
Average number of students who get an item right	50%	80%
Compares a student's performance to:	The performance of other students	Standards indicative of mastery
Breadth of content sampled	Broad—covers many objectives	Narrow—covers a few objectives
Comprehensiveness of content sampled	Shallow—usually one or two items per objective	Comprehensive—usually three or more items per objective
Variability	Because the meaningfulness of a norm-referenced score basically depends on the relative position of the score in comparison with other scores, the more variability or spread of scores, the better	The meaning of the score does not depend on comparison with other scores; it flows directly from the connection between the items and the criterion; variability may be minimal
Item construction	Items are chosen to promote variance or spread. Items that are "too easy" or "too hard" are avoided; one aim is to produce good "distractor options"	Items are chosen to reflect the criterion behavior; emphasis is placed upon identifying the domain of relevant responses
Reporting and interpreting considerations	Percentile rank and standard scores used (relative rankings)	Number succeeding or failing or range of acceptable performance used (e.g., 90% proficiency achieved, or 80% of class reached 90% proficiency)

Source: Educational testing and measurement (p. 348), by T. Kubiszyn and G. Borich, Copyright © 2003, Wiley: New York. This material is used by permission of John Wiley & Sons, Inc.

although highly valued by parents and teachers, seldom becomes a basis for assigning grades.

Over the years, measurement experts have attempted to develop techniques for considering growth when assigning final grades (Kubiszyn & Borich, 2003). For example, one obvious problem occurs with the student who begins instruction with a great deal of knowledge about what is being taught. Improvement for this student is likely to be less overall than for a student who begins instruction with considerable deficiencies

APPLICATION 3.1

You are preparing to talk to parents for the first back-to-school night of the year. Write some "talking points" below about which frame of reference (norm-, criterion-, or growth-reference) you will use to assess their child's performance for the following:

Classroom assignments:

Classroom tests:

Standardized tests:

Homework:

in the area being taught. Some authors believe growth-referenced interpretations should be used to supplement norm- and criterion-referenced interpretations of learning.

In Application 3.1 show your understanding of norm-, criterion-, and growth-referenced assessment by preparing some "talking points" for a brief presentation to parents at back-to-school night.

Purposes of Assessment

Whether you adopt a norm-, criterion-, or growth-referenced frame of reference, or more likely a combination of these, your choice will be influenced by the purposes or functions your data are to serve. Grading is one of those purposes. Traditionally, four purposes have been assigned to classroom assessment: (a) setting expectations, (b) making a diagnosis, (c) monitoring learning, (d) and assigning grades.

Setting Expectations

Most teachers seek information about learner performance before instruction begins. Traditional classroom testing programs often use this information to set expectations for individual students. For example, knowing at the start of the school year that a learner's math skills rank in the bottom 25 percent of the class will influence your expectations for that learner. In doing so, you are making norm-referenced interpretations of the learner's performance.

Criterion-referenced interpretations can also be used to establish expectations. For example, let's say that a teacher's final goal for a three-week, third-grade multiplication unit is that a learner will solve multicolumn multiplication problems with 95 percent mastery. This teacher will have different expectations of mastery for those students who know their times tables and math facts before the lesson than for those learners who don't.

Like criterion-referenced assessment, growth-referenced assessment makes use of learner performance before instruction, but not for setting expectations. The basic assumption underlying growth-referenced assessment is that all learners will learn. The purpose of growth-referenced assessment is to help them do so—not to set expectations for how much or how little growth will occur. Consequently, growth-referenced assessment uses learner information from tests and observations before and after instruction to discover obstacles to learning that can be removed in subsequent instruction.

Making a Diagnosis

Diagnosis can occur before, during, or after instruction to determine the source or potential source of a learning problem. In many schools and classrooms diagnosis invariably begins after a learning problem has been detected. It is usually carried out by someone other than the classroom teacher, such as an educational diagnostician or school psychologist. In these cases diagnosis focuses on determining weaknesses in the abilities or aptitudes that are presumed to underlie successful reading, spelling, writing, math problem solving, and so forth. Often norm-referenced interpretations are made of the data generated by these diagnostic tests.

Some specialists also use diagnostic tests that assess whether the learner has the prerequisite skills to spell, write, or read effectively. In such cases the assumption is that learners are experiencing learning problems because they are not prepared for the instruction. Criterion-referenced interpretations are made of the results of these tests.

Growth-referenced assessment also uses measurement for diagnostic purposes but with two important differences. In growth-referenced assessment diagnosis is carried out by the teacher to uncover learning problems before and during instruction, not just after it. As you will recall from chapter 2, cognitive learning theory places emphasis on what learners know in a specific area prior to instruction. The purpose of instruction, therefore, is to develop, organize, and increase the complexity and efficiency of the learner's knowledge base. Diagnosis helps the teacher determine what misinformation or misconceptions, such as any error-prone or "buggy" math rules, the learner brings to instruction. Instruction and assessment focus on correcting the misinformation and modifying the misconceptions, as in debugging and amending the math rules seen in Figure 3.2. Growth-referenced assessment assumes that learning problems are caused by misconceptions or inadequacies in how learners think about or represent problems, not by inadequate abilities or prerequisite skills.

Monitoring Learning

In traditional classroom assessments, teachers monitor learning by making informal observations and asking questions. Such monitoring focuses on the products of learning or observable outcomes, such as precisely spelled words, answers to math problems, grammatically correct sentences, accurately read sight words, or correctly answered reading comprehension questions. Ideally, such information should be used to decide if instruction in an area should be altered in some way or continue. But teachers may monitor learning more for reasons of giving praise and feedback to students than for what it may indicate about their instruction. Both criterion- and growth-referenced interpretations are made of these data gathered from monitoring.

Monitoring learning is an integral part of growth-referenced assessment; but in contrast to more traditional testing practices, growth-referenced assessment uses monitoring to focus on the processes underlying learning as well as on the observable performances or products that suggest learning has occurred. Growth-referenced assessment begins with an analysis of the knowledge and thinking skills required for competence in a particular subject area. How the student becomes competent is as important as the proof of competence.

Consequently, assessment comprises specific questioning strategies, like verbal prompts and hints, which may include techniques called student "think-alouds" and "cognitive maps" during instruction to systematically monitor the learning and use of cognitive strategies and the increasing complexity and organization of the knowledge base. We will present examples of these assessment techniques in the chapters ahead. Information gained from them provides learners with feedback that enhances student motivation and provides the teacher with feedback on whether to revise, continue, or begin a new lesson.

Assigning Grades

Nearly all classrooms assign some number, letter, or label to represent the sum total of a student's learning at the end of a term or semester. These summative judgments can be derived from criterion- or norm-referenced assessment data. However, these grading practices have a number of problems: They assume equal amounts of learning have occurred for individuals who achieve the same grade, fail to acknowledge continuous progress or development in learning, and may mask an individual student's unique learning strengths and needs.

APPLICATION 3.2

Provide one key understanding you would want your parents to have concerning how you will accomplish each of the following purposes of assessment.

Setting expectations:

Making a diagnosis of a potential learning problem:

Monitoring learning:

Assigning grades:

Growth-referenced assessment can also result in a letter grade, but growth-referenced assessment requires that a learner's performance be described in terms of what was learned, how it was learned, and the changes that came about in the learner's knowledge base and use of cognitive strategies. Thus, descriptions of a child's learning that are richly textured with work examples, products, oral accomplishments, anecdotes, and brief stories about what and how the child is learning take precedence over single indicators of achievement whether in terms of averages, percentiles, letters, or category labels. We will discuss the variety of grading systems that will be available to you in chapter 12.

Now that we have reviewed the four purposes of assessment, in Application 3.2, try articulating to your learners' parents which one you will use in your classroom.

Determining Learning Outcomes

The focus of your assessments will depend on what you want your students to learn. Unfortunately, most textbooks that cover how to identify goals and objectives for teaching do not always make this clear. The result is that some teachers teach and construct an assessment that does not match the kinds of learning they value.

Traditional approaches to assessment derive from behavioral learning theory (Sulzer-Azaroff, Drabman, Greer, Hall, Iwata, & O'Leary, 1988). This theory holds that the focus of instruction should be on observable behaviors and skills. These learning skills are hierarchically sequenced such that more advanced skills cannot be learned before less advanced ones. There is a correct sequence for teaching these skills that applies to all learners. Learning involves the accumulation of these skills. The difference between more complex and less complex learning and problem solving is a matter of the number of observable skills that the learner has mastered. According to behavioral learning theory, teaching and assessment should focus exclusively on these observable outcomes and not on the unobservable cognitive processes (e.g., the use of thinking strategies) and metacognitive skills (e.g., being aware of and monitoring the effectiveness of thinking strategies) that underlie observable changes in behaviors and skills.

Two systems for identifying the outcomes of classroom instruction have been influenced to varying degrees by this perspective: the taxonomies of educational objectives in the cognitive, affective, and psychomotor domains (Bloom, Engelhart, Furst, Hill, & Krathwohl, 1984; Harrow, 1972; Krathwohl, Bloom, & Masia, 1999) and learning hierarchies (R. Gagné, 1985). The influence of these two systems on learner assessment has been considerable. We present an overview of these systems and then compare and contrast them with assessments based on cognitive learning theory.

Taxonomies of Educational Objectives

Bloom and his associates (1984) have developed a system for helping teachers identify the types of learning they can expect from their students. They refer to their classification schemes as **taxonomies of educational objectives**. These taxonomies are most helpful to teachers when they are planning their lessons. They help teachers focus on the outcomes, specifically behavioral objectives, that they want students to attain as a result of their instruction. The taxonomies also facilitate standards-based assessment. Teachers simply need to prepare behavioral objectives and construct measurement tools aligned with their curriculum standards. Anderson (2000) provides a version of the *Taxonomy of Educational Objectives* by Bloom et al. that helps teachers better understand, implement, and assess standards-based curricula.

The taxonomies cover three domains of learning: cognitive, affective, and psychomotor. The *cognitive* domain deals with thinking skills, the *affective* domain with attitudes and emotions, and the *psychomotor* domain with physical abilities. Let's look at each of these to see how they can help plan and assess learning outcomes.

The Cognitive Domain.   The *Taxonomy of Educational Objectives in the Cognitive Domain* (Bloom et al., 1984) illustrates the focus and purpose of the taxonomies. This widely used taxonomy organizes cognitive outcomes of teaching into six categories: knowledge, comprehension, application, analysis, synthesis, and evaluation. According to Bloom and associates (1984), attaining higher level outcomes can occur only after lower level outcomes have been mastered. Learners cannot tackle analysis (e.g., in a science class) unless they have previously acquired knowledge of facts and principles, comprehension of those facts and principles, and the ability to apply them. Only then can they be expected to be able to analyze. Likewise, if a learner lacks the skill to analyze empirical results, he cannot be expected to synthesize or evaluate the significance of scientific experiments and research findings.

Let's look more closely at each of the six outcomes in the cognitive domain.

Knowledge.   The knowledge category covers lesson objectives that require learners to remember information such as facts, definitions, terms, rules, words of a poem, and so forth. The taxonomy includes verbs that describe observable actions which provide evidence that the student has acquired knowledge. Some observable learner actions that suggest knowledge include recall, defines, labels, selects, states, and names.

Example knowledge objectives would be

- The student will recall the four major food groups, without error, by Friday.
- From memory the student should be able to name the primary colors with 80 percent accuracy.

Comprehension.   Objectives at the comprehension level require some degree of understanding. Reciting a rule does not show understanding, but restating it in one's own words does, as would comparing one rule with another rule. Some learner actions that suggest understanding are summarizing, comparing and contrasting, explaining, and paraphrasing.

Example comprehension objectives would be

- By the end of the period, the student will summarize the main events of the story in grammatically correct English.
- After reading the story assigned, the student will be able to orally explain the difference between there and their.

Application.   Application objectives ask learners to use information previously learned in one context in a different context. If a student can borrow in subtraction, reduce a fraction to its least common denominator, or test for the presence of sugar in a chemistry class, and does this with material he has never seen before, the requirements for application have been met. Learner actions that suggest application are prepare, compute, use, modify, and demonstrate.

Example application objectives would be

- By the end of the science unit, the student will be able to demonstrate for the class the law of conservation.
- Given fractions not covered in class, the student will multiply them on the board with 85 percent accuracy.

Analysis.   Analysis requires a student to examine, read, or listen to something; identify or break it down into its important elements or constituent parts; and point out relationships and organizing principles. You can analyze an essay into themes, arguments, main ideas, conclusions, and so forth. Learner actions indicating analysis are deduce, outline, break down, infer, diagram, and point out.

Example analysis objectives would be

- Given a presidential speech, the student will be able to point out the positions that attack an individual rather than that individual's program.
- Given contradictory statements (e.g., A man had the flu twice. The first time it killed him. The second time he got well quickly.), the student will be able to point out the contradiction.

Synthesis. Synthesis objectives ask learners to create something original or organize something in a unique way. A learner shows that he can synthesize when he discovers a new way to solve a math problem or design a science experiment. Learner actions that indicate synthesis are compile, devise, design, create, develop, and produce.

Example synthesis objectives would be

- Given a short story, the student will devise a different but logical ending.
- Given a statement of a community problem, the student will design on paper a practical solution to the problem.

Evaluation. Evaluation objectives ask learners to examine a product that they have never seen before and judge its worth according to some set of criteria. For example, after students have learned how to judge an effective political campaign speech, they demonstrate evaluation by critiquing an unfamiliar speech. Learner actions indicating evaluation include appraise, criticize, judge, validate, justify, and defend.

Example evaluation objectives would be

- Given a previously unread paragraph, the student will judge its value according to the five criteria discussed in class.
- Given a description of a new law, the student will defend it, basing arguments on principles of democracy.

The Affective Domain. Another method of categorizing objectives was devised by Krathwohl, Bloom, and Masia (1999). This taxonomy delineates five levels of affective behavior ranging from the receiving level to the characterization level. As in the cognitive domain, these levels are presumed to be hierarchical—higher level objectives are assumed to include and be dependent on lower level affective skills. As one moves up the hierarchy, more involvement, commitment, and reliance on one's self occurs, as opposed to having one's feelings, attitudes, and values dictated by others.

Let's look more closely at each of the levels of the affective domain.

Receiving. Objectives at the receiving level require the student to be aware of, or to passively attend to, certain phenomena and stimuli. At this level students are expected simply to listen or be attentive. Some action verbs describing outcomes at the receiving level are attend, listen, look, be aware, and, notice.

Example receiving objectives would be

- The student will be able to notice a change from small-group discussion to large-group lecture by following the lead of others in the class.

- The student will be able to listen to all of a Mozart concerto without leaving his or her seat.

Responding.   Objectives at the responding level require the student to comply with given expectations by attending or reacting to certain stimuli. Students are expected to obey, participate, or respond willingly when asked or directed to do something. Some action verbs that describe outcomes at the responding level are comply, follow, practice, discuss, and participate.

Example responding objectives would be

- The student will follow the directions given in the book without argument when asked to do so.
- The student will practice a musical instrument when asked to do so.

Valuing.   Objectives at the valuing level require the student to display behavior consistent with a single belief or attitude in situations where she is neither forced nor asked to comply. Students are expected to demonstrate a preference or display a high degree of certainty and conviction. Some action verbs describing outcomes at the valuing level are debate, display, express an opinion, and argue.

Example valuing objectives would be

- The student will express an opinion about nuclear disarmament whenever national events raise the issue.
- The student will display an opinion about the elimination of pornography when discussing this social issue.

Organization.   Objectives at the organization level require a commitment to a set of values. This level of the affective domain involves (a) forming a reason why one values certain things and not others and (b) making appropriate choices between things that are and are not valued. Students are expected to organize their likes and preferences into a value system and then decide which ones will be dominant. Some action verbs describing outcomes at the organization level are compare, formulate, decide, define, and select.

Example organization objectives that use these verbs are

- The student will be able to compare alternatives to the death penalty and decide which ones are compatible with her beliefs.
- The student will be able to formulate the reasons why she supports civil rights legislation and will be able to identify legislation that does not support her beliefs.

Characterization.   Objectives at the characterization level require that all behavior displayed by the student be consistent with her values. At this level the student not only has acquired the behaviors at all previous levels but also has integrated her values into a system representing a complete and pervasive philosophy that never allows expressions out of character with these values. Evaluations of this level of behavior involve the extent to which the student has developed a consistent philosophy of life (e.g., exhibits respect for the worth and dignity of human beings in all situations). Some action verbs describing outcomes at this level are display, exhibit, internalize, resolve, and revise.

Example characterization objectives would be

- The student will exhibit a helping and caring attitude toward students with disabilities by assisting with their mobility both in and out of classrooms.
- The student will display a scientific attitude by stating and then testing hypotheses whenever the choice of alternatives is unclear.

The Psychomotor Domain.   A third method of categorizing objectives has been devised by Harrow (1972) and by Moore (1992). Harrow's taxonomy delineates five levels of psychomotor behavior ranging from the imitation level (least complex and least authentic) to the naturalization level (most complex and most authentic). These behaviors place primary emphasis on neuromuscular skills involving various degrees of physical dexterity. As behaviors in the taxonomy move from least to most complex and authentic, behavior changes from gross to fine motor skills.

Let's look more closely at each of the outcomes in the psychomotor domain.

Imitation.   Objectives at the imitation level require that the student be exposed to an observable action and then overtly imitate it, such as when an instructor demonstrates the use of a microscope by placing a slide on the specimen tray. Performance at this level usually lacks neuromuscular coordination (e.g., the slide may hit the side of the tray or be improperly aligned beneath the lens). Thus, the behavior generally is crude and imperfect. At this level students are expected to observe and be able to repeat (although imperfectly) the action being visually demonstrated. Some action verbs that describe outcomes at this level are align, repeat, reproduce, follow, and balance.

Example imitation objectives would be

- After being shown a safe method for heating a beaker of water to boiling temperature, the student will be able to repeat the action.
- After being shown a freehand drawing of a triangle, the student will be able to reproduce the drawing.

Manipulation.   Objectives at the manipulation level require the student to perform selected actions from written or verbal directions without the aid of a visual model or direct observation, as in the previous (imitation) level. Students are expected to complete the action from reading or listening to instructions, although the behavior still may be performed crudely and without neuromuscular coordination. Useful expressions to describe outcomes at the manipulation level are the same as those at the imitation level, using the same action verbs, except they are performed from spoken or written instructions.

Here are example manipulation objectives:

- Based on the picture provided in the textbook, type a salutation to a prospective employer using the format shown.
- With the instructions on the handout in front of you, practice focusing your microscope until the outline of the specimen can be seen.

Precision.   Objectives at the precision level require the student to perform an action independent of either a visual model or a written set of directions. Proficiency in reproducing the action at this level reaches a higher level of refinement. Accuracy, proportion, balance, and exactness in performance accompany the action. Students are expected to reproduce the action with control and to reduce errors to a minimum. Expressions that describe outcomes at this level include performing the behavior accurately, without error, independently, proficiently, and with control.

Example precision objectives would be

- The student will be able to accurately place the specimen on the microscope tray and use the high-power focus with proficiency as determined by the correct identification of three out of four easily recognizable objects.

- The student will be able to balance a light pen sufficiently to place it against the computer screen to identify misspelled words.

Articulation.   Objectives at the articulation level require the student to display coordination of a series of related acts by establishing the appropriate sequence and performing the acts accurately, with control as well as with speed and timing. Expressions that describe outcomes at this level include performing the behaviors with timing, smoothness, confidence, coordination, integration, and speed.

Example articulation objectives would be

- Students will be able to write all the letters of the alphabet, displaying the appropriate proportion between uppercase and lowercase, in 10 minutes.

- Students will be able to accurately complete 10 simple arithmetic problems on a handheld electronic calculator quickly and smoothly within 90 seconds.

Naturalization.   Objectives at the naturalization level require a high level of proficiency in the skill or performance being taught. At this level the behavior is performed with the least expenditure of energy and becomes routine, automatic, and spontaneous. Students are expected to repeat the behavior naturally and effortlessly time and again. Some expressions describing this level of behavior are automatically, effortlessly, naturally, spontaneously, and routinely.

Here are example naturalization objectives:

- At the end of the semester, students will be able to write routinely all the letters of the alphabet and all the numbers up to 100 each time requested.

- After the first grading period, students will be able to automatically draw correct isosceles, equilateral, and right triangles, without the aid of a template, for each homework assignment that requires this task.

The taxonomies of educational objectives are useful reminders to teachers of the variety of ways that students can show simple or complex learning. After you have decided on the content of a lesson, it is worthwhile to ask yourself about the kinds of learning you want your learners to acquire and the indicators you will use to measure this learning.

Several cautions, however, are associated with using taxonomies for deciding what you will teach and assess. First, it might be questioned whether the six levels of the cognitive domain are distinct from one another. Although the distinction between knowing something, understanding it, and using it appears obvious, the notion that analysis, synthesis, and evaluation represent distinct and increasingly higher degrees of complex thinking may be problematic. For example, on what basis would you conclude that evaluating a piece of writing is a more rigorous intellectual accomplishment than creating or analyzing one? The assumption that analysis is a less complex form of thinking than evaluation may persuade some teachers to ignore the former in favor of the latter (Anderson, 2000).

Furthermore, the assumption that lower levels of a taxonomy must be mastered before higher levels can be achieved is unproved and contradicted in practice. Although it makes sense that someone cannot read with understanding unless they know the meaning of the words, it is possible for someone to be able to evaluate what they have read and not be able to synthesize or analyze a piece of writing. Coaches coach without being expert players at the game, playwrights write plays without being able to act, and foremen supervise employees who have skills that they themselves may not possess. The assumption that higher levels of thinking cannot be expected until lower levels of learning have been acquired may influence teachers to ignore higher levels of learning for certain individuals or classes when, in fact, some research suggests that students can sometimes learn higher levels of thinking faster than lower levels (Anderson, 2000; Resnick, 1976).

Finally, categorizing behaviors into cognitive, affective, and psychomotor domains does not mean that behaviors in one domain are mutually exclusive of those in the other domains. For example, it is not possible to think without having some feeling or emotion about what we are thinking, or have some emotion without some cognition about what we are feeling. Also, much thinking involves psychomotor movements and bodily performances that require procedural skills and abilities. Conducting a laboratory experiment requires not only thought but also pouring from one test tube to another, safely igniting a Bunsen burner, adjusting a microscope correctly, and so forth. It may be convenient for an objective to contain behavior from only the cognitive, affective, or psychomotor domain, but one or more behaviors from other domains are often required for a successful performance. The categorization of desired outcomes into discrete domains may underrepresent the simultaneous importance of multiple outcomes and processes of learning.

Gagné's Learning Hierarchies

Like Bloom and his colleagues (1984), Robert Gagné (1985) sought to develop a system that identifies learning goals in terms of their underlying thought processes and organizes them into categories from simple to complex. But Bloom and Gagné took different roads. Gagné's **learning hierarchies** organize learning outcomes into six categories: verbal information, intellectual skills, generalizations, cognitive strategies, attitudes, and motor skills. The last two categories resemble the affective domain and psychomotor domain developed by Bloom and associates. The first four categories encompass learning types that are both similar to and different from those included in Bloom et al.'s cognitive domain. Let's focus on these four categories.

Verbal Information.   Like Bloom et al.'s (1984) knowledge category, verbal information includes skills such as knowing the names of explorers, dates, definitions of words, the letters of the alphabet, or the multiplication tables. It also includes the ability to state a rule, such as "When two vowels go walking, the first one does the talking." Verbal information does not assume that the learner understands or can apply the rule (e.g., when sounding out new words). Instead, verbal information provides many of the building blocks for the development of concepts, rules, and generalizations that are covered by Gagné's intellectual skills category.

Intellectual Skills.   Intellectual skills cover what the person does with information. Intellectual skills involve making *discriminations,* or being able to recognize one thing as different from another. For example, you make discriminations when you recognize that *b* is different from *d*, a horse is different from a mule, pig sounds different than big, or an x-ray of a compound bone fracture looks different from an x-ray of a stress fracture.

The ability to make discriminations is prerequisite to the ability to *form concepts.* A person shows an understanding of concepts when he can label a concrete object (table) or an abstraction (justice) based on specific characteristics or he can make discriminations between concepts (point out that red is different from orange). But he does not have a concept of red or orange until he can correctly identify all the examples of red as red and not mix them up with examples of orange. Concrete concepts are easier to acquire than abstract or defined concepts. You can teach what an apatosaur is by showing examples of dinosaurs that are and are not apatosaurs, but the concept "democracy" must be defined for a person using words.

A third level of intellectual skills, according to Gagné (1985), involves *rule learning.* An example of a general rule is, "*i* before *e* except after *c*." To learn and use this rule, one must already know the concepts *i, e,* except, after, and *c.* So, concept learning must precede rule learning. We know that learners have acquired rules when they consistently read certain vowel combinations correctly, solve physics problems by applying Bernoulli's principle, bisect an angle, or write grammatically correct sentences.

Generalizations.   The fourth and highest level of intellectual skills involves generalizations. Generalizations are complex or higher order rules such as laws of supply and demand, gravitational forces, principles that apply to the rise and fall of civilizations, or laws that help explain geological events such as earthquakes.

Intellectual skills form learning hierarchies. Any school task—whether reading for comprehension, solving an algebra equation, writing an essay, or proving a theorem in geometry—can be broken down (or task analyzed) into the knowledge, discriminations, concepts, rules, and generalizations that are required to master the task. These skills form a hierarchy in that lower level skills must be learned before higher level skills. Once you correctly classify a task as one involving rule learning, for example, you automatically know that certain verbal information, discriminations, and concepts must first be learned. Figure 3.4 displays a learning hierarchy for conservation skills.

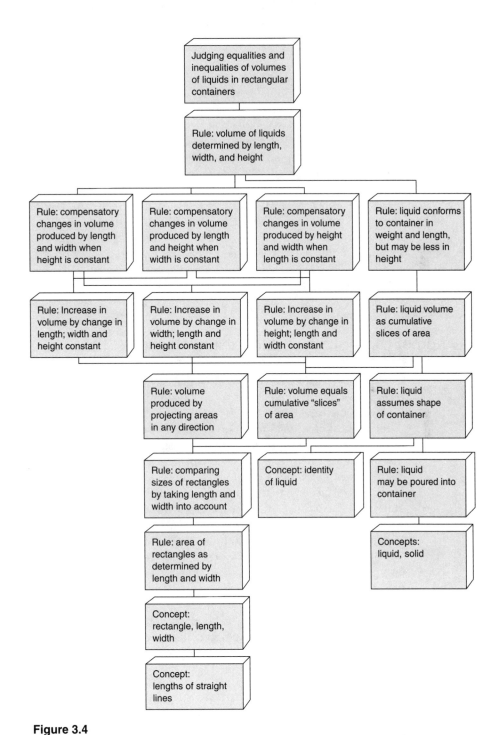

Figure 3.4

A learning hierarchy for conservation skills

Source: From "Contributions of Learning to Human Development" by Robert M. Gagné, 1968, *Psychological Review, 75*, p. 184. Copyright © 1968 by the American Psychological Association. Reprinted with permission.

Cognitive Strategies.   As you will recall from chapter 2, cognitive strategies are skills we learn to help us read, write, or solve problems that go beyond the immediate requirements of the task. Although Gagné (1985) does not explicitly say so, the learning of cognitive strategies requires the prior learning of certain intellectual skills. For example, learning a strategy to solve four-column subtraction problems involving regrouping and zeros in the second and third columns will require prior learning of certain spatial concepts such as "right side" as well as the concepts of numbers.

Some concerns with Bloom's (1984) taxonomies also apply to Gagné's: assumptions that certain learning is required before other learning can take place, and ambiguity in the meaning and distinctions among terms such as concepts, rules, and generalizations. Moreover, research fails to support the notion that, for all children, higher levels of learning can be attained only after lower levels have been mastered (Mayer, 1987; Resnick, 1976).

Evaluation of the Systems of Bloom and Gagné

Bloom and colleagues (1984) and Gagné (1985) have made major contributions to our understanding of what is involved in simple and complex forms of learning, and both systems can embrace some of the outcomes identified by cognitive learning theory. The knowledge and comprehension levels of Bloom et al. represent the declarative knowledge so important for establishing a knowledge base for building toward higher order thinking, whereas their analysis, synthesis, and evaluation levels represent the genesis of cognitive strategies. Gagné's "cognitive strategies" provide an even closer link to more recent cognitive learning theory. The work of both authors has added to our ability to clarify what we mean by learning and to develop valid indicators of learner achievement. It has also underscored the importance of the link between instruction and assessment.

Both systems reflect a theory or school of learning that primarily derives from a behavioral science tradition, the assumptions of which may not always provide valid explanations of complex human learning (Lieberman, 1992). In particular, the taxonomies of Bloom et al. and Gagné may view learning as too sequential, hierarchical, and outside the control of the learner to account for some important types of learning, such as the role of problem solving, decision making, critical thinking, and valuing.

Research in cognitive science points out that learners are constantly trying to make sense out of the information they learn as well as trying to develop new learnings and understandings in ways that cannot be neatly mapped into rigid sequences and hierarchies (Bransford et al., 1999). Cognitive approaches to school learning, similar to those by Bloom and colleagues and Gagné, underscore the importance of information, higher level thinking, and cognitive strategies. But, unlike behavioral conceptions of learning, the cognitive view stresses that learners often derive or construct different meanings from the same information and experiences and end up in different places than might be predicted from learning sequences or hierarchies as suggested by constructivist views of teaching and learning.

APPLICATION 3.3

Using either the same or different lesson topics you will be teaching, see if you can differentiate the taxonomy of Gagné from the taxonomy of Bloom by preparing an oral or written test question for each of the following:

Knowledge:

Application:

Verbal Information:

Generalizations:

This text takes an approach that preserves the strengths of the systems of Bloom et al. and Gagné, but also acknowledges the constructive nature of the learner's own contribution to the learning process. In other words, we want to maintain the emphasis on clearly specifying what is meant by learning. In addition, we want lesson planning to recognize that learning does not always proceed in neat, linear steps that require mastery of one skill before moving to another, more complex form of learning.

In Application 3.3, check your understanding of the taxonomies of Gagné and Bloom by discriminating the type of learning each emphasizes with some lesson topics you will be teaching.

A Cognitive Learning Model for Determining Outcomes

Let's look in on the planning process used by sixth-grade teacher Lori Copeland to see how a lesson based on a cognitive model of learning differs from one based on a behavioral model. The main point of Lori's lesson is to help students understand that plants use light to make their own food through a process called photosynthesis. Were she to use a behavioral model, her lesson planning might go something like this:

> Let's see. What do I want my students to be able to do at the end of the photosynthesis lesson? Well, I want them to understand the process of photosynthesis. Understanding is at the comprehension level of the taxonomy, and students can show understanding by explaining photosynthesis in their own words, summarizing the steps in the process using their own words, or predicting what would happen if plants weren't exposed to light. So, I'll focus on the following objectives which I can test with a short essay: On an essay test, students will (a) summarize in their own words the steps involved in the process of photosynthesis; and (b) predict and explain what would happen to a plant if it got water and some plant food, but was put in a basement for two weeks where there was very little light.
>
> In order for students to be able to achieve these objectives, they're going to have to have some knowledge. They'll have to know relevant terms such as root system, catalyst, and phototropism. They'll have to be able to identify the parts of a plant that produce food. They also must memorize in sequence the steps in the process of food making. So, my knowledge objectives in this area will be that students will (a) recognize the correct meaning of the following words: root system, catalyst, phototropism, stoma, veins, food, energy, and chlorophyll; (b) label the parts of a plant and parts of a leaf; and (c) list the steps in the process of photosynthesis.
>
> I'll start my lesson with activities to help them acquire knowledge for understanding photosynthesis. Once they have all the important concepts, I'll describe the process of photosynthesis. I have a film for them to watch, and we can examine some plants to point out the structures. Then, I'll ask questions to see if they understand what I've told them, and we'll have an objective test at the end of class.

Were Lori to plan from a cognitive learning model, her lesson planning might go something like this:

> At the end of this lesson, I want my students to know what it means when we say that plants make their own food. If they understand what it means for plants to make their own food, then they should be able to explain why some plants live and some die, why some are strong and some are weak, and they should be able to make predictions about how certain circumstances will affect plant growth.
>
> But I also want them to do some scientific thinking by raising questions or forming hypotheses and finding out how to support or disprove them. So, knowing how to ask questions and how to observe and collect information to answer those questions is also an important outcome of this lesson.
>
> Good scientific thinking also involves a willingness to challenge your beliefs about things. Another goal will be to get learners to reflect on what they know now about how plants make food and to challenge what they know.
>
> I'm sure the students all have ideas about what makes plants grow, what food is, and how plants get food. If they're like previous students, they'll have some misconceptions, too. So, another goal will be to see how their knowledge of things like food and energy changes over the course of the lesson. They need to see that food means one thing for human beings and another thing for plants, but there are some common concepts.
>
> I'll start my lesson with a discussion of what is a living thing, what is and is not food, and then ask students how they think plants get food. From that I'll gradually build to the idea that plants have to make their own food. Then, we can discuss how they do this while I model the scientific way of thinking by my questions. I'll see if

their own thinking is becoming increasingly scientific by observing if they pattern their questions after mine. If I can get them to ask questions that challenge one another's ideas, I will know I'm accomplishing my goal.

At the end of the lesson, I'll develop a test that measures some facts about photosynthesis. But I'll also ask students to solve some real-life problems pertaining to photosynthesis in the laboratory. I'll ask them not only to solve these problems but also to show me how they arrived at a solution. This way I can evaluate not just their answers but also the processes they used to arrive at an answer.

As you can see, both the behavioral and cognitive approaches place importance on objectives and activities to accomplish them. Although each model includes the learning of information, the cognitive model also emphasizes the processes by which information is acquired, qualitative changes in the knowledge base (e.g., better knowledge organization) and in problem solving, and includes assessment over the course of the lesson, not just at the end. The behavioral approach measures products, discrete behaviors, and answers on a paper-and-pencil test in ways that require that knowledge be taught first, followed by understanding. The cognitive model stresses that learners will arrive at their own understanding if the teacher provides a learning context that involves providing real-world examples, giving information, eliciting misconceptions, challenging ideas, modeling problem-solving strategies, and giving learners skill in monitoring their own learning. What guides these teaching processes in the cognitive model of learning is an analysis of the task that identifies the necessary knowledge, thought processes, and mental representations learners must use to meet an objective.

Summary

This chapter has shown you how to establish a frame of reference and purpose for your assessment and how to determine learning outcomes. Establishing your assessment frame of reference involves choosing the proper balance among the norm-, criterion-, and growth-referenced frames of reference and establishing how you will set expectations, make a diagnosis, monitor learning, and assign grades. This chapter also introduced the *Taxonomy of Educational Objectives* by Bloom and colleagues and Gagné's (1985) *Learning Hierarchy* to help you plan a learning assessment. Finally, this chapter reinforces the importance of four important areas of learning: declarative knowledge, procedural knowledge, cognitive strategies, and metacognition. We will revisit each of these important areas of learning in the chapters ahead.

Activities

1. Using the taxonomies of Bloom and or Gagné as a guide, identify some learning outcomes for a lesson or unit you will teach.

2. Give examples of assessments that you have taken or know of that were (a) norm-referenced, (b) criterion-referenced, and (c) growth-referenced. In your opinion, what is one advantage and one disadvantage of each of these frames of reference?

3. How would you answer someone who said, "You can't be a good coach unless you've been a good player, but you can be a good teacher without having been a good student." Explain whether you agree or disagree using the concept of learning by either Bloom et al. or Gagné.

4. Using Lori Copeland's two lesson plans from this chapter as an example, write a brief summary of two new lesson plans that are on the same topic, one representing the behavioral model of learning and the other the cognitive model. Which plan do you believe will be most effective for achieving the goals of your lesson?

5. For the two scenarios you have outlined, identify any declarative knowledge, procedural knowledge, cognitive strategies, and metacognitive skills that will be necessary for achieving the goal of your lesson.

Suggested Readings

Borich, G. (2004). *Effective teaching methods* (5th ed). Upper Saddle River, NJ: Merrill/Prentice Hall.
   This book discusses ways to categorize learning outcomes using the cognitive learning categories of Bloom et al., Gagné, and others.

Orfield, G., & Kornhaber, M. (Eds.). (2001). *Raising standards or raising barriers?: Inequality and high stakes testing in public education.* New York: The Century Foundation.
   This report discusses how standardized tests inadvertently provide a gate-keeping function with unintended side effects and how this effects public education.

Quality Assurance: Determining Reliability and Validity

The initial chapters of this book have emphasized that teaching and assessment co-exist in dynamic interaction. They have the same mission, to enhance student learning, and the same goals, to develop knowledge, thinking skills, and motivation to learn. Teachers set goals and objectives that assessment measures, and assessment informs teachers about learner progress and the usefulness of their teaching methods.

This chapter introduces some concepts that will help your assessment accomplish its mission. **Quality assurance** is the process that ensures that it will. It addresses two related questions:

1. How do you know that your assessment is measuring what it is supposed to measure?

   OR: What is the validity of your assessment?
2. How do you know that your assessment is dependable?

   OR: What is the reliability of your assessment?

The **validity** of an assessment is the degree to which it measures what you say it measures. You may develop an assessment activity to evaluate how well a student can think critically. But how do you know that it is measuring critical thinking and not memorization? A test's **reliability** is its ability to produce the same results if assessed at a different time. How do you know that your conclusions about a learner's ability to think critically, based on observations and questions asked during Wednesday's lesson, would be the same as those based on observations and questions during Friday's lesson? This chapter identifies indicators of validity and reliability and suggests methods of achieving them as you construct your own assessments.

Validity

In chapter 3 you learned about different approaches to determining the outcomes of your learning assessment system. These outcomes are typically inside the heads of your learners, such as knowledge, organization of knowledge, cognitive strategies, problem solving, and metacognition. You cannot see any of these, therefore, you need to identify observable signs that suggest that these behaviors are being learned. An "assessment" is a vehicle for measuring these behaviors. An assessment can consist of objective test items, essay questions, a written sample of your students' work, observations of their behavior, an oral question and answer session, their performance in an authentic setting, or any combination of these. Validity concerns how well such assessments measure what you want your students to learn.

Validity encompasses three important questions.

1. To what degree am I assessing the behaviors that I want my students to learn?
2. To what degree am I assessing what I teach?
3. To what degree does my assessment accomplish its purpose?

The first question measures a type of validity called *construct validity;* the second measures *instructional validity*. The third question concerns the ultimate purpose for which you are doing the assessment and is called *consequence validity*.

Let's examine each of these questions and point out what you can do to assure that these types of validity are a part of every assessment you make.

Construct Validity

The following question was asked of a fourth-grade class during a presidential election:

> Imagine that you could vote. Because you are interested and concerned about the country's future, you try to keep yourself well informed. You have just heard "replays" of the two candidates' speeches. Your cousin, who has not listened to the speeches, asks you about some of the problems facing the nation.
>
> Tell the class some of the things your cousin should understand. Your answer should be based on (a) the specific facts you know about each candidate, and (b) the past discussions we have had in class about the coming election.

This question was designed to assess the acquisition, organization, interpretation, and application of knowledge (Baker, 1994). On the surface, the question appears to require these thought processes of learners. So the answer to the question, "Does this assessment measure the qualities of thinking that the teacher intended?" seems to deserve a "yes."

But does it? Suppose that the class discussion preceding this assessment included a review and discussion of excerpts of each candidate's speech, and class exchanges about the most important ideas and issues pertinent to the election. If this were the context in which the question was asked, then all a learner would need to do is recall what was said in class and parrot that back. In these circumstances, the answer demands mostly memorization, which is a far cry from the understanding that the question was designed to measure. In other words, under these circumstances the assessment task lacks construct validity.

An assessment has **construct validity** when it produces learner behaviors that bear a direct link to the cognitive activity you want to assess. If you want to determine how well one acquires new knowledge and applies it to solve a problem, then you must design an assessment context that requires those cognitive processes. The assessment context is more than the written or oral question. It involves prior exposure to test content, limits placed on the learner's response (called test constraints), and the nature of the response being required. In this example the way the question was asked suggests it has construct validity for assessing understanding. But this understanding also depends on the cognitive processes actually required by the learner to answer the question correctly.

Looks can be deceiving. An assessment, oral or written, which appears to be assessing one type of cognitive learning, like analysis or application, may actually require a different type of cognitive activity. Asking a learner to tell you who is running for president may tell you little about whether the learner understands anything the candidates might have said. Likewise, labeling the states on a map is no indication of whether someone knows how to travel from North Dakota to Iowa.

Construct validity is more difficult to achieve as the cognitive activity you want to assess becomes more complex. Assessing whether a learner has basic knowledge of people, places, dates, and events about an election may be relatively easy. Determining how organized and related the learner's information is about the election is more demanding, and assessing whether the learner can draw on this knowledge to compose a response in a real-life setting may be a challenge to any teacher's assessment skills.

Assuring Construct Validity. The challenge to achieving construct validity is ensuring that the behaviors you decide to observe and to measure are valid indicators of what a student knows and thinks. Here are some important steps for doing this.

Step 1. Specify the construct domain. This is the first and most essential part of ensuring construct validity. It requires that you delineate the type of cognitive activity you want to assess. The question about the election from which the teacher wanted to assess understanding could require the following cognitive activities: knowledge acquisition, knowledge organization, interpretation, and application of specific content knowledge in new contexts.

The more indicators of the behavior you want to measure, the better. You might start with terms such as knowledge, comprehension, analysis, concept formation, problem solving, and so forth introduced in chapter 3. Don't forget to consider the thought processes used by experts when they are engaged in problem solving, writing an article, solving a math problem, interpreting historical events, or designing an experiment to see how well your questions match their questions.

Some cognitive outcomes are more difficult to specify or delineate than others. If you want to assess content-specific knowledge, it is appropriate to ask students to recall facts, recognize important dates, or give definitions on paper-and-pencil tests. If you want to assess whether your students know how to follow a certain procedure, you might specify the steps of the procedure and then use a checklist to see how well it is followed. With constructs such as making connections, becoming a math problem-solver, communicating complex ideas, and deep understanding, specifying precise cognitive activities can be a more challenging task. Choosing from the behaviors identified by Bloom et al. (1984) and Gagné (1985) in chapter 3 can get you started.

Step 2. Choose as many indicators of the domain as possible.   When specifying the construct domain, identify all the behaviors that represent it. For example, let's say that you are teaching fourth-grade math and want to assess your students' deep understanding of fractions. You decide that deep understanding involves problem solving, reasoning, and communication. You break down these activities further into seeing mathematical relations, organizing information, using and discovering procedures, formulating hypotheses, evaluating the reasonableness of answers, justifying an answer or procedure, and explaining your solutions to someone else.

The best way to ensure construct validity for assessing deep understanding is to design a task that requires as many of these indicators as possible. Developing a fraction assessment task which requires using a procedure and justifying an answer only would not have as much construct validity as one requiring three or four indicators.

Notice the number of indicators of deep understanding in the election question: (a) acquisition of knowledge, (b) organization of knowledge, (c) interpretation, and (d) application. All four of these indicators could be rated or judged from the students' oral responses making it more construct valid.

Elementary school teachers who wish to assess reading comprehension can ask their learners to do several of the following: summarize what was read in their own words, predict what would happen next, describe the main idea of the passage, or relate the surprise ending to an event in their own life. All of these represent multiple indicators of the cognitive activity being measured.

Step 3. Design the assessment task so that it requires only the cognitive skills relevant to the construct you wish to assess.   When designing an assessment task, we sometimes inadvertently measure, or require students to use skills that are not relevant to the construct being measured. For example, the election question was designed to measure understanding, which was defined as acquisition, organization, interpretation, and application of knowledge. But what if the assessment task included reading material that was too difficult for many learners to understand? In that case, the assessment would not measure the construct of understanding, but rather reading comprehension. If the scoring standards for a student's answer gave more importance to *how* the student said it than *what* the student said, this question would measure the student's speaking ability more than his thinking ability. The relevancy of the behaviors you are assessing is determined by the purpose for the assessment as identified in step 1.

Remember to design an assessment context that requires construct-relevant skills, and avoid contexts that make the assessment tasks unrelated to your instruction. After you have designed the assessment task, ask yourself or a colleague whether it requires thought processes or constructs irrelevant to your instruction. These may include reading ability, writing ability, memory, or background knowledge that gives unfair advantage to learners who happen to have had particular experiences.

Step 4. Write task directions that require the thought processes that you intend to assess. You should phrase the assessment question or task with words that clearly identify the desired thought processes that underlie an acceptable response. In other words, you should select terms and phrases that precisely communicate what you want the learner to do. The question about the election, for example, should clearly communicate to the learner what she was expected to do: "Explain the most important issues," "Base your answer on what you learned in our previous class discussion," and "Tell how you acquired the opinions you express."

When giving or writing directions, we sometimes use words and expressions that are ambiguous to learners, however clear they may be to us. Here are some ambiguous words and expressions which may fail to lead the learner to the higher cognitive processes that you may want. Below them are some alternative expressions that focus and direct the student to a higher level response:

Tell me...about the story. (description)
What role did Tom have in the story? (analysis)

What do you think...about the ending? (opinion)
Could you tell me another way in which the story might have ended? (prediction)

Who was the boy who got in trouble? (identification)
Why was Josh always getting in trouble? (analysis)

What did Josh do wrong? (recall)
How would you have acted, if you were Josh? (valuing)

One way to check the clarity of your questions is to write out a model answer or set of guidelines and then revise the directions to better lead the learner to your response or to follow the guidelines. This usually results in some revision of the directions or the task.

In Box 4.1 we have asked Mr. Wilson to follow the four steps above to assure construct validity in preparing a math assessment for his third-grade students. Using his responses as a guide, try applying these four steps to a lesson of your own choosing in Application 4.1.

Gathering Evidence of Construct Validity. If your assessments have construct validity, then after you have rated or scored them and have come to conclusions about what your students know, you will observe the following:

1. *The students who do best should be among those learners you know to be more knowledgeable and expert.* You have lots of prior information about your learners' knowledge and academic background. This will come from previous grades, listening to their answers in class, and reading their homework and class work. All other things being equal, those whom you judge to know more in a particular content area

---

BOX 4.1   Mr. Wilson's Steps for Assuring Construct Validity

Step 1: Specify the construct domain.

The cognitive domain I want to assess is the application of basic mathematics to everyday life.

Step 2: Choose as many indicators of the domain as possible.

I will assess knowledge of multiplication and division with two- and three-digit numbers, the application of this knowledge in a new context, and its interpretation for decision making in a real world setting.

Step 3: Design the assessment task so that it requires only the cognitive skills relevant to the construct you wish to assess.

I will use a practical example in every-day life, such as miles per gallon in determining how far you can travel, and ask students to show their knowledge of multiplication and division. Then I will ask them to make a decision based on their interpretation of the results.

Step 4: Write task instructions that require the thought processes that you intend to assess.

The assessment question I will ask is:

You are on vacation and want to drive from Chicago to St. Louis on your way home. The distance between these cities is 300 miles. Your car gets 20 miles per gallon on the highway.

1. How many gallons of gas will it take to make the trip?
2. How many gallons would you have left if you filled up your 23-gallon tank before leaving?
3. If you got only 15 miles per gallon instead of 20 because of some city driving along the way, could you continue to Hannibal, MO, to stay the night with your grandmother, which is another 90 miles from St. Louis?

---

should do better on your assessment. If not, it may indicate that your assessment is unrelated to your instruction.

2. *Learners should do significantly better on assessments given at the end of a lesson or unit than on similar assessments given at the start of the unit.* In other words, evidence of the construct validity of an assessment is whether learners who have had instruction perform better than learners who have not.

3. *Other assessment data that measure similar abilities or constructs should agree with the conclusions about learners that you make from your assessment.* For example, students take standardized achievement tests of reading and math. All things being equal, students who show strong reading comprehension or math

---

APPLICATION 4.1

Design an assessment question or task that measures your learners' deep understanding of a topic, following the four steps below for ensuring the construct validity of your task. Tell what you will do to accomplish each step.

Step 1: Specify the construct domain.

Step 2: Choose indicators of the domain.

Step 3: Include only relevant cognitive skills.

Step 4: Write task directions that require the relevant thought processes.

---

problem-solving skills on these tests should also be among those who do well on your tests that measure the same skills.

Instructional Validity

In chapter 1 we said that the link between assessment and teaching is a principal influence on academic motivation. The kind of assessment validity that relates to this link is called **instructional validity**.

Whereas most teachers are certain that they assess what they teach, their learners are sometimes not as convinced. One of the most common complaints of students, whether in grade school or college, is that their tests do not measure what was taught (Tuckman, 1988). When a tenuous link exists between assessment and teaching, two problems occur: (a) students who have learned what was taught are unable to demonstrate it, and (b) students are evaluated on topics for which they have received little or no instruction. When these problems occur the assessment can be said to lack content validity. A test's content can be said to be valid when it adequately samples a desired body of knowledge. Our discussion of instructional validity will subsume the topic of content validity and the procedures for ensuring it.

Teachers often fall into two traps when designing assessments. The first is that they assess content areas or skills that they did not teach. This often occurs when teachers hold their students accountable for textbook content or skills that were not discussed and practiced in class, assigned for homework, or encountered in workbook exercises. Teachers may think that, although some content was not covered, "good students will learn it anyway."

The second trap occurs when the assessment places more emphasis on certain domains of knowledge or skills than was reflected during instruction. A common student complaint is that the test covered too many areas that were discussed only briefly in class and ignored much of what the teacher presented during lessons. Thus, an assessment has instructional validity when it asks learners to do what was taught during their lessons and with the same degree of emphasis. If students saw a teacher demonstrate how to reduce fractions to their least common denominator, practiced this, and solved similar problems for homework, then an assessment that is valid for assessing this skill should ask them to reduce fractions and not to transform them into decimals. Mr. Wilson's math questions would have instructional validity if he had prepared them before the test to use the same cognitive processes they needed to do well on the test.

Assuring Instructional Validity.   An assessment that has instructional validity meets two standards:

1. It reflects the goals and objectives of your lessons.
2. It gives the same emphasis to specific goals and objectives as did your lessons.

One way to ensure instructional validity is to construct an assessment blueprint. An **assessment blueprint** is a table used to identify the type of behavior and content to be assessed. Figure 4.1 shows a teacher's assessment blueprint for a unit on how the earth's surface changes. The content (topics covered) is listed down the first column, and the cognitive learning outcomes emphasized in class are identified across the top. This particular unit requires memory or the accumulation of domain-specific declarative knowledge, conceptual understanding, and some application and analysis. The percentages given in the column headings indicate the teacher's emphasis for these cognitive behaviors. The cells within the table identify assessment formats that measure the content and behaviors taught and the points assigned to each type of assessment. The percentages in column 1 reflect how much weight or importance each assessment format will be given in the overall evaluation or grade. The totals for rows and columns reflect the emphasis (in points) that the assessment must have to match the instructional emphasis in class. In the chapters ahead you will acquire an increasingly varied menu of formats for completing an assessment blueprint, including portfolios, oral performances, products and exhibits, and performance assessments.

Gathering Evidence of Instructional Validity.   There are a variety of systems for constructing assessment blueprints (Gronlund, 1993; Kubiszyn & Borich, 2003; Oosterhof, 1996). Ideally, assessment blueprints should be constructed when you plan your

| Test Blueprint for a Physical Science Test | | | |
Topics	Memory for Facts and Terms 25%	Understanding of Concepts 40%	Application and Analysis of Data 35%	Totals
Weathering (15%)	5 fill-ins (1 pt each)	5 multiple-choice (2 pts each)		15 pts
Physical weathering (15%)	5 true-false (1 pt each)	5 multiple-choice (2 pts each)		15 pts
Volcanic activity (25%)	5 fill-ins (1 pt each)	5 multiple-choice (2 pts each)	1 essay (10 pts)	25 pts
Folded structures (15%)	5 fill-ins (1 pt each)		1 essay (10 pts)	15 pts
Faults (30%)	5 fill-ins (1 pt each)	5 multiple-choice (2 pts each)	1 essay (15 pts)	30 pts
TOTALS	25 pts	40 pts	35 pts	100 pts

Figure 4.1
Teacher's assessment blueprint for a three-week unit on how the earth's surface changes

lessons. That way, what you teach and its emphasis in your class activities is easily remembered.

When you design your assessment, follow this procedure:

1. Have the blueprint in front of you. Do not rely on memory to tell you if you emphasized knowledge acquisition or problem solving and to what degree.

2. Write your assessment questions, tasks, and specifications from a learner's perspective. Ask yourself: What information and cognitive skills are required to do these tasks? Did I prepare my learners for these tasks?

3. For each assessment task that you develop, refer to the cognitive learning outcome(s) that the task is intended to assess. Ask yourself: Does this question reflect the level of cognitive complexity indicated in the learning outcome(s)?

In college teaching, most of the evidence for instructional validity comes from comments that students make on course evaluation surveys. Specific questions address the relevance of test content to instructional objectives. In the elementary and middle school, much of the evidence for this type of validity comes to your attention informally: You overhear students griping about how unfair the test is or they complain to you directly. Take these comments seriously. They suggest that you should routinely assess the instructional validity of your assessment by asking

	Strongly Agree	Agree	Not Sure	Disagree	Strongly Disagree
Class and text adequately prepared me for the test.	☐	☐	☐	☐	☐
A lot of questions on the test came as a real surprise.	☐	☐	☐	☐	☐
Too many questions asked about things we didn't cover in class.	☐	☐	☐	☐	☐
Overall, this test was fair.	☐	☐	☐	☐	☐

Figure 4.2
Test evaluation survey

learners after a test to anonymously agree or disagree with statements such as those in Figure 4.2.

Imagine that Mr. Wilson did a good job of teaching multiplication and division of two-, three-, and even four-digit numbers involving fractions, but never asked his learners to practice on a problem that included *both* multiplication and division and to interpret the result. Do you think his students would have gotten to Hannibal, MO, to visit their grandmother without running out of gas?

In Application 4.2, practice applying the concept of instructional validity to several tests you recall taking recently.

APPLICATION 4.2

Think of two tests that you have recently taken: one which you felt had instructional validity and another which you felt did not. Describe the tests and list the distinguishing features that could account for their validity or lack of validity.

Distinguishing characteristics of the instructionally valid test:

Distinguishing characteristics of the instructionally invalid test:

Consequence Validity

Until recently, discussions about the importance and meaning of test validity focused primarily on construct and instructional validity. Many assessment experts now believe that validity considerations should also include the *use* made of test scores and the *consequences* they have (Gipps, 1995; Messick, 1989). This type of validity is called **consequence validity** (AERA, APA, NCME, 1999). In other words, validity also encompasses whether the assessments you design change both you and your students' behavior.

If the purpose of your assessment is to facilitate learning and motivation, then consequence validity requires evidence of this: Were you able to improve learning and motivation from the decisions you made from the assessment data? When a significant number of learners do not become more motivated, increase the size and complexity of their knowledge base, or learn how to think better, then your assessment lacks evidence of this type of validity. If you want your assessment to be used to help you adjust your teaching methods to become a better teacher, then there should be some evidence that your teaching has changed as well. The best way to ensure consequence validity is to have a plan that specifically describes how you will use the results of your assessments.

What we have been saying is that your assessment can only be valid for its intended purpose. Consider the situation in which the purpose of a test is to assess students over a unit of mathematics instruction. A valid test in this case would accomplish its purpose by identifying those who had mastered the skills taught during the unit and those who had not. In other words, its purpose is to measure how well certain concepts had been taught and mastered. But, what if this test was being considered by the school's administration to identify students for an advanced mathematics class the following semester? In this situation the classroom teacher was only interested in finding out how well her students mastered a particular body of knowledge. She constructed her test to find out whether her students could (a) use models to add, subtract, multiply, and divide integers and connect the actions to algorithms; (b) use division to find unit rates and ratios in proportional relationships such as speed, density, price, recipes; and (c) simplify numerical expressions involving order of operations and exponents. Here a test would do the job and have consequence validity if it tells the teacher what students need more instruction and what kinds of errors they need remediated. It would, however, have little or no validity for selecting who should be assigned to the advanced math class. Such a test, if specifically constructed to select students for an advanced math class, would likely have little or no validity for assessing the content of this teacher's mathematics unit. Figure 4.3 provides a checklist to help determine the consequence validity of your assessments.

To summarize:

1. Evidence of construct validity tells you that you are measuring what you say you are measuring.
2. Evidence of instructional validity tells you that you are measuring what you are teaching.

1. Describe how you intend to use the results of your assessment. Check all that apply:
   __a. Grading
   __b. Improving teaching
   __c. Improving learning
   __d. Monitoring learner development
   __e. Enhancing motivation
   __ f. Informing parents

2. For each purpose named in step 1, identify what evidence you will gather to show that the purpose is being achieved.

	Purpose					
	a	b	c	d	e	f
Percentages of answers correct	☐	☐	☐	☐	☐	☐
Changes in test scores across the semester	☐	☐	☐	☐	☐	☐
Opinion surveys of learners and parents	☐	☐	☐	☐	☐	☐
Motivational assessment	☐	☐	☐	☐	☐	☐
Ratings of teaching effectiveness and improvement	☐	☐	☐	☐	☐	☐
Other (describe):	☐	☐	☐	☐	☐	☐

3. For each purpose, describe how you will use the evidence to achieve it.
   a.
   b.
   c.
   d.
   e.
   f.

Figure 4.3
Checklist for ensuring consequence validity

3. Evidence of consequence validity tells you that your assessment has provided evidence that it has accomplished its purpose by changing both you and your students.

Reliability

Assuring validity means that your assessment methods are measuring what you want them to measure, but validity is only one aspect of quality assurance. Another aspect concerns the accuracy of the scores, grades, ratings, or judgments that you make about a learner from your assessments. You can make a paper-and-pencil test or construct a performance task that has the potential to measure what you want; however, it may not *reliably* measure your learner's behavior.

For example, take the question about the election presented earlier. The question appears valid for assessing understanding, but after students answer the question, the teacher has to reflect on their answers and make judgments about the degree to which they show "understanding." If two teachers read the same essay and each assigned a grade without consulting one another, would they agree?

Why Assessments Lack Reliability

Here are some assessment situations. As you read them, reflect on how comfortable you would feel if you were the teacher described.

A fifth-grade teacher developed a five-question true–false test to determine her learners' factual knowledge of U.S. geography. The questions covered four chapters. Sean got a C because he missed two questions. He told the teacher that he knows a lot more but that the questions on the test were not enough to reflect what he knows. The test just asked questions over the areas in which he was the weakest.

Rose, a second grader, got an "unsatisfactory" on her 6-week report card for "works cooperatively with others." Her mother questioned the teacher. The teacher explained that she based her judgment on how Rose behaved during cooperative learning groups, which met for 45 minutes every Friday. The parent explained that Rose was absent for all but two of these groups and wondered whether the teacher saw enough of Rose to come to such a judgment.

Ozzie, a sixth grader, was upset about getting only 13 of 20 points on one of the essay questions regarding a story about Lewis and Clark they had read. The essay question read: "What were some of the biggest reasons contributing to the Lewis and Clark expedition not attaining some of their goals?" The teacher explained that he failed to discuss the issue of illness as a factor in the Lewis and Clark expedition. Ozzie said he knew about that but did not know he was supposed to have it as a part of his answer.

Mr. Snead, a fourth-grade teacher, used the following method to grade his students' reading journals: They would be graded from A to F, with pluses and minuses. After reading a journal, Mr. Snead would make a global judgment about how good it was and put it in one of six piles corresponding to the letter grade. Then, he would go to each pile and assign pluses or minuses. Laura got a C minus and wanted to know exactly what the difference was between a C minus and a C and what she needed to do to get a B.

Each of these vignettes portrays a reason why assessment judgments made by a teacher can be unreliable: limited sample of behavior, small number of observations, unclear tasks, and scoring imprecision. Let's consider each one.

Limited Sample of Behavior.   For many practical reasons, assessments have to adhere to certain time constraints. Thus, the number of questions on an assessment is limited, but this comes at a cost. The fewer questions or tasks that you observe, the more likely it is that your judgments of the learner based on those tasks will be unreliable. Imagine trying to make a judgment of someone's dart-throwing ability based on one toss at a target. Maybe a finger slipped, the person sneezed, someone bumped into her, or a clap of thunder startled her and shook the target.

Random influences also affect a learner during an academic assessment, whether that assessment is a test, an observation, or a project. The more the learner is asked to do, the more likely you can rule out these random influences on performance. With a five-question quiz, it is more likely that momentary lapses of attention, anxiety, classroom disturbances, or other random influences will affect performance. Perhaps several questions pertain to areas in which the student forgot to study or for which she wasn't in class. With a 30-question test, such factors would play a less prominent role.

Small Number of Observations.   Learners have good and bad days just like teachers. A test, a one-time observation, a single opportunity to do a science procedure, or a no-revision policy for a writing assignment each increases the likelihood that factors other than the learner's knowledge, thinking skills, or writing ability will affect performance.

Judgments about noncognitive attributes such as motivation, attitude, or getting along with others are especially susceptible to unreliability due to limited opportunities to observe. Thus, the more occasions on which you base your observations, the more reliable they will be.

Unclear Tasks.   Ambiguity and lack of clarity are major hazards to reliability. If a learner performs poorly on a test of knowledge, it should be because she lacks knowledge and not because she did not understand the questions. Likewise, if a student fails to show evidence of problem solving during a science experiment, it should be due to his lack of this cognitive skill, not because he didn't understand what was expected of him.

Vague questions, ambiguous requirements, or unclear directions allow learners to interpret the task in ways that you did not intend. In such cases, your judgments about what is lacking or missing in the learner's performance may say more about your test development skills than the learner's cognitive abilities.

Scoring Imprecision.   Scoring contributes significantly to unreliability, especially for essay questions, writing assignments, history projects, or science experiments that are designed to assess complex thinking or deep understanding. Vague scoring standards increase the likelihood that a teacher's judgment will be influenced by factors unrelated to what the students actually wrote, said, or did.

For example, some questions after a reading assignment might be designed to assess knowledge acquisition, organization, interpretation, and application. But, without a detailed scoring guide to evaluate learner answers, a teacher could be unduly influenced by writing style over substance. Moreover, lack of a scoring guide may cause factors such as teacher fatigue to play a prominent role in the measurement process. As we will see in future chapters, this threat to reliability can be diminished by creating a model answer which includes all the essential ingredients required for assigning different numerical values or grades.

Assuring Reliability

Certain assessment goals present a greater challenge to validity than others. This also is true for reliability. Building reliability into a project or test to assess problem-solving ability and critical thinking presents a greater challenge to your assessment than constructing a paper-and-pencil test to assess factual knowledge. Still, regardless of the learning outcomes you wish to assess, there are some general strategies that you can use to ensure reliability: increasing the number of performances to be scored or rated, increasing the number of occasions on which to score or rate, writing clear task specifications, and increasing scoring objectivity. Let's take a closer look at each of these.

Increasing the Number of Performances.   If you wanted to find out how the parents of students in your school feel about homework, and you could not ask them all, you would be concerned about two issues of relevance to reliability: number of parents sampled and their representativeness. You would want to make sure that the parents you surveyed were not from only one segment of the community and that you had enough parents to adequately represent all segments.

The same considerations apply when designing an assessment. Because you can not ask questions to cover all the content, you must ask enough questions to adequately represent the most important aspects. For example, if you are trying to assess knowledge of some science concepts to determine misconceptions, you might identify some of the most important misconceptions, randomly sample from these misconceptions, and write true–false or multiple-choice questions about them. Say you discover 15 misconceptions your learners have about motion, gravity, magnets, electricity, and so forth. You randomly sample five of them and put them into question form. Someone who has misconceptions of most of the five would probably have exhibited misconceptions about most of the 15 had you included them all on the test.

Thus, you need to do three things to satisfy this standard for reliability pertaining to assessment length: (a) define the domain of important knowledge, (b) select an appropriate number of bits of knowledge or information from this domain, and (c) randomly sample from this domain.

The difficulty of doing this comes when you are trying to assess domains other than simple knowledge, such as understanding, problem solving, or the skilled use of cognitive strategies. Designing more than one or two tasks to assess these areas would take too long. Thus, when designing an assessment to measure complex skills, you should make sure that you observe or rate these skills on more than one occasion.

Increasing the Number of Observations.   When you conclude that a learner is a good problem solver in math, or a strategic thinker in science, or an effective communicator in writing based on one observation, one essay question, or one short story, ask yourself this question: Would I come to the same conclusion about this person's understanding, problem-solving, or writing ability if I were to observe the student on a different but related task on another day? For example, a student's writing can be expected to differ according to whether they are responding to a persuasive, informative, or narrative writing assignment. These types of writing would need to be assessed on a number of occasions to justify an overall inference of "good" writing.

The only way to ensure that your judgments based on one observation generalize to other occasions is to plan other opportunities to observe. Sometimes this occurs naturally, for example, when evaluating a piece of writing where multiple drafts are turned in for feedback. In this situation the reliability of the teacher's judgments or ratings about a written work is increased due to the multiple opportunities to rate it. At other times you will need to create alternative situations to determine if your learners have mastered instructional routines without understanding the underlying concepts. For example, a first grader may be able to add one pile of 3 blocks to another pile of 7 blocks and come to a total of 10 blocks; but, when given this same problem on paper ($3 + 7 =$ __), supplies the answer of 11. Learners often do not see the difference because one problem is in blocks and the other in numbers. This child has yet to gain the concept of numeracy, and relying on only the first problem would not reveal the misconception. You can enhance the reliability of scoring science, social studies projects, arithmetic tasks, or oral presentations by giving learners multiple opportunities to present and improve their work using different contexts, and when differences occur, using the opportunity to develop a deeper understanding.

When repeated measurements of the same task are not practical or feasible, then it is important to plan for several observations at different times. In such cases the tasks and context should be different but should assess the same underlying construct, such as acquisition and communication of knowledge or application of scientific procedures. This method might be used when assessing math problem solving, answering open-ended essay questions, using particular scientific procedures or methods, or designing an experiment.

Writing Clear Task Specifications.   Reducing task ambiguity can be accomplished by writing clear and concise questions, tasks, and directions. Your students will find it difficult to respond to an assessment task if they do not fully understand the task. The most important part of an assessment task is the directions you provide. Your directions should get students thinking in the right direction and set out the limitations and criteria that must be responded to if a satisfactory score is to be achieved. For example, if you wrote the following essay item, expect a wide range of answers, only some of which may be in the "ballpark" you are expecting.

> "In 500 words, discuss democracy in the United States."

Contrast this question with the following which includes criteria that prompts the student to focus a response on the specific outcomes (e.g., comparison and contrast, classification, prediction) that are most desired and that make scoring more reliable:

> "Describe the executive, judicial, and legislative branches of the United States government and provide examples of the checks and balances they have on one another."

The following chapters provide many examples of how to improve the clarity of your paper-and-pencil, oral, and performance tasks.

Increasing Scoring Objectivity. Some assessment formats present a greater challenge to scoring objectivity than others. Essay questions are more difficult to score reliably than true–false or multiple-choice questions, but, even in the latter cases, scoring keys are important.

Essay questions and performance assessments can be scored in a variety of ways, including holistic techniques, rating scales, and analytic scoring procedures. Each technique has its advantages and disadvantages which are described in subsequent chapters. Whichever method you choose, you should design a scoring plan—called a **rubric**—that defines the degree of accomplishment that is achieved for products (e.g., poems, essays, drawings, maps), complex cognitive processes (e.g., skills in acquiring, organizing, and using knowledge), use of procedures (e.g., physical movements, use of specialized equipment, oral presentations), and attitudes and social skills (e.g., habits of mind, cooperative group work). In the chapters to come we provide examples of these scoring techniques.

Summary

Your learning assessment system will accomplish its mission if it meets standards of validity and reliability. The checklist in Figure 4.4 summarizes the various aspects of these two considerations. You will want to review it before administering each test, observation, or performance assessment that you design.

Activities

1. Explain the difference between construct validity, instructional validity, and consequence validity. Now imagine that you just discovered that an assessment you gave lacked each of these. What could you do to improve each before you gave the test the next time?
2. For the assessment in question 1, explain how you would show evidence of (a) construct validity and (b) instructional validity.
3. Show that the assessment in question 1 has consequence validity by describing (a) how you intend to use the results, and (b) what evidence you will gather to indicate that your purpose for this assessment has been achieved.
4. Using Figure 4.1 as your guide, construct an assessment blueprint for a unit in your subject or grade. Provide percentages that indicate your intended emphasis for subject-matter content and learning outcomes, and be sure the total points for rows and columns reflect your instructional emphasis.
5. Describe a test you would like to develop using Figure 4.4, the quality assurance checklist, as your guide. Provide as much detail in your description as the checklist calls for.

1. Validity
   A. Construct Validity
      ☐ Have you identified the construct domain?
      ☐ Have you specified a number of indicators of the domain?
      ☐ Have you chosen several of these indicators for which you will design tasks?
         Example indicators:
         1. Writing skill
         2. Memorization
         3. Reading ability
         4. Prior knowledge
      ☐ Have you constructed tasks that assess only those indicators?
      ☐ Have you asked a colleague for an opinion on what skills the tasks require?
      ☐ Have you taken steps to make sure that the task directions require the thought processes that you want to assess?
         Example steps:
         1. Model answers
         2. Review by colleagues
   B. Instructional Validity
      ☐ Have you defined the goals and objectives of your lesson?
      ☐ Do your assessment tasks measure only those goals and objectives?
      ☐ Have you estimated the extent of class time devoted to those goals and objectives?
      ☐ Does the relative importance assigned to each assessment task match the extent of instructional time devoted to them?
      ☐ Have you developed an assessment blueprint?
   C. Consequence Validity
      ☐ Have you identified the uses to which your assessment results will be put?
         Example uses:
         1. Grading
         2. Improve teaching
         3. Improve learning
         4. Monitor development
         5. Enhance motivation
         6. Inform parents
         7. Other:
      ☐ Have you taken steps to ensure that your assessment results accomplish the purpose(s) identified?
II. Reliability
   ☐ Have you adequately defined the domain of knowledge or skills that you wish to assess?
   ☐ Have you included sufficient numbers of tasks or questions to adequately represent or sample this domain?
   ☐ Are you observing the learner on more than one occasion while he/she is displaying the learning?
   ☐ Do you observe more for complex than simple learning?
   ☐ Have you taken steps to ensure that your tasks, questions, and directions are unambiguous?

Figure 4.4
Quality assurance checklist

Suggested Reading

Gipps, C. V. (1995). *Beyond testing: Towards a theory of educational assessment.* Washington, DC: Farmer Press.
This book provides an excellent discussion of traditional psychometric notions of reliability and validity. Gipps also discusses these notions as they apply to current concerns about the usefulness of educational assessment.

5

Assessing Declarative Knowledge: The Objective Test

One of the frequently heard criticisms of American education is that learners spend too much time memorizing information and too little time learning to use it (National Research Council, 2001). These criticisms have had an impact on teacher training, curriculum, and testing. Today, a much greater emphasis is placed on such outcomes as critical thinking, learning to learn skills, and deep understanding.

Although these worthy efforts have led teachers to assign greater importance to higher order thinking, they have often led them to underrate the significance of knowledge acquisition (Bruer, 1993). One of the most important findings of cognitive learning theorists is that knowledge is indispensable for good thinking. What has convinced them of this? Let's look into an influential study about the importance of knowledge for complex thinking.

Knowledge Versus IQ

Most people believe that to be a good thinker, to solve problems like an expert, you have to be smart—you have to have a high IQ. Ceci and Liker (1986) conducted research on this issue. They wanted to know how important IQ was for complex thinking or problem solving in comparison to knowledge. If you had to choose the better problem solver in a specific area of expertise, would you pick the person with the high IQ but little knowledge or the person with average IQ and a lot of knowledge?

The specific area of expertise that Ceci and Liker studied was horse-race handicapping. Expert handicappers consider many factors when deciding which horses in a race are likely winners. They study statistics pertaining to the jockey, horse, and track including lifetime earnings, lifetime speed, racetrack size, track surface conditions, and purse size. Fourteen variables in all were examined for each horse in a race. An expert has to understand all these statistics and engage in a complex reasoning process to decide which horse is likely to win, place, or show. Ceci and Liker selected 30 men who were avid racetrack patrons for their 3-year study. Fourteen of them were classified as experts based on their ability to pick the top horse in 9 out of 10 races and the top three horses in at least 5 out of 10 races. The 16 nonexperts were nowhere near as capable of picking the top horses.

Ceci and Liker took great pains to make sure that the only difference between the experts and nonexperts was handicapping ability. Both groups had similar IQs (average of nonexperts = 99.3, experts = 100.8), occupational prestige, average years of education (nonexperts = 10.1, experts = 10.2), and average years of track experience (nonexperts = 17.4, experts = 15.1).

The researchers gave both groups an array of statistics related to 50 horses. Each horse was pitted against a "standard horse" in 50 two-horse races. The task was to pick the winner. As expected, the experts did much better at picking winners than the nonexperts and displayed much more sophisticated reasoning. In fact, their handicapping ability and reasoning matched those of a professional handicapper included in the study.

What was unexpected was the relationship between reasoning ability and IQ. IQ had nothing to do with picking winners or complex reasoning. Lower IQ experts, in some cases with IQs as low as 81, 82, and 84, clearly surpassed higher IQ nonexperts, some with IQs of 113, 118, and 130. What the former group had that the latter group lacked was knowledge of how to handicap. The experts knew exactly which statistics were important and which were not and the relationship among all these facts. Ceci and Liker concluded that in a specific area of expertise, IQ is unrelated to good thinking. Knowledge and how to use it in decision making separate the skilled performer from the unskilled.

Does this conclusion hold true for skills like reading comprehension in school-age children? A group of German researchers have provided some convincing evidence that it does (Schneider, Korkel, & Weinert, 1989). Working with children in grades 3, 5, and 7, they identified those who had a lot of information about topics like soccer and those who did not but were comparable in IQ. The learners with more knowledge were much more capable of detecting inconsistencies and contradictions in reading passages about soccer than learners with less knowledge, regardless of IQ.

In this country Walker (1987) showed that lower IQ learners who knew a lot about baseball got more out of a baseball passage than higher IQ learners who knew little about the sport. Hall and Edmondson (1992) found similar results with basketball expertise. What all these studies point to is that those of your learners with substantive knowledge about a specific subject will be your best thinkers. Those who know little will not reason well regardless of their IQs. The learners who get most out of reading about the weather, photosynthesis, or the legislative process will be those who have the most information at the time they are reading (Macintosh, 1998; Reber, Walkenfeld, & Hernstadt, 1991).

Research from the Rightstart program (Griffin & Case, 1975) referred to in chapter 2 makes a similar point. It has shown that low socioeconomic status learners are at risk for low math achievement because they come to first grade without particular math information, not because they have lower aptitude for math. In the area of science instruction, Hunt and Minstrell (1994) and Smith (1990) have shown that prior misinformation detracts from learning new information and impedes complex reasoning.

Thus, if you are asking your students to read about plants and animals, first make sure they have acquired some basic knowledge about these topics. Your students will not be good thinkers in science if they lack information about forces, motion, and gravity. Your best thinkers in civics will be those who know something about forms of government and the legislative process, and your best third-grade math problem solvers will be those who know their math facts.

The Domain-Specific Knowledge Base

Learners know lots of things about history, geography, movies, baseball, inventors, religions, and so forth. If you could look inside someone's head to find out what they know, just as you might browse through an encyclopedia, what might you see? Researchers have evidence that the brain compartmentalizes knowledge. One spot is active when you think about history; another, when you think about math. The sciences have their niche as well as reading and literature. The math spot is further organized into related domains like double-column subtraction, fractions, or division.

Cognitive neuropsychologists are fairly convinced that these knowledge domains and their subdomains are really networks of nerve cells with connections running from one neuron to another (Kosslyn & Koenig, 1992). With estimates of over 100 billion of these nerve cells in the brain's cortex, and hundreds to thousands of connections associated with each nerve cell, that leaves a lot of room for information to be stored (Squire & Kandel, 1999).

What if you could surgically remove one domain of knowledge, for example, science, and put it under an electron microscope which was connected to a computer system that let you see finer and finer neural networks? If you were looking at the science domain of a middle-school learner after reading a story on rocks and how they are formed, you might see a network like that in Figure 5.1 (Champagne, Klopfer, Desta, & Squires, 1988).

Notice the hierarchical arrangement in Figure 5.1 This domain-specific knowledge base contains facts about rocks, such as terms and their definitions (metamorphic, igneous, sedimentary). It contains concepts such as instances of igneous rocks clustered together and separated from instances of metamorphic rock.

What does this learner know about rocks? Quite a bit! First, as we pointed out, he knows the names of different rocks (limestone, shale, pumice). Not only does he know facts about rocks, but he also has concepts: metamorphic, igneous, and sedimentary are different classes of rocks, of which there are many examples. He knows how different rocks are classified and that some rocks share the same characteristics.

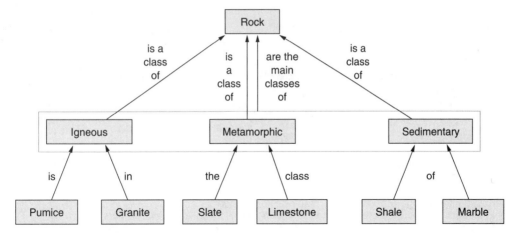

Figure 5.1
Preinstruction knowledge organization of geology knowledge
Source: From *Structural representations of students' knowledge before and after science instruction,*
by A. B. Champagne, L. E. Klopfer, A. T. Desta, and D. A. Squires, 1988, *Journal of Research in
Science Teaching, 18,* p. 97. Copyright © 1988 by John Wiley & Sons, Inc. Reprinted by permission of
Wiley-Liss, Inc., a subsidiary of John Wiley & Sons, Inc.

Every domain-specific knowledge base has a similar structure: facts, concepts, and connections among concepts that lead to rules and generalizations. A **knowledge base** contains every bit of information that we have ever learned about something and the connections among these bits. These knowledge bases are dynamic and ever changing. They increase in size as the student acquires more information, but, more important, they grow increasingly organized to allow the learner to learn new information and remember old information.

To better appreciate this changing nature of knowledge networks, look at Figure 5.2. This network represents the same student's rock knowledge base as before, but, after additional reading and class discussion on rocks, new information has been added to the learner's knowledge base. What's different? What does this knowledge base tell us about what the student knows about rocks after more instruction? Now concepts are connected to form principles of how rocks are formed; for example, weathering changes metamorphic rock into sedimentary rock, and magma and lava, which come out of volcanoes, are made of igneous rock. In other words there are more connections among the concepts, indicating that the student is aware of the relationships among the different rocks and how one type of rock is formed from another. He knows a lot about the dynamics of rock formation.

What can we conclude about the characteristics of a knowledge base from Figures 5.1 and 5.2? First, a knowledge base has breadth: It contains a wide array of information, concepts, and rules. Second, it becomes gradually more elaborate as a result of instruction. It acquires more information and ideas. The learner associates more and more examples with particular concepts and more and more concepts with one another. Third, it has a certain hierarchical organization that changes over time

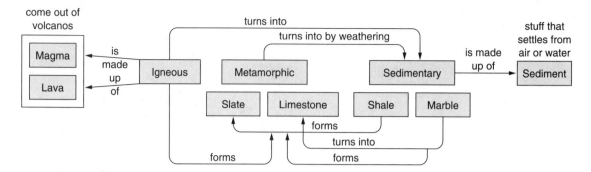

Figure 5.2
Postinstruction knowledge organization of geology knowledge
Source: From *Structural representations of students' knowledge before and after science instruction,*
by A. B. Champagne, L. E. Klopfer, A. T. Desta, and D. A. Squires, 1988, *Journal of Research in
Science Teaching, 18,* p. 97. Copyright © 1988 by John Wiley & Sons, Inc. Reprinted by permission
of Wiley-Liss, Inc., a subsidiary of John Wiley & Sons, Inc.

by dividing information into more subsets and establishing the relationship among
the subsets.

These changes in the student's rock knowledge base illustrate what it means to
"know more." When we say that someone knows more about rocks after instruction
than before, or that an expert race handicapper knows more than a novice, or that
a college English major knows more than an 11th-grade American literature student,
we mean that person has more bits of information. We also mean that this information is more elaborate and organized, as in Figure 5.2. It is precisely this elaboration
and organization that allows more knowledgeable learners to think and problem-
solve better in a given domain than the less-informed learner, regardless of IQ (Mack-
intosh, 1998).

How a Knowledge Base Develops

What causes domain-specific knowledge bases to acquire more information and to
become more elaborate and organized? Are these changes that teachers alone can
bring about, or do learners also play a role in elaborating and organizing their knowledge base? Modern cognitive learning theory stresses the role of the learners themselves in constructing knowledge networks.

Cognitive learning theory holds as fundamental the principle that learners and
not teachers construct knowledge networks (Bransford et al., 1999; Richardson,
1997). As Figures 5.1 and 5.2 show, the breath, elaboration, and organization of a
learner's knowledge base can increase from instruction. The mind spontaneously
constructs and enlarges knowledge bases from your instruction. The hierarchical
organization is a natural transformation that occurs without the learner even being

aware of it. The hierarchy was not created by lessons systematically organized to present a fixed sequence of facts, discriminations, concepts, rules, and generalizations—a teaching strategy that behaviorists, who were only interested in the outward manifestations of behavior, used to recommend. It was created by instruction that taught learners the cognitive and metacognitive processes that provided them the tools to create these organized networks on their own.

The role of instruction is to arrange learning environments so that learners gain access to information and have the opportunities to relate it to what they already know. They associate new bits of information with pieces they already possess to form concepts and connections among concepts, and they gradually develop deeper and deeper understanding with support and guidance from you. Where initially their knowledge domains contained information that was organized based on surface features (e.g., the texture or color of rocks), eventually it becomes organized on the basis of higher order principles of thinking (e.g., the way rocks are formed). With the proper instruction, it is the learner who constructs this organization.

Assessing What Learners Know

Given that learners construct their own knowledge networks or domains from classroom and other experiences, the assessment role of the classroom teacher is clear—monitor knowledge construction. This involves assessing prior information, the acquisition of new information (breadth), and its transformation (elaboration and organization).

Using the rock knowledge example, let's say that one goal of an interdisciplinary unit in reading and science is to develop an understanding of rocks and how they are formed in the context of a mystery adventure story that takes our protagonists through rugged mountain terrain on the island of Hawaii. One of the principle concepts to be learned is that the rocks that make up the earth's crust all have a common source, volcanic activity. Students come to the unit with some knowledge, but much of it consists of unconnected, isolated pieces of information, some of which is misinformation. For example, many naive learners believe that all rocks are essentially the same: They just look different because of the effects of weathering. Others believe that all rocks were formed under a vast ocean that once covered the earth. Others, when asked why different rocks are heavier than one another, or have larger crystals than others, reason that "that's how they looked before the volcanoes threw them out." The notion that the rate of cooling can cause molten rock to be different is absent and, to them, counterintuitive.

Misconceptions can seriously impede the types of learning and conceptual change that you desire. To promote and monitor conceptual change, therefore, you will want to assess not only learners' new information and its conceptual structure but also its changing elaboration and organization.

To assess what learners know, you will have to do the following:

1. Assess simple factual knowledge before, during, and after instruction.

2. Assess elaboration as new pieces of information are added to old to help form concepts.

3. Assess organization as concepts become connected to one another to form rules, principles, and generalizations.

Let's look at how you can accomplish these goals.

Assessing Simple Factual Knowledge

Simple factual knowledge refers to the facts, dates, names, expressions, or labels a person knows without much concern for depth of understanding or ability to use this information. Before you teach about rocks, fractions, or political parties, you will want to determine whether your students know such things as the names of different rocks, how to write a fraction, and what a political party is. As your lesson progresses, you give tests and ask questions to determine whether the knowledge base is growing or is acquiring more breadth.

You should consider two issues when assessing the extent of someone's factual knowledge. These issues are the sampling of content and assessment of recall versus recognition. Let's look at these to see how they can help assess your learners' knowledge base.

Sampling

Whether before or after a lesson, learners know more bits of information than you can practically assess. Science contains more technical terms; social studies, more names and dates; language arts, more spelling vocabulary; and basic math, more number facts than could possibly be measured on a paper-and-pencil test. So, the question becomes: Which information do I include on my test, and how many questions need I ask?

This question pertains to sampling. Just as pollsters sample voters to make inferences about how the nation feels about a particular political candidate, so also do teachers sample information to make inferences about what someone knows. In fact, any test is really only a sample of what someone knows. The challenge is in drawing the best possible sample—asking the right questions to allow correct inferences about the knowledge base to be made.

Sometimes knowledge domains are so small we do not need to sample. In math, for example, there are so few types of angles and geometric shapes that we can ask questions about all of them. There are several common misconceptions that learners have about plants and how they make food. You can assess all of these and changes in the misconceptions after a story on photosynthesis. But some knowledge domains are too vast to be exhaustively surveyed. Examples of these are math and geography facts, and spelling, reading, vocabulary, and grammar rules. For example, if the names of states and their capitals are being assessed, need students supply all 50 in order to make a reasonable inference that students know their states and capitals? Would 5 or 10 be sufficient for determining if students know those facts? In such cases we test on a random sample of facts. If a learner gets 70 or 90 percent correct, we infer a moderate or extensive knowledge base. Thus, when knowledge bases are extensive and we want to draw inferences about how informed or knowledgeable someone is, we have to sample from the knowledge domain and write or ask questions about the sample.

From a cognitive learning perspective, knowledge is not important for its own sake, that is, knowing for the sake of knowing, unless you aspire to be a game show expert. Knowledge is important because it is the foundation of deeper understanding and more complex problem solving. Teachers want to assess a learner's knowledge base about rocks, plants, or fractions because knowing about certain terms, concepts, and their connections is important for deeper understanding and problem solving in these areas. In other words knowledge is only a vehicle to some greater end and not important in and of itself.

The question you must ask in deciding which knowledge to assess, then, is: What knowledge is essential to helping my learners solve the important problems that are the focus of my curriculum? In other words, what knowledge is required to get my learners to the next step on the learning ladder in a particular content area? When this knowledge is limited, as in our rock example, you need not sample. You can assess all the important pieces of information. But when this knowledge is extensive, as is the case of vocabulary for reading comprehension, math facts for automatically solving division problems, and grammar rules for fluent writing, you must sample and make inferences about how much someone knows.

Chapter 3 discussed the significance of goals and objectives for teaching and testing. These goals and objectives will help you decide which knowledge is and is not essential to accomplish them. If your goal is deep understanding of division problems, and you have defined the important knowledge as that which is contained in the math workbook, then you can ask questions that comprehensively cover that knowledge. On the other hand, if you want to measure your learners' acquisition of knowledge from many sources, such as readings, class discussion, book chapters, and computer-assisted software, it is more than likely you will have to compose a sample of questions from these sources.

Recall Versus Recognition

When trying to determine spelling knowledge before or after a spelling unit, you can use either of these procedures:

1. Give the students a list of words and have them circle all those that are spelled incorrectly,
   OR
2. Dictate the words and have the students spell them on a piece of paper.

Both techniques assess knowledge, but the former measures recognition and the latter measures recall. The second procedure is a more demanding task for most learners than the former. Which is the better measure of knowledge? Before answering this question, consider another example.

How would you assess whether students know the names of famous explorers and their discoveries? Here are three ways:

1. List the names of 10 explorers and their discoveries.
2. Answer true or false: DeGama explored the Amazon River.
3. The Spanish explorer who discovered the Mississippi River was named
_____.

All assess knowledge, but questions 1 and 3 require recall, whereas question 2 requires recognition.

Tasks that ask learners to *fill in* blanks; *list* things in order; write down words; outline; or *recite* facts, names, or dates require **recall. Recognition** is elicited by tasks that ask learners to choose, select, or match.

The answer to whether recall or recognition gives a better measure of knowledge depends on your goal. In spelling, you may want learners to recognize their own writing errors and consult a dictionary. In this case a recognition test will meet your needs. On the other hand, if you want your learners to write quickly, automatically, and correctly without depending on a dictionary, then the recall test is the better choice. If a learner in math will have access to calculators, then recalling number facts or steps in solving a problem is less a concern than if the learner must provide quick and automatic answers to basic skill problems.

In general, when deciding whether to use a recall or recognition test to assess knowledge, remember first that recall is more demanding. Then ask yourself whether, given the goals of the lesson, it is more important for learners to recall information from memory or to recognize accurate information when they see it. It is more important that they have the information at their fingertips or that they know it when they see it?

Ways to Measure Recall and Recognition

Simple factual knowledge is typically assessed with *objective-type* item formats. The word objective refers to the objectivity with which it is scored. These item formats avoid subjectivity or bias in how the item is scored by having a single correct answer. Objective test item formats include true–false, completion, matching, and multiple choice. True–false, matching, and multiple choice are also called *selected-response* items, because the learner selects from alternatives that are provided in the question. Let us look at some rules for developing test items that measure the recall and recognition of factual knowledge using these formats.

True-False Items.   True–false items are popular because they are quick and easy to write, or at least they seem to be. Although they do take less time to write than good objective items of any other format, well-written true–false items are not so easy to prepare.

As you know from your own experience, every true–false item, regardless of how well or poorly written, gives the student a 50 percent chance of guessing correctly even without reading the item. In other words, on a 50-item true–false test, we would expect individuals who were totally unfamiliar with the test content to answer about 25 items correctly.

Fortunately, the effects of guessing can be reduced by following these guidelines:

- Encourage *all* students to guess when they do not know the correct answer. Because it is virtually impossible to prevent certain students from guessing, encouraging all students to guess equalizes the effects of guessing. The test scores will then reflect a more or less equal "guessing factor" plus the actual level of each student's knowledge. This also will prevent test-wise students from having an unfair advantage over students who are not test-wise.

- Require revision of statements that are false. In this approach, you provide space at the end of an item for students to alter false items to make them true. Ask the student to first underline or circle the false part of the item and then add the correct wording, as in these examples:

T	<u>F</u>	High IQ students <u>always</u> get good grades.
		sometimes
T	<u>F</u>	Panama *is* <u>north</u> of Cuba.
		south
T	<u>F</u>	<u>September</u> has an extra day during leap year.
		February

If you are asking true–false questions orally of younger learners, you can simply ask them to write the number of each of the items and a T or F alongside the number. If you are asking them to require revision of a true–false item, tell them or write on the board which word may be true or false, then they may provide a word or choose an alternative word from a list.

With this strategy, full credit is awarded only if the revision is correct. The disadvantage of such an approach is that more test time is required for the same number of items, and scoring time is increased.

Here are some suggestions to keep in mind when writing true–false test items:

- Tell students clearly how to mark true or false (e.g., circle or underline the T or F) before they begin the test. Also orally explain and/or write this instruction at the top of the test.

- Construct statements that are definitely true or definitely false, without qualifications. If the item is true or false on the basis of someone's opinion, identify the opinion's source as part of the item, for example, "According to our city government, more citizens are recycling than ever before."

- Keep true and false statements approximately the same length and be sure that there are approximately equal numbers of true and false items.

- Avoid using double-negative statements. They take extra time to decipher and are difficult to interpret. For example, avoid statements such as "It is not true that subtraction cannot precede addition in the problem $7 - 2 + 5$."

- Avoid terms denoting indefinite degree (e.g., large, long time, regularly) or absolutes (never, only, always). For example, "A students never get a poor grade." Students tend to consider these responses wrong because they are indefinite.
- Avoid placing items in a systematic pattern that some students might detect (e.g., True-True-False-False, TFTF, etc.).
- Do not take statements directly from the text without first making sure that you are not taking them out of context.

Completion Items.   Contrary to true–false items, completion items measure recall. Like true–false items, completion items are relatively easy to write. The first tests constructed by classroom teachers and taken by students often are completion tests. Like items of all other formats, completion items may be well written or poorly written. Completion items such as true–false can also be orally delivered, which is often an advantage for younger learners who are just learning to read. It also eliminates the advantage better or faster readers have over those who may know the answer but may not be able to respond as quickly. Here are some suggestions for writing completion items:

- Require a single-word answer or a brief, definite statement. Avoid items so indefinite that they may be logically answered by several terms:
  Poor item: The next President will be elected in _____.
  Better item: The next President will be elected in the year _____.
- Be sure the item poses a problem. A direct question often is better than an incomplete statement because it provides more structure for an answer.
  Poor item: The main character in the story "Lilies of the Field" was called

  _____.

  Better item: Who was the main character in the story "Lilies of the Field?"

  _____.
- Be sure the answer is factually correct. For example, can the answer be found in the text, workbook, a class presentation, or class notes taken by students?
- Omit only key words; do not eliminate so many elements that the sense or order of the content is impaired.
  Poor item: Multiplication precedes _____,
  _____ precedes _____, and
  _____ precedes _____.
  Better item: In problems involving addition, subtraction, division, and multiplication, the first operation (from left to right) should be

  _____.
- Word the statement so the blank is near the end. This prevents awkward sentences.
- If the problem requires a numerical answer, indicate the units in which it is to be expressed (e.g., years, pounds, ounces, minutes).

Matching Items.   Like true–false, matching items are a popular and convenient testing format for assessing recognition, but they are not easy to write. Imagine your students are reading about some events in our country's history and you give them the following item to check on their factual knowledge:

Directions: Match A and B.

A	B
1. Lincoln	a. President during the twentieth century
2. Nixon	b. Invented the telephone
3. Whitney	c. Delivered the Emancipation Proclamation
4. Ford	d. Only president to resign from office
5. Bell	e. Civil rights leader
6. King	f. Invented the cotton gin
7. Washington	g. Our first president
8. Roosevelt	h. Only president elected for more than two terms

See any problems? Compare the problems you identify with the descriptions of faults that follow.

No homogeneity.   The lists are not homogeneous. Column A contains names of presidents, inventors, and a civil rights leader. Unless they are specifically taught as a set of related men or ideas, this is too wide a variety for a matching exercise.

Poor list order.   The lists are reversed: Column A should be in place of column B, and column B should be in place of column A. As the exercise is now written, the student reads a name and then has to read through all or many of the more lengthy descriptions to find the answer, a time-consuming process. It also is a good idea to introduce some sort of order—chronological, numerical, or alphabetical—to your list of options. This saves the student time.

Easy guessing.   Notice that there are equal numbers of options and descriptions. This increases the chances of guessing correctly through elimination. If there are at least three more options than descriptions, the chance of guessing correctly is reduced to one in four.

Poor directions.   The instructions are too brief. Matching directions should specify the basis for matching.

Multiple correct responses.   The description "President during the twentieth century" has three defensible answers: Nixon, Roosevelt, Ford. Also, always include first and last names to enhance recall and avoid ambiguities.

No response space.   Notice that the only way a student could connect the descriptions with the proper option would be to draw a line connecting them. These can be difficult to follow among intersecting lines and a nightmare to grade.

Here is a corrected version of the directions and matching items:

Column A contains brief descriptions of U.S. presidents. Column B contains the names of U.S. presidents. Indicate which president is being described by placing the appropriate letter to the left of the number in column A. Options may be used only once.

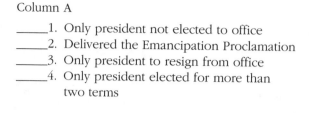

Column A

_____1. Only president not elected to office
_____2. Delivered the Emancipation Proclamation
_____3. Only president to resign from office
_____4. Only president elected for more than
      two terms

Column B

a. Gerald Ford
b. Thomas Jefferson
c. Abraham Lincoln
d. Richard Nixon
e. Franklin Roosevelt
f. Theodore Roosevelt
g. George Washington
h. Woodrow Wilson

Notice that this exercise has complete directions, more options than descriptions, homogeneous lists (all items in column A are about U.S. presidents, and all the items in column B are names of presidents), and unambiguous alternatives.

Here are some suggestions to keep in mind when writing matching items:

- Keep both the descriptions list and the options list short and homogeneous. They should fit together on the same page. Title the lists to ensure homogeneity (e.g., Column A, Column B) and arrange the options in a logical (e.g., alphabetical) order.

- Make sure that all the options are plausible *distracters* (wrong answer choices) for each description to ensure homogeneity of lists.

- The descriptions list should contain the longer phrases or statements, whereas the options should consist of short phrases, words, or symbols.

- Number each description (1, 2, 3, etc.) and letter each option (a, b, c, etc.).

- Include more options than descriptions, or some that match more than one.

- In the directions specify the basis for matching and whether options can be used more than once.

- Provide spaces to the left of the descriptions list for students to place their answers.

Multiple-Choice Items.   Another popular recognition item format is the multiple-choice question. Multiple-choice tests are more common in the middle school and upper elementary than lower elementary due to their heavier reliance on reading comprehension. Because these items are so prominent in later grades and on standardized tests, all students should have some early practice in taking them. When writing multiple-choice items, be careful not to give away answers by inadvertently providing students with any of the following types of clues.

Stem clue.   The statement portion of a multiple-choice item is called the *stem,* and the answer choices are called *options* or *response alternatives.* A stem clue occurs when the same word or a close derivative occurs in both the stem and an option, thereby clueing the test taker to the correct answer. For example:

> In the story *Hawaiian Mystery* the name of the volcanic structure Mark and Alisha had to cross to get free was called _____.
>
> A. volcanic ridge   C. caldron
> B. tectonic plate   D. lava

In this item the correct option and the stem both contain the word volcanic. Thus, the wise test taker has a good chance of answering the item correctly without mastery of the content being measured.

Grammatical clue. Consider this item:

> U. S. Grant was an _____.
>
> A. army general   C. cavalry commander
> B. navy admiral   D. senator

Most students would pick up on the easy grammatical clue in the stem. The article *an* eliminates options B, C, and D, which require the article *a*. Option A is the only one that forms a grammatical sentence. A way to eliminate the grammatical clue is to replace *an* with *a/an*. Similar examples are is/are, was/were, his/her, and so forth. Alternatively, place the article (or verb or pronoun) in the options list:

> Christopher Columbus came to America in _____.
>
> A. a car   C. an airplane
> B. a boat   D. a balloon

Redundant words/unequal length. Two very common faults in multiple-choice construction are illustrated in this item:

> In the story *Hawaiian Mystery*, when Mark and Alisha were held hostage at the top of the volcano,
>
> A. the police could not see them to free them
> B. the police called for more help
> C. the police attempted to free them by going behind the volcano and risking a rescue
> D. the police asked them to jump to the rock below

The phrase "the police" is included in each option. To save space and time, add it to the stem: "When Mark and Alisha were held hostage at the top of the volcano, the police" _____. Second, the length of options could be a giveaway. Multiple-choice item writers have a tendency to include more information in the correct option than in the incorrect options. Test-wise students know that more often than not, the longer option is the correct one. Avoid making correct answers more than one and a half times the length of incorrect options.

All of the above/none of the above. In general, use *none of the above* sparingly. Some item writers use none of the above only when there is no clearly correct option presented. However, students catch on to this practice and guess that none of the above is the correct answer without knowledge of the content being measured. Also, at times it may be justified to use multiple correct answers, such as *both a and c* or *both b and c*. Again, use such options sparingly, because inconsistencies among alternatives may allow students to easily eliminate some from consideration. This most frequently occurs when an alternative cannot possibly be right in two instances (e.g., option A paired with C and option B paired with C), leading the test taker to correctly reject both alternatives without actually knowing why they are wrong. Avoid using *all of the above,* because test items should encourage discrimination, not discourage it.

In Application 5.1, try writing some objective test items of your own that distinguish recognition from recall.

Higher Order Multiple-Choice Questions.   Multiple-choice items are unique among objective test items because if properly written, they enable you to measure some limited types of higher level cognitive objectives. Unfortunately, most multiple-choice items are written at the knowledge level in the taxonomy of educational objectives in the cognitive domain. As a new item writer, you will tend to write items at this level, but you will also need to write some multiple-choice items that measure cognitive objectives beyond the simple factual knowledge level. The

---

APPLICATION 5.1

Write two test items to measure recall and two to measure recognition. Choose the best format for your purpose. Make each of your four questions measure simple factual knowledge for lessons you will be teaching.

Recall

Test item 1:

Test item 2:

Recognition

Test item 1:

Test item 2:

following are some suggestions that can help you write higher order multiple-choice questions.

Use justification to assess reasons behind an answer. Questions that follow a multiple-choice item can ask for specifics as to why a particular answer was chosen. For example:

Directions: Choose the most appropriate answer and cite evidence for your selection in the space below.

The principal value of a balanced diet is that it

A. increases your intelligence
B. cures disease
C. promotes mental health
D. promotes physical health
E. improves self-discipline

Present evidence from the text as to why you choose your answer.

Use pictorial, graphical, or tabular stimuli. Pictures, drawings, graphs, and tables can require the student to think at least at the application level in the taxonomy of educational objectives and may involve even higher cognitive processes. Also, such stimuli often can generate several higher level multiple-choice items, as the following questions about Figure 5.3 illustrate.

Directions: Refer to the map (Figure 5.3) to answer these questions.

1. Which of the following cities would be the best location for a steel mill?

   A. Li (3A)   C. Cot (3D)
   B. Um (3B)   D. Dube (4B)

2. Approximately how many miles is it from Dube to Rag?

   A. 100 miles   C. 200 miles
   B. 150 miles   D. 250 miles

3. In what direction would someone have to travel to get from Wog to Um?

   A. northwest   C. southwest
   B. northeast   D. southeast

Use analogies to show relationships between terms. To answer analogies correctly, students must not only be familiar with the terms but also be able to understand how the terms relate to each other. For example:

Physician is to humans as veterinarian is to

   A. fruits   C. minerals
   B. animals   D. vegetables

Require application of principles or procedures. To test whether students comprehend the implications of a procedure, have them use the principle or procedure with new information or in a novel way. This requires them to do more than just follow the steps in solving a problem. It has them demonstrate an ability to go beyond

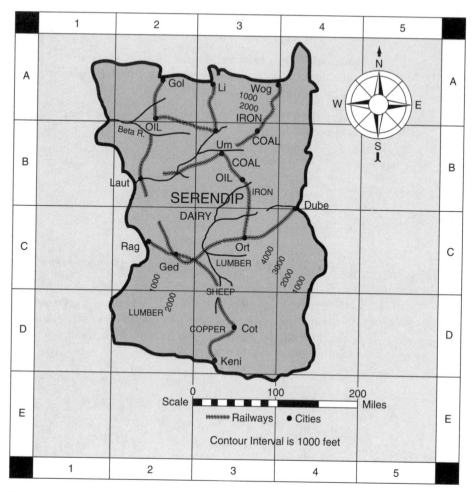

Figure 5.3
Use of a pictorial stimulus to measure a higher level cognitive process
Source: From *Educational Psychology: A Contemporary Approach* (2nd ed., p. 407) by G. Borich and M.
Tombari, 1997, New York: Longman. Copyright © 1997 by Addison-Wesley Educational Publishers, Inc.

the context within which they originally learned a principle or procedure. Consider
this example from a lesson on computation of ratios and proportions:

> After filling the car's tank with 18 gallons of gasoline, Mr. Watts said to his
> son, "We've come 450 miles since the last fill-up. What kind of gas
> mileage are we getting?" Circle the best answer.
>
> A. 4 miles per gallon   C. between 30 and
> B. 25 miles per gallon   35 miles per gallon
>   D. it can't be determined from the
>   information given

This item tests not only knowledge of division but also application skills in a real-world context.

Writing Multiple-Choice Items That Diagnose Learning Problems

Multiple-choice items can yield more than a percentage correct score. By carefully writing response alternatives as sets of related pieces of knowledge, multiple-choice items can also diagnose degrees of learner competence (Hunt and Minstrell, 1994; Minstrell, 2000). The results can alert the teacher to the causes behind errors so that they can be corrected. Let's look at an example for young readers.

Informal reading inventories given individually by the teacher may yield a student's reading level, but not what the learner needs to know. Let's look at how a series of multiple-choice items on a classroom assessment can reveal related pieces of knowledge about reading decoding skills.

1. Which of the following words has the long **O** sound?

    A. coat
    B. cot
    C. job
    D. loop

If the student correctly chooses A, the teacher can assume that he knows the rule about two vowels next to each other taking the long vowel sound of the first vowel. If the learner chooses either B, cot, or C, job, she has confused long and short vowel patterns and/or sounds. Choice D, loop, shows she almost has the concept but needs instruction about some exceptions that have pairs of vowels.

2. Which word makes the long **A** sound?

    A. marker
    B. make
    C. camp
    D. matter

If the student chooses B, the teacher can assume he knows the rule about the long vowel pattern of vowel, consonant, silent e. Choices A, marker, and D, matter, indicate she needs to be reminded that a single consonant comes between a long vowel and a silent e. Choice C, camp, shows confusion over long and short vowel sounds or patterns.

3. Which word has a short vowel sound?

    A. soon
    B. dirt
    C. lump
    D. cape

If the student chooses C, lump, the teacher can assume he knows the rule about the short vowel pattern of a vowel followed by a double consonant. Choice B, dirt, shows the student may need reminding about the special influence of the letter *r* on vowels next to it. Choice D, cape, shows confusion about short and long vowel sounds or patterns. Choice A, soon, indicates reteaching the various sounds of the double *o* combination.

> 4. Which word makes the **g** sound?
>   A. gnaw
>   B. sign
>   C. eight
>   D. gate

The correct answer D, gate, shows that the student knows enough about the silent letter combinations *gn* and *gh* to eliminate gnaw, sign, and eight. Students who choose A, gnaw, may need to learn that the g is silent when it is followed by the letter *n*. This same pattern applies to the *gn* combination within as well as at the beginning of a word, for those who choose B, sign. Those who choose C, eight, should be taught that *gh* in the middle of a word is often silent.

Notice how the careful preparation of wrong answers to these carefully crafted multiple-choice questions indicate which specific areas of decoding need to be retaught or reviewed, and, the teacher can look at the results across all the items together to determine which areas to emphasize with the whole class. These profiles of learning are more diagnostically useful than simply knowing that a student missed some combination of items.

Here are some suggestions to keep in mind when writing multiple-choice items:

- Be sure that there is one and only one correct or clearly best answer.
- Be sure all wrong answer choices (distracters) are plausible. Eliminate unintentional grammatical clues and keep the length and form of all the answer choices equal. Rotate the position of the correct answer from item to item randomly.
- Use negative questions or statements only if the knowledge being tested requires it. In most cases it is more important for the student to know what the correct answer is rather than what it is not.
- Include four to five options (three to four distracters plus one correct answer) to optimize testing for knowledge, comprehension, or application rather than encouraging guessing. It is not necessary to provide additional distracters for an item simply to maintain the same number of distracters for each item.
- Use the option none of the above sparingly and only when all the answers can be classified unequivocally as wrong.
- Avoid using all of the above. It usually is the correct answer and makes the item too easy for students who have only partial information.

In Application 5.2, check your understanding of good multiple-choice item writing practices by preparing two multiple-choice questions that assess higher order thinking.

APPLICATION 5.2

Write two multiple-choice items that demonstrate your ability to use an objective test format to assess higher order thinking. Indicate any pictorial or tabular information you will provide learners for answering your questions

1.

2.

Mistakes to Avoid

Although answers to true–false, completion, matching, and multiple-choice test items are easier to score than answers to essay questions, they still present significant problems for the reliability and validity of your test. Recall that the reliability of your test is its capacity to dependably and consistently provide the same or similar score on a subsequent testing occasion. And, its validity is whether your test measures what you say it measures. When questions are poorly written, conclusions based on test results about what someone does or does not know can be invalid and unreliable. Here are some common writing mistakes, that if avoided, can protect the reliability and validity of your assessment.

1. *Ambiguous or unclear presentation of question.* Write test instructions and questions in simple, uncomplicated language. This way, your learners will not have to struggle to untangle complicated phrases or clauses. When in doubt, have a student in a lower grade read the item and tell you what the question means.

2. *Not enough questions.* Include enough test questions to adequately cover all that the learner is expected to know. The more items, the greater the sample of performance obtained and the higher your test's reliability.

3. *Not enough time.* Allow students sufficient time to take the test. A rushed student is more likely to make careless errors, which will lower the reliability of the test.

4. *Uncomfortable conditions.* Make sure the testing conditions (temperature of the room, noise level, seating arrangements) are conducive to maximum performance. If the test situation is uncomfortable, learners are more easily distracted and less likely to demonstrate what they really know.

5. *No test blueprint.*   Follow a test blueprint so that you adequately sample all that has been taught—all that the learner knows. The test blueprint will enable you to coordinate the alignment of test items with the taught material to ensure its adequate measurement.

6. *Ambiguous answers.*   Write objective questions that have easily identifiable right and wrong answers. This way, the correct answer will be scored "right" every time.

Following the construction and first administration of your multiple choice test, you can examine each question to determine if it meets two important standards: appropriate level of difficulty and whether each item reflects the overall trait or ability that the test is presumed to measure. You can determine the extent to which these two standards are met by calculating the **index of item difficulty** and **index of item discrimination**. These indices are described in Boxes 5.1 and 5.2. The index of item difficulty indicates the proportion of learners who answered the test question correctly. The index of item discrimination compares the answers to individual items of students who did well on the entire test to the answers of students who did poorly on the entire test. It allows the test developer to distinguish items that measure the competency underlying the test from those that do not.

BOX 5.1   Calculating the Index of Item Difficulty

To determine the difficulty index (indicated with the letter p) for a particular test item, the test developer divides the number of students selecting the correct answer for a test item by the total number of students attempting the item. For example, suppose students chose the options to a four-alternative multiple-choice item the following numbers of times, with option C the correct answer (indicated with *)

A	B	C*	D
3	0	18	9

$$p = \frac{\text{number of students selecting correct answer}}{\text{total number of students attempting answer}}$$

$$p = \frac{18}{30} = .60$$

We learn from this index that the item was moderately difficult (60 percent of the class got it right) and that option B should be modified. When p levels are less than about .25, the item is considered relatively difficult. When p levels are about .75, the item is considered relatively easy. Test developers try to build tests that have most items between p levels of .20 and .80, with an average p level of about .50.

Additional information and applications of these indexes can be found in Kubiszyn and Borich (2003).

The issues confronting you when you assess simple factual knowledge often represent trade-offs. Although some item formats give you greater content coverage (like true–false), they are also more susceptible to guessing. Multiple-choice items are less susceptible to guessing, but they take longer to write. Completion items require recall and are less susceptible to guessing, but they are more difficult and time consuming to score. Table 5.1 lists the advantages and disadvantages of each objective-type item.

BOX 5.2   Calculating the Index of Item Discrimination

To determine the discrimination index (indicated by the letter D for a particular test item), the test developer follows these steps:

1. Arranges the scores on the total test from highest to lowest.
2. Divides the total test scores into the top half and bottom half (or similar division, such as top third and bottom third).
3. Counts the number in the upper group and the number in the lower group that chose each response alternative for that item.
4. Records the information in the following format:

EXAMPLE FOR ITEM X

Options	A	B	C*	D
Upper	1	0	11	3
Lower	2	0	7	6

5. Computes the discrimination index with the following formula:

$$D = \frac{\text{(number who got item correct in upper group)} - \text{(number who got item correct in lower group)}}{\text{number of students in upper (or lower) group}}$$

Using the numbers above for test item X,

$$D = \frac{11 - 7}{15} = .267$$

The discrimination index is .267, which is positive. This means that more students who did well on the overall test answered the item correctly than students who did poorly on the overall test. A test item with a D = .267 would be considered a moderately difficult item that has positive (desirable) discrimination. Generally, test items that have positive D values are considered adequate. Other factors being equal, a test's discrimination will be greatest when the average p level (difficulty) is about .50.

TABLE 5.1
Advantages and Disadvantages of Various Objective-Item Formats

Advantages	Disadvantages
True–False Tests	

Advantages	Disadvantages
Tend to be short, so more material can be covered than with any other format; thus, use true–false items when extensive content has been covered.	Tend to emphasize rote memorization of knowledge (although complex questions sometimes can be asked using true–false items).
Faster to construct (but avoid creating an item by taking statements out of context or slightly modifying them).	They assume an unequivocally true or false answer (it is unfair to make students guess at your criteria for evaluating the truth of a statement).
Scoring is easier (tip: provide a "T" and an "F" for them to circle, because a student's handwritten "T" or "F" can be hard to decipher).	Allow and may even encourage a high degree of guessing (generally, longer examinations compensate for this).

Matching Tests	

Advantages	Disadvantages
Simple to construct and score. Ideal for measuring associations between facts.	Tend to ask trivial information.
Can be more efficient than multiple-choice questions because they avoid repetition of options in measuring association.	Emphasize memorization.
	Most commercial answer sheets can accommodate only five options, thus limiting the size of a matching item.
Reduce the effects of guessing.	

Multiple-Choice Tests	

Advantages	Disadvantages
Versatile in measuring objectives, from the knowledge level to the application level.	Time-consuming to write.
Since writing is minimal, considerable course material can be sampled quickly.	If not carefully written, can have more than one defensible correct answer.
Scoring is highly objective, requiring only a count of correct responses.	
Can be written so students must discriminate between options varying in correctness, avoiding the absolute judgments of true–false tests.	
Reduce effects of guessing.	
Amenable to statistical analysis, so you can determine which items are ambiguous, or too difficult (see Kubiszyn and Borich, 2003, chapter 10).	

Completion Tests	

Advantages	Disadvantages
Question construction is relatively easy.	Encourage a low level of reponse complexity
Guessing is reduced because the question requires a specific response.	Can be difficult to score (the stem must be general enough to not communicate the answer, leading unintentionally to multiple defensible answers).
Less time is needed to complete than multiple-choice items, so more content can be covered.	Very short answers tend to measure recall of specific facts, names, places, and events instead of more complex behaviors.

Source: From *Effective Teaching Methods* (5th ed.) by G. Borich, 2004, Upper Saddle River, NJ: Merrill/Prentice Hall.

Summary

This chapter presented some of the ways you can assess your learners' simple understanding with selected-response and completion items. It presented formats for testing simple factual knowledge with the true–false, completion, matching, and multiple-choice item formats. These assessment formats were examined for their content sampling requirements and contribution to measuring recall versus recognition. It also presented formats for measuring simple understanding with higher order multiple-choice formats and for writing multiple-choice items that diagnose learning problems.

Activities

Before completing the activities, review the Lesson Contexts section at the end of each chapter. These lesson contexts contain examples that apply the assessment practices discussed in the chapter to grades K–2, 3–5, and 6–8 in the areas of reading and language arts, social studies, science, mathematics, and health. For this chapter these examples illustrate questions for assessing your learners' declarative knowledge with objective tests. Review them as a guide for completing the following activities.

1. What implications for your classroom teaching and assessment can be drawn from Ceci and Liker's (1986) study of horse-race handicapping with respect to the relative emphasis you might want to place on building your learners' domain-specific and domain-general knowledge base?
2. Select a topic for which you would like your learners to exhibit simple factual understanding. Using a higher order multiple-choice format, prepare an item that goes beyond simple recall and recognition to elicit evidence of more complex learning.
3. For your grade or subject, construct a multiple-choice item with response options that could diagnose the nature of a particular learning problem. Critique your item for its capacity to direct your attention to what should be remediated.
4. Using the lesson contexts and template at the end of this chapter as a guide, create three questions of your own that assess your learners' use of declarative knowledge with objective test items.

Suggested Reading

Kubiszyn, T., & Borich, G. (2003). *Educational testing and measurement: Classroom applications and practice* (7th ed.). New York: Longman.
   Chapters 15 and 16 cover all of the methods traditionally used to determine the validity and reliability of objective tests and how to interpret their meaning. Chapter 10 provides examples of the index of item difficulty and index of item discrimination.

Lesson Contexts

K–2 EXAMPLE LESSON CONTEXTS FOR ASSESSING DECLARATIVE KNOWLEDGE WITH OBJECTIVE TEST ITEMS

Grade	Subject	Topic	Assessment Questions
K–2	Language Arts	Fact vs. fiction	Do you think *Little Red Riding Hood* is fact or fiction?
		Onomatopoeia	Select the word that sounds like its name in the story *Little Toot.*
K–2	Math	Measurement	Circle the coins that are larger in size than the nickel.
		Measurement	Match the activities below with whether they would occur in one second, one minute, or one hour by putting an **S, M**, or **H** in front of them.
K–2	Science	Living and non-living organisms	Separate these pictures taken on a walk through the countryside into two piles—living and nonliving organisms.
		Basic needs of organisms	From the following list, circle three ways that animals protect themselves from the cold (possible examples—birds, mice, horses).
K–2	Social Studies	History	Place the pictures that represent the celebration of Thanksgiving into one pile and the pictures that represent the celebration of Christmas into another.
		Geography	Circle the ways in which our class has helped to conserve and replenish natural resources.
K–2	Health	Hygiene	Point to the pictures on the table that show how cold germs are spread.
		Safety	Match pictures of the proper protective equipment on the left with the sport or activity on the right.

GRADES 3–5 EXAMPLE LESSON CONTEXTS FOR ASSESSING DECLARATIVE KNOWLEDGE WITH
OBJECTIVE TEST ITEMS

Grade	Subject	Topic	Assessment Questions
3–5	Language Arts	Analyze characters	In the first chapter of *Charlotte's Web* we meet Fern. Circle all the words that correctly describe her (persuasive, lazy, fair-minded, emotional, hardhearted).
		Compare text events with student experience	Like Fern in *Charlotte's Web,* circle the other characters in the stories we have read that were concerned with "injustice."
3–5	Social Studies/ Math	Temperature/ measurement	Match the average daily temperatures on the map with the month of the year for the following cities: New York, Sao Paulo, Nome.
		Geometry and spatial reasoning	Select by placing an "X" all the lines that are parallel in the geometric shapes pictured below.
3–5	Science	Concepts: physical properties	Read the list below and put an **L** next to liquids, **S** next to solids, and **G** next to gases.
		Concepts: the needs of living organisms	Which of the following descriptions best explains how the beaver modifies its environment to meet its needs.
3–5	Social Studies	Geography	Select the map with the best scale for measuring the distance between Chicago and St. Louis.
		Science, technology, and society	Match the inventor with his/her invention by writing the correct letter next to the name of the inventor.
3–5	Health	Health behaviors	From the list, fill in the blanks in the food pyramid to represent a healthy, well-balanced diet.
		Physical activity and health	Label what each physical activity listed below promotes by writing **S** for strength, **E** for endurance, and **F** for flexibility.

GRADES 6–8 EXAMPLE LESSON CONTEXTS FOR ASSESSING DECLARATIVE KNOWLEDGE WITH
OBJECTIVE TEST ITEMS

Grade	Subject	Topic	Assessment Questions
6–8	Language Arts	Denotation, connotation	Words may mean or denote the same things, but have different emotional overtones or connotations. Put a plus, check, or a minus next to each word to indicate a positive, neutral, or negative connotation (overweight, fat, plump; thrifty, economical, cheap; determined, obstinate, steady).
		Using references	Indicate which reference source you should use to locate the following information by putting **T** for Table of Contents, **I** for Index, and **G** for Glossary.
6–8	Math	Probability and statistics	Choose the correct mean, median, and mode for each set of numbers listed below.
		Patterns, relationships, and algebraic thinking	Match the patterns of data given below to the correct table, graph, and verbal description.
6–8	Science	Scientific process	Read the paragraph below describing a laboratory experiment. From the list circle all the unsafe practices that can be found.
		Science concepts: generational change	Label each offspring characteristic in the table that most likely would be a result of **A** for asexual reproduction or **S** for sexual reproduction.
6–8	Social Studies	History: Civil War	Below are several events that led up to the Civil War. Put them in the proper sequence by numbering from 1 to 10.
		History: Revolutionary War	Read the following statements about the causes of the Revolutionary War. Mark them either as true or false.
6–8	Health	Interpersonal skills	Put a check in front of each healthy and effective way to reduce stress.
			Put the letter **U** for use and **A** for abuse next to each statement concerning a prescription or over-the-counter medication.

TEMPLATE FOR YOUR LESSON CONTEXTS FOR ASSESSING DECLARATIVE KNOWLEDGE WITH OBJECTIVE TEST ITEMS

Grade	Subject	Topic	Assessment Questions

6

Assessing Declarative Knowledge: The Constructed-Response Test

When measuring declarative knowledge, we want to determine more than whether learners know the names of rocks, the parts of a leaf, the names of presidents, or the definition of cleave. We want to ascertain if they have acquired a concept: whether they know what a word or expression (shale, stem, democracy, "to split along the grain") means. Can they give examples of it, tell how it is different from or similar to another term or expression, and explain what it means using their own words? We must determine if they know or can represent information as an idea or if they simply know it by rote memorization.

The expression declarative knowledge represents different degrees of understanding—understanding deepens as the knowledge base grows more complex. For example, your understanding of assessment is richer and deeper now than when you first began this book. So, too, a learner's understanding of the word rock deepens as he learns more about the different kinds of rocks and how they were derived.

You can assess your learners' understanding of terms and expressions using higher order multiple-choice questions or constructed oral and written responses. We have just shown some examples of higher order multiple-choice questions. Now, we will provide some examples of test items that require a constructed written or oral response.

The Restricted–Response Question

A constructed-response question that poses a specific problem for which the student must recall proper information, organize it in a suitable manner, derive a defensible conclusion, and express it according to specific criteria is called a

restricted-response question or short essay. A restricted-response item is one for which the student supplies, rather than selects, the correct answer. The student must compose a response to a question for which no single response or pattern of responses can be cited as correct to the exclusion of all others. The accuracy and quality of such a response can often be judged only by a person skilled and informed in the subject area being tested. Like selected-response test items, restricted-response questions may be well constructed or poorly constructed. The well-constructed item aims to test knowledge and understanding by requiring the student to organize, integrate, and synthesize knowledge. The poorly constructed restricted-response item may require the student to do no more than recall information as it was presented in the textbook or a class presentation. Worse, the poorly constructed restricted-response question may not even let the student know what is required for a satisfactory response.

Restricted-response questions can be written or posed orally to the learner. They usually require a minute or so of an oral response or a paragraph or two that is written. The statement of the problem given orally or as part of the written question specifies the response limitations that guide the student in responding and provides criteria for scoring. The following are some examples of restricted-response questions that assess student understanding:

> In your own words, explain two differences between igneous and sedimentary rock and give one example of each not given in class.

> In the story "Ben Franklin's Childhood" give some examples of how he was a born leader and always knew what to do.

> Now that we've studied about the Gold Rush, imagine you are on a wagon train going to California. Write a letter to your relatives back home telling them of some of the hardships you have suffered and the dangers you have experienced.

To demonstrate that they know igneous and sedimentary as concepts and not just simple knowledge, your learners must do two things: They must use their own words to explain the differences and not simply recall what their text said or what they copied from an overhead, and they must give original examples of each rock. If they can do this, then you can correctly say that they have the concepts.

A constructed-response question that allows the student to determine the length and complexity of an answer is called an **extended-response response** question. This type of question is most useful for assessing behaviors at the analysis, synthesis, and evaluation levels of the cognitive domain and for assessing deep understanding that often takes the form of extended papers completed out of the classroom or a take-home test. We will review these types of outcomes and the extended-response question in later chapters.

When to Use Restricted-Response Questions

The following list describes some of the conditions for which restricted-response questions are best suited.

- The instructional objectives require supplying information rather than simply recognizing information. These latter processes often cannot be measured with selected-response items.

- Relatively few areas of content need to be tested. If you have 30 students and design a test with six restricted-response questions, you will spend a great deal of time scoring. Use restricted responses sparingly or in conjunction with objective items.

- Test security is a consideration. If you are afraid multiple-choice test questions will be passed on or told to other students, it is better to use a restricted-response question. In general, a good restricted-response question takes less time to construct than a good objective test.

Some examples of restricted-response questions and learning outcomes for which they are best suited include the following:

Express relationships.   The colors blue and gray are related to cool temperatures. What are some other colors related to? How would these colors be shown on a picture you might draw? (K–3, Art)

Compare and contrast positions.   Compare and contrast two characters from stories you have read. How did the two characters respond differently to the conditions in the stories? (Grades 4–6, Reading)

State necessary assumptions.   When Columbus landed on San Salvador, what did he assume about the land he had discovered? Were his assumptions correct? (Grades 4–6, Social Studies)

Identify appropriate conclusions.   What are some of the reasons for and against building a landfill near homes? (Grades 7–8, Social Studies)

Explain cause-and-effect relations.   What might have caused early Americans to travel west in the 1800s. Choose one of the pioneers we have studied (like Daniel Boone) and give some of the reasons they traveled west. (Grades 7–8, U.S. History)

Make predictions.   What can you predict about a coming storm by observing clouds? Explain what it is about the clouds that helps you predict rain. (Grades 4–6, Science)

Organize data to support a viewpoint.   On the board you will find the numbers of new homes built and autos purchased for each month over the past year. Use these data to support the viewpoint that our economy is either growing larger or smaller. (Grades 7–8, Math)

Point out strengths and weaknesses.   What is either a strength or a limitation of the following musical instruments for a marching band: oboe, trumpet, tuba, violin? (Grades 4–6, Music)

Integrate data from several sources.   Imagine you are celebrating your birthday with nine of your friends. Two pizzas arrive but each is cut into four pieces. What problem do you have? What method would you choose for seeing that everyone gets a piece of the pizza? (K–3, Mathematics)

Know the quality or worth of an item, product, or action. What should be considered in choosing a balanced meal from the basic food groups? (K–3, Health)

Additional examples for the curriculum at your grade are provided in the Lesson Contexts section at the end of the chapter. Here are some suggestions to keep in mind when preparing restricted-response questions, delivered orally or in writing:

- Have clearly in mind what mental processes you want the student to use before starting to write the question. Refer to the mental processes required at the various levels of the taxonomies of Bloom et al. (1984) and/or of Gagné (1985) described in chapter 3. For example, if you want students to apply what they have learned, determine what mental processes would be needed in the application process.

  Poor item: Describe the escape routes considered by Mark and Alisha in the story *Hawaiian Mystery*.

  Better item: Consider the story about Mark and Alisha. Remember the part where they had to escape over the volcanic ridge? Compare the advantages of Mark's plan of escape with that of Alisha's plan. Which plan of escape would get them home the quickest?

- Write the question to clearly and unambiguously define the task to the student. Tasks should be explained (a) orally, (b) in the overall instructions preceding the questions, and/or (c) in the test items themselves. Include instructions about whether spelling and grammar will be counted, and whether organization of the response will be an important scoring element. Also, indicate to the student the point value of the question, because restricted-response items are often worth more than a single-objective item, and not all restricted-response questions need to be worth the same point value.

  Poor item: Discuss the choices Mark and Alisha had to make in the story *Hawaiian Mystery*.

  Better item: Mark and Alisha had to make three decisions on their journey home. Identify each of them and indicate if you disagree with any of these decisions and why you disagree. Organize your response into three or four paragraphs and check your spelling.

- Start restricted-response questions with such words or phrases as compare, contrast, give reasons for, give original examples of, predict what would happen if, and so forth. Do not begin with such words as what, who, when, and list, because these words generally lead to tasks that require only recall of information, which could be more efficiently assessed by a selected-response question.

  Poor item: Who made the decision to take the path by the sea?

  Better item: Give three reasons why Alisha decided to take the path by the sea and predict what would have happened if they had stayed on the mountain for another night.

- A question dealing with a controversial issue should ask for and be evaluated in terms of the presentation of evidence for a position rather than the position taken. It is not defensible to demand that a student accept a specific conclusion or solution, but it is reasonable to assess how well the student has learned to use the evidence upon which a specific conclusion is based.

    Poor item: What laws should Congress pass to improve the medical care of all citizens in the United States?

    Better item: Some feel that the cost of all medical care should be the responsibility of the federal government. Do you agree or disagree? Support your position with at least three reasons.

- Establish reasonable time and/or page limits for each restricted-response question to help the student complete the question and to indicate the level of detail for the response you have in mind. Indicate such limits orally *and* in the statement of the question.

- Use time limits instead of page limits for younger learners who are just learning to write. Students who write in larger letters may only be able to write half as much on a page as students who write in smaller letters.

- Use restricted-response questions with content and objectives that cannot be satisfactorily measured by objective items.

Scoring Restricted-Response Questions

Restricted-response questions are difficult to score consistently across individuals. That is, the same answer may be given an A by one scorer and a B or C by another scorer. The same answer may even be graded A on one occasion but B or C on another occasion by the same scorer. What can you do to avoid such scoring problems?

1. Write good restricted-response questions. Poorly written questions are one source of scorer inconsistency. Questions that do not specify response length are another. Depending on the grade, long (e.g., three-page) responses generally are more difficult to score consistently than shorter responses (e.g., one page). This is due to student fatigue and subsequent clerical errors as well as to a tendency for grading criteria to vary from response to response, or for that matter, from page to page or paragraph to paragraph within the same response.

2. Use several restricted-response questions. Rather than a single comprehensive restricted-response question, use several smaller more specific and detailed ones. This will provide a greater variety of criteria to respond to and thus give students a greater opportunity to show off their skills.

3. Prepare a model answer that identifies the criteria for a correct or acceptable response to each of your questions. All too often, questions are graded without the scorer having specified in advance the criteria for a "good" answer. If you do not specify the criteria beforehand, whether given orally or written,

your scoring consistency will be greatly reduced. If these criteria are not readily available (written down) for scoring each question, the criteria themselves may change (you may grade harder or easier after scoring several papers, even if the answers do not change), or your ability to keep these criteria in mind will be influenced by fatigue, distractions, frame of mind, and so forth. Because we are all human, we are all subject to these factors.

Figure 6.1 provides example responses to a restricted-response essay question for fifth-grade social studies representing three levels of proficiency. Many times it is

---

An Illustration of a Restricted-Response Question with Tiered Responses

Question: Explain why cities so often developed along rivers. Be sure to discuss the relationship between rivers and city growth, energy, economics, water supply, and transportation. Use examples to support your points. Your response will be graded for its accuracy, organization, and examples.

Response Earning a High Score

Probably the first reason for cities growing along rivers is because the rivers provided a supply of water for washing, drinking, and maybe even watering crops. They might supply food in the form of fish and probably made hunting or trapping easier because animals would come down to the river for a drink. As the towns grew into larger cities, the rivers also helped supply water for factories. Some of the early examples of cities using river water for these reasons are Chicago, Philadelphia, and Cincinnati.

Another reason cities grew up along rivers is because of transportation. People could move the crops they raised on boats or barges to sell them down river. For instance, the corn grown in Iowa could be moved down the Mississippi and sold to people in St. Louis. Products could also be moved on the rivers. A St. Louis dressmaker could ship her dresses to shops in New Orleans. Steel from Chicago could go down the Illinois River to be sold in southern Illinois.

Finally, cities developed along rivers because of the energy the moving water provided. At first it was just simple power to run things like mills to grind corn or turn wheat into flour. In the Midwest, the corn and wheat were plentiful. Later on, the water turned machines that created electricity. An example of a large electric-producing plant is Hoover Dam on the Colorado River near Las Vegas.

This response gets a high score because it answers the question with well-thought-out reasons and explains with well-chosen examples. The use of a fresh water supply, transportation, and energy are three of the most important links between rivers and city growth. The student also showed accurate knowledge of geography by correctly identifying river cities and corresponding rivers.

(continued)

Figure 6.1
An illustration of a restricted-response question with tiered responses

Response Earning an Average Score

Cities grew up along rivers because people needed water. They used it to drink, clean up, and even to have a little fun. Sure, they could dig a well or collect rainwater from their roofs, but being near a river was much easier. The people who started St. Louis probably used some river for water to drink and wash up.

Another reason cities grew up near rivers is because the rivers were like roads. And you didn't need to have horses to pull you. You could just put your stuff on a boat and let the river current float you downstream to wherever you needed to go. Just like Huck Finn floating down the raft in Missouri. Maybe you could move things you grew, too, like cotton.

Rivers are really beautiful, too. There's nothing prettier or more fun than sitting along a riverbank, listening to nature and seeing the clouds reflected in the water. You could go fishing there too, which is not only fun, but also could help put food on the table.

This response earns an average score because it touches on at least two of the most important links between city growth and rivers, fresh water supply and transportation. However, the writer does not explain fully and examples are not always accurate or illuminating. The river next to St. Louis is not named, and the example about Huck floating down a raft in Missouri tells us little or about his hometown of Hannibal where he grew up along the Mississippi. A few of his reasons, such as the river as a source for fun or beauty are true, but more bonuses of riverside living, not the cause of it.

Responses Earning a Low Score

We have cities next to rivers because of all the sports. You can go swimming right out of your backyard, or maybe fish off your porch. Not to mention water skiing and in the winter ice skating, but you have to be careful not to fall through the ice like that little boy in Chicago did last January. I really like to ski on the Fox River, but the fishing there is not too good. For fishing, it is better to go to a lake.

I guess you can use the water in the rivers for stuff like drinking, but it looks pretty dirty, especially after a rain. Watering your lawn is okay though.

This response earns a low score because it uses poorly chosen reasons with little or no explanation. The examples chosen seem to be gleaned from personal experience rather than from an understanding of history or geography. The incident about the boy falling through the ice in Chicago as well as the mention of the fishing potential of a lake do not support or develop his ideas. This response is essentially an account of emotional associations instead of a reasoned and focused response to the question.

Figure 6.1
(*continued*)

helpful to see side by side both more and less proficient answers that may represent a high, average, and low score. You can prepare tiered responses in advance or choose them from previous responses of students to help keep in mind what a good, average, and poor response looks like. Tiered responses are also diagnostically

BOX 6.1   The Computer-Based Assessment of Restricted-Response Questions

Computer software has been developed that can reliably score restricted-response essays. For example, a computer program has been used to estimate the similarity between an essay response written by a student with that of a model response written by the teacher and to compare a student's essay with a set of pre-graded essays at varying levels of proficiency (Landuaer, Foltz, & Laham, 1998). Studies reveal that scores obtained with this method are as reliable as those produced by pairs of human raters (Landuaer, 1998). One of the advantages of this method is that, in addition to a single overall score, it can provide multiple scores for a constructed response compared with a model response at various levels of proficiency, such as those in Figure 6.1. These multiple scores can then be used for diagnostic purposes to direct specific learners to examples at the next and higher levels proficiency.

useful for giving feedback to the student and providing examples with which learners can compare their own work.

See Box 6.1 for the latest developments in the computer assessment of restricted-response questions.

In Application 6.1, practice writing a restricted-response question and identifying the cognitive processes you want to assess.

APPLICATION 6.1

Identify some cognitive outcomes (e.g., comparison and contrast, analysis, application, discrimination, etc.) you want to assess. Then, write a constructed-response question that assesses whether your learners have acquired these outcomes.

Cognitive processes you want to measure:

Constructed-response question:

Assessing Knowledge Organization

In Figures 5.1 and 5.2 at the beginning of the previous chapter we saw how a learner's mind spontaneously organized a knowledge base about rocks as it was being learned. As students attend and listen to lectures and discussions, or read from their books, they link this new information with prior learning, and this linking helps them to learn concepts, principles, and generalizations. Over time, as their knowledge base grows, it becomes increasingly organized in a hierarchical fashion.

Even though learners construct this organization on their own, teachers can facilitate it in these ways.

1. At the start of a lesson, you can ask questions that get learners to recall previous learning.

2. During the lesson you can ask questions and provide activities that help learners see similarities and differences and to detect patterns and relationships among the pieces of information that they are hearing or reading.

3. You can also construct outlines or mind maps that visually remind learners of how new information is organized and relates to previously learned information.

Figures 6.2 and 6.3 represent visual interdisciplinary thematic units developed by an elementary and a middle-school teacher. These teachers used a graphic format to help them organize knowledge for instruction and to assess it in ways that emphasize interrelationships that build to more important themes and concepts. Knowledge organization was an important goal of their instruction in the belief that an organized knowledge base would help their students acquire new information, learn it in a meaningful way, remember it, and better solve problems that require it. When knowledge organization is a goal for your learners, what are some ways to assess it?

First of all, assessing knowledge organization and assessing concepts are not the same. The assessment procedures previously discussed let you determine understanding of terms and expressions like photosynthesis, plants, and chlorophyll; but they may not tell you much about how well the student understands the relationships among the concepts. Again, recall the rock knowledge base represented in Figures 5.1 and 5.2 in the previous chapter. Before much instruction the knowledge base was there but the pieces were disjointed and unrelated to one another in the mind of the learner; but after further instruction not only were the concepts understood but also connections between them were made. It is these connections that we want to assess when we assess knowledge organization.

The connections between and among concepts represent the student's knowledge and understanding of rules, principles, and generalizations. Now the learner has moved from simple knowledge (recall and recognition) to understanding (the learner can give examples, tell how it is different from and similar to other terms and expressions, and explain what it means in their own words) to the organization of

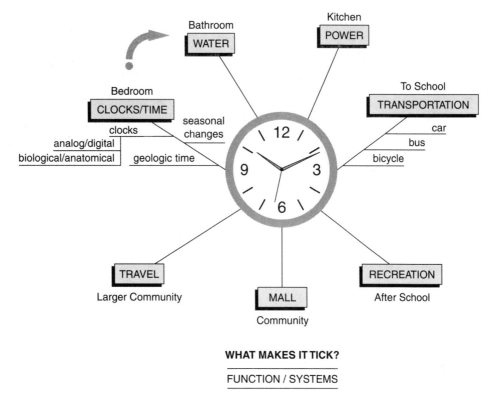

WHAT MAKES IT TICK?

FUNCTION / SYSTEMS

Figure 6.2
Visual representation of interdisciplinary unit theme "dimensions of time"
Source: From *ITI: The Model* by S. Kovalik, 1994, Kent, WA: Books for Educators. Copyright © 1994 by S. Kovalik. Reprinted with permission.

knowledge (not only does the learner know the pieces, but also the pieces are connected to one another and ordered hierarchically). For example, the learner knows not only about the California Gold Rush but also about its connections to the food the pioneers ate, the songs they sang, how they calculated the amount they traveled each day, the diaries they kept, and how they weighed and measured the gold. In other words, they constructed concepts, principles, and generalizations that connected the gold rush experience to larger concepts found in everyday life, representing knowledge organization.

Learners construct these concepts, principles, and generalizations as a result of instruction that allows them to gather information through direct experience, to explore similarities and differences, and to establish relationships and connections. Learners of all ages spontaneously organize information and form orderly knowledge bases in this way.

Thus, assessing for knowledge organization requires identifying the connections among concepts, or the sets and subsets of knowledge, just as our two

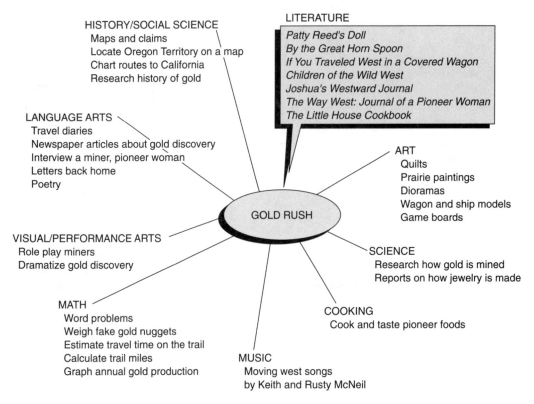

Figure 6.3
Teacher's visual representation of the interdisciplinary unit theme "Gold Rush"
Source: Developed by Cynthia Kiel, teacher, Glandora, California.

teachers did in their interdisciplinary thematic units. But how can *learners* display their organization of knowledge—of cause-and-effect relationships, similarities and contrasts, or problems and solutions? Traditional outlines in which major topics and subtopics are grouped in a I, II, III, A, B, C order may not reveal knowledge organization. Some educators (Goetz, Alexander, & Ash, 1992) believe such outlines emphasize categories of things over relationships that can impose a structure that differs from the way knowledge should actually be organized for understanding.

Dansereau (1988) urges teachers to model alternate strategies to help learners when they listen to presentations or read from books, which, in turn, can be used to assess the depth of understanding and organization of their knowledge base. He advocates graphic outlines displayed as webs, much like the visual interdisciplinary thematic unit plans made by teachers shown in Figures 6.2 and 6.3—but this time prepared by students. Webbing is a free-form outline technique that learners can use to display their level of understanding of class discussions or textbook content,

CAUSES OF WATER POLLUTION—HIGH SCORE

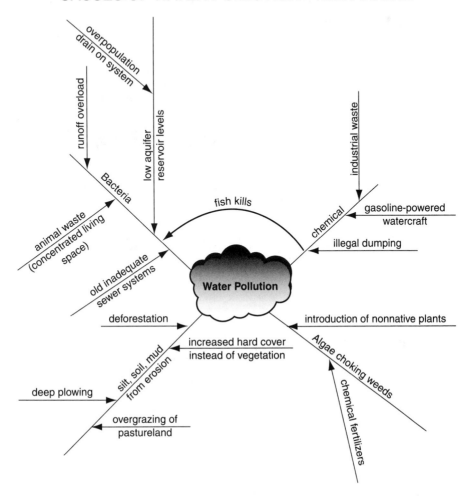

This web indicates the complex and interactive causes of water pollution. Four major areas are identified—chemical, algae, soil, and bacteria—with underlying causes linked to each spoke. In one case a linking dynamic is shown. Chemical pollution kills fish, which in turn, creates bacterial contamination.

Figure 6.4a
Thorough and accurate web showing a high level of understanding

as displayed in Figures 6.4 a–c. Notice in each of these how the learners who drew them rose on the learning ladder from basic knowledge, requiring the memorization of facts, to understanding, requiring conceptualization and an understanding of relationships. Mind maps such as these allow the teacher to diagnose the degree to which learners have organized their knowledge and know the relationships among

CAUSES OF WATER POLLUTION—AVERAGE SCORE

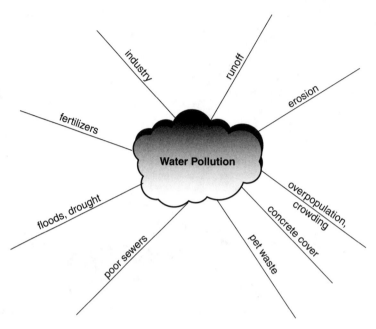

This web shows an initial understanding of contributors to water pollution but does not display some of the important interrelated causes of it. In most cases the source of the pollution, was named without identifying the type of pollutant, that is, "pet waste" without mention of bacteria, "industry" without mention of chemicals.

Figure 6.4b
Web showing initial understanding

concepts. The following are four simple rules for communicating to your learners how to construct webs, networks, or maps for assessing their organization of knowledge.

- Display only essential information or big ideas or concepts.
- Assign the central idea or concept to a central location.
- Draw arrows from the main ideas to show relationships.
- Label the arrows with key words or code letters to describe their relationship.

See Box 6.2 for recent developments in the computer-based assessment of knowledge organization

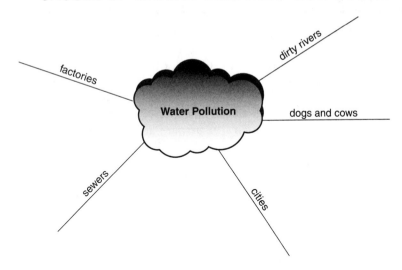

CAUSES OF WATER POLLUTION—LOW SCORE

This incomplete web shows a superficial understanding of the causes of water pollution. One entry, "dirty rivers," is more a description or type of pollution rather than a cause of it. Others are vague as to reasoning. Just how do dogs and cows pollute water? What specifically is it about the existence of cities and factories that pollutes water? Finally, one could argue that sewers keep water clean. The insertion of the words "poor," "old," or "inadequate" before sewer would clarify this.

Figure 6.4c
Superficial and incomplete web showing poor understanding

BOX 6.2   The Computer-Based Assessment of Knowledge Organization

Software is now available that enables students, working alone or in groups, to create knowledge organization maps on the computer. This software can be used to display graphical representations of important relationships and an understanding of the conceptual structure of a domain of knowledge (Edmondson, 2000; Mintzes, Wandersee, & Novak, 2000; Shavelson & Ruiz-Primo, 2000). It can also provide timely feedback by immediately scoring students' concept maps by comparing them to the characteristics found in concept maps developed by the teacher (O'Neil & Klein, 1997). Computer-generated grades on individually produced concept maps have had a high degree of correspondence with grades on written student essays intended to convey the same information (National Research Council, 1999).

The Open-Book Constructed-Response Test

After selecting a topic area and identifying the cognitive outcomes that you wish to assess, you have the choice to give the questions you want your learners to answer in an open-book format. Ideas for these questions can come from the text but also newspapers, news programs, technical reports, journals related to your curriculum, and your experiences with a variety of real-life situations in which the behaviors you want to assess are used. Your open-book questions may ask students or collaborative groups of students to prepare an outline of a presentation to a city planning board using reference material from the text, simulate an experiment or laboratory task using data from resource tables, develop specifications for a product using a published list of industry standards, or develop a mass transit plan, given maps and budgetary information. You can get started on developing open-book questions by asking yourself the following questions:

> What do the jobs of professionals who make their livings as mathematicians, electronic technicians, journalists, food processing supervisors, television newscasters, and so forth look and feel like?

> Which of the projects and tasks of these professionals can be adapted to the knowledge and skills required by your curriculum?

> Which of these skills are enhanced by being able to refer to existing data, resources, tables, charts, diagrams, and so forth without having to memorize them?

Once you answer these questions, a host of ideas arise. The task is then one of developing the open-book exam questions. The examples below illustrate different types of open-book questions.

Some Open-Book Techniques

Here is an example open-book question with explicit directions for a middle school science class. It allows students to use a table and a portion of their text to formulate a response.

> On pages 70 to 74 of your text you will find a description of a static electricity experiment. Read the description carefully. Then, using your understanding of the experiment and the principles of the electroscope shown in Table 5, answer the following questions:
>   1. What would happen to the leaves of the electroscope as the charged ruler is brought closer or farther away from it? Explain why this happens.
>   2. What would happen to the leaves when you touch the electroscope with the charged ruler and then touch it with your finger? Explain why this happens.
>   3. What would happen when you pass the charged ruler close to the leaves but do not make contact with them? Explain why this happens.
>   4. What would happen to the charged leaves when you heat the air next to them with a match? Explain why this happens.

For each question:

(a) Make a prediction about what would happen.

(b) What you would observe.

(c) How your prediction could be supported.

Because you want the answer to show evidence of particular reasoning strategies and not memorization, be sure to include explicit cues to learners to show evidence of the strategy they are using or the thinking and reasoning they went through on the way to solving the problem. Reminders like, "Show all work," "Be sure to list the steps involved," and so on, will allow you better to assess both cognitive and metacognitive strategies.

Quellmalz (1991) recommends that, particularly with questions that assess analysis and comparison, you include the question, "So what?" Rather than simply list elements in an analysis or develop a laundry list of similarities and differences, learners should be asked to explain the significance of the analysis or points of comparison. Thus, questions should explicitly cue learners to explain why the various aspects of the analysis or comparison are important (e.g., Why should the reader care about the things you analyzed? or Why are the similarities and differences that you discussed important for an understanding of this event.)

Dialectical Journals

Another way of encouraging and assessing higher level thinking skills with open-book exams is through dialectical journals. The word *dialectical* comes from a method of argumentation originating with the ancient Greeks. This process involves the art of examining opinions or ideas logically, often by the method of question and answer to determine their validity. It was the practice of Socrates and his followers to conduct this process through oral discourse, but many of the same positive results can be achieved by implementing this structure into a written journal form.

In a sense, the dialectical journal is a conversation with oneself over the concepts of a given text. Here is one suggested format. Divide your examination in half vertically and title two columns as follows:

Quotation, Summary, or Paraphrase	Reaction, Prediction, or Analysis
(From text)	(From student)

A quotation, summary, or paraphrase from the text or related reading (e.g., relevant magazine or newspaper article) is chosen by you. A reaction, prediction, or analysis to your quotation, summarization, or paraphrasing is written by the student in the column on the right. Just like the professional on the job, your students are allowed to consult the text to find material for composing their response.

This journal format should be modeled with examples and practiced with students before using it for assessment purposes. Initially students unfamiliar with this procedure may make shallow or superficial comments, often thinking that simple explication or explanation is what is wanted. Learning to use the text in this manner can increase the accuracy and depth of responses and encourage higher level cognition.

Dialectical journals can be practiced in the *initial* stages of a new topic or unit to encourage active reading, at *midpoint* to see if early ideas were valid, and at the *conclusion,* as an open-book exam in which new perspectives and greater understanding can be assessed. A good rule of thumb is to use the early dialectical journals for modeling and feedback, to generate the exchange of ideas, and for assessment purposes at the conclusion of a topic or unit. Therefore, they can be used as an instructional tool as well as an assessment device. Here are two sample dialectical entries in the form of an open-book exam in math and reading. These begin with a quotation, summary, or paraphrase from the text, followed by a related question to which students provide a reaction, prediction, or analysis.

DIALECTICAL OPEN-BOOK QUESTIONS

Quotation, Summary, or Paraphrase	Student Reaction, Prediction, or Analysis
"A triangle with given sides can have only one shape. A rectangle formed by four bars joined at their ends can flatten into a parallelogram, but the structural integrity of a triangle cannot be deformed except by bending or stretching the bars." (Quote from text or resource on geometric shapes.)	
From the pyramids of ancient Egypt to the Eiffel Tower in France, extending to the modest tripod of photography, or the tallest of radio towers, we see the ever-present tower. Using examples from the text, what other building or structural uses can be made of the simple triangle?	

Quotation, Summary, or Paraphrase	Student Reaction, Prediction, or Analysis
"Never read feverishly, never read as though you were racing against time— unless you wish to derive neither pleasure nor profit from your reading." (Quote from the introduction to a middle-school reader.)	
Could it be that pleasure and profit are connected? Do we remember things more if we take the time to enjoy them? How important are emotions to learning? According to this author, the conventional advice to read faster and more efficiently may not be so good. Can you show from examples in any of the stories you have read that slowing down and enjoying what you are doing can increase your understanding and ability to apply what you have read?	

Because the student self-selects the material to answer the question from the text or resource, there is already inherent interest in the content and meaning for the student. This journal technique may be refined to meet an individual instructor's needs. For example, students may be asked to choose entries that relate to a single theme or concept, such as the application of conservation practices, future uses of known scientific principles, or analysis of an historical event.

Here is another type of dialectical question. This one reverses the process by asking the student to find a quotation, paraphrase, or summary from the text that exhibits a certain principle or concept provided by you.

Directions: Read the following passage and *choose* three quotations from the story we have studied that supports this theme.

Machines and tools have always been created in the image of man. The hammer grew from the balled fist, the rake from the hand with fingers outstretched for scratching, the shovel from the hand hollowed to scoop. As machines became more than simple tools, outstripping the creators in performance, demanding and obtaining increasing amounts of power, and acquiring superhuman speed and accuracies, their outward resemblance to the natural model disappeared; only the names of the machines' parts show vestiges of the human origin. The highly complex machinery of the industrial age has arms that swing, fingers that fold, legs that support, and teeth that grind. Machines feed on material, run when things go well, and spit and cough when they don't.

Quotation, Summary, or Paraphrase from the Text That Supports the Previous Passage	Pg.
1.	
2.	
3.	

In Application 6.2, compose a dialectical open-book question that promotes higher order thinking.

Now that we have studied ways of writing good constructed-response questions in the form of restricted-response questions, knowledge organization maps, open-book exams, and dialectical journals, let's summarize with some guidelines that can help you write good constructed-response questions in all of these formats.

APPLICATION 6.2

From a text you will be teaching, compose an open-book question that requires your learners to find specific instances of a particular concept, principle, or generalization (e.g., in a science text, from a story, or in different newspapers and magazines) which corresponds with what is being expressed in a quotation, summary, or paraphrase that you provide. Provide one example of a possible student response to your quotation, summary, or paraphrase.

Your stimulus quotation, summary, or paraphrase:

An example student response and source:

Guidelines for Planning Constructed-Response and Open-Book Exams

1. *Make clear the requirements for answering your questions, but not the solution itself.* Although your questions should be complex, learners should not have to question whether they are finished, or whether they have provided what you want. They should, however, have to think long and hard about how to answer a question. As you refine your questions, make sure you can visualize what an acceptable answer looks like and identify the skills you can infer from it.

2. *The questions should represent a valid sample from which you can make generalizations about the learner's knowledge, thinking ability, and attitudes.* What essay tests lack in breadth of coverage, they make up in depth. In other words, they get your students to exhibit higher order thinking behavior in a narrow domain or skill. Thus, the type of questions you choose should be complex enough and rich enough in detail to allow you to draw conclusions about transfer and generalization to other tasks. In other words, they should be representative of other important skills that assess the essential performance outcomes you wish your learners to achieve (Shavelson & Baxter, 1992).

3. *The questions should be complex enough to allow for multiple correct answers.* Most assessment tends to depend on a single right answer. Constructed-response questions, however, are designed to allow learners to demonstrate learning through a variety of paths. In science, for example, a student might choose to answer a

question by emphasizing the results of an experiment from the text, showing the solution by explaining how laboratory equipment would be used to arrive at it, or by simulating data and conclusions from an experiment that would answer the question. Allowing for multiple paths to the correct answer will be more time consuming than a multiple-choice test, but it will provide unique information about your learners' achievement untapped by other assessment methods. Shavelson and Baxter (1992) have shown that examination procedures that allow teachers to draw different conclusions about a learner's problem-solving ability lead to more analysis, interpretation, and evaluation behavior than do multiple-choice tests or restricted-response essay tests.

4. *The questions should yield multiple solutions when possible, each with costs and benefits.* Essay questions are not a form of practice or drill. They should involve more than simple tasks for which there is one solution. Constructed-response questions should be nonalgorithmic (the path of action is not fully specified in advance), complex (the total solution cannot be seen from any one vantage point), and should involve judgment and interpretation.

5. *The questions should require self-regulated learning.* Constructed-response questions should require considerable mental effort and place high demands on the persistence and determination of the individual learner. The learner should be required to use cognitive strategies to arrive at a solution rather than depend on memorized content at various points in the assessment process.

6. *The questions should have clear directions.* Constructed-response questions should be complex, require higher level thinking, assess multiple goals, and permit considerable latitude about how to reach these goals. Nevertheless, your questions should leave no doubt in the minds of learners about what is expected. Although your students need to think long and hard about how to answer the question, they should be clear about what a good answer looks like. In other words, they should be able to explain exactly what you expect them to turn in when the exam is over.

Summary

This chapter presented some ways you can assess your learners' understanding and knowledge organization with constructed-response items. This chapter also illustrated how to measure knowledge organization through the vehicles of visual webs, networks, and concept maps. This chapter has also introduced you to the flexibility and motivating nature of open-book exams and dialectical journals that can capture the degree to which you have taught and your learners have acquired the relationships among bits of knowledge necessary for building higher order concepts and themes. It is to these higher order concepts and themes, built from the knowledge bases studied in this and the previous chapter, that we now turn.

Activities

Review the lesson contexts and example questions at the end of this chapter. For this chapter these examples illustrate questions for assessing your learners' declarative knowledge with constructed-response items. Review them as a guide for completing the following activities.

1. Distinguish between a restricted-response and an extended-response question by citing examples of each from your recent academic experience. Which do you feel represented the more valid assessment of what you knew and could do—and why?
2. Identify three potential threats to the scoring of a restricted response question. What would you do to protect your scoring from them?
3. Using the web format illustrated in this chapter, draw three diagrams representing poor, adequate, and good knowledge organization for a topic you believe knowledge organization is important.
4. Using the lesson contexts and template at the end of this chapter as a guide, create three questions of your own that assess your learners' use of declarative knowledge with constructed-response items.

Suggested Readings

Quellmalz, E. S., & Hoskyn, J. (1997). Classroom assessment of reasoning strategies. In G. D. Phye (Ed.), *Handbook of classroom assessment: Learning, adjustment, achievement* (pp. 103–130). San Diego: Academic Press.
The authors lay a foundation for the importance of building upon declarative knowledge to achieve higher order outcomes, including reasoning, problem-solving and decision-making skills.

Shavelson, R. J., & Ruiz-Primo, M. A. (2000). On the psychometrics of assessing science understanding. In J. Mintzes, J. Wandersee, & J. Novak (Eds.), *Assessing science understanding: A human constructivist view* (pp. 303–341). San Diego: Academic Press.
This chapter sets out guidelines for measuring science understanding that considers the learner's contribution to the learning process.

Lesson Contexts

K–2 EXAMPLE LESSON CONTEXTS FOR ASSESSING DECLARATIVE KNOWLEDGE WITH
CONSTRUCTED-RESPONSE QUESTIONS

Grade	Subject	Topic	Assessment Questions
K–2	Language Arts	Fact vs. fiction	Do you think *Little Red Riding Hood* is fact or fiction?
		Onomatopoeia	What word sounds like its name in the story *Little Toot*? What words name the sounds that different animals make?
K–2	Mathematics	Measurement	Look at all the coins on the table. Which coins are larger in size than the nickel and which are larger than the others?
		Measurement	What activities have you done this past week that took one second, one minute, and one hour.
K–2	Science	Living and non-living organisms	Which pictures on the table show living organisms and which show nonliving organisms.
		Basic needs of organisms	Recall three ways that animals protect themselves from the cold (possible examples—birds, mice, horses).
K–2	Social Studies	History	Recall the reasons behind the celebration of Thanksgiving. What customs do we have and why?
		Geography	Recall ways in which our class has helped to conserve and replenish natural resources.
K–2	Health	Hygiene	Which pictures show how cold germs are spread?
		Safety	What protective equipment should be worn while playing the following sports: football, rollerblading, snowboarding, horseback riding? Be ready to explain how this makes you safer.

GRADES 3–5 EXAMPLE LESSON CONTEXTS FOR ASSESSING DECLARATIVE KNOWLEDGE
WITH CONSTRUCTED-RESPONSE TESTS

Grade	Subject	Topic	Assessment Questions
3–5	Language Arts	Analyze characters	In the first chapter of *Charlotte's Web* we meet Fern. What words would you use to describe her (e.g., persuasive, lazy, fair-minded, emotional, hardhearted)?
		Compare text events with student experience	Tell or write about a time that you, like Fern in *Charlotte's Web*, were concerned with "injustice."
3–5	Mathematics	Measurement: Temperature	Read and record the temperature from the thermometer outside the classroom each day at the same time for a week. Chart it on the graph in your workbook.
		Geometry and spatial reasoning	Draw two parallel lines that could be used to construct a geometric shape.
3–5	Science	Concepts: Physical properties	Name all the liquids, solids, and gases that were used in our study of the greenhouse effect.
		Concepts: The needs of living organisms	Explain how the beaver modifies its environment to meet its needs.
3–5	Social Studies	Geography	Explain how to use the scale on the map to measure the distance between Chicago and St. Louis.
		Science, technology, and society	Describe two inventions and their inventors that have most influenced the way we travel. Write a sentence describing the impact of each of these.
3–5	Health	Health behaviors	Fill in the blanks in the food pyramid to represent a healthy, well-balanced diet.
		Physical activity and health	Describe one physical activity each that can be expected to promote strength, endurance, and flexibility.

GRADES 6–8 EXAMPLE LESSON CONTEXTS FOR ASSESSING DECLARATIVE KNOWLEDGE
WITH CONSTRUCTED-RESPONSE TESTS

Grade	Subject	Topic	Assessment Questions
6–8	Language Arts	Denotation, connotation	Identify five words from our story that mean or denote the same things, but have different emotional overtones or connotations (e.g., overweight, fat, plump; thrifty, economical, cheap; determined, obstinate, steady).
		Using references	Indicate which reference source you should use to locate the following information: Table of Contents, Index, and Glossary.
6–8	Mathematics	Probability and statistics	Calculate the mean, median, and the mode for each set of numbers listed below.
		Patterns, relationships, and algebraic thinking	Create a set of data that matches the graph, and verbal description below.
6–8	Science	Scientific process	Read the paragraph below describing a laboratory experiment. Identify all the unsafe practices and rewrite the paragraph implementing safe ones.
		Science concepts: Generational change	After reading the section in the text on reproduction, which offspring characteristic is most likely to be a result of asexual reproduction and which sexual reproduction?
6–8	Social Studies	History: Civil War	Describe the most important events that led up to the Civil War. Put them in the proper sequence by numbering from one to ten.
		History: Revolutionary War	Read the following statements about the causes of the Revolutionary War. Describe why they are true or false.
6–8	Health	Interpersonal skills	Describe some unhealthy ways to reduce stress. Then describe the bad consequences of each.
			Choose two prescription or over-the-counter medications and show how they can be abused.

TEMPLATE FOR YOUR LESSON CONTEXTS FOR ASSESSING DECLARATIVE KNOWLEDGE
WITH CONSTRUCTED-RESPONSE QUESTIONS

Grade	Subject	Topic	Assessment Questions

7

Assessing Procedural Knowledge

In chapters 5 and 6 you learned about methods for assessing what learners know. As you will recall, learners know facts, concepts, rules, and generalizations. Their knowledge base is organized to make it easier to remember and recall information. You can assess this knowledge base with a variety of measurement tools, such as completion, short-answer, true–false, and multiple-choice items, and its degree of organization with restricted-response questions, concept maps, and open-book exams.

Often teachers are interested in assessing not only what learners know but also what they can do. They want to know if their learners can use the information they possess. For example, it is important to find out what learners know about microscopes and whether they can use one. Learners should know not only about fractions but also about how to add, subtract, and reduce them. They should know about the parts of speech and be able to write a sentence, paragraph, or essay.

It is possible to know about things and not be able to apply what you know. For example, you might be able to tell a friend how to bake bread yet be unable to do it yourself, or you might be able to describe clearly how to make parallel turns when skiing but fall head over heels the first time you try yourself. Similarly, a learner may correctly state the rule for adding fractions with unlike denominators but not be able to arrive at the right answer when applying the rule.

As we saw from earlier chapters, cognitive psychologists distinguish between knowledge about things, or declarative knowledge, and knowledge of how to perform activities, or procedural knowledge. This distinction is important because different teaching conditions are required for students to learn procedural knowledge than for students to learn declarative knowledge. Also, different methods are used to assess these knowledge bases. In this chapter we will study the learning conditions and assessment methods associated with procedural knowledge.

Procedural Knowledge

Top professional basketball player Karl Malone is called the "Mailman" because he delivers. Experts in any field "deliver." They not only know how to do the job, but also they get the job done. To use a popular expression, they "talk the talk and walk the walk." Experts deliver because they have extensive, organized networks of procedural knowledge. They know not only *about* reading, writing, geometry, anatomy, or mathematics, but also about *how* to read, produce a short story, bisect a line, dissect a specimen, or solve an equation.

An expert's knowledge of how to do things, of how to get the job done, is stored in long-term memory just like declarative knowledge. Cognitive psychologists speculate that there are separate information stores or networks of neurons for declarative and procedural knowledge. They also speculate that the organizational properties of the two types of knowledge are different (Squire & Kandel, 1999).

Declarative knowledge appears to be organized hierarchically, like a pyramid with larger concepts on the top and bits and pieces that support them on the bottom. Procedural knowledge, on the other hand, seems to be organized into networks or sequences of if–then rules. An if–then rule identifies a condition and an action. The *if* component specifies the condition needed for a particular action to take place (the *then* component). For example, procedural knowledge about adding fractions is organized into a network of if–then rules: If the denominators are the same, then add the numerators; if the denominators are different, then first reduce the denominators to their least common multiple, and so forth.

Much of our procedural knowledge is used so automatically that we do not have to think consciously about it, for example, reading. When students first learn to read, they consciously think through and act out if–then rules: If the letters *t* and *h* are next to one another, then say a *th* sound; if the vowels *e* and *a* are next to each other, then pronounce the combination as long *e*, and so forth. With practice, learners read the vowel and consonant combinations automatically. Cognitive psychologists speculate that procedural knowledge started as declarative knowledge (Anderson, 1983; Squire & Kandel, 1999). In other words, we first learn *about* something. We learn about vowels and vowel sounds and combinations; then we learn *how* to read them. We learn about parts of speech; then we learn how to write a sentence. We learn about bisecting angles; then we learn how to do it. We learn about swinging a golf club, or hitting a backhand in tennis, or doing a handstand; then we learn how to do these actions. In each of these examples, declarative knowledge (knowledge about something) preceded procedural knowledge (knowledge of how to do something).

Although declarative knowledge and procedural knowledge occupy different locations in the brain's long-term memory and are organized in different ways, they work together to produce expert performance. Your classroom management skills depend on what you know about appropriate and inappropriate learner behavior. They also depend on how well you communicate rules, encourage good behavior, and prevent inappropriate behavior. Likewise, you need extensive declarative knowledge about U.S. history to develop a lesson plan. But you also must know how to get a learner's attention, model good thinking, coach learning, and fade out your direct involvement to allow for learner independence.

How Procedural Knowledge Develops

The development of procedural knowledge is one of the most important missions of schooling. Children should leave the early elementary grades able to read and write fluently—or automatically. They should be able to perform basic procedures of addition, subtraction, division, and multiplication without thinking. They should know how to read a story and comprehend what it is about. They should know how to use some basic strategies for solving math and science problems. When they reach middle school, they should be beginning to learn procedures to automatically write essays, carry out experiments, analyze a piece of writing, and so forth.

Learners pass through a series of stages on their way to automatically carrying out procedural knowledge. These stages are called cognitive, associative, and autonomous (Gagné, Yekovich, & Yekovich, 1993).

Cognitive Stage. During the cognitive stage the learner is a novice and is dependent on declarative knowledge to cue her about how to do something. When she sees on a worksheet the problem:

$$5/6 + 1/3 =$$

she might have to consult a handout or her textbook to recall the procedure:

1. Find the least common denominator.
2. Divide the denominator of the second fraction into the least common denominator.
3. Multiply the numerator of the first fraction by the number found in step 2.
4. . . . and so forth.

The learner might then verbally state to herself each step before carrying it out. She consciously executes all the steps in the procedure.

If you have ever skied and are just learning to execute a turn, you probably start by saying to yourself:

> Now slide across the slope. Keep your weight on your downhill ski. Pick up and step out your uphill ski into a wedge. Point that ski in the direction you want to turn. Now plant your inside pole and shift all your weight onto your outside ski. Now pick up the inside ski, lay it in parallel to the outside ski, and skid around the turn. Keep your hands forward and knees flexed.

At this point in your development you move slowly; are conscious of weight shifts, hand positions, and pole placements; and must cue yourself to perform every movement.

Associative Stage. During the associative stage the learner's performance gradually changes from a sequence of actions controlled by cues or reminders guided by declarative knowledge to a sequence of actions that are less conscious. Performance slowly becomes smooth and rapid. Two changes bring this about. First, several steps are collapsed into one step. The learner combines several individual actions or movements. In the fraction example this could involve one set of cues that quickly elicit steps 1 to 3, followed by another set of cues that elicit steps 4 to 6, rather than a separate set of cues for each step. In the skiing example, it might involve one fluid movement to the point where the inside pole is planted.

The second change which occurs during this stage is the dropping out of the declarative knowledge cues. The learner no longer has to pause and think about what comes next or hesitate before executing the next movement. The learner no longer consciously searches for the next thing to do. Rather, she automatically executes the action sequence, although not as smoothly as an expert.

Autonomous Stage.   A continuation of the associative stage, the autonomous stage, is characterized by a finely tuned action sequence performed with little hesitation. One action follows the other in a smooth, effortless movement or motion. It is as if the learner is on automatic pilot. You can detect almost no thinking by the learner about what to do next. The only conscious thought is that of the goal: solving the problem of getting down the hill. Actions are so automatic that the learner can think about something else as she is performing them. While completing a fraction worksheet, the learner thinks about recess. The skier admires the breathtaking landscape as she plunges down the slope. While walking down the stairs, you think of nothing but the friends you are going to meet. Your actions have become so natural you no longer have to think about them.

Types of Procedural Knowledge

Just as we have seen that there are different types of declarative knowledge (facts, concepts, rules, generalizations), there are also different types of procedural knowledge that schools seek to develop. These are domain-specific basic *skills,* which will be the focus of this chapter, and domain-specific and domain-general *strategies,* which will be the focus of the chapters that follow (Gagné et al., 1993). Before we begin, let's review each of these types of procedural knowledge.

Domain-Specific Basic Skills.   As you will recall from chapter 2, a knowledge domain is any defined subject-matter area that can vary in breadth. Math is a knowledge domain that is very broad. American history is a knowledge domain that has many subdomains, as does science. Procedural knowledge that is specific to a knowledge domain or subdomain is referred to as a **domain-specific basic skill**. Examples of such procedural knowledge would be adding fractions, bisecting an angle, making parallel skiing turns, and baking bread. These examples of procedural knowledge lie within the domains of addition, geometry, skiing, and cooking. Other examples include three-digit multiplication, computing a square root, proving a geometric theorem, constructing a map, focusing a telescope, tying shoelaces, riding a bicycle, starting a car, saving information to a floppy disk, and taping a television program on a videocassette recorder.

The goal of teaching domain-specific basic skills is to enable learners to reach the autonomous stage of procedural knowledge development. In other words, once a learner recognizes that the task before her requires a certain sequence of actions, she then *spontaneously* executes these actions *automatically*.

Domain-Specific Strategies. Procedural knowledge specific to a knowledge domain (such as math) which requires the conscious, controlled, and deliberate execution of problem-solving, thinking, and reasoning behaviors is referred to as a **domain-specific strategy**. When your students start a composition assignment, they are probably using a domain-specific strategy you have taught them. For example, as part of writing instruction, your students may learn to execute a routine that involves (a) generating a topic sentence, (b) noting reasons, (c) examining the reasons to see if readers will accept each reason, and (d) coming up with an ending (Scardamalia & Bereiter, 1986). This strategy is domain-specific because it is taught as a writing tool that is consciously and deliberately applied to a specific content area. Unlike domain-specific procedural skills, domain-specific strategies are problem solving, thinking, and reasoning routines that are executed by *consciously* thinking about them and applying them in a controlled and deliberate manner. They do not occur spontaneously and automatically; they require deliberation and thought. Another example of a domain-specific strategy would be safe driving techniques. As you drive, you monitor traffic conditions such as speed, the distance between your car and the one in front of you, road conditions, congestion, and so forth. To be effective this strategy should be consciously and deliberately applied.

Domain-General Strategies. Procedural knowledge which encompasses routines or sequences of actions that are useful in *any* knowledge domain (e.g., across writing, social studies, and reading) is referred to as a **domain-general strategy**. When your students learn to become aware of the problem-solving strategy they are using, monitor its effectiveness while using it, and make a conscious commitment to use the strategy, they are applying a domain-general strategy that can apply to any knowledge domain or content area.

For example, teachers seek to improve a student's ability to learn or think regardless of whether the subject is history, science, geography, or mathematics. A student should be able to set goals for learning, come up with a plan to achieve the goal, monitor learning, and evaluate her progress. This "learning to learn" strategy can be used regardless of the content area a student is trying to master.

Domain-specific strategies and domain-general strategies represent what are called problem-solving, thinking, or reasoning strategies that will be the topic of our next chapter. In this chapter we will focus our attention on procedural knowledge that represents a skill—or sequence of actions—specific to a knowledge domain that is spontaneously and automatically executed.

Teaching Domain-Specific Procedural Knowledge

When making distinctions among domain-specific skills, domain-specific strategies, and domain-general strategies, keep in mind that all three represent types of procedural knowledge in which the learner knows how to successfully perform in some way. In other words, procedural knowledge is not just a matter of knowing something. Procedural knowledge is more than just an academic exercise; it involves not only teaching rules and sequences of actions but also knowing when and how to use these rules and actions until they become automatic. Learners must be able to recognize the situation or problem to which a sequence of actions apply, choose the appropriate sequence of actions that fits the context, and execute the required actions spontaneously and automatically. Learners must know not only how to perform a procedure but also when to do so. Motivation is a key factor in the learning and the expert execution of procedural knowledge.

When teaching and assessing domain-specific procedural skills, keep in mind the notion of knowledge construction. Your task is to set up meaningful contexts within a domain of knowledge in which learners recognize the need for constructing a particular procedure or routine rather than to train a rote sequence of actions. Once you have provided learners with a meaningful context in which to learn a specific procedure, then the challenge is to provide the conditions that allow them to reach the autonomous stage of procedural knowledge development—where the learner executes the procedure automatically. To accomplish this you will have to model the sequence of actions in a systematic, step-by-step manner. For example, if you want to teach your learners how to meaningfully read a poem, operate an electronic calculator, or follow the steps in long division, learners must imitate your actions and practice the steps under your guidance and coaching. Remember that the purpose of practice is spontaneous and automatic use of the procedure. This will require extensive repetition in conjunction with your specific feedback. The more examples and contexts you provide, the more learners will recognize when and how to use the procedure.

Now let's look at some assessment techniques that can help your students acquire procedural knowledge that is domain-specific.

Assessing Domain-Specific Procedural Knowledge

Whereas evidence of declarative knowledge can come in a variety of ways (short-answer questions, objective-type test items, recall or recognition exercises), procedural knowledge has to be performed. It has to be observed to be assessed. For example, the only way to know if Sarah can ride a bike is to see her do it. Her telling you how it is done is not enough. You say you know how to manage classroom behavior? Well, let's see you do it! You say you can teach learners how to subtract? Well, show me!

We want to stress, however, that procedural knowledge, as pointed out earlier, has a declarative knowledge foundation. Knowing how to subtract depends on knowing what subtraction is. Knowing how to manage classroom behavior depends on knowing something about behavior. The following sections focus on the "how-to" aspect of procedural knowledge in specific domains—on ways to determine if learners spontaneously and automatically know how to do something.

Assessing Processes and Products

A *process* is the sequence of actions, routines, or steps that a learner takes to complete an activity. The *product* is the concrete, tangible outcome that results from those actions. In math, for example, the product might be the written solution, with the process being the logical sequence of steps that the student followed. A loaf of bread is a product. The process involves mixing the ingredients, kneading the dough, and so forth.

It is usually easier to evaluate a product—a book report, map, drawing, science project, or essay—than it is to evaluate the process of developing these concrete outcomes. You have a single object to compare to other products or to some standard, and you can take your time while doing so. Processes, however, consist of a series of steps that you usually have to observe being performed.

Most of classroom assessment concerns itself with products. When the product is competently completed in a timely fashion, the correct processes are usually assumed. But when the product is faulty and/or takes an unreasonably short or long time to complete, a product assessment by itself does not tell why. This is where process assessment becomes important. When the product is flawed or unacceptable, a process assessment helps you determine what steps may have been completed improperly or were omitted. If your goal is automatic performance that consistently leads to an acceptable product, process assessment is essential to assure that the procedures taught have been properly applied. Table 7.1 is an example of a process assessment designed to discover and diagnose procedural errors in subtraction.

Brown and Burton (1978) and Brown and VanLehn (1980) have discovered that the majority of students who have problems with subtraction exhibit "bugs" in the process of executing a problem that prevent them from attaining the right answer. The same has been found with fractions (Resnick, Nesher, Leonard, Magone, Omanson, & Peled, 1989) and science concepts (diSessa and Minstrell, 1998) across a wide range of languages and instructional settings. Typically, the teacher assesses knowledge in a certain area with a set of problems. The student's score is usually a tally of the number of correct answers and the percentage correct. Although this may tell us that the student got 60 percent of the items correct, it does not tell us about the processes used by the student to arrive at those answers.

Now, consider the information that would be gained from the set of problems in Table 7.1. These were specifically chosen to determine which, if any, subtraction bugs were contributing to the learner's incorrect answers. From this set of problems a pattern of errors would emerge that, with subsequent practice and instruction, could be easily and quickly remedied, because the teacher would know exactly what the learner is doing wrong. In a less carefully constructed set of items, we would know only that the learner has gotten a certain percentage correct but not what to do to make the learner competent. The interpretation of the learner's ability to do subtraction could be considerably different in these two instances. In this chapter we will cover ways of constructing this type of process assessment.

TABLE 7.1
Subtraction Bugs Assessment

$$\begin{array}{r} 143 \\ -\ 28 \\ \hline 125 \end{array}$$
The student subtracts the smaller digit in each column from the larger digit regardless of which is on top.

$$\begin{array}{r} 14\overset{1}{3} \\ -\ 28 \\ \hline 125 \end{array}$$
The student adds 10 to the top digit of the current column without subtracting 1 from the next column to the left, when needing to borrow.

$$\begin{array}{r} \overset{9}{13\cancel{0}\cancel{0}} \\ -\ 522 \\ \hline 878 \end{array}$$
The student writes 9 above the column whose top digit is 0, but does not continue borrowing from the column to the left of the 0.

$$\begin{array}{r} 140 \\ -\ 21 \\ \hline 121 \end{array}$$
The student writes the bottom digit in the answer, whenever the top digit in a column is 0.

$$\begin{array}{r} 140 \\ -\ 21 \\ \hline 120 \end{array}$$
The student writes 0 in the answer, whenver the top digit in a column is 0.

$$\begin{array}{r} \overset{10}{13\cancel{0}\cancel{0}} \\ -\ 522 \\ \hline 788 \end{array}$$
The student borrows from the next column to the left correctly, when borrowing from a column where the top digit is 0. But then the student writes 10 instead of 9 in this column.

$$\begin{array}{r} \overset{10}{32\cancel{1}} \\ -\ 89 \\ \hline 231 \end{array}$$
The student gets 10 instead of 11 when borrowing into a column whose top digit is 1.

$$\begin{array}{r} 5\overset{5}{\cancel{5}}\overset{1}{\cancel{1}} \\ \cancel{6}\cancel{6}2 \\ -\ 357 \\ \hline 205 \end{array}$$
The student continues to borrow from every column whether she needs to or not, after borrowing from a column.

$$\begin{array}{r} \overset{4}{\cancel{6}}\overset{1}{6}2 \\ -\ 357 \\ \hline 115 \end{array}$$
The student always subtracts all borrows from the leftmost digit in the top number.

Note. Results of a subtraction test derived from a test plan indicating specific skills to be remediated. *Source:* Adapted from Brown, J., & Burton, R. (1978). Diagnostic models for procedural bugs in basic mathematical skills. *Cognitive Science, 2,* 156–192.

Steps in Assessing Procedural Knowledge

As you begin designing an assessment to evaluate your learner's procedural knowledge of a domain-specific basic skill, reflect on what you have learned thus far about this type of knowledge.

- Procedural knowledge shows what a learner can do.
- It should be executed spontaneously and automatically.

- It is acquired through stages.
- It is developed by learners from contexts or situations that are important to them and to you.

Now you are ready to follow the steps to design a process assessment.

Step 1. Clarify the Procedure and the Reasons for Assessing It

When you decide to conduct a procedural assessment, you are making a substantial commitment of your time and energy as well as that of your learners. You want to have a clear reason for doing so. Ask yourself why it is important for you to assess how someone goes about doing the task instead of just examining and rating the final product. What will you do differently with the results of a procedural assessment in comparison to the results of a product assessment? The following are some possible reasons:

- *Individual diagnosis.* You want to observe the strengths and needs of individual learners as they carry out the procedure on their way to developing automatic performance.
- *Group needs assessment.* You want to determine the strengths and needs of the entire class and use this information to group learners according to their level of mastery.
- *Grading.* You want to base a learner's grade on both product and process outcomes.
- *Certification.* You want to verify that individual learners have mastered certain procedures before moving on to other more complex action sequences.

Examples

1. I will conduct an assessment of how the learner uses an electronic calculator in order to diagnose individual strengths and needs.
2. I will conduct an assessment of the steps involved in long division to allow me to group learners to meet their learning needs.
3. I will assess how the learner sets up an experiment in order to include this as part of the science grade.

Notice in each of the examples that it was the process, not the product (or result) that was of interest. You will want to assess both process and product, but without knowing how well the process was executed by the learner you will not know if she successfully achieves the product for the wrong reason, and may not be able to repeat her good fortune again. Being able to consistently execute the process assures you and your learners that they can consistently achieve the same high standard of excellence again and again.

In Box 7.1 you will find a classroom example of domain-specific procedural knowledge in Mrs. Watkins middle-school English class. Using Mrs. Watkins's responses as a guide, complete step 1 in Application 7.1 for a domain-specific procedure you would like to assess.

BOX 7.1   An Example of Domain-Specific Procedural Knowledge

Mrs. Watkins's classroom has decided to do a process assessment of a domain-specific basic skill she has just taught her middle-school English class. We have asked her to identify the procedure she will be assessing and the reasons for assessing it.

Step 1: Clarify the Procedure and the Reasons for a Process Assessment

The procedure I will be assessing:

To introduce a unit on poetry, I will teach my students a procedure that will help them orally read a poem. The procedure has four simple steps. I will teach my students (a) the correct posture for oral reading, (b) the correct rhythm for breathing while reading a poem, (c) how to keep your place in the text when establishing eye contact with the audience, and (d) when to pause to establish the meaning of a poem.

My reasons for assessing this procedure is to:

Determine if my students can successfully apply this procedure to help convey the meaning of a poem in future assignments.

APPLICATION 7.1

Step 1. Clarify the procedure and the reasons for a process assessment you might want to conduct.

The procedure I will be assessing is:

My reason(s) for assessing this procedure is/are:

Step 2.   Describe the Assessment Context

This step involves three components: (a) specifying the setting and level of obtrusiveness, (b) specifying who will observe the performance, and (c) specifying how much evidence is needed.

To specify the setting and level of obtrusiveness, you must decide whether you will use a natural, structured, or simulated situation for observing the learner's performance. A **natural setting** is one in which process assessment occurs without the observer intervening or interrupting the normal flow of events. One way to do this is to embed the assessment in a lesson. Because practice is a necessary feature of any lesson designed to teach a procedure, assessment should occur during this time. For example, the most authentic way to assess the processes involved in long division, oral reading, focusing a microscope, using a balance scale, or booting a floppy disk would be as the learner is practicing these skills.

However, on some occasions it is not practical or feasible to use natural classroom settings as the assessment context. At these times you may tell the learner that you want to observe her performing a procedure in a particular place and at a certain time, or in a **structured setting**. You ask the learner to do something rather than wait for it to happen.

Structured settings can benefit both student and teacher by providing a private context that minimizes outside distractions. The learner may be distracted and anxious about being assessed when peers are around. The teacher may find that lesson-embedded assessment detracts from her ability to monitor class behavior, especially in large classes.

In choosing between natural and structured situations, the issue of *best* versus *typical* performance arises. Do you want to assess what the learner typically does when she reads, types, measures, calculates, plays the trombone, or speaks? Or do you want to know what she can do when she is consciously trying to do her best? Natural situations tend to elicit the former performance and structured settings the latter.

In a **simulated setting**, the learner performs the procedure in a controlled but authentic environment. Assessment in a simulated setting is usually necessary when the procedure being taught is one that naturally occurs outside a classroom context and therefore is unavailable for assessment, such as job interviewing, speaking before the schoolboard, ordering food in a restaurant, or planning a route for a two-week backpacking adventure. Again, a desire to make the assessment authentic would place a premium on putting the learner in a realistic context.

You will also need to decide if the learners will know that they are being assessed. In structured and simulated situations that occur outside the natural rhythm of the classroom lesson, most learners will be aware that they are being assessed. This is not always the case in natural situations. You must decide whether to tell the students that their oral reading or calculator skills will be rated as they are practicing the skill. In making this decision, you should weigh considerations of anxiety and motivation. Telling students that their performance will be assessed often enhances motivation and allows you to assess a student's best performance. For some learners, this may create anxiety that limits them from doing their best. In such a situation you may want to assess unobtrusively to reduce a student's anxiety and measurement error or bias.

Examples

1. Oral reading assessments will be done in a private area of the classroom. The students will know that they are being assessed and that this will be part of their reading grade.
2. Computer literacy will be assessed during the lesson. The learners will not be aware that I am rating their performance.
3. I will tell the music students that their sheet music reading skills will be assessed on Friday.

The second component of this step is specifying who will observe the performance. Typically, teachers assess procedures, but learners can self-assess, peers can rate one another's skills, another teacher or aide can assess, or any combination of the above.

Consider the teacher or other expert observer when

- the procedure is one that requires the specialized knowledge or skill that only an expert possesses, and/or
- the assessment will be used for high-stakes purposes such as deciding the winner of a competition, a final course grade, or when district and/or state accountability standards are to be met.

Consider peer or self-ratings when

- the learners themselves are capable of mastering and applying the scoring criteria, and/or
- time constraints prevent you from observing the procedures and giving the learners timely feedback, and/or
- the learners themselves have nothing to gain from artificially inflating or deflating their performance.

Consider using more than one rater when

- the assessment will be used for high-stakes purposes and the reliability of the ratings is of critical importance, and/or
- assessment requires a high degree of judgment. We will discuss this point further when we examine how to construct a process assessment instrument.

Examples

1. Learners will rate one another on the quality of their oral class presentations.
2. The industrial arts teacher will assess the use of proper safety procedures when working with power tools.
3. With a checklist learners will self-evaluate their use of a sequence of steps for booting a floppy disk and shutting down the computer system.

The last component of this step is specifying how much evidence is needed. Here you have several choices:

- Collect one sample of performance on one occasion.
- Collect more than one sample of performance on one occasion.
- Collect more than one sample of performance on different occasions.

The least time-consuming choice is the first one, but remember that all learners have good and bad days. How critical is it that your assessment be a reliable and valid one? Consider:

1. *The importance of the decision.*   If the skill is one that places a premium on safety, or the equipment being used is expensive and easily damaged, then more than one sample of behavior may be needed to be certain that the learner possesses the skill.

2. *The context.*   If the skill is one that is used in a variety of contexts, each of which can affect differently the learner's performance, you will have to assess the behavior in these different contexts. Oral presentations before familiar and unfamiliar peers, and familiar and unfamiliar adults, can elicit different types of performance. Also student's subject-matter interests will be related to performance. Assessment in only one of these situations is unlikely to indicate how the learner will perform under different conditions.

3. *Time constraints.*   If assessment time is limited, you simply may not have time to observe more than one performance.

Examples
1. Use of safe procedures when working with power tools will be observed three times on three different days.
2. Proper use of the coloring pens will be observed for two separate drawings during one class.

Let's look in again on Mrs. Watkins in Box 7.2, who is teaching a domain-specific procedure to her middle school English students. This time we have asked her to describe the context in which she would be assessing her students on the procedure taught. Using Mrs. Watkins's responses as a guide, in Application 7.2 describe the assessment context for the domain-specific procedure you chose in step 1.

Step 3.   List Important Behaviors and Characteristics of the Performance, Including Common Errors and Mistakes

If you are assessing physical movements (e.g., using coloring pens; booting a disk), specify the observable behaviors that must occur to skillfully execute the procedure. Word the statements which designate the behaviors in such a way that they can be answered yes or no, present or absent. Try to make the list of behaviors as inclusive as possible without being too lengthy.

In making the list, do not include behaviors that all students perform without a need for instruction. For example, when setting up a microscope every learner will "hold the slide between thumb and forefinger." Do not include this behavior on your

BOX 7.2   Mrs. Watkins's Assessment Context

Step 2: Describe the Assessment Context

Specify the setting and level of obtrusiveness

The setting I will use for assessing my students' oral reading will be group work in which each of five groups will be assigned a short poem and each member of the group will practice reading the poem to the others Each group will be expected to work in helping each member follow the four steps taught and to improve his oral reading by providing and receiving feedback from other members of the group.

Describe who will rate the performance

The groups will rate each other's final oral presentation with regard to their execution of each step and I will rate each group's cooperative behavior. Each member of a group will receive the average of the ratings from myself and their peers.

Describe how much evidence you will gather

This activity and its assessment will be repeated consecutively for two poems to provide the groups with a variety of examples.

APPLICATION 7.2

Step 2. Describe the assessment context for the procedure you identified in Application 7.1.

Specify the setting and level of obtrusiveness:

Describe who will rate the performance:

Describe how much evidence you will gather:

list. In addition, try to identify behaviors that are clearly inappropriate and for which feedback must be given if they occur. In making an oral presentation, for example, it is important not to use sarcasm when answering a question.

Some processes, including oral performances, cannot always be defined in terms of clearly observable behaviors that lend themselves to yes/no kinds of judgments. In these cases try as best as possible to identify characteristics with an observable quality. For example, clear articulation is important during an oral presentation. The statement "Articulates clearly" does not lend itself to a yes or no decision as readily as a statement like "Wipes the slide with lens paper." We will discuss how to rate these statements shortly.

Be as specific as you can when identifying the attributes of a skilled performance. Resist the temptation to say, "I'll know a good oral presentation when I see one." Identifying the critical attributes of a procedure in observable terms in advance and sharing them with your students is the single most important thing you can do to ensure the quality of your assessment. It will focus the observations of you and your students on important aspects of the procedure that might be ignored had you not gone through this step (Wiggins & McTighe, 2000).

Examples
1. Using an electronic calculator, students should be able to add, subtract, multiply, and divide two-digit numbers with decimals without mistakes.
2. Using audio–video technology, students should read a script on camera without pauses or hesitations due to their unfamiliarity with the script.
3. Using a balance scale, students should weigh three objects in grams.
4. Students should demonstrate their application of basic electrical principles by constructing a series circuit with switch, battery, and bulb.
5. Students should be able to choreograph and perform a dance routine.

The critical behaviors Mrs. Watkins will assess appear in Box 7.3. Using her responses as a guide, describe the critical behaviors you will assess in Application 7.3 for the domain-specific procedure you have chosen in steps 1 and 2.

Step 4.   Design the Procedure Rating Plan
Choose a scoring system best suited for the purpose of assessment (identified in step 1) and for the process you wish to assess. You have four options: checklists, rating scales, holistic scoring, and anecdotal records. Each has certain strengths and limitations that make it more or less suitable for different purposes and processes. Let's look at each of them.

Checklists.   Checklists are suitable for processes that can be described in terms of discrete, observable behaviors, such as those exhibited when using a calculator or balance scale. With a checklist, the observer need only observe the process and mark on an observation form whether the behavior occurred or not. Checklists are efficient. They can be scored while the behavior is taking place and, because they require simple judgments, can assess a relatively large number of attributes. They are

---

BOX 7.3   Mrs. Watkins's Critical Behaviors

Step 3: List the critical behaviors or attributes of the performance.

I will look for evidence of the four steps for orally reading a poem in assessing each of the group presentations and evidence that the students have used these steps while assessing the presentations of their peers. The critical behaviors are:

1. Did each student stand erect and confident during the oral reading?
2. Did each student draw a deep breath before beginning and breathe from the abdomen to maintain a slow and deliberate rhythm?
3. Did each student keep their place in the text when creating eye contact with the audience?
4. Did each student pause at each punctuation point to emphasize the meaning of the poem?

---

also useful for providing diagnostic information to learners. Their principal drawback is that not all procedures lend themselves to such a detailed, observable behavior analysis and they may not provide adequate feedback as to why a behavior was or was not observed. Here are some examples:

Checklist for Social Skills (Assign 1 or 0)

☐ Gave praise to a peer

☐ Asked for clarification

☐ Used expressions like, "what I meant to say was..."

☐ Was constructive in clarifying another's explanation

☐ Waited for another to finish before responding

APPLICATION 7.3

Step 3. List the critical behaviors or attributes of the procedure you want to assess:

Checklist for Using the Hand Calculator (Assign 1 or 0)

Student knows how to:

☐ Turn calculator on

☐ Key in 10 numbers consecutively without hitting adjacent keys

☐ Add three 2-digit numbers without error

☐ Position keyboard; rest arm and elbow for maximum comfort and accuracy

☐ Push keys with positive, firm motion

☐ Tell when a key touch is insufficiently firm to activate calculator

Rating Scales.   Rating scales are suitable for processes that cannot be neatly broken down into behaviors that can be scored as present or absent. Making a presentation and giving a speech are best assessed with a rating scale. The most common type of rating scale assigns values to the components of the procedure on a continuum that indicates the frequency or quality of the behavior, thereby providing greater feedback than that of a checklist. These scales can offer a variety of ways to record the assessment, such as circling verbal descriptions, circling a number, or placing a check on a line. Here are some examples.

Uses proper safety procedures when handling cutting tools (assign 1–5).
Never   Seldom   Occasionally   Often   Always

Uses appropriate voice volume when addressing the class.
Never   Seldom   Occasionally   Often   Always

Rate the quality of the student's introduction to the presentation
Inadequate   1   2   3   4   5   6   7   Superb

Rate the efficiency of the subtraction routine (assign 1–7 points)
Hesitant _____ _____ _____ _____ _____ _____ _____ Smooth

Holds the class's attention while speaking.
Inadequate _____ _____ _____ _____ _____ _____ _____ Adequate

Is sensitive to the needs of the audience.
Unaware   Attuned to
of Audience _____ _____ _____ _____ _____ _____ _____ Audience

Persuasiveness.
Lacks
Enthusiasm _____ _____ _____ _____ _____ _____ _____ Convincing

The job of the rater is to focus on the various aspects of the performance and make a judgment along some qualitative dimension. This judgment is made by circling the number or word on the scale that best corresponds to the observer's judgment or by placing an *X* on a line between bipolar opposites to indicate the proximity of the performance to either pole of the continuum. This judgment often can be made after the procedure or performance has been executed. Because rating scales are more time-consuming to score than checklists, the number of critical attributes that you can practically assess is limited.

Holistic Scoring.   Holistic scoring is used when the rater observes the procedure, notes the different attributes (as defined in step 3) and their qualities, and then assigns a numerical value to the overall quality. Holistic scoring gives an overall index of performance and is appropriate when a grade is the purpose of the assessment. It is less time-consuming than checklists and rating scales. These latter techniques require many individual judgments, whereas holistic scoring requires only one. However, holistic scoring cannot serve a diagnostic purpose because specific strengths and weaknesses are not noted.

The most common examples of the holistic scoring of performances occur in areas such as science fair competition, diving competition, gymnastics, and band recitals. Generally, numbers are assigned on a 3-, 5-, or 7-point scale, with additional numbers between unlabeled points on the scale used to indicate finer gradations of performance. For example:

What is your overall impression of the accuracy of this student's ability to subtract with three-digit numbers?

1	2	3
Below Average	Average	Clearly Outstanding

What is your overall impression of this student's ability to complete the steps for preparing a 10-minute speech?

1	2	3	4	5
Very Poor		About Average		Very Competent

Checklists, rating scales, and holistic scoring are the most efficient assessment techniques for large classes and for procedures that have many attributes. They provide a quick, accurate, and easily interpretable means of recording data. We will have more to say about how to construct these assessment techniques in the next chapter.

Anecdotal Records.   Anecdotal records can add important details to checklists, ratings, and holistic scoring. An anecdotal record is a written account of a procedure: It describes what the learner did and makes evaluative judgments about the performance of critical attributes. Such a record does not include numerical values, but it does provide a richness of detail and information that is often missing in a checklist or rating scale. Although anecdotal records are more time-consuming than these checklist or rating scales they can record improvement when completed on several different occasions. Anecdotal records are best made when important details can be brought to light that explain why a procedure was improperly executed or omitted.

BOX 7.4   Mrs. Watkins's Anecdotal Report

Teacher/Observer: Watkins
Class: 8th grade
Subject: English
January 17
Purpose: To observe the domain-specific procedure: Oral reading: poetry
Observed: Group A
Part A: Description:

As the rest of the class formed into their groups, group A was already taking their turns reading the poem "Man is Mortal." Kloe read the first line and Matt interrupted to remind Kloe to stand up while reading. Pat and Erika stayed at the table reading the poem to each other. When Matt and Kloe finished, they returned to the table and talked about how each could improve on their reading. Matt looked up a word of which he was unsure in the dictionary. There was an argument over the meaning of "mortal" so Rick, who hadn't participated yet, told them the correct meaning was the second, not first, meaning listed in the dictionary—to be vulnerable, not human. Everyone agreed. Matt decided to read the poem for the others so everyone could agree on its meaning. Kloe and Rick made some good suggestions as to how to establish eye contact when pausing for a punctuation mark, after noting that Matt looked down most of the time.

Part B: Assessment

Group A worked very well together with most members contributing something meaningful to each other's performance. Matt and Kloe did a particularly good job using the dictionary, and Matt gave a strong reading that served as a good model for the others. However, Matt is not yet comfortable with making eye contact and may need more practice with steps 3 and 4. Pat and Erika were enthusiastic, although contributed less, caring instead to be supportive to the efforts of others. From what I observed, this group has a firm grasp of the procedure for orally interpreting a poem and should do well on the next assignment.

To maintain the objectivity of the observation, anecdotal reports are usually divided into two distinct parts: facts and the interpretation of the facts.

An example anecdotal report written by Mrs. Watkins after observing one of her groups practicing the steps of orally reading a poem appears in Box 7.4. Notice how she is careful to divide her record into two sections: a description and her interpretation.

Notice how Mrs. Watkins recorded her observations separately from her judgments. This way she or a dispassionate reader could always go back to the facts to see if they agreed with Mrs. Watkins's evaluative statements about this group. For example, the accuracy of Mrs. Watkins's judgment that Matt needed more practice with steps 3 and 4 could be linked to Kloe and Rick's observation that Matt looked down most of the time. It could also provide a basis for her next observation of Matt.

Anecdotal reports are most useful when they occur over time. For example, after an observer makes an initial interpretation, she returns to the classroom at a later date (perhaps several times) to clarify that interpretation. The focus of later observations is to expand on the interpretation's usefulness and validity. Later anecdotal reports should help clarify ambiguities, identify misinterpretations in past reports, and update and enhance factual descriptions with more recent data. Most important, when anecdotal reports focus on the same target behaviors over time (e.g., Matt's eye contact with his audience), they can reveal patterns and regularities that may reveal a continuing problem or the smooth, efficient, and automatic use of a procedure. Anecdotal reports can be especially helpful at parent–teacher nights and during parent conferences, when parents ask for specific instances of the behavior of their child.

Let's consult Box 7.5 to see what Mrs. Watkins did in completing step 4 to design the rating plan. Using Mrs. Watkins's rating plan as a guide, complete a plan of your own in Application 7.4 for the domain-specific procedure you have chosen.

If you are using a checklist or rating scale, organize the behaviors or characteristics you are rating in the sequence that is likely to be followed by the learner and encountered by the observer. This list should be easy to read and contain space where checks can be made, numbers circled, time recorded, frequencies counted, and ratings computed that fit the purpose of the instrument. Once the checklist or rating scale is completed, the instrument should be interpreted based on the purpose(s) specified in step 1.

BOX 7.5   Mrs. Watkins's Rating Plan

Step 4: Design the Procedure Rating Plan

A. Describe a checklist you would use to assess the procedure.

The checklist I will use to record if each member of the group followed the four steps to orally reciting a poem is as follows:

- ❑ Posture erect and confident
- ❑ Breathed deeply and comfortably
- ❑ Established eye contact at critical points
- ❑ Paused at punctuation to establish meaning

B. Describe a rating scale you would use to assess the four steps.

The rating scale I will use to holistically assess the performance of each group is as follows:

This group's application of the procedure was:

Outstanding	Above Average	Average	Below Average	Poor
5	4	3	2	1

APPLICATION 7.4

Step 4. Design the procedure rating plan

A. Show a checklist you would use to assess the procedure.

B. Show a rating scale you would use to assess the procedure.

Summary

This chapter presented methods for assessing how well learners perform sequences of actions or behaviors within a content domain. Your goal in teaching these skills is that learners be able to spontaneously perform them smoothly, efficiently, and automatically. The techniques in this chapter, when used at regular intervals, will allow you to assess learner development of domain-specific procedural skills.

These techniques can be used by themselves to assess the development of procedural knowledge or in combination with other techniques to assess complex performances that show deep understanding in a subject area. These performances can involve projects, products, or demonstrations that incorporate processes of which the purpose is to allow learners the opportunity to demonstrate high levels of thinking and problem solving. We examine this type of learning and the techniques used to assess it in the next chapter.

Activities

Review the lesson contexts and example questions at the end of this chapter. These lesson contexts and examples illustrate questions for assessing your learners' domain-specific procedural skills. Review them as a guide for completing the following activities.

1. Using an example of a unit you are likely to teach, illustrate how procedural knowledge develops from the cognitive stage, through the associative stage, to the autonomous stage.
2. For the example in activity 1, describe some domain-specific procedures that a learner might need to achieve the goals of your unit.

3. Describe an appropriate assessment context for the procedural knowledge described in activity 1. Specify the number of samples of performance you will observe, the specific behaviors you will observe, and the type of scale you will use to assess the behavior.

4. Provide a holistic scale you would use to assess the behaviors described in activity 3. Be sure to add a sufficient number of descriptive words to your scale to reliably measure the behavior.

5. Using the lesson contexts and template at the end of this chapter as a guide, create three questions of your own that assess domain-specific procedural skills.

Suggested Readings

Gagné, E. D., Yekovich, C. W., & Yekovich, F. R. (1993). *The cognitive psychology of school learning* (2nd ed.). New York: HarperCollins.

A comprehensive treatment of cognitive learning theory and cognitive learning outcomes. The discussion of procedural knowledge and how it is acquired is especially illuminating.

Wiggins, G., & McTighe, J. (2000). *Understanding by design.* Upper Saddle River, NJ: Prentice Hall.

This reading will help you identify the critical observable attributes of a procedure in advance and show you how to share them with your students to insure the quality of your procedural assessment.

Lesson Contexts

K–2 EXAMPLE LESSON CONTEXTS FOR ASSESSING PROCEDURAL KNOWLEDGE

Grade	Subject	Topic	Assessment Questions
K–2	Language Arts	Listening skills	Model what a good listener looks like: good body posture, alert facial expressions sensitive to content, eye contact with storyteller. A good listener might smile or laugh quietly in funny parts, or look serious or sad in dramatic parts.
		Reading/print awareness	Move your hand over text to show the proper direction of reading—from left to right, from the top to the bottom of the page.
K–2	Mathematics	Number, operation, and quantitative reasoning	Use blocks to model addition and subtraction problems.
		Patterns, relationships, and algebraic reasoning	Count orally to 100, first by twos, then by fives, and finally, by tens.
K–2	Science	Scientific process	Demonstrate how to calculate the weight and length of several objects.
		Scientific process	Show how to use the lines on a thermometer to determine an accurate temperature reading.
K–2	Social Studies	Geography	Locate places on a simple map by following directions such as above, below, next to, and underneath.
		Social Studies skills	Demonstrate how to use a Table of Contents, Glossary, and Index to locate information.
K–2	Health	Health behaviors	Demonstrate the proper way to wash hands in order to avoid the spread of germs.
		Health behaviors	Demonstrate the proper way to brush your teeth.

GRADES 3–5 EXAMPLE LESSON CONTEXTS FOR ASSESSING PROCEDURAL KNOWLEDGE

Grade	Subject	Topic	Assessment Questions
3–5	Language Arts	Reading: Word identification	Blend initial letter sounds with common vowel spelling patterns to read words.
		Reading: Vocabulary development	Use the dictionary to determine word meaning and correct pronunciation.
3–5	Mathematics	Geometry and spatial reasoning	Locate and name points on a line using whole numbers and fractions such as halves.
		Number, operation, and quantitative reasoning	Change fractions to lowest common denominator.
3–5	Science	Scientific process	Construct simple graphs, tables, and charts to organize, examine, and evaluate information.
		Scientific process	Demonstrate correct and safe procedures for collecting soil and water samples.
3–5	Social Studies	History: Time and chronology	Put the historical events from a history chapter on a timeline.
		Geography	Use the degrees of latitude and longitude to locate cities and regions on the globe.
3–5	Health	Personal / interpersonal skills	Demonstrate the use of refusal skills in unsafe situations such as peer pressure to smoke, drink alcohol, or take drugs.
		Health behaviors	Demonstrate safe procedures for escaping from a burning building, including how to deal with smoke and blocked exits.

GRADES 6–8 EXAMPLE LESSON CONTEXTS FOR ASSESSING PROCEDURAL KNOWLEDGE

Grade	Subject	Topic	Assessment Questions
6–8	Language Arts	Reading / vocabulary development	Demonstrate how the meaning of root words and affixes such as *happy* and *un* work to create word meaning.
		Writing: Grammar and usage	Combine simple sentences into compound and complex sentences by using appropriate punctuation and conjunctions.
6–8	Mathematics	Number, operation, and quantitative reasoning	Estimate and round numbers to approximate reasonable results to solve problems where exact answers are not required.
		Geometry and spatial reasoning	Locate and name points on a coordinate plane using ordered pairs of integers.
6–8	Science	Scientific processes	Demonstrate safe and effective procedures for growing biological specimens in petri dishes.
		Scientific processes	Show your familiarity with the computer Internet by collecting information on a given topic.
6–8	Social Studies	Geography	Illustrate your interpretive skill at map reading by writing a verbal description of the information communicated on the map of a specified region.
		Social Studies skills	Locate and use primary and secondary sources such as computer software, databases, media, and news services to acquire information about a given topic.
6–8	Health	Influencing factors	Apply your knowledge of the use of conflict resolution to resolve common peer disturbances.
		Health information	Demonstrate your knowledge of procedures for preventive health measures by filling in appropriate measures on a time chart for one year in the life of a 13 year old.

TEMPLATE FOR YOUR LESSON CONTEXTS FOR ASSESSING DOMAIN-SPECIFIC
PROCEDURAL SKILLS

Grade	Subject	Topic	Assessment Questions

8

Assessing Problem-Solving Strategies

In chapter 2 we defined cognitive strategies as ways of thinking that help a student learn. Cognitive strategies go beyond the processes naturally required to learn or carry out a task. For example, when writing an essay you naturally spell correctly, form complete sentences, and link sentences and paragraphs with transition words. These are not strategies. A writing strategy would involve *consciously* cueing yourself to identify a goal for writing, asking yourself whether something you wrote could be said better, or weighing whether the words you use communicate to a particular audience.

Cognitive learning specialists believe that explicit strategy instruction, along with the teaching of a knowledge base and the skills to transfer knowledge to new contexts, is essential for helping learners become good thinkers. Their research on the importance of explicit strategy instruction is reflected in almost every educational reform movement of the past two decades. In its report, "Building a Nation of Thinkers," the National Educational Goals Panel (1993) urged American schools to give learners skills to learn on their own, to think deeply about challenging subject matter, and to transfer what they know to new problems. In this and the following two chapters we will present assessment tools that will allow you to assess transfer of knowledge, as well as other higher order classroom goals.

Cognitive psychologists and educators use a variety of terms to describe these cognitive strategies. They use such expressions as "reasoning strategies," "problem-solving methods," "decision-making skills," "higher order thinking skills," "critical-thinking skills," and "metacognitive skills."

Cognitive strategies, like domain-specific basic skills studied in the previous chapter, are types of procedural knowledge that lead to action. The procedural knowledge studied in chapter 7 was knowledge that learners have about how to ride a bike, deliver a poem, focus a microscope, tie their shoes, or use a balance scale—all domain-specific basic skills that can be executed *spontaneously* when needed in an *automatic* manner. The procedural knowledge discussed in this chapter is knowledge about how to solve problems in a *deliberate, conscious* manner, referred to as problem-solving strategies. These problem-solving strategies may be either domain-specific, for use primarily within a subject or content area, or domain-general, for use across any subject or content area.

Domain-general and domain-specific cognitive strategies are used for a variety of accomplishments, not just problem solving. They are used to weigh alternative choices and help make decisions, hence the term "decision-making strategies." They are used to critique literature or scientific experiments and are sometimes called "critical-thinking skills." Some educators make a distinction between decision-making, critical-thinking, and problem-solving strategies (Crowl, Kaminsky, & Podell, 1997). They believe that problem-solving strategies should be used with narrowly defined problems that have one or two specific solutions, whereas decision-making and critical-thinking strategies should be used when the problem confronting the learner is ambiguous, open-ended, and has multiple solutions.

In this chapter we consider both decision making and critical thinking to be types of problem solving, regardless of the complexity of the problem. Consequently, the term "problem-solving strategies" encompasses thinking and reasoning skills used to solve problems that teachers present to learners in class. Sometimes these problems are well defined, as in third- or fourth-grade mathematics word problems. At other times the problems confronting learners are more unstructured, as when fifth graders must come up with solutions for coping with global warming or when sixth graders must plan the details of a cross-country trip.

We focus on problem solving for a number of reasons. Teachers and educators consider problem solving to be one of the most important goals of instruction. In addition, many recent curriculum reforms recommend that teachers approach classroom learning from a problem-solving perspective. Thus, many language arts teachers teach writing as a form of problem solving, or teach reading comprehension from a problem-solving perspective.

This chapter focuses on assessing the type of procedural knowledge that makes learners facile problem-solvers. Basically, when challenged with a problem, this knowledge allows learners:

- to understand the problem by forming a verbal or pictorial representation of it,
- search the problem space for ways to solve it,
- gather or collect relevant information, and
- monitor or evaluate their progress toward finding an answer or solution.

The goal of this chapter is to help you develop your learners' problem-solving strategies and to give you the procedural knowledge about how to assess them.

Who Will Defend the Country: An Illustration

Imagine that you are the president of a small, peace-loving, independent nation that sits next to an aggressive country itching to expand its borders. Your country is unprepared for military conflict. So, somehow, you must outwit your belligerent neighbor. You must choose someone as a national security advisor. It just so happens that the reigning world chess champion is a citizen of your nation. Because he is a person of gifted intelligence who possesses superior tactical and strategic problem-solving ability, you consider choosing him as your national security advisor.

Who you select has a lot to do with your beliefs about expertise. Do you think that an expert is someone of superior intelligence and problem-solving abilities who can transfer these strengths to any domain? If so, you might be inclined to choose the chess champion. On the other hand, you may believe that expertise is domain-specific and that only someone with extensive training and education in a specific field and years of experience can ever be considered an expert. In this case, you might be highly skeptical of the chess champion's ability to protect your country.

This same debate about general or specific expertise has been going on in American education for a long time. At certain times the generalists held sway, and at others the specialists were ascendant. The debate has important implications for the teaching and assessment of problem-solving strategies. Let's review the evolution of this controversy to better appreciate current thinking on the extent to which problem-solving expertise is a matter of domain-general or domain-specific procedural knowledge.

At the start of the twentieth century, the view that certain subjects exercised and strengthened the mind like a universal weight machine exercises and strengthens muscles was prominent. In particular, the study of Latin, Greek, Aristotelian logic, and the classics was viewed as essential to the development of deep thinkers. Edward Thorndike, an eminent educational psychologist, systematically and convincingly debunked this theory during the 1910s and 1920s. An early behaviorist, Thorndike so influenced educators that for decades they abandoned any serious study of the mind and how it works to promote learning.

Research focus changed in the early 1970s with a boon in computer technology and a new generation of educational psychologists interested in studying how the mind works. Their initial work supported the notion that general reasoning and problem-solving skills lie at the heart of intelligence and expertise. Had you been familiar with their work, at that time, you might have chosen the chess champion as your national security advisor.

However, researchers' attempts to teach general cognitive strategies to learners in one context and have them transfer this knowledge to different contexts failed. They discovered that learning strategies to improve memory for foreign language vocabulary did not improve memory for history facts or even English vocabulary. Mastering such problem-solving strategies like brainstorming or reasoning by analogy helped learners solve familiar but not novel problems.

Thus, by the late 1970s and early 1980s, the generality–specificity pendulum took a pronounced swing to the specificity side. Cognitive psychologists were becoming convinced that expertise was not due to general thinking skills. In addition, they were skeptical of classes in junior and senior high schools that taught study skills such as note taking, outlining, how to listen to a lecture, or underlining. Their research suggested that such general learning strategy classes didn't improve listening, reading comprehension or memory beyond simply rereading the material several times over. During that time our chess champion would have been told to stick to what he knows best.

In the 1980s cognitive psychologists developed an interesting research methodology called the **expert–novice study**. They would give an expert and a novice the same problem to solve or task to master and then ask them to describe out loud or in writing what they were thinking as they engaged in the activity. Thus, they could compare the problem-solving thinking of a historian or physicist with that of an amateur. They also gave experts problems to solve or tasks to master outside their area of expertise and told them to describe their thought processes. Out of this research came several important findings.

It was confirmed that experts employ a specific set of problem-solving strategies when working in their areas of expertise. Their ability to flexibly use these strategies hinged on a well-organized and elaborate domain-specific knowledge base. In addition, experts who had excellent recall for facts in their field did not necessarily remember information outside their field better than novices. Chess champions whose memory for chess positions was remarkable had memories for vocabulary words or strings of numbers that were unremarkable. Experts were not much better at problem solving outside their field than novices to that field. After reading these findings, we could conclude that our chess champion would be no better at defending the country than a person picked at random.

But the expert–novice research also turned up something unexpected. It seems that some novices learn unfamiliar material more quickly than others, regardless of the knowledge domain. In other words, whether they are studying unfamiliar material about astronomy, chess, hockey, photovoltaics, or Mesopotamian civilization, some novices acquire information faster than others. Regardless of what they read, these intelligent novices are aware when they do not understand something, know which parts of the text are more difficult for them, are aware of the differences between memorizing something and understanding something, and change strategies depending on their goal (Bruer, 1993). These novices were more aware of themselves as learners and more aware of their thought processes. They were using domain-general strategies to master new fields.

Cognitive psychologists used the term **metacognition** to describe these "thinking about thinking" mental competencies. Basically, metacognition encompasses the skills of knowing when you do and do not understand something, knowing when to use a learning strategy to improve your understanding, being aware of whether you are experiencing more or less difficulty learning as you try out a particular strategy, and being able to compare the effects that different strategies are having on your learning. Cognitive psychologists found out that these metacognitive strategies could be taught to school-age children and that they actually improved their ability to learn in any academic area (Pressley, 1995).

Thus, as we approached the 21st century and continuing through today, a synthesis has come about in the debate over the significance of domain-general or domain-specific strategies. This new perspective holds that domain-specific strategies, domain-general strategies, and metacognition are all important for knowing how to learn in any given domain (Bransford, et al., 1999). Thus, if you are a history or math teacher, you can teach your learners three types of procedural knowledge to help them become better thinkers and problem solvers: (a) problem-solving strategies specific to the domain of history or math, (b) general cognitive strategies to improve their recall of information or comprehension of text across domains, and (c) metacognitive skills that will remind them to use both general and specific strategies and monitor their effectiveness as they are learning.

So, how do we resolve the problem posed at the start of this section? Our current knowledge about problem solving leads us to conclude that the chess champion's detailed knowledge about chess and chess strategies will not help him in the field of international diplomacy. In other words, if all he knows about is chess, he will not make a good national security advisor. However, if he knows how to learn new things, if he has the metacognitive knowledge to be a rapid learner, if he is aware of how to monitor his learning, then with a crash course on foreign affairs and some on-the-job training he could become an effective diplomat.

Cognitive Components of Problem Solving

Figure 8.1 depicts the cognitive components of problem solving that you can directly teach and assess. We have left out domain-specific basic skills, such as those studied in the previous chapter, not because they are unimportant; rather, they serve problem solving indirectly by providing the spontaneously executed and automatic routines that often support problem-solving activity. For the components in Figure 8.1, there is strong consensus concerning their direct influence on effective problem solving and their application to teaching, learning, and assessment. Let's look at them more closely.

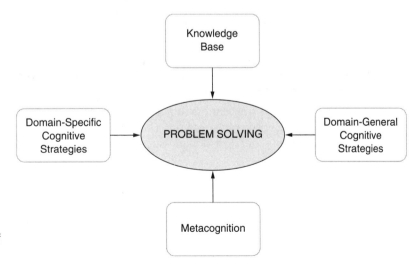

Figure 8.1
Cognitive components of
problem solving

Knowledge Base

Cognitive psychologists almost unanimously agree that skilled problem solving in any domain depends on an extensive, elaborate, and well-organized knowledge base. Chapters 5 and 6 presented ways to assess this knowledge base.

Domain-Specific Strategies

Each knowledge domain has strategies specific to it that learners must master to become good problem solvers. There are strategies specific to good reading, writing, math problem solving, historical analysis, and reasoning about science.

Domain-General Strategies

This knowledge includes strategies such as recognizing when a problem exists, identifying the elements of a problem, searching your memory for what you know, brainstorming, and forming images of the problem that work regardless of the topics or content to which they are applied. Students can learn these strategies and thus improve their problem solving across many domains—provided they also receive instruction in metacognition.

Metacognition

Students must (a) know when to use strategies (whether domain-general or domain-specific), (b) monitor their effectiveness, (c) make judgments about the relative effectiveness of different strategies, and (d) make a commitment to use the more effective strategies in future problem solving. They must be aware of themselves as problem solvers, planners, decision makers, monitors, and evaluators. Without metacognition, strategy use does not generalize to novel contexts. Most cognitive psychologists treat metacognition as a type of procedural knowledge.

In the remainder of this chapter, you will learn how to assess strategies for problem solving and metacognition.

Characteristics of Effective Problem-Solving Assessment Tasks

Effective measurement instruments for assessing problem solving have several general characteristics in common. These characteristics apply whether you are assessing domain-general or domain-specific problem-solving skills.

Novelty

The tasks that you give your learners to solve and the situations to which you ask them to respond should be new and unfamiliar. Otherwise, problems that appear to demand complex reasoning of learners may be eliciting only rehearsal or recall of a routine learned in class. For example, analysis is a problem-solving strategy that learners must master to solve a variety of problems. This strategy typically is taught by explanation, modeling, and practice. However, an assessment which asks students to model an analysis that was practiced in class is measuring only recall. Here is an assessment question in the context of a lesson that would require novel responses from your class:

> Select three dinosaurs from the story which we have read that have characteristics that you believe would help them survive and that you would like to see in animals today. Create a new dinosaur that combines these qualities. (K–3, Reading)

Authenticity

Recall what has been said in previous chapters about the importance of learners constructing their own knowledge bases and memory structures. The same applies to problem-solving strategies. You want to challenge your learners with problems that grab their attention and make them want to find a solution. You want their problem solving to be goal-directed and not done simply to please the teacher. The best way to ensure that learners construct their own solutions to problems and learn problem-solving strategies is to make the problem-solving tasks authentic—ones that real writers, geographers, historians, mathematicians, literary critics, or scientists face. The following assessment question is authentic because it is what real professionals do.

> Our world is increasingly being polluted in many different ways. Look around you and identify one type of pollution we all see every day. Generate the best solution to eliminating this type of pollutant. (Grades 4–6, Social Studies)

Sustained, Purposeful Problem Solving

The assessment task should require prolonged effort and thought. A problem that can be solved in a few minutes is probably not demanding enough of the problem-solving skills of your learners. A math problem should require several problem-solving strategies rather than a listing of a series of required computations. A problem built around an historical event should ask learners to analyze and interpret, not just identify some key point. Here is an example of an assessment question that might keep your learners thinking and problem solving for a long time:

> Some say that Native Americans should be given back the land that was taken from their ancestors. If you were a lawyer for these Native Americans, what reasons would you present in court to help them gain their land back. If you were a lawyer for the U.S. government, what reasons would you offer for not giving the land back. Can you suggest a compromise? (Grades 4–6, U.S. History)

Problems with Multiple Solutions

In the real world we rarely encounter problems that have one solution. When writing an article for a newspaper, a journalist can approach the task in a variety of ways. The good writer makes intelligent choices about the best way to reach the target audience.

Likewise, there are a variety of ways to choose a building location, locate a solid-waste disposal plant, plan an exploration, increase voter registration, and so forth. Thus, the problems you ask learners to solve should, like that below, have multiple solutions, which the learner should identify and analyze based on their relative merits.

> At the end of the year our school librarian found that many books which have been checked out during the year have not been returned. Think of as many things as you can to prevent this from happening. Compare the cost and extra time that might be needed for each of the alternatives you propose. (Grades 4–6, Library Use)

Evidence of the Problem-Solving Process

The problem-solving format that you design should require an answer and its explanation. Learners should be required to explain or show how they arrived at an answer. This is the only way that you can judge if they have learned the problem-solving strategy. Open-ended questions and extended-response formats rather than objective-type formats are best for eliciting this type of response.

Chapter 7 introduced the idea of ratings to judge the proficiency with which learners exhibit certain procedures. Likewise, assessing problem-solving strategies will require skillfully designed rating systems. Such assessment by its very nature requires judgment. True–false, completion, or multiple-choice items cannot elicit authentic problem solving from your learners. Instead, you will have to make a judgment about how well they reason with the use of well-worded questions and rating procedures, such as the following:

> The Mississippi River has been compared to a major highway in which goods, products, and people are transported. Is this a good comparison to make? If so, how could we make better highways from studying the flow of traffic on the Mississippi River, and how might we improve the Mississippi River by studying the flow of traffic on our highways? (Grades 4–6, Social Studies)

Do you believe this question would encourage your learners to reason?

Assessing General Problem-Solving Strategies

A Taxonomy of General Problem-Solving Strategies

Since the late 1960s many educational psychologists have developed systems for describing reasoning and problem solving. The *Taxonomy of Educational Objectives* by Bloom et al., updated in Anderson and Krathwohl (2001), was one of the first and most influential examples of these classification systems. As you will recall, Bloom and his colleagues classified the cognitive domain into six categories of learning: knowledge and comprehension (which represent lower level reasoning), application, analysis, synthesis, and evaluation (which represent increasingly higher levels of reasoning).

Ellen Gagné (Gagné et al., 1993) defines problem solving as a situation where one has a goal and has not yet figured out a way to reach it. The goal may be to resolve a controversy about the origins of your local community, to solve a problem involving geometric shapes, or to write a letter to the editor of the local newspaper. Problem solving for Gagné involves four cognitive processes, regardless of the specific nature of the problem. Her cognitive processes and an assessment question requiring their application are reviewed next.

1. *Forming a representation of the problem.*   The learner must think about the information given and what she is being asked to do. For example,

> On the board are written the freezing temperatures for both the centigrade and Fahrenheit scale. Create a third scale using any numbers you like representing both freezing points in proper distance to one another. (Grades 6–8, Mathematics)

2. *Searching the problem space.*   The learner searches his memory for what he knows about the problem and different ways to solve it. For example,

> When we look around our city, we see many different types of businesses and industries from small shops in our malls to big companies, each with their own customers and products to sell. Pick out two different businesses and indicate what factors you believe were considered in locating them at their respective locations. (Grades 6–8, Social Studies)

3. *Choosing a solution.*   The learner applies her knowledge to solve the problem. For example,

> We have studied several types of geometric shapes, such as the rectangle, square, parallelogram, and triangle. Which shape would most frequently be used in building a 50-story-tall skyscraper? Explain your reasons for choosing this shape. (Grades 7–8, Mathematics)

4. *Evaluation.*   The learner judges whether his application worked. For example,

> Draw a picture of what you think the Native American tepee looked like in the story "Westward Trails." From paper and sticks, construct a miniature model of what you drew. Do you believe your model looks like the tepee in the story. Based on what you have learned from your model, make any changes in your drawing that would make it more realistic. (Grades 4–6, U.S. History)

These extended-response questions are more open ended than the restricted-response questions illustrated in chapter 6. They ask for more elaborate answers, investigation, creativity, and reasoning from students and allow for multiple correct solutions.

Quellmalz and Hoskyn (1997) and Quellmalz (1987, 1991) have placed problem-solving activities, such as those previously mentioned, into a problem-solving taxonomy that has been used over the past decade in numerous curriculum and assessment programs. Quellmalz (1991) classifies problem solving into four categories of reasoning strategies: analysis, comparison, inference and interpretation, and evaluation. She states that problem solving involves the deliberate use of these fundamental cognitive strategies. These strategies are nonhierarchical, unlike those proposed by Bloom and colleagues (1984). Quellmalz (1991) has also identified four categories of metacognitive strategies that learners apply when they are problem solving: planning, draft and tryout, monitor and revise, evaluate and reflect.

Quellmalz and Hoskyn (1997) stipulate that these cognitive and metacognitive operations are carried out in all problem solving, regardless of the content area. However, she also underscores that learners apply these processes in specific contexts such as biology, history, or writing. Consequently, the best way to teach general problem solving is by presenting significant, authentic, and meaningful problems to learners within the context of academic disciplines. In the remainder of this section we demonstrate how to assess general problem-solving strategies using Quellmalz's taxonomy. But, before doing so, we briefly address how to teach them.

Teaching General Problem-Solving Strategies

Research on the teaching of problem-solving strategies underscores that the teacher plays a direct role in helping learners construct strategies. The teacher does this by giving direct explanations of the strategies and allowing learners to actively learn from them. Pressley (1995) refers to this as "direct explanation teaching." The basic features of direct explanation teaching of general and domain-specific problem-solving strategies are the following (Borich & Tombari, 1997, pp. 143–147):

- *Up-front demonstration and explanation.*   The teacher tells learners the goal of the problem-solving lesson and what is expected of them. The teacher then presents a significant task that requires the use of a problem-solving strategy and informs the learners that they will need to learn the strategy to solve the problem.

- *Mental modeling.*   The teacher thinks through the strategy aloud and, as learners watch and listen, demonstrates its use.

- *Guided practice.*   The teacher provides an authentic task and uses hints, prompts, and questions to get learners to use the modeled strategy. Feedback, praise, and encouragement accompany the learners' efforts.

- *Metacognitive information.*   The teacher points out to learners when and where to use the problem-solving strategy and how to notice or monitor whether it is helping them.

Let's listen in on Mr. Martinez's class as he is teaching a problem-solving strategy with direct explanation teaching. The topic of his lesson is how to build a greenhouse.

Teacher: Today we're going to think about how to build a greenhouse and the problems we'll face in getting our flowers and vegetables to grow in this environment. I'll show you a strategy for solving problems. One of the problems I see is how the plants will get the food they need to grow. Anybody see any other problems?

Ronni: I see a problem: What about when it gets cold?

Teacher: So, what's the problem?

Ronni: Well, it's how we make sure they have the right temperature to grow.

Teacher: Good. The first step of our problem-solving strategy is to identify a problem. The second step is to obtain any information we might need to solve the problem. Is there any information that we need?

Jenni: I think we need to know how warm we must keep the plants so that they grow just like they would if they were outside in the summer.

Teacher: Rowan, could you take the responsibility of getting that information for us from this book on building a greenhouse? Now, the third thing we do when we think about solving a problem is to explore strategies. What would be an example of a strategy for keeping plants in the greenhouse from freezing in the winter?

Alex: We could shut out the cold air with glass. That will let the sun shine in to heat the plants.

Teacher: Good. We could create what's called "the greenhouse effect." That way we can save on using a heater, except on cloudy days. Our fourth step is to test out our strategy. So, I guess we better devise a way to see how much the temperature rises when we place our plants in the greenhouse.

Trena: We could measure it with a thermometer.

Teacher: That's our fifth step—studying the results of our strategy. These are the five steps we will use to solve problems in building our greenhouse. Remember what they are: identify the problem, define terms, explore strategies, act on the strategy, and look at the effects of the strategy. Ready to begin?

Teachers who incorporate problem-solving strategies into their lessons have two broad goals: (a) enhance learner acquisition of declarative and procedural knowledge and (b) enhance cognitive processes. Teachers accomplish these goals when they design instruction that helps learners when they are studying and participating in lessons. Teachers further increase the likelihood of achieving these two goals when they teach problem-solving strategies to their students.

Steps in Assessment

Once you have made a commitment to incorporate problem-solving strategies into your curriculum, then the following steps can be followed to assess them.

Step 1. Identify and Define the General Problem-Solving Strategies. Before you can teach problem solving and assess how well your students have learned the strategies, you first need to be clear about what the strategies are. We will use Quellmalz's taxonomy as a guide for the assessment of general problem-solving strategies. Quellmalz advocates teaching all the components of problem solving and metacognition.

She also stresses that one component is not a prerequisite for learning another. You can teach these components in any particular order, selecting some but not others. The component strategies are identified and defined as follows:

Cognitive Strategies

- *Analysis* is a strategy that involves perceiving the whole task or problem; identifying the distinctive elements, aspects, or terms associated with the problem; and understanding the relationship of each distinctive element to the whole task. An example of an assessment task at this level might be:

Examine the three branches of government—the judicial, executive, and legislative. Why is each branch necessary for the functioning of our country? How does each relate to one another? (Grades 7–8, Social Studies)

- *Comparison* is a strategy that involves identifying the similarities and differences among the various elements or aspects of some task, choosing the dimensions along which to make comparisons or contrasts, and understanding the significance of the comparison for solving the problem presented.

Compare the characteristics of reptiles and amphibians. What features would you find in common and what features would you see that are different? (Grades 4–6, Science)

- *Inference and interpretation* involve gathering information or evidence to solve a problem, using inductive or deductive reasoning, and applying certain rules or heuristics to reach a conclusion.

"Smoking is hazardous to your health" is a phrase that appears on every package of cigarettes. To whom do you think these words are written and from where did they come? (Grades 4–6, Health)

- *Evaluation* requires learners to take a position or arrive at a conclusion, identify certain criteria for judging the adequacy of the position or conclusion, present evidence of how well the solution or position meets or does not meet the various criteria, and come to some judgment about the adequacy of the conclusion or solution.

In the story *Jack and the Beanstalk*, what do you think Jack should have considered when he traded the cow for the beans, took the hen from the giant, and climbed the beanstalk a second time? Would you have done these same things? Why or why not? (K–3, Reading)

Metacognitive Strategies

- *Planning* occurs when learners analyze the problem, compare the problem to problems they have encountered previously, and identify strategies to solve the problem.
- *Draft and tryout* involves several attempts to solve the problem.
- *Monitor and revise* occurs when the learner makes preliminary checks on whether goals are achieved and strategies are working.

■ *Evaluate and reflect* involves the learner examining the adequacy of the problem solution and the effectiveness of strategies used to reach a solution.

The preceding definitions are by no means inclusive of all that is involved in analysis, evaluation, planning, and so forth. You may want to expand each definition to fit better with how you teach these skills in a particular content area. In any case, you should be clear about what each strategy entails before teaching and assessing it. This step of the assessment process is completed by identifying what your learners must do to demonstrate the skill you wish to teach. Figure 8.2 presents a higher order thinking and problem-solving checklist that can help you select and prioritize some of the strategies you may want to teach. We will return to this task in step 4 when we explain how to rate the quality of your learners' problem-solving strategies.

The Higher Order Thinking and Problem-solving Checklist

Check each column below indicating (a) the extent to which your curriculum requires students to achieve the following outcomes, and (b) the extent to which you are teaching your students to achieve these outcomes.

Assign the number 5 to each checkmark under "Great Extent," a 4 to "Fair Extent," a 3 to "Some Extent," a 2 to "A Little," and a 1 to "Not at All." Subtract your assigned values for the Degree of Implementation column from the Degree of Importance column for each behavior to arrive at your highest priorities.

	Degree of Importance					Degree of Implementation				
	Should your curriculum require students to achieve the following: (Check one)					Does your curriculum require students to achieve the following: (Check one)				
	1	2	3	4	5	1	2	3	4	5
APPLICATION OF KNOWLEDGE										
1. Search his/her memory for what is already known about a problem.										
2. Draw a picture or diagram that shows what was learned or observed.										
3. Construct and interpret graphs, charts, and tables.										
4. Classify/categorize things into definable attributes.										

(continued)

Figure 8.2
Higher order thinking and problem-solving checklist

5. Communicate the results of what was observed in written and oral format.										
6. Apply given rules to reach a conclusion.										
7. Consult a variety of knowledge sources to gather information.										
ANALYTICAL SKILLS										
8. Identify the similarities and differences among various elements.										
9. Compare a problem to problems encountered previously.										
10. Understand the relationship of each component to the whole.										
11. Make reasonable conclusions from observation or analysis of data.										
12. Identify and articulate errors in their own thinking or in that of others.										
13. Explain the reasons for a conclusion.										
14. Predict what will happen given the information you have.										
15. Plan a way to test one's prediction.										
16. Distinguish the most important elements of a problem.										
17. Organize a conclusion about a problem in a logical fashion.										
18. Identify criteria for evaluating a problem solution.										
19. Gather information or evidence to solve a problem.										
20. Find corroborating evidence from among different data sources.										
21. Determine the reliability of the evidence.										
22. Place an interpretation of a problem in the context of prevailing circumstances.										

Figure 8.2
(*continued*)

SYNTHESIS/CREATIVITY												
23. Generate new ways of viewing a situation outside the boundaries of standard conventions.												
24. Reformulate a problem to make it more manageable.												
25. Brainstorm new applications of content.												
26. Anticipate potential problems.												
27. Accurately summarize what is read or others have said, orally and in writing.												
EVALUATION/METACOGNITION												
28. Ignore distractions that interfere with goal attainment.												
29. Make appropriate revisions on basis of feedback.												
30. Assess risks involved in a solution.												
31. Monitor the outcome and revise a strategy where appropriate.												
32. Judge the credibility of evidence.												
33. Evaluate and revise what is written.												
34. Ask questions to oneself about ideas he/she is unsure of.												
35. Catch fallacies and contradictions.												
DISPOSITIONS												
36. Meaningfully praise the performance of others.												
37. Share and take turns.												
38. Help keep others on task.												
39. Provide assistance to others when needed.												
40. Engage in tasks even when answers or solutions are not immediately apparent.												

Figure 8.2
(*continued*)

41. Seek accuracy.											
42. Be flexible to change view-point to match the facts.											
43. Demonstrate restraint over impulsive behaviors.											
44. Compose draft and tryouts in attempts to solve a problem.											
45. Demonstrate persistence in tackling difficult tasks.											
46. Use a constructive tone when responding to others.											
47. Display enthusiasm for learning.											
48. Ask for feedback when needed.											
49. Collaborate with others in team.											
50. Provide assistance to others when asked.											
51. Demonstrate independence in completing a project.											
52. Listens attentively to others.											
53. Ignore distractions that interfere with goal attainment.											
54. Keep record of one's own progress toward important goals.											
55. Realistically evaluate own performance.											
56. Set goals that are achievable within a specific span of time.											
VALUES											
57. Demonstrate awareness of ethical concerns and conflicts.											
58. Adhere to codes of conduct.											
59. Show an ability to resolve ethical dilemmas and conflicts.											
60. Maintain self-discipline in dealing with difficult situations.											
61. Behave in a manner that communicates care and concern for others.											
62. Act responsibly in dealing with tasks and people.											

Figure 8.2
(*continued*)

BOX 8.1   Ms. Defluer's Metacognitive Strategy and Student Behaviors

In preparation for their science exhibits, I would like to teach my students the ability to be able to systematically plan solutions to problems in science.

They would demonstrate that skill when they:

1. Identify the scientific principles of the problem that are the most relevant.
2. Compare the problem to similar problems and solutions that have been encountered in the past.
3. Identify strategies to solve the problem that are practical, cost-effective, and within the time allocated to solving the problem.

In Box 8.1, we asked Ms. Defluer to identify a particular metacognitive strategy that her eighth-grade science students could use in preparing for a subsequent science exhibit and what they would do to demonstrate their use of that strategy. Using Ms. Defluer's lesson as an example, complete Application 8.1 for a cognitive or metacognitive strategy you would like to teach.

APPLICATION 8.1

Identify a particular problem-solving strategy that you want to teach.

Learners demonstrate this strategy when they perform the following problem-solving behaviors:

1.

2.

3.

Step 2. Select the Context for Demonstrating Strategies.   Once you have decided which strategies you want to teach and assess, you must select a context that motivates the student to demonstrate knowledge of the strategy. An authentic context is preferable, but a novel context is mandatory. The cognitive strategies of analysis, comparison, inference, and evaluation are challenging to learners when they are asked to use them to solve newly encountered problems. Suggestions in specific content areas would be the following.

Cognitive strategies: Literature.   Give your learners an unfamiliar narrative story and have them identify the key story elements, settings, plot events, and character traits (analysis); or give them a newspaper editorial and have them analyze the content for positions, reasons, evidence, and conclusions. Assess comparison by giving several editorials and asking students to compare and contrast points of view, evidence, accuracy, and organization.

Cognitive strategies: History/civics.   Have your learners read an important historical document such as Lincoln's Gettysburg Address, and have them deduce causes and events, predict future effects, and infer consequences; or have them read about a particular school policy and evaluate its significance, practicality, impact, and lasting effects.

Metacognitive strategies: Science.   You can assess how thoroughly learners plan an investigation to study the effects of climatic change, or how adequately they plan a project to assess the effect of gravity on the speed of a flying object. The problem-solving strategy of draft and tryout can be assessed in an electrical conductance experiment where learners have to determine which of a variety of substances conduct electricity the best.

Metacognitive strategies: Social science.   You can assess the problem-solving strategy of monitoring air pollution. Your learners can monitor changes in the atmosphere and make adjustments if their goals are not being met. In the same context they can evaluate the final outcome of the study and reflect on what they could have done differently.

In Box 8.2 we asked Ms. Defluer to specify the instructional context in which her students would demonstrate a metacognitive skill. Using her context as a guide, describe in Application 8.2 a suitable context for teaching and assessing the cognitive or metacognitive strategy you have identified.

BOX 8.2   Mrs. Defluer's Instructional Context for Metacognition

I will teach and assess the metacognitive strategy of planning with an assignment that asks students to plan the construction of a vehicle that can escape from the gravitational forces of earth. I will expect their planning to include a draft description of their vehicle and a model or drawing of what it might look like.

APPLICATION 8.2

Specify the particular task or assignment you will use to teach and assess the problem-solving strategy identified in step 1.

Step 3. Design the Assessment Task.   In designing the assessment task, you will need to answer two questions: (a) What type of outcome or performance will you observe to assess the learner's problem-solving strategies? and (b) What type of instructions will you give the learner for carrying out the task?

You can assess problem solving as it occurs by observing learners and rating the extent to which you see evidence of analysis, evaluation, planning, revision, or other strategy. An obvious example would be observing learners as they carry out a science experiment or solve a math problem; or you could observe learners as they engage in a mock classroom political debate and assess such reasoning strategies as analysis, evaluation, inference, planning, or reflection. In addition to observing and rating, you could ask questions of your learners that elicit their thinking and reasoning.

Cognitive and metacognitive processes can be difficult to evaluate. They require on-the-spot judgments and are best suited for assessment when they result in a performance or product. The better choice is to design an assessment task that results in some product that requires use of the cognitive or metacognitive strategy you have taught. The product may be a written essay that you will read and assess for evidence of the desired strategies. This type of product often works well for middle-school learners, but it does not work as well for younger learners. For them, an exhibit or scale model and a demonstration or oral performance, which includes visual maps, outlines, timelines, flowcharts, drawings, graphs, pie charts, and genealogical charts in which the student displays his use of the strategy in more pictorial or visual detail, are more conducive for the assessment of cognitive and metacognitive strategies. Let's look at some examples of each of these.

Visual maps.   Assess how well learners can analyze the elements of a story by having them draw characters, settings, and events with the use of arrows to depict sequences. Captions can be included that identify plot elements, episodes, goals, or outcomes. Figure 8.3 shows a visual story map for *The Three Little Pigs*. Such visual techniques can be used to show evidence of the metacognitive skills of planning and revision. Webbing formats, as we saw in chapter 6, can also be used to assess the cognitive strategy of compare and contrast as noted in Figure 8.4.

Timelines, flowcharts, drawings, graphs, pie charts, and genealogical charts. Learners can demonstrate planning by constructing a timeline that depicts important milestones in the process of completing a science project. A genealogical chart

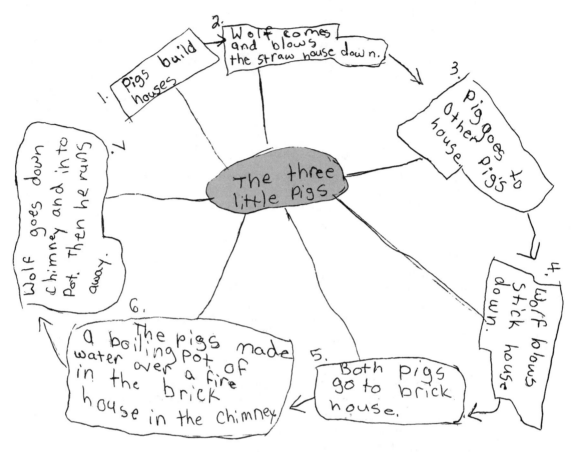

Figure 8.3
Story map of the three pigs
Source: Grace Tober, third-grade student

can show skill in analyzing a story dealing with generations of family members. Flowcharts can be used to assess analysis, planning, and inference. Students can be asked to construct graphs or pie charts as part of a math problem solving activity. Such graphs or pie charts can be examined for evidence of inference and interpretive problem-solving strategies. Following a science unit on prehistoric animals, learners can be requested to draw the skeleton of an animal who could perform certain kinds of actions, such as run exceptionally fast or climb trees. Some of these assessment tasks with visual and pictorial detail are illustrated in Figures 8.5, 8.6, and 8.7

Once you have decided on the outcome or performance you will observe, you can concentrate on communicating the proper task instructions. Because you want the product to show evidence of particular reasoning strategies, be sure to include

Directions: Write who or what is being compared in each box.
          List differences in the outside circles. List likenesses in the overlapping circles.

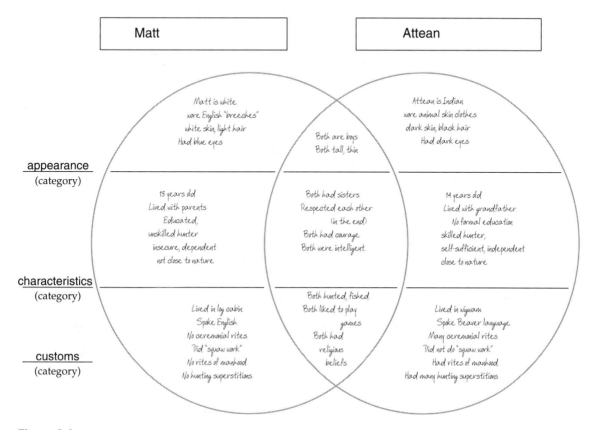

Figure 8.4
Comparison map
Source: From "Classroom Assessment of Reasoning Strategies" by E. Quellmalz and J. Hoskyn, in *Handbook of Classroom Assessment: Learning, Adjustment and Achievement* (pp. 103–130), by G. D. Phye (Ed.), 1997, San Diego: Academic Press. Copyright © 1997 by Academic Press, Inc. Reprinted with permission.

explicit cues to learners to show evidence of the strategy they are using or the thinking and reasoning they went through on the way to solving the problem. Reminders such as "Show all work" and "Be sure to list the steps involved" will allow you better to assess both cognitive and metacognitive strategies.

Quellmalz and Hoskyn (1997) strongly recommend that, particularly with tasks that assess analysis and comparison, you include the question, "So what?" Rather than simply list elements in an analysis or develop a laundry list of similarities and differences, learners should be asked to explain the significance of the analysis or points of comparison. Thus, task directions should explicitly cue learners to explain why

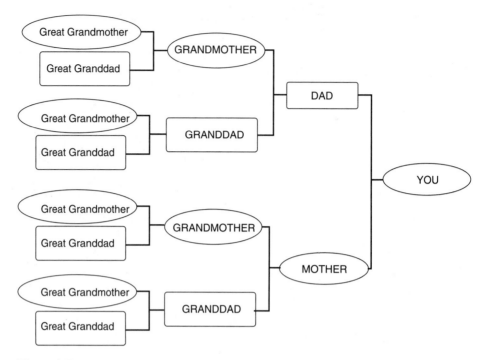

Figure 8.5
Draw a flow chart with a genealogical family tree starting with your Great Granddad

the various aspects of the analysis or comparison are important for the story as a whole (e.g., "Why should the reader care about the things you analyzed?" or "Why are the similarities and differences that you discussed important for an understanding of this historical event?").

In Box 8.3 we asked Ms. Defluer to describe the task and directions to her students for demonstrating the metacognitive activity of planning described in step 1. Using her instructions as a guide, in Application 8.3 describe an assessment task and instructions to your students for the cognitive or metacognitive strategy you have chosen in step 1.

Figure 8.6
Draw a pie chart dividing up 4 pieces of pie, make 2 one color and 2 another and then connect them with an arrow showing "2 + 2 = 4"

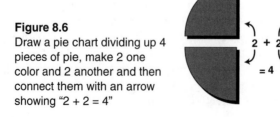

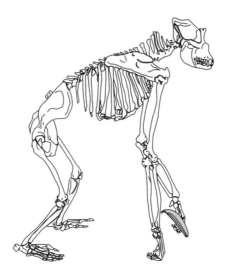

Figure 8.7
Draw a skeleton of an animal
tall and agile enough to raise
a stick to knock a banana off
a tree

Step 4. Develop the Scoring Procedure.   Open-ended or extended written answers, story maps, diagrams, and the like should be scored according to explicit criteria. These criteria define the important problem-solving skills that the learner is expected to demonstrate and the range of quality exhibited by the product. Your scoring guide can simply list the components of the skill, as defined in step 1, and include a rating scale for each element.

BOX 8.3   Ms. Defluer's Task and Student Directions for Her Metacognitive Activity

I have asked my students to show their planning skills with a science project in which they will demonstrate their knowledge of gravitation by creating a practical means of overcoming it. The following are the instructions to my students.

"Each of you will be asked to prepare a science exhibit showing your understanding of gravity by demonstrating the principles by which gravity can be overcome. To do this, you will create a model or drawing of a vehicle that can escape the earth's gravitational pull and describe the principles by which it works in a 5-minute presentation to the class. As you give your presentation and show your model or drawing that supports it, I want you to be sure and point out (a) the scientific principles relevant to the problem, (b) your comparison with similar problems and their solutions, and (c) why your solution is practical in escaping the earth's gravitational forces."

APPLICATION 8.3

Describe the specific task that will direct your learners to demonstrate the problem-solving strategy you specified in step 1. Include the directions for what you want your learners to do.

For example, let's say that in the step 1, Application 8.1, you listed the following as elements of narrative story analysis:

> Learners demonstrate the cognitive strategy of story analysis when they do the following things:
> 1. Name or identify the important elements of a story (plot, character, etc.).
> 2. Describe, explain, or give detail about each element.
> 3. Explain how each element is important to the story as a whole.
> 4. Organize the analysis in some logical fashion.

Your scoring guide for assessing their story analysis might look like Figure 8.8. The points on the rating scale and the terms associated with them define the range of quality of each feature or aspect of the cognitive strategy. Rating scales are typically constructed with 3, 5, or 7 points.

Assessing Narrative Story Analysis

1. Names/defines the important elements of the story

1	2	3	4	⑤
Lists some elements but fails to define		Names all elements and defines some		Names/defines all elements

2. Gives details about each element

1	2	③	4	5
Lacks detail		Adequate detail		Abundant detail

3. Explains how each element is important to the story

1	2	③	4	5
Not at all		Some explanation		Full explanations

4. Organizes analysis

1	2	3	4	⑤
Disorganized		Some organization		Logical presentation

Figure 8.8
Sample rating scale to assess analysis

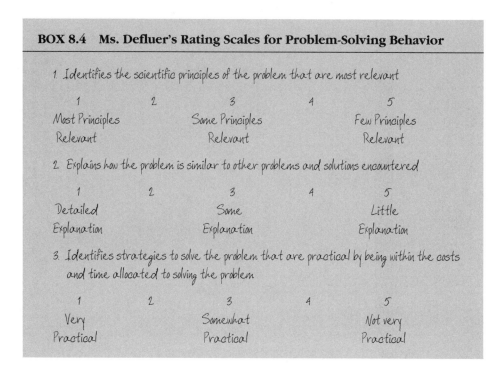

BOX 8.4   Ms. Defluer's Rating Scales for Problem-Solving Behavior

1. Identifies the scientific principles of the problem that are most relevant

1	2	3	4	5
Most Principles Relevant		Some Principles Relevant		Few Principles Relevant

2. Explains how the problem is similar to other problems and solutions encountered

1	2	3	4	5
Detailed Explanation		Some Explanation		Little Explanation

3. Identifies strategies to solve the problem that are practical by being within the costs and time allocated to solving the problem

1	2	3	4	5
Very Practical		Somewhat Practical		Not very Practical

For each cognitive and metacognitive problem-solving strategy that you wish to assess, you could construct similar rating scales. Your scoring task involves examining the product thoroughly and then circling the number on the rating scale that best reflects your judgment of how well the product meets the criteria. You then add up the total points earned to provide feedback to the learner as to his strengths and needed areas of improvement and, if needed, apply this total to construction of an overall grade to be discussed in chapter 12. For the story analysis completed by a learner named Markus, using the rating scale in Figure 8.8, a teacher might write the following feedback:

Markus:

"You did an excellent job of naming each element in the story, *The Wizard of Oz,* but you could have added more detail to the character of the Wicked Witch and how this character's narration of the story may have colored our perception of the other characters. Your writing was well organized which made your analysis easy to understand and readable."

To complete step 4, we asked Ms. Defluer to construct a rating scale for each problem-solving behavior identified in step 1. Box 8.4 shows the scales she developed for measuring her students' ability to be able to systematically plan solutions to problems in science. For Application 8.4 create a rating scale for each dimension of the cognitive or metacognitive behavior you have chosen in step 1.

APPLICATION 8.4

Construct a rating scale for each problem-solving behavior identified in step 1 that you expect your learners to exhibit.

Rating scale for behavior 1:

Rating scale for behavior 2:

Rating scale for behavior 3:

Assessing Specific Problem-Solving Strategies

General strategies such as analysis or planning can be applied to solving problems in any domain or discipline. As pointed out earlier, recent research shows that many learners are intelligent novices; that is, they have learned general ways to think, reason, and problem solve that help them learn new skills and information quickly. We also stressed that each knowledge domain, for example, reading, science or mathematics has specific problem-solving strategies associated with it that experts in these domains know and use. These domain-specific strategies can also be taught and assessed.

Identifying Specific Problem-Solving Strategies

Educational psychologists starting from the time of Bloom et al. (1984) have been developing systems or taxonomies of general problem-solving strategies. We know about specific problem-solving strategies from studying how experts in domains like physics, mathematics, writing, or history solve problems. We discussed some of these expert studies in the first section of this chapter.

Thus, there are two basic ways to find out about specific problem-solving strategies: If you are an expert in a particular area, write down exactly how you go about solving problems, or consult textbooks that specifically deal with strategies in the subject areas (see, e.g., McGilly, 1994).

For example, experts in solving science problems dealing with motion and forces do the following:

1. Draw a diagram that depicts all the forces given in the problem.
2. Indicate how the forces interact.
3. Apply mathematical operations to information given in the problem to generate new knowledge.
4. Review the problem question and solve it.

Expert readers do the following as they are reading texts:

1. Summarize what they have read.
2. Ask questions to themselves about ideas of which they are unsure.
3. Clarify uncertainties.
4. Predict what occurs next.

Expert writers do the following:

1. Plan (search long-term memory for what they know, organize information, set goals).
2. Translate (generate text).
3. Review (evaluate and revise their writing).

Expert historians do the following as they study past events:

1. Corroborate evidence from different sources.
2. Consider the credibility of the source.
3. Place their interpretation in the context of what they are studying.

Expert mathematicians do the following to solve estimation problems:

1. Reformulate (round off numbers to make them more manageable).
2. Translate (change the structure of the problem from the one originally given).
3. Compensate (compensate for one adjustment by making an equal and opposite adjustment).

Figure 8.2, *The Higher Thinking and Problem-solving Checklist*, can help you identify other specific problem-solving behaviors.

The procedures for assessing specific strategies are similar to those for assessing general reasoning strategies: identify the strategy, select the context for demonstrating the strategy, design the assessment context, and design the scoring procedure. Figure 8.9 shows how these steps might be applied in designing an assessment of a learner's ability to design a scientific experiment.

Step 1. Identify the Strategy
The strategy to be assessed is the learner's skill in designing an investigation. The steps involved are as follows:

1. Generates a question
2. Generates an hypothesis
3. Makes a prediction
4. Conducts an investigation to test the prediction
5. Collects, organizes, and interprets relevant data
6. Draws reasonable conclusions from the data

Step 2. Select the Context for Demonstrating the Strategy
The learner will demonstrate the strategy. The problem will be the following. Under normal atmospheric conditions, an object is placed on a scale and the scale reads 10 pounds. If there were no gravity, what would the scale read?

Step 3. Design the Assessment Context
The learner will carry out the investigation keeping a detailed log of all the steps involved in the investigation and the reasoning behind each step. He will show all work and calculations. Drawings will be made of all aspects of the procedure. While the learner is conducting the investigation, the teacher will question him about his reasoning. Both process and product assessment procedures will be used.

Step 4. Design the Scoring Procedure
The following will be assessed based on oral questions and responses:

1. Explains the reasoning behind hypotheses
2. Makes reasonable predictions
3. Explains the basis of the prediction

The following will be assessed based on the written report:

1. States a question
2. Conducts an investigation
3. Collects, organizes, and interprets relevant data
4. Draws reasonable conclusions

Figure 8.9
Sample assessment plan for designing a scientific experiment

An Example of an Online Assessment of Problem-Solving Skills

A number of school-based programs have been developed recently to teach and assess problem-solving behavior from kindergarden to Grade 12. Among the most successful have been the AmericaQuest program and its technology-based MashpeeQuest performance task, and a middle-school computer-enhanced science curriculum called ThinkerTools. Their Web sites may be found at: quest.classroom.com/america2000/home.asp?DayofTrip=1&Language=English and thinkertools.soe.berkeley.edu.

MashpeeQuest is an example of an online performance task used as a tool to assess problem-solving behavior within the context of an instructional program, called AmericaQuest, which teaches learners the reasoning and problem-solving skills used by professional historians and archaeologists (Mislevy, Steinberg, Almond, Haertel, & Penuel, 2000). The MashpeeQuest performance task is designed to assess the following problem-solving skills taught by the AmericaQuest program:

- Ability to synthesize disparate ideas through reasoning in a problem-solving context.
- Ability to offer reasoned arguments rather than brief guesses.
- Ability to formulate creative, well-founded theories for unsolved questions in science and history.

The online performance task, described by Mislevy et al. (2000) and the National Research Council (2001), is as follows:

> During instruction, students participate via the Internet in an expedition with archeologists and historians who are uncovering clues about the fate of a Native American tribe, the Anasazi, who are believed to have abandoned their magnificent cliff dwellings in large numbers between 1200 and 1300 A.D. To collect observations of students' acquisition of the targeted skills, the MashpeeQuest assessment task engages students in deciding a court case involving recognition of another tribe, the Mashpee Wampanoags, who some believe disappeared just as the Anasazi did. A band of people claiming Wampanoag ancestry has been trying for some years to gain recognition from the federal government as a tribe that still exists. Students are asked to investigate the evidence, select Web sites that provide evidence to support their claim, and justify their choices based on the evidence. They are also asked to identify one place to go to find evidence that does not support their claim, and to address how their theory of what happened to the Mashpee is still justified. (National Research Council, 2001, p. 268)

One of the goals of the AmericaQuest program is to assist students in learning persuasive arguments for problem solving supported by evidence from the program's Web site and their own research. Because the problem-solving skills and data that serve as evidence are embedded in the Web site, some of the assessments of student performance are made automatically by counting the number of sources used and time spent examining each source. Other assessments involving the organization of evidence and presenting it orally are made by the teacher using a structured format provided by the program. The MashpeeQuest problem-solving task is a good example of the role technology can play in assessment and in presenting an authentic learning task. Similar problem-solving tasks can be teacher-prepared in the Internet-connected classroom.

ThinkerTools is another example of a program that harnesses the computer for teaching and assessment—this time to promote metacognitive skills with which students assess their own and others' work (White & Frederiksen, 2000). ThinkerTools is a middle-school science curriculum that teaches students how to formulate and test competing theories with experiments simulated on the computer. Software enables each learner to simulate experiments to accurately measure distances, times, and velocities, and to compare findings and reach a consensus about the best explanation for different naturally occurring phenomena. As with the MashpeeQuest problem-solving task, feedback is provided to the student by the computer.

Most important, ThinkerTools focuses on development of the metacognitive skills needed to create and revise scientific explanations from evidence. The curriculum encourages students to reflect on their own procedures and choices to evaluate their research using established scientific criteria, such as reasoning, problem-solving, and collaborative skills. The ThinkerTools program has been found to be effective in improving students inquiry and problem-solving skills and in reducing the performance gap between low and high achievers in urban classrooms (White & Frederiksen, 2000).

Summary

In this chapter you have learned how to identify and assess domain-general and domain-specific problem-solving strategies. We want to emphasize two points. First, do not underestimate the amount of time it takes to teach these strategies. Too often teachers explain and model a problem-solving strategy on one occasion and expect learners to use it from then on. You should not only model the strategy but also provide relevant practice and give learners metacognitive knowledge about when to use it and how to monitor its effectiveness. Second, use authentic contexts to teach and assess problem-solving strategies. Learners will master these strategies and want to show off what they have learned when the contexts for learning and assessment are important ones. The next chapter focuses on developing assessments that use some other real-world contexts to assess learner acquisition of knowledge, procedural skills, and problem-solving strategies.

Activities

Review the lesson contexts and example questions at the end of this chapter. These lesson contexts and examples illustrate questions for assessing your learners' problem-solving and metacognitive strategies. Review them as a guide for completing the following activities.

1. Imagine that you have been chosen by your superintendent to interview four candidates for the principal of your school. Compose a list of domain-specific and domain-general questions that you will ask each candidate to determine who is the best person for the job. Indicate whether you will place more emphasis on domain-specific (e.g., knowledge of the school and community) or domain-general (e.g., decision-making and problem-solving strategies) questions or whether you will consider them both equally. Explain your choice.

2. Assume that after the first round of interviews two of the candidates are tied for the position of principal. You have been asked to interview both candidates, this time with instructions from the superintendent to determine which candidate is more aware of herself as a problem solver and of her own decision-making processes. Which candidate is likely to be more in tune with her own management techniques and strategies and their desired effects and flexible enough to change? What questions would you now ask the candidate to provide the information requested?

3. Using the lesson contexts and template at the end of this chapter as a guide, create three questions of your own that assess your learners' use of problem-solving or metacognitive strategies.

Suggested Reading

Quellmalz, E. S., & Hoskyn, J. (1997). Classroom assessment of reasoning strategies. In G. D. Phye (Ed.), *Handbook of classroom assessment: Learning, adjustment, achievement* (pp. 103–130). San Diego: Academic Press.
The authors describe nearly two decades of work in helping teachers to teach and assess reasoning strategies. Their chapter presents actual examples of assessments developed by classroom teachers.

Lesson Contexts

K–2 EXAMPLE LESSON CONTEXTS FOR ASSESSING PROBLEM SOLVING

Grade	Subject	Topic	Assessment Questions
K–2	Language Arts	Listening critically to interpret and evaluate	What do we learn about each of the three pigs by the kind of house each builds? Compare and contrast the three brothers. Who would be the best worker, the best parent, and the most fun to be with?
		Analyzing characters	If Little Red Riding Hood looked back over her visit to Grandma's house at the end of the day, what changes would she have made in her actions. What things did she do that reflected poor judgment, carelessness, and slow thinking? Explain with reasons.
K–2	Mathematics	Geometry and spatial reasoning	Most American houses are shaped by joining rectangles. Eskimo's igloos are circular, and Native American tepees are triangular. Why do you think each shape became so popular with each group? What specific advantages did each shape offer that fit the group's needs and climate? Explain.
		Patterns, relationships, and algebraic thinking	Our number system is based on the number 10, but a lot of what we measure is in groups of 12—12 inches to 1 foot, 12 numbers on a clock, 12 months to a year. What are some of the problems with two different number bases being used? Do you have any solutions?
K–2	Science	Science concepts	Explain the way desert animals cope with the problems that intense heat and dryness cause.
		Scientific processes	One way to conserve our resources is through recycling such things as metal, glass, and paper. What other items can or should be recycled? Brainstorm creative ways to reuse them.
K–2	Social Studies	Science, technology, and society	Talk to an older person such as a grandparent or elderly neighbor and ask what life was like before television, computers, and cell phones? Compare to life today. What have we lost? What have we gained? Explain.
		Economics	Why do we use money? Why is it better than trading property or work? Explain.
K–2	Health	Health behaviors	Technology, such as computers, automobiles, and television, makes our lives more comfortable and pleasant, but it has also allowed us to become couch potatoes. Brainstorm ways that technology can be used to help us become more fit.
		Health behaviors	"An ounce of prevention is worth a pound of cure." Explain the truth of this statement with examples.

GRADES 3–5 EXAMPLE LESSON CONTEXTS FOR ASSESSING PROBLEM SOLVING

Grade	Subject	Topic	Assessment Questions
3–5	Language Arts	Connecting experiences	Cinderella was poor and unloved but had a fairy godmother to help her out. Wilbur from *Charlotte's Web* was the runt of a litter saved from death first by Fern and then by Charlotte. But most of us who are poor, little, or unloved do not have such magical or determined protectors. What are some ways to overcome these problems by yourself? Can you name people from stories, movies, or real life who tapped the magic in themselves to make their dreams come true?
		Writing process	Look over a piece of writing from the beginning of the year. Evaluate its strengths and weaknesses and revise it according to strategies for coherence and elaboration that you have learned since then.
3–5	Mathematics	Underlying processes and mathematical tools	What are some of the advantages and disadvantages of having calculators and computers perform everyday mathematical functions for us? Explain.
		Probability and statistics	Use your math skills to plan our school vegetable garden. Look up the average date for the first freeze of the year. Read the seed packet information of at least three different vegetables to find out how long it will take your plant to mature. Calculate the latest dates it is safe to plant each vegetable for a fall crop.
3–5	Science	Science concepts	With increased urban development, many wild populations such as deer have increased to the point of becoming nuisances. Brainstorm some new and creative solutions to this problem.
		Science concepts	We once thought antibiotics were the magic bullet that removed the threat of infectious diseases. Now we know that this has helped create new dangerous and resistant strains of bacteria. Brainstorm some other "scientific advancements" that have solved one problem but created another.
3–5	Social Studies	Government	Some judges are elected; some are appointed. Discuss the advantages and disadvantages of each system. Explain some abuses of either system.
	Social Studies	Economics	With changes in technology and economics, many jobs have been eliminated. We no longer have elevator operators or gas station attendants. Even travel agents are in danger of losing their customers to the Internet. Predict some other jobs that may fade away and some that may come into existence with new technological advancements.
3–5	Health	Health information	Analyze advertisements in magazines that might contribute to unrealistic body images and could result in eating disorders.
		Health behaviors	Stress sometimes makes us lose our tempers, keeps us from sleeping, or sets off unhealthy eating habits. Brainstorm some healthier ways to handle stressful situations.

GRADES 6–8 EXAMPLE LESSON CONTEXTS FOR ASSESSING PROBLEM SOLVING

Grade	Subject	Topic	Assessment Questions
6–8	Language Arts	Critical listening	Listen to television advertisements and analyze the use of persuasive and propaganda techniques to sell products. Be able to expose their flaws.
		Literary structures	Demonstrate your ability to interpret character and point of view by rewriting a well-known tale through the villain's point of view, such as the wolf telling the story of *Little Red Riding Hood,* or the Wicked Witch narrating *The Wizard of Oz.*
6–8	Mathematics	Patterns, relationships, and algebraic thinking	Start with an equation and identify several problems that could have generated it.
		Probability and statistics	Describe situations in which the preferred average would be (a) the mean, (b) the median, or (c) the mode. Explain the appropriate use of each construct.
6–8	Science	Scientific processes	Use the scientific process to design an experiment to test the effect of soil conditions on plant growth.
		Science concepts	Read and evaluate the two schools of thought concerning the existence of global warming.
6–8	Social Studies	Geography	Using your knowledge of how physical processes such as erosion, ocean circulation, and earthquakes have resulted in physical patterns on the Earth's surface, draw a map predicting the modified topography of the United States in the 25th century.
		Economy	Analyze various magazine advertisements for automobiles and decide which segment of the market is being courted and why. Be prepared to back up your conclusions with details and reasoning.
6–8	Health	Health behaviors	In spite of increased awareness of the dangers of cigarette smoking, as well as a campaign to curtail advertising to young people, more and more adolescents are smoking. Explain what you believe to be the cause of this trend and several creative ways to reverse it.
		Influencing factors	Describe the underlying causes for drug use and some creative and nonconventional ways to curb it.

TEMPLATE FOR YOUR LESSON CONTEXTS FOR ASSESSING PROBLEM-SOLVING STRATEGIES

Grade	Subject	Topic	Assessment Questions

9

Assessing Deep Understanding

In chapters 5 and 6 you learned how to construct objective and constructed-response questions to measure a learner's knowledge. Here are four assessment activities that show a different type of learning:

> We have just read *Oh, The Thinks You Could Think* by Dr. Seuss. In this story how did Dr. Seuss say that new ideas could be created from old ideas? Do you think this is really possible? Let us see if this is true. I want each of you to create some ideas of your own just the way Dr. Seuss does.

> The *Courier* is interested in its readers' opinions of a city tax proposed to help offset the cost of a new football stadium for the city's NFL team. The story shown below is based on a poll taken by the *Courier* of a random sample of 200 readers surveyed on three separate occasions. [The story is about a decline in support of the tax. The decline became even more pronounced when the NFL team failed to make the playoffs.] Write a letter to the editor about this story that reflects your opinion of whether or not there should be a tax based on the percentage of games won and lost.

> Choose a neighborhood from the city map on your table and identify its important features. From the information available to you, identify any significant problems, such as poor housing, crime, or traffic congestion. Consider various plans for improving the neighborhood and decide how to implement them. Select one plan that addresses at least one problem and prepare an outline for a presentation to the city council. Be sure to include any alternate plans and why you rejected them. Your plan must be ready a week from today.

> On the table are batteries, wires, alligator clips, light bulbs, paper clips, and plastic and wooden spoons. Find out which materials make the bulb light and be prepared to orally explain what a conductor is and why it conducts.

Learners who address these problems correctly have accomplished some significant learning feats. They have acquired a knowledge base in reading, math, geography, or science. This knowledge base undoubtedly has some organization or structure to it that allows learners to quickly recall important concepts, rules, and generalizations. They have learned procedures for exacting meaning from text, doing math problems, drawing diagrams, or constructing maps. In addition, these students have learned certain problem-solving strategies such as analysis, inference, evaluation, planning, tryout, and revision. In other words, these learners, even at an early age, draw upon their declarative and procedural knowledge, problem-solving strategies, and metacognition to demonstrate deep understanding of an academic discipline.

What exactly do we mean by "deep understanding?" **Deep understanding** is unique because it requires the ability to construct and organize new knowledge to solve novel problems. In everyday language, deep understanding means that you "really know" something. When you really know something like addition and subtraction with three-digit numbers, a law governing physical force, African history, Spanish, or map reading, you have the initiative and commitment to learn new things in these areas and construct new knowledge for yourself. You can organize this new knowledge into concepts and generalizations and see relationships and patterns. More important, you can apply this knowledge to solve novel problems in authentic, lifelike contexts.

This chapter gives you the techniques to assess deep understanding. Such assessment will require you to use much of what you have learned about assessing declarative and procedural knowledge and problem-solving strategies in the previous chapters to assess still more complex outcomes in authentic, real-life contexts. These techniques involve the observation and measurement of a student process or product, referred to as performance assessment. Before clarifying exactly what performance assessment is, let us take a critical look at how deep understanding has typically been assessed in schools.

The Extended-Response Essay Question

You have undoubtedly taken many essay exams by now. Perhaps you were asked to "compare and contrast," "discuss thoroughly," "take a position and defend it," or "weigh alternatives." Most teachers choose to write essay questions because they believe that they capture types of learning that objective-type questions miss. In chapter 6 we learned that restricted-response essay questions require the student to draw upon past learning to demonstrate higher order thinking. In this chapter we will consider extended-response questions and performance assessments. Features of these types of questions are that, like the restricted-response item, they can be posed orally to younger learners or in writing to older students. But, unlike restricted-response questions, extended-response and performance questions give the student considerable latitude in how she responds to the question, because there is no single right or best answer.

An often-cited disadvantage of essay items, especially extended essays, is their low scoring reliability. Studies comparing how experts score the same essay sometimes show poor agreement between or among the raters (Thorndike et al., 1997). More recently, however, many educators have concluded that the principal problem with the traditional essay test is poor construct relevancy (Alleman & Brophy, 1997).

If your test measures only the behavior you want it to measure, it has **construct relevancy**. The principal threat to construct relevancy for objective-type items is the reading level of the question. If the reading level is too high, then your test will measure reading comprehension more than simple factual knowledge. Often children cannot demonstrate their knowledge of math because they do not understand the question they are reading. When these tests and their contexts are closely examined, it appears that they are measuring something different from what was intended (Baker, 1994; Cizek, 1997; Newman, 1997). Unless you specifically intend to measure reading ability, you must make the reading level of the test at or below that of the test takers.

For example, let us say you want to determine a student's ability to understand new information and apply it to novel problems in real-life contexts at the end of reading a story on the geological formation of rocks. You write the following essay question:

> Identify the principal types of rocks Mark and Alisha found in the story *Hawaiian Mystery* and compare and contrast their features. What type of rock did Alisha tell Mark they had to cross to escape from the volcano?

This task presents some serious obstacles to the valid assessment of ability to understand and apply new information. First, understanding and application of new content will be difficult to separate from writing skill. A learner could comprehend the story yet be unable to express this learning satisfactorily in writing, given the time and space constraints of this essay question. But a greater challenge to construct relevancy is that no new information was given to the learner to apply in a real-life context. The task depends completely on old information and is almost completely dependent on memory. Added to this, the student may have discussed the story in class or talked about it with others. Thus, based on this question, the teacher has no way of judging a learner's ability to apply what was learned.

A task cannot measure a learner's ability to acquire, organize, and make sense of new knowledge (i.e., construct new knowledge) and to apply this knowledge to novel problems in real-life contexts if the task depends almost exclusively on the recall of old knowledge. Thus, with its time limitations, restrictions on answers, reliance on writing skill, and dependence on old information, a restricted and sometimes even extended-response essay question can be unsuited to the assessment of *deep* understanding. A different type of assessment task is required.

Features of Performance Assessment

Performance Assessments Can Be Activities or Tests

Look again at the sample tasks that began this chapter. Are these the activities used to teach deep understanding or are they used to assess it? A more important question is: Should there be a difference?

The traditional restricted-response question or essay test takes place after a lesson or unit of study is completed. This practice can lead to some unfortunate results. Learners miss the connection between what happens in class and what happens on test day, reducing the motivation both to learn in class and to study for tests. In addition, learners often do not receive feedback on the adequacy of their answers until long after their actual performance. One of the key features of performance assessment, therefore, is that it serves as both a classroom activity and a test.

Performance Assessments Are Direct Measures of Learning

With most educational and psychological assessments, the behavior that you see is not what you want to measure. The behavior that you see on a multiple-choice test in history is a learner drawing a circle around the letter that represents the best answer. Depending on how many correct choices the learner makes, the teacher judges the degree to which learning has or has not taken place. In other words, learning is measured indirectly. It is inferred from observing the learner's test-taking behavior.

Performance assessments, however, elicit the very behavior that the instructor wants to see. For example, in a diving or gymnastics competition, the behavior that the judges see is the same behavior that they want to assess. A performance test asks learners to do the things you want to measure—not things that just look like what you want to measure in the absence of the real thing. You might set up situations that allow you to directly observe and assess the learning of a problem-solving strategy or of a scientific procedure. With performance assessments you need to make less of an inference—or leap of faith—that the learner can analyze, compare, plan, or evaluate a product, project, or oral response than if you had used traditional assessment measures. The reason is that your assessment is an activity that asks the learner to do the things that result in a tangible product or performance (not just tell or write about them), and you observe and make judgments from preestablished standards about the quality of the product or performance that you see.

Performance Assessments Measure Processes and Products

A **performance assessment** should record not only what learners can do but also how they accomplished a task. To assess writing competence, we ask learners to produce a story or essay of some kind. But we also want to assess the process of writing—the planning, translating, and revising that goes into a good writing product. Likewise, in science we want to see that the learner can produce a science project and, while doing so, use good scientific thinking.

Thus, the typical performance assessment assesses the products of learning—a report, project, painting, video, scale model, experiment and so forth—*and* the processes that produced them. It assesses knowledge use, skill use, strategy use, and the products resulting from these processes. In judging the quality of these two types of learning, you will make use of checklists and rating scales to record your judgments of what you observe.

Performance Assessments Can Be Embedded in Lessons

Although performance activities and their assessment can occur during an examination period at the end of a term, ideally they should be integrated with classroom lessons or activities. In fact, as indicated earlier, the ideal performance test is also a good teaching activity. Figure 9.1 shows a performance activity and assessment that is part of a science lesson on electricity (Shavelson & Baxter, 1992). While the students learn important principles about electricity, the teacher observes and rates the learners on the methods they use to solve the problems. This can also provide feedback to the learner as to what was

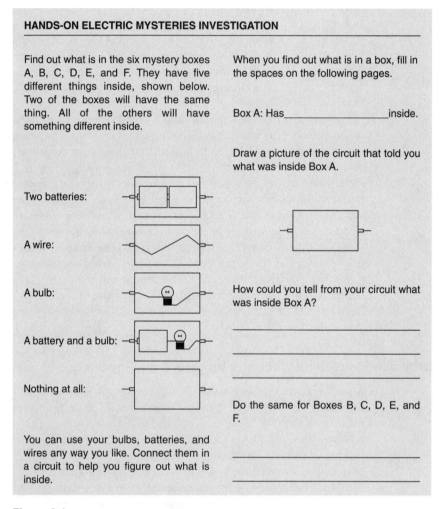

HANDS-ON ELECTRIC MYSTERIES INVESTIGATION

Find out what is in the six mystery boxes A, B, C, D, E, and F. They have five different things inside, shown below. Two of the boxes will have the same thing. All of the others will have something different inside.

Two batteries:

A wire:

A bulb:

A battery and a bulb:

Nothing at all:

You can use your bulbs, batteries, and wires any way you like. Connect them in a circuit to help you figure out what is inside.

When you find out what is in a box, fill in the spaces on the following pages.

Box A: Has_____inside.

Draw a picture of the circuit that told you what was inside Box A.

How could you tell from your circuit what was inside Box A?

_____

_____

_____

Do the same for Boxes B, C, D, E, and F.

_____

_____

Figure 9.1
Example of a performance activity and assessment
Source: From "What We've Learned about Hands-on Science," by R. Shavelson and G. Baxter, 1992, *Educational Leadership, 49*(8), pp. 20–25. Copyright © 1992 by ASCD. Reprinted with permission. All rights reserved.

done right or wrong. This type of assessment allows the teacher to give immediate feedback to learners and makes the link between teaching and testing explicit to learners.

To get an idea of what some performance activities might be like, let us look at a sample of what some teachers are doing in their classrooms to assess deep understanding. Here are some of their assessment activities and questions:

> Different forms of pollution can be found in many parts of our neighborhood. Choose one source of pollution and think of as many possible ways of preventing it as you can. Prepare to give your conclusions to the class orally. (K–3, Health)

> In our story about Christopher Columbus we learned that he arrived at the island of San Salvador. What did he find there and what was it that he expected to find? Show the difference by drawing two pictures of the island: the one that he actually discovered and a second showing what he expected to be there. In your second drawing, use special colors to highlight what he expected but did not find. (K–3, Social Studies)

> In the story *The Big Wave* by Pearl Buck, a tidal wave destroys a village and leaves Jiya alone without his family. This left Kino and his relatives with several problems. Choose what you believe was their biggest problem and tell the class how, if you were Kino, you would have solved this problem. Write out your solution to this problem along side Kino's solution. (Grades 4–6, Reading)

> Using each of the three ways of starting a letter we discussed, write a letter requesting a favor from (a) your best friend, (b) a teacher at school, and (c) the owner of a downtown department store, whom you have never met. (Grades 4–6, Writing)

> We have read various accounts of slavery in the South before the Civil War. One of these accounts was from a slave owner, another from a son of a slave owner who played with other African American children on the plantation, and a third from stories about life on the plantation from a historical museum. Which of these would you consider to be the most accurate and which the least accurate. Write three paragraphs indicating the most important piece of information from each of these three accounts. (Grades 7–8, American History)

> We have studied some games, such as a coin toss, which follow the laws of chance. Following the examples discussed, create a simple game you can play with your classmates in which the chances of winning are less than 50 percent. Play the game for 10 minutes with a partner recording the rate at which you have won and lost. Prepare to show the game to the class and play it with your teacher to confirm your predictions (Grades 7–8, Math).

Performance Assessments Can Assess Social Skills

Although performance activities such as these are ideally suited to assess deep understanding, they can also be used to assess a learner's work habits and social skills such as cooperation, sharing, and negotiation. Many performance assessments are group projects in which learners have different but interdependent roles and tasks to fulfill. Because the ability to get along and work with others is important for most professions—journalist, weather forecaster, historian, mechanic, or park ranger—performance assessments are ideal opportunities to teach and assess these competencies. Keep in mind that these skills are a part of many performance assessments that require a cooperative activity or the gathering of information from others.

Authentic Assessments and Performance Assessments

Not all performance assessments may be authentic assessments. A performance assessment is an authentic assessment when it is carried out in a real-world context. It measures the behaviors exhibited by those in the community, on the job, or in advanced grades, as part of their normal work, rather than as a specific task for assessment. An example of an authentic assessment would be a portfolio—the portfolio contains examples of actual student performance indicating "best" performance elicited under real-world conditions. In using the term "authentic assessment" it should be specified in which ways the assessment is authentic with respect to task complexity (e.g., the learner must consider different viewpoints); degree of independence of the learner (e.g., the learner is free to gather own data); available resources (e.g., the learner can consult the Internet and seek the advice of experts); and conditions under which the task is completed in the real world (e.g., the learner must work under deadlines), because many performance tests vary in how they represent these dimensions, making them either more or less authentic. A performance assessment that is authentic should have value to the student beyond simply getting a grade that shows competence on a particular task. It should represent a project, product, or oral performance that is completed with tasks embedding the assessment in a context that has some meaning or purpose beyond school or beyond the bounds of the immediate classroom lesson or unit. Let us look at some of the ways a performance assessment can be authentic.

Developing an Authentic Performance Assessment

When you decide to design a performance assessment that is authentic, you are committing yourself to several assumptions about deep learning. These assumptions include the belief that

1. Students learn best in contexts where they struggle with tasks under the guidance of a teacher, often with support from other learners that are relevant and meaningful to them. In other words, they learn best when they can take ownership in what they are producing rather than simply giving something back that someone else has already created and told to them.

2. Your learners' minds spontaneously store and organize information and create strategies for using this information. In other words, they construct their own declarative and procedural knowledge bases through their experiences with the world around them. Your instruction can inhibit or promote this knowledge construction, but it is not its only source.

3. Students are most motivated to learn when they are asked to demonstrate to others, perform orally, create a product, or perform. In other words, when students become actively engaged in the process of learning under lifelike conditions that prevail in the real world they see around them and rise to the occasion to provide their best performance.

4. Students perform at their best when they are being assessed in the context of a learning activity, not at the end of a long sequence of instruction. In other words, to the eye of the student, the learning activity and its assessment should be indistinguishable because what is being "tested" is what they have been taught to do and have had opportunities to practice.

Performance assessment is one way of meeting these four avenues to deep learning. Let us examine some general principles for designing performance assessments that you can incorporate in your classroom.

Performance Assessments Should Require Knowledge Construction

Performance assessments embedded in lessons accomplish two purposes. By being an integral part of the learning process, they help learners acquire and construct new knowledge. In addition, they are a means of assessing cognitive activity by which real-world products and performances are achieved.

Constructing knowledge involves identifying relationships among bits of information, making comparisons, drawing inferences, or evaluating. We make comparisons, draw inferences, and evaluate what we read or hear. We also extract generalizations, rules, or principles that are not explicitly pointed out in the oral or written text. The only way to assess learners' ability to construct knowledge during a performance assessment is to give them new knowledge and ask them to extend it or reformulate it to create a new product or performance. Knowledge construction uses the general cognitive strategies of analysis, comparison, inference and interpretation, and evaluation to create a finished product or performance.

Thus, an essential feature of any performance assessment is a task that requires learners to acquire and then construct new information—perhaps by hearing you read a story, reading from text, examining a graph or chart, viewing a film, listening to a debate, hearing a speech or searching through an encyclopedia. If the assessment task does not ask for something new, but requires solely the recall or application of prior information, then knowledge construction and deep understanding are not being measured.

Performance Assessments Should Require Strategic Thinking

When historians are given an original historical document to interpret, or an historical analysis to critique, they engage in what is called strategic thinking or disciplined inquiry (Newman, 1997). Likewise an anthropologist would interpret, critique, and engage in strategic thinking to determine the origin of an ancient relic. In other words, they draw upon their extensive prior knowledge and engage in certain problem-solving processes (e.g., evaluate the credibility of the source, corroborate evidence, and apply interpretations to a specific context). The same is true of mathematicians, journalists, and geographers.

Thus, a performance assessment that is valid for assessing deep understanding requires learners to draw upon their prior knowledge base (both declarative and procedural) and use both general and specific problem-solving strategies. It must explicitly cue students that they are to demonstrate their strategic knowledge. You practiced how to do this in chapter 8.

Performance Assessments Should Require Clear Communication

The end result of a performance assessment should be a product of some kind. This product may be a written document; a map; a diagram; a demonstration that includes visual, written, and spoken material; or an oral presentation. Something tangible that enables the teacher to judge knowledge construction, strategic thinking, and skill in communicating ideas must be produced.

Performance Assessments Should Strive for Authenticity

The word "authenticity" has numerous meanings. As we have seen, one meaning is that the assessment task must relate to what real people do outside of the classroom. For instance, a math performance test would assess what scientists, engineers, and mathematicians sometimes do as part of their job. The reading performance test would assess what good readers at a given grade routinely do. But this definition is unduly restrictive. The authentic task that you use in your performance assessment should have value to the student beyond simply getting a grade that shows competence on a particular task. A task is authentic if it has relevance to job or life skills. It also is authentic if it builds toward and prepares your learners for some higher learning occurring later in the school year or in succeeding grades.

Designing the Performance Assessment Task

As with any test, there are steps that must be taken to develop a valid and reliable performance test. These steps include the clear identification of the cognitive processes you want your test to measure, specifying the performance task that will measure these processes and objectively scoring your student's responses. Let us look closely at five steps that can help you design an authentic assessment of your learner's deep understanding.

Step 1. Decide on a Specific Subject Area

The best way to get started is to pick a topic in your subject area for which your students have the basic knowledge, problem-solving skills, and metacognitive behaviors necessary for deep understanding. If you are teaching science, you might choose photosynthesis. If you are a fourth-grade math teacher, you might choose fractions. If you are teaching geography you might select how to locate a city. Or, if you are teaching a history lesson you might assess deep understanding of the causes of the Revolutionary War.

BOX 9.1   The Topic of Mr. Lee's Performance Assessment

The topic of my performance assessment is third-grade mathematics skills. My students have just learned how to use decimals to two places. I want them to organize this new knowledge in a novel situation. I would like them to work in small collaborative groups to create a pretend store with items priced in dollars and cents. They can create play money to make purchases and demonstrate their new knowledge of decimals.

In Box 9.1 we asked Mr. Lee what he would like to propose for a performance assessment to assess deep learning in his third-grade classroom. Follow his lead in Application 9.1 by identifying a topic of your own for which you would like to design a performance assessment to assess deep understanding.

Step 2. Define Cognitive Processes and Social Skills You Want to Assess

We develop performance assessments because we want to tap into a learner's higher order thinking or problem-solving skills. At this stage you should have identified which higher order thinking or problem-solving skills you want to assess. Typically,

---

APPLICATION 9.1

Identify a lesson or unit topic in which you would like to assess your learners' deep understanding with a performance task. Describe the content you will teach and the performance task (e.g., writing a letter, conducting an experiment, playing store, buying a train ticket, etc.) through which your learners can display their understanding of what you have taught.

Lesson or unit topic:

Content you will teach:

Performance task:

performance tests assess cognitive processes involved in the acquisition and organization of information, the use of problem-solving strategies, and communication. For example, if you are interested in assessing how well your learners have acquired and organized information that they have just read or heard about (knowledge construction) and whether they can communicate it clearly, you could ask them to do the following:

> Read Senator Sharp's proposal on dealing with legal and illegal immigration. Identify the key principles underlying his proposal and compare them to those studied in class. Pretend you are writing a letter to a friend in another country. Explain why immigration is a major issue in this country, and how Senator Sharp's proposal compares to others that you have studied.

This task requires students to extract the important elements of a proposal that they have never read before, make distinctions with what they already know, put the proposal in a cultural context, and draw comparisons with other immigration policies.

Performance assessments such as this can be designed to assess the cognitive processes of:

- Understanding and representing problems
- Discovering mathematical relations
- Organizing information
- Discovering and using strategies
- Making predictions
- Evaluating the reasonableness of answers
- Generalizing results
- Communicating

Here is an example of a mathematics performance assessment:

B&O Railroad Fares

One way	$2.00
Weekly pass	$18.00

> Sheryl is trying to decide if she should buy a weekly train pass. Three days a week, on Monday, Wednesday, and Thursday, she takes the train to and from work. On the other two days she takes the train to work but gets a ride home with her sister. Should Sheryl buy a weekly train pass? Justify your answer with a flow chart of decision points that others could follow to make a similar judgment.

This problem assesses understanding and representing problems, evaluating the reasonableness of an answer, and clear communication.

The following example of a science performance task assesses knowledge acquisition and organization, strategic thinking (analysis and comparison), and clear communication.

On the table in front of you are rocks of shale, marble, limestone, slate, granite, lava, and magma. Design a chart that identifies the different types of rocks and the classes they belong to showing the relationships among the rocks. Draw arrows to show the relationships. Present your chart to the class, making sure to point out what each of these relationships means and why they are important.

Performance tests often are implemented in a group learning format. In such cases, you want learners to demonstrate collaborative or cooperative social skills. These can involve group members assigning and carrying out different roles as researcher, checker, recorder, troubleshooter, runner, and summarizer (Johnson & Johnson, 1991). If you choose to use a group context for your performance assessment, then you should specify the collaborative skills you want your learners to exhibit in the process of completing the performance task.

Learners need four types of skills to work well in small group learning formats. They must have basic interaction skills, getting-along skills, coaching skills, and skills in fulfilling particular roles (Hoy & Gregg, 1994). Figures 9.2 to 9.4 present examples

Collaborative Skills Rating Scale

Setting: _____   Date: _____
Total time observed: _____

Directions: Rate the extent to which each group member demonstrated the listed categories of skill. Use the following scale:

5 = Highly competent at these skills
4 = Pretty good in using these skills
3 = Moderately good at these skills
2 = Awkward in using these skills
1 = Lacks these skills

1. *Basic interaction skills.* Student shows that he/she likes and respects other members of the group.
2. *Getting-along skills.* Student shows that he/she can make and keep friends in a group.
3. *Coaching.* Student shows that he/she can help and explain things to other group members.
4. *Role fulfilling.* Student carries out his/her assigned responsibilities.

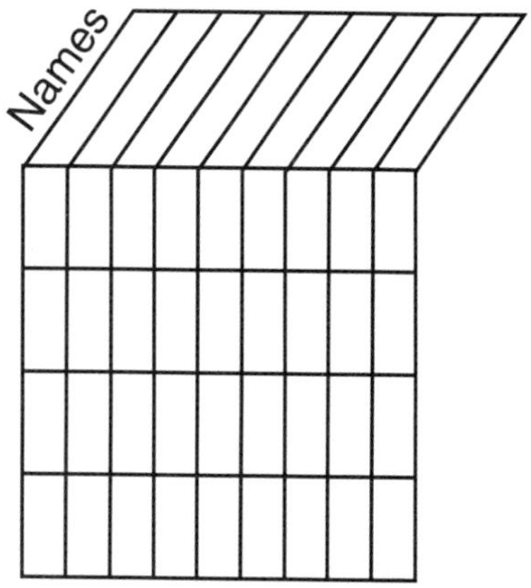

Figure 9.2
Sample rating scale for collaborative skills

Collaborative Skills Rating Scale

Setting: _____   Date: _____

Total time observed: _____

Directions: Read the statements and, in the boxes below each name, indicate how well a group member performed the stated skill. Use the following scoring code:

5 = Didn't miss an opportunity to do this
4 = Almost always did this
3 = Usually did this
2 = Seldom did this
1 = Never did this

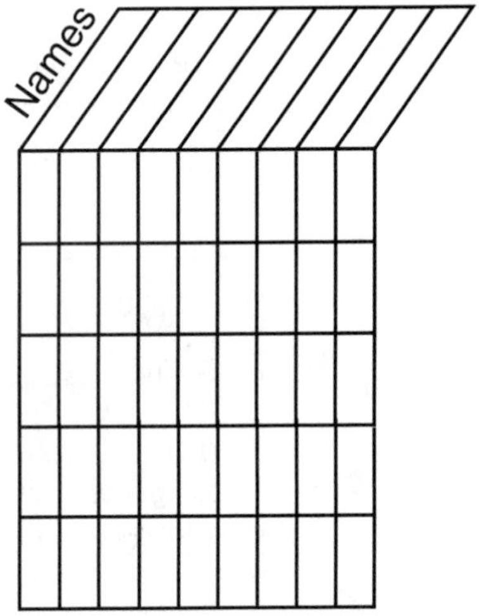

Names

1. Spoke to group members in an appropriate tone of voice

2. Acknowledged compliments coming from peers

3. Gave appropriate help when asked

4. Told others when they did something good

5. Clearly explained how to do something when asked

Figure 9.3
Sample rating scale for collaborative skills

of two rating scales and a checklist for assessing these and other collaborative skills. Figure 9.5 summarizes from these scales the collaborative skills of a learner in the form of an anecdotal report. As noted in chapter 7, anecdotal reports can be an important aid for refreshing your memory about a learner's collaborative behavior before parent–teacher night or a parent conference.

   If you were to build a performance assessment to assess deep understanding of a fifth-grade science lesson on static electricity, you might be interested in assessing understanding of the principles of attraction and repulsion; the ability to extract a principle concerning the movement of electrons; the cognitive strategies of planning, hypothesis testing, and prediction; and skill in communicating the results of an experiment. If the assessment was conducted in a group context, you would also want to assess collaborative skills with some of the tools provided in Figures 9.2 to 9.5.

Collaborative Skills Checklist

Setting: _____   Date: _____

Total time observed: _____

Directions: Place a check (√) in the appropriate box if you saw the student demonstrate this skill as the small group was working:

1. *Praising.* Student complimented the work or contribution of a peer.
2. *Listening.* Student attended to others when they were speaking and acknowledged that he/she heard what was said.
3. *Followed rules.* Student complied with all group rules.
4. *Assisting.* Student gave help when asked.

Figure 9.4
Collaborative skills checklist

Anecdotal Report of Collaborative Skills

Student's name: Brandon _____   Date: _____

Rater: Mrs. Antoine _____   Setting: Small collaborative group ____

Time observed: 10 minutes ____

Description:

I observed Brandon for about 10 minutes today during the small reading group. During this time he assisted two of his classmates, but his frustration with one was clearly evident when she didn't understand what he was saying. During the group presentations he listened attentively to what others were saying but did not volunteer information or ask questions. When I asked Brandon to say or explain something, he did so very clearly, and this is a significant improvement over a month ago.

Interpretation:

Brandon still needs to be more patient when giving directions to peers who don't understand something and to express himself even when not being asked a question. He continues to be very responsible in carrying out his group assignment.

Figure 9.5
An example anecdotal report summarizing collaborative skills

BOX 9.2   Mr. Lee's Cognitive Processes and Collaborative Skills

The cognitive processes I expect my students to learn from this assignment are to:

Plan: Search their memory for what they know about decimals, organize that information to create prices and play money of different denominations, and prepare to demonstrate simulated purchases.

Translate: Translate what they know about decimals to two places to prices in dollars and cents. Also translate what they know about decimals to the value of the coins needed to make up the prices.

Communicate: Communicate their new knowledge of decimals in the demonstration of several purchases at a pretend store, explaining to the class the mathematical steps and processes involved.

In Box 9.2, we have asked Mr. Lee to identify the cognitive processes and collaborative skills he would like to assess to determine his students' deep understanding. In Application 9.2, describe some of the cognitive processes and social skills you would like your performance task to assess.

Step 3. Design the Task and Task Directions

Having selected a topic area and identified the cognitive and social outcomes that you wish to assess, your next step is to create an authentic task for learners to show what they can do. You have seen several of these situations earlier in this chapter. A task may be a mock presentation to a school board or city council, a reenactment of an historical event, a laboratory task, a science experiment, or development of a travel brochure or a mass-transit plan. Many teachers get started on developing the assessment task by asking themselves the following questions (Wiggins, 1993; Wiggins & McTighe, 1998):

1. What do the jobs of professionals who make their living as mathematicians, writers, geographers, artists, or historians look and feel like?
2. Which of the projects and tasks of these professionals can be adapted for school instruction for my learners in this age group?
3. What skills do these professionals acquire that my learners can begin to practice in the classroom?

Once you start asking these questions, a host of ideas for different assessment tasks and contexts arise. The problem then becomes one of developing the task specifications for the skills and/or strategies you want to assess. Next are some criteria that you should keep in mind when planning and implementing the performance task.

APPLICATION 9.2

Imagine you are designing a performance task on the topic you identified in step 1. Describe the cognitive processes and any social skills in the following categories that you are interested in assessing.

Knowledge construction:

Strategic thinking:

Clear communication:

Social skills:

Goal Relevance.   Will your learners see the assessment as an integral part of classroom instruction or something that gets them a grade and little else? Do the assessment tasks reflect what you and your learners value? Do they ask for skills that learners have learned about and practiced in their lessons? This is probably the single most important design consideration.

Level of Difficulty.   Just as the track coach asks his sprinters to run 100- and 200-meter dashes in competition and not 800-meter runs, so too must teachers aim their assessment tasks within the optimal range of learner competence. The tasks must be novel but familiar, representing something that was practiced but not identical to it. The activities should be challenging but with content to which learners are accustomed. The purpose of the assessment is to have learners demonstrate the higher level thinking skills they learned during instruction. If the procedures and content are too difficult, your learners will not be able to show what they can do.

Multiple Goals.   Real-world tasks require a variety of thinking skills: analysis, interpretation, evaluation, planning, revision, clear communication, and self-monitoring. The same is true for a performance assessment. Although these assessments can measure one of these skills, a focus on multiple goals is preferable. Learners find complex activities more engaging. Furthermore, performance assessments take time to develop. Teachers use them more efficiently when they accomplish many goals rather than one.

Performance assessments are ideally suited to incorporating content and skills from a variety of academic disciplines to accomplish these goals. They can require learners to integrate math, writing, science, and art skills to produce a project or demonstration as part of interdisciplinary thematic lessons and units. Figure 9.6 shows the visual organization of a unit theme requiring interdisciplinary content and skills.

This interdisciplinary unit, Adventures of Lewis and Clark, draws concepts from social studies, math, science, art, writing, and reading. It therefore requires a performance task requiring some knowledge and cognitive strategies from all of these disciplines. How might this be done? This teacher had her students create imaginary journals of their own, just like Lewis and Clark did during their journey. The students were instructed to assume the roles of Lewis and Clark and to write a letter home, recording the birds, foliage, and outstanding landmarks they saw along the way and to draw pictures to document what they wrote.

Multiple Solutions.   A performance assessment should require learners to wrestle with a complex problem that can be solved in a number of ways. They must make

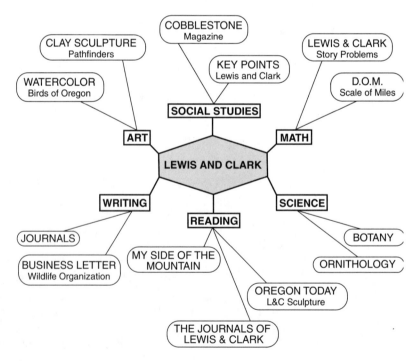

Figure 9.6
Visual representation of the interdisciplinary unit theme Adventures of Lewis and Clark
Source: Adapted from *The Classroom of the 21st Century,* by S. Kovalik, 1994, Kent, WA: Books for Educators. Copyright © 1994 by S. Kovalik

and defend their choices of strategies to solve problems and methods used to communicate their solution. At times, learners should be able to select their own data sources (experts, magazines, encyclopedias, newspapers, scientific journals) and presentation formats (videotape, audiotape, persuasive essay, oral explanation, dramatic reenactments, graphic displays, stories, dialogs), which can inspire a sense of ownership in the task. A key goal should be to adapt the assessment to the strengths and needs of the learner.

Self-Regulated Learning. As was pointed out at the end of chapter 1, one of the most important outcomes of classroom lessons should be your students' feelings about themselves as learners. Deci and colleagues (1991) believe that learners feel good about themselves when they are allowed to master and demonstrate their competence at completing a complex task largely with their own intellectual resources with some assistance from peers and teachers. In other words, when they are allowed to regulate their own behavior by being given the flexibility to make some choices for themselves with regard to the nature of the task and their response to it, they become self-determined. Remember, your learners will bring to the task a lot of declarative and procedural knowledge acquired from the world around them. They spontaneously store and organize information and strategies. Your performance task should invoke them to use this information. Performance assessments should be designed with self-regulation in mind. In other words, they should allow for a considerable degree of learner autonomy (choices), provide sufficient time and resources to allow learners to show their competence, and permit consultation with peers and adults.

Clear Directions. Performance assessments should be complex, require higher level thinking in an authentic, real-world context, assess multiple goals, and permit considerable latitude about how to reach these goals. Nevertheless, your directions and descriptions of the project should leave "no surprises, no excuses" (Wiggins, 1998) in the minds of learners about what is expected. Your students may need to think long and hard about how to carry out the task, but they should be clear about what a finished product looks like. They should be able to explain exactly what you expect them to turn in when the assessment is over.

Here are some example task specifications for a middle-school performance assessment on static electricity:

> The material in this box can be used to construct an electroscope similar to the one you have used in our class lessons. Construct an electroscope with your group. It can be built in a lot of different ways. Assign roles (e.g., researcher, checker, recorder, troubleshooter, runner, and summarizer) to different group members for carrying out this project. Once you have done this, use the plastic ruler and the wool cloth to solve the following problems:
> 1. What will happen to the leaves of the electroscope as the charged ruler is brought closer to or farther away from it? Explain why this happens.
> 2. What will happen to the leaves when you touch the electroscope with the charged ruler and then touch it with your finger? Explain why this happens.

3. What will happen when you pass the charged ruler close to the leaves but do not make contact with them? Explain why this happens.
4. What will happen to the charged leaves when you heat the air next to them with a match? Explain why this happens.

For each question, fill out the appropriate section on your lab sheet:
a. Make a prediction about what will happen.
b. What did you observe?
c. Was your prediction supported?
d. Explain what you saw using the important terms that we studied in class.
e. Make a drawing that shows the electrical forces at work.

Now you be the judge of whether the above tasks meet the criteria for designing a good performance task: goal relevance, level of difficulty, multiple goals, multiple solutions, self-regulated learning, and clear directions.

In Box 9.3, we have asked Mr. Lee to prepare instructions to his students for completing his performance task. In Application 9.3, follow Mr. Lee's example and write the directions for the performance task that you will give to your students.

Step 4. Specify the Scoring Rubrics

Performance tests like the static electricity and decimal example can be scored reliably, but it takes the use of rubrics to do so. Recall that a rubric represents a detailed

---

BOX 9.3   Mr. Lee's Instructions to His Students

Instructions to my students:

You and your group members are to demonstrate your understanding of decimals and what they mean by creating a fantasy store with items priced in dollars and cents. You can make the store any kind you like. It can be a candy store, a bakery, a toy store, or even a school store. You can sell anything from donuts to dolls, nuts to notebooks, or gummy bears to drawing paper.

Draw pictures of your sale merchandise or use real objects. Decide on a fair price and mark each item in dollars and cents, using your knowledge of decimals. Next, create both paper and coin money of different amounts for your customers to use.

Finally, communicate that you know what the numbered prices and money stand for as you act out several purchases. Have one person explain the math behind the buying and selling, or each customer or clerk can explain his or her own part. This can be kind of like a Sesame Street episode explaining "How Decimals Work." Be prepared to answer questions from the rest of the class.

APPLICATION 9.3

Using Mr. Lee's instructions to his students as a guide, write the task directions for the performance assessment you are planning.

description of the preestablished standards or criteria that will guide your rating of a performance task. Unlike objective-type test questions, performance assessments have no simple right or wrong answer. You must identify beforehand the specific performance characteristics for the processes and products that you want to assess and the relative importance of each of these characteristics in your overall evaluation of learner performance.

Given the time and effort this might take, it is tempting to limit your scoring criteria to those aspects of performance that are easiest to rate (e.g., Did the learner make a drawing? Did the learner complete the lab sheet? Did the learner complete the project on time?). Such yes/no judgments ignore the more important characteristics that you identified in step 2: clear communication, knowledge construction, strategic thinking, planning and revision, and so forth. By focusing on these processes, you guard against turning a performance assessment into a knowledge test. Thus, your goal when designing a scoring system is to do justice to the effort that you expended in developing the performance assessment and that your learners exerted when taking it.

By giving careful consideration to this step, you will minimize scoring subjectivity and bias while also holding learners to high standards of achievement. Let us examine some of the important considerations in developing rubrics for a performance test.

Measure Your Goals. In Application 9.2 you identified the learning outcomes that you want to assess with your performance test. Your rubrics should fit these accomplishments. Will you be expecting evidence of knowledge acquisition and organization? If so, you will need to design a rating scale reflecting this. Do you wish to assess the use of problem-solving strategies? If so, you will need rating scales to assess their use. Will you be observing the processes that learners employ as they complete the assessment? If so, you may need to construct checklists that record whether the processes were used. You will be expecting a product of some kind. Therefore, you will need to construct rating scales that assess the qualities that you desire in the poem, written essay, exhibit, map, graph, or other product. In chapters 7 and 8 you learned how to develop a variety of scales and checklists to make assessments such as these. Shortly we will show you some examples of others.

Select an Appropriate Scoring System.   Choose a scoring method suited for the type of outcome that you want to measure. There are three methods to consider: checklists, rating scales, and holistic scoring, as shown in Figure 9.7. Recall that when they provide the detailed standards or criteria to guide the assessment of a performance task, they are called rubrics. Rubrics serve as scoring guides that provide preestablished criteria for evaluating student products, processes, and performances. Rubrics control subjectivity of scoring with the use of precise language and definitions by which the quality of a learner's performance is judged against specific criteria. Because performance tasks often have multiple learning outcomes, you may need more than a single scoring method. Figure 9.8 shows how these scoring principles were applied in a combination checklist and rating scale to assess the static electricity performance tasks described earlier.

Checklists.   Recall that checklists contain lists of behaviors, traits, or characteristics that can be scored as present or absent. They are best suited for complex behaviors or performances that can be divided into a series of clearly defined specific actions that are either present or absent. You saw examples of these in chapters 7 and 8. They take time to develop but have good scoring reliability.

Rating scales.   Rating scale rubrics are typically used for assessing products, processes, and performances that do not lend themselves to yes/no or present/absent type of judgments. As you learned in chapter 8, the most common type of rating scale assigns numbers to certain levels or degrees of performance. These scales focus the rater's attention on certain aspects—or component parts—of the product or process to which the rater assigns a number which provides a benchmark or anchor for what is being rated.

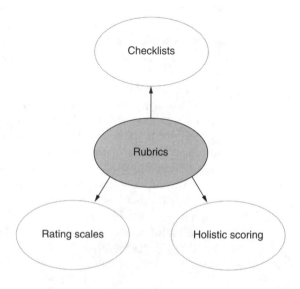

Figure 9.7
Types of scoring rubrics

Scoring Rubric for Static Electricity Performance Assessment

Checklist for Social Skills *(Assign 1 or 0 points.)*

———— Role differentiation was accomplished

———— *Gave praise to a peer*

———— Carried out role

———— Asked for clarification

———— Used expressions like, "What I meant to say was . . ." or "Do you agree with what I suggested?"

Points: _____

Rating Scales for Cognitive Processes

Knowledge of Basic Concepts of Static Electricity *(Assign 1–5 points.)*

Scale	Description
5	Firm command of basic concepts
	Uses terminology correctly
	Identifies important principles
4	Shows nearly complete understandig of basics
	Most terms used correctly
	Has identified most important principles
3	Has only tentative grasp of concepts
	Some terms used incorrectly
	Some inference evident
2	Lacks command of most of the important concepts
	Uses little relevant terminology
	Little evidence of ability to abstract principles
1	Shows no understanding of basic concepts
	No attempt to use relevant terminology
	No evidence of abstraction or inference

Points: _____

Carrying Out the Task *(Assign 1–5 points.)*

Scale	Description
5	Very carefully planned project
	Stated clear hypotheses
	All predictions are explicitly stated
4	Thorough planning and anticipation of most problems
	Hypotheses are for the most part clear
	Most predictions are clear and explicit
3	Evidence of some planning
	Hypotheses stated but vague
	Attempted to make clear predictions
2	Little planning went into this
	Hypotheses incomplete and unclear
	Some vague predictions made
1	No evidence of planning
	Does not make hypotheses
	No predicted results

Points: _____   *(continued)*

Figure 9.8

Scoring rubric for static electricity performance assessment

Rating Scale for Communication *(Assign 1–5 points.)*

Scale	Description
5	Gives a complete, clear, unambiguous report
	Includes diagrams and other visual aids
	Uses good organization and mechanics
4	Gives a fairly complete report that is generally clear
	Uses some visual aids
	Organization and mechanics are generally good
3	Report is somewhat ambiguous and not always clear
	Could use more visuals that are clear
	Presentation is a little disorganized and writing weak
2	Report is difficult to follow
	Very limited visuals; hard to understand
	Poor organization with noticeably poor
	writing mechanics
1	Ineffective communication; incomprehensible
	No visuals of any kind
	No evidence of any organization; numerous
	spelling and grammatical errors

Points: _____

TOTAL POINTS: _____ (Maximum of 20)

Figure 9.8
(*continued*)

The key question to ask when designing a rating scale is: What are the most important characteristics that show to a high degree the thinking process, learning, or trait being measured? In other words, what are the important aspects of, for example, clear communication, knowledge construction, problem solving, or metacognition that I want to assess? Therefore, with rating scale rubrics multiple components of an overall product, process, or performance are being rated. Students receive specific feedback on their performance with respect to each individual scoring criteria and, therefore, considerable feedback can be provided to both student and teacher which can form a profile of specific student strengths (Mertler, 2001).

Holistic scoring. Holistic scoring is used when the rater estimates the *overall* quality of the product, demonstration, or exhibit and assigns a numerical value to that quality. Table 9.1 is an example of holistic scoring. Holistic scoring is typically used in evaluating extended written products such as stories and research papers or artistic performances like a dance, skit, or reading interpretation. You may decide to score your class term papers holistically on an Excellent to Needs Improvement scale. In such a case, it is important that you have models that show the varying degrees of such a scale. After creating or selecting these models from the set to be rated, you

TABLE 9.1
Sample Grades and Categories for a Holistic Rubric

Rubric Score	Grade	Category
7	A+	Excellent
6	A	Excellent
5	B+	Good
4	B	Good
3	C+	Fair
2	C	Fair
1	D	Needs Improvement

can assign each of them to one of the categories. A model for each category helps to ensure that all the products and performances assigned to a given category are of comparable quality.

Holistic scoring can be more difficult to use for processes and performances than for products. For the former, experience in rating the process or performance is necessary (e.g., rating a dramatic rendition of a poem, oral interpretation of a story, or debate). Here you may need to integrate and make a summary judgment from many complex parts. You may find it helpful to make audio- or videotapes of the performance, which you can use in subsequent classes as models representing different degrees of competence. Because a holistic rubric is an overall or summary judgment, it provides no means of giving the learner detailed feedback on the quality of the performance as does the rating scale rubric. On the other hand, holistic rubrics can be scored more quickly.

Good performance tests require learners to achieve multiple goals in alternative ways. Thus, a comprehensive performance assessment might combine all three rubric scoring systems. Figure 9.9 provides some step-by-step procedures you can follow to design scoring rubrics (Mertler, 2001).

Assigning Point Values.   You will have to decide how many points to assign to the project as a whole and how many points to assign to each component of the project (communication, understanding, planning, presentation, etc.). It is a good idea to limit the number of points for each component to that which can be reliably discriminated. For example, if you assign 20 points to how well the person communicates the results of the project, you are implying that you can reliably grade 20 degrees of communication quality. Few raters can discriminate 10 degrees of quality on any trait, much less 20.

You have two related goals in assigning points: (a) Assign enough points to a component or trait so that you do justice to varying degrees of quality, but (b) avoid assigning so many points that you start assigning points arbitrarily. We recommend that you assign no fewer than 3 and no more than 7 points to any one component

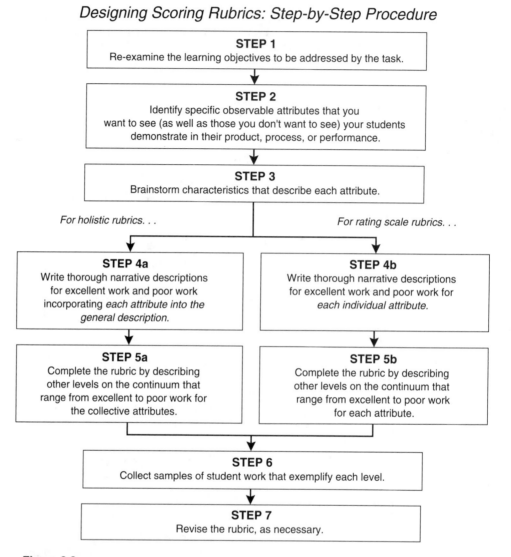

Designing Scoring Rubrics: Step-by-Step Procedure

STEP 1
Re-examine the learning objectives to be addressed by the task.

STEP 2
Identify specific observable attributes that you
want to see (as well as those you don't want to see) your students
demonstrate in their product, process, or performance.

STEP 3
Brainstorm characteristics that describe each attribute.

For holistic rubrics. . .   *For rating scale rubrics. . .*

STEP 4a
Write thorough narrative descriptions
for excellent work and poor work
incorporating *each attribute into the
general description.*

STEP 4b
Write thorough narrative descriptions
for excellent work and poor work for
each individual attribute.

STEP 5a
Complete the rubric by describing
other levels on the continuum that
range from excellent to poor work for
the collective attributes.

STEP 5b
Complete the rubric by describing
other levels on the continuum that
range from excellent to poor work
for each attribute.

STEP 6
Collect samples of student work that exemplify each level.

STEP 7
Revise the rubric, as necessary.

Figure 9.9
Designing scoring rubrics: Step-by-step procedures
Adapted from Mertler, C. A. (2001). Designing scoring rubrics for your classroom. *Practical Assessment, Research, and Evaluation, 7*(25). Available online: http://ericae.net/pare/getvn.asp?= 7&n=25

of a performance assessment. Three-, five-, and seven-point scales are often preferred to provide a middle point.

The scoring rubric Mr. Lee has chosen for his third-grade performance task appears in Figure 9.10. In Application 9.4 create one or more scoring rubrics, as needed, for assessing the performance task you have identified in step 3.

Rubric for Composition Outline

5   Firm command of outlining
     Correctly uses roman numerals and subordinate letters
     Excellent distinction between major and minor details
4   Shows nearly complete understanding of outlining
     Most roman numerals and subordinate letters used correctly
     Good distinction between major and minor details
3   Has only tentative grasp of outlining
     Some roman numerals and subordinate letters used incorrectly
     Some distinction between major and minor details
2   Lacks command of most principles of outlining
     Uses few roman numerals and subordinate letters correctly
     Little distinction between major and minor details
1   Shows no understanding of outlining
     No attempt to use roman numerals correctly
     No distinction between major and minor details

Rubric for Composition

5   Use of writing conventions very effective, no errors
     No mistakes in spelling, punctuation, grammar; sentence structure excellent
4   Use of writing conventions effective, a few errors
     Only a few mistakes in spelling, punctuation, grammar, and sentence structure
3   Use of writing conventions somewhat effective, some errors
     Several mistakes in spelling, punctuation, grammar, and sentence structure
2   Use of writing conventions somewhat ineffective, many errors
     Many mistakes in spelling, punctuation, grammar, and sentence structure
1   Use of writing conventions ineffective, major errors
     Lacks command of basics of spelling, punctuation, grammar, and sentence structure

Rating Scale for Revisions

0   Made no attempt to revise
1   Made some revisions that improved composition
2   Made many revisions that improved composition

Sum of Ratings ——-
Comments:

Figure 9.10
Scoring rubric for Mr. Lee's third-grade writing performance activity

Step 5. Identify Important Implementation Considerations

In carrying out steps 1 through 4, you have created the performance task. Now it is time to think through how you will implement it. Two major considerations are (a) specifying testing constraints, and (b) planning how you will deliver the assessment activity to your learners.

APPLICATION 9.4

Prepare a set of scoring rubrics for your performance assessment identified in step 3, using a checklist, rating, holistic rubric, or combination of these.

Identifying Testing Constraints.   Your testing constraints will be the conditions under which learners are allowed to demonstrate their deep understanding. Some of the most common conditions are

- *Time.* How much time should a learner or group of learners have to plan, revise, and finish the task?
- *Reference material.* What resources (dictionaries, textbooks, class notes, CD-ROMs) will learners be able to consult while they are completing the assessment task?
- *Other people.* Will your learners be able to ask for help from peers, teachers, and experts as they take a test or complete a project?
- *Equipment.* Will your learners have access to computers, calculators, spell checkers, or other aids or materials as they complete the assignment?
- *Scoring criteria.* Will you inform your learners about the explicit standards that you use to evaluate the product or performance?

In deciding which of these constraints to impose during a performance assessment, ask yourself the following questions: What constraints do people in the real world face when they do these types of tasks? What kinds of constraints tend to elicit the best performance in apprentice performers? What are the appropriate limits a teacher should impose on the availability of the five resources listed above?

If you were Mr. Lee, what limits would you impose on the availability of the five resources listed above? In Box 9.4, we asked Mr. Lee to identify the conditions under which his learners would be allowed to complete the performance task. In Application 9.5, respond to the five conditions by identifying those under which learners will complete your performance task.

Delivering the Assessment.   To successfully implement a performance assessment, you must consider these issues: structuring the task, motivation, initial coaching, independent work, and debriefing.

BOX 9.4   Mr. Lee's Assessment Constraints

Time:

Students will have one hour before lunch to plan their store, price their products, and create their play money. Each group will demonstrate purchases after lunch. The demonstration should take about ten minutes with some time for questions.

Reference material:

Students will have access to art supplies, magazines, and any objects they may wish to bring from home. They can use the classroom dictionaries to check their spelling.

Other people:

The teacher will arrange small groups of four to six students each. Students will show courtesy and cooperation with other group members.

Equipment:

Students will have at their disposal colored paper and scissors for making paper money and drawing pictures of the products to be sold and personal calculators for making change.

Scoring criteria:

Students will receive up to five points if the priced items and play money are clearly marked and accurate. Another five points will come from the demonstrated purchases. Full credit will depend on accuracy and explanation. Bonuses of up to two points may be awarded for exceptional work or answers to student or teacher questions.

Structuring. How will you describe the performance task to your learners? What words and expressions will you use to communicate the goals and purposes of the activity? At the start of the activity, review relevant prior knowledge and cognitive strategies they will need to successfully complete the task. Make sure that the students understand the task requirements before they begin the assessment (what they will be doing, what product they will produce, and how their performance will be evaluated).

Motivation. The key to an effective performance assessment is learner engagement, not simply performing physical actions or the time spent on the task. At the start of the activity give your learners some encouraging words that will stimulate their curiosity and interest and help them to become self-motivated learners.

Coaching. What explanations and modeling will you give before setting learners out to work on their own or in small groups? It is a good idea to guide your learners through several examples before they work independently.

APPLICATION 9.5

Identify the testing constraints that identify the conditions under which your learners can demonstrate their deep understanding during your performance assessment. Add any that are not listed below.

Time:

Reference material:

Other people:

Equipment:

Scoring criteria:

Independent work.   What monitoring will you do once learners are working on their own? Will they be able to learn from their mistakes? You should give your learners formative feedback while they are completing the assessment task and be close to the action to handle any confusion or misconceptions that may arise while learners are completing the task.

Debriefing.   How will you tie your learners' performance to the goals and purposes of other related classroom activities? At the end of the activity you should help learners reflect on what they have learned and interpret their accomplishments in light of the big picture beyond the immediate task requirements. In other words, help them link the performance assessment with the larger unit or curriculum strand, later learning, or the world outside the classroom.

In Application 9.6 describe how you will give feedback to your learners on their performance task. What follow-up activities might you propose for learners who perform below expectations?

APPLICATION 9.6

Describe the procedures you will use to provide feedback to your learners on how well they performed. Identify some ways you will help them learn from their mistakes.

Procedures for providing feedback:

Suggestions that will help them improve and learn from their mistakes:

Summary

This chapter presented some ways of measuring deep understanding using a performance assessment. You saw that a well-designed and implemented performance assessment is a five-step process: deciding on a specific subject area, defining the cognitive processes and social skills you will measure, designing the task and task directions, developing scoring rubrics, and identifying testing constraints.

A well-designed and implemented performance assessment will tell you things about your students' understanding and achievement that no other type of assessment can rival. But, even more importantly, it can represent a type of motivating exercise that can inspire self-regulated learning. When performance assessments are authentic, they become as highly motivating to learners as track championships or band competitions are for their contestants.

Activities

Review the lesson contexts and example questions at the end of this chapter. For this chapter these lesson contexts and examples illustrate questions for assessing your learners' deep understanding. Review them as a guide for completing the activities below.

1. If you were to assess your learners for deep understanding, what steps would you follow to guide the development of a performance assessment?

2. In chapter 3 you studied lists of behaviors developed by Bloom and colleagues and Gagné, some of which purport to measure higher order thinking. If you were to build a taxonomy of your own to represent deep understanding using terms from *The Higher Order Thinking and Problem-solving Checklist* in chapter 8, what might your selections be?

3. Assume you are planning a unit to teach deep understanding. Describe what your unit would ask your learners to do to: (a) be authentic, (b) encourage knowledge construction, (c) require strategic thinking, and (d) exhibit clear communication.

5. Identify a behavior a worker in the real world is likely to use on the job related to a subject you are teaching. Develop a checklist, rating scale rubric, or holistic scale to assess whether or not your learners can perform this behavior in the context of a real-life task in your classroom.

6. Using the lesson contexts and template at the end of this chapter as a guide, create three questions of your own that assess your learners' deep understanding.

Suggested Readings

Mitchell, R. (1992). *Testing for learning: How new approaches to evaluation can improve American schools*. New York: Free Press.
  This is an excellent primer on performance assessment that clearly explains the different types of performance tests and how they can be used to evaluate instruction.
Wiggins, G., & McTighe, J. (2000). *Understanding by design*. Upper Saddle River, NJ: Prentice Hall.
  This book provides many good suggestions on how to design a performance assessment that will inspire your students to become self-motivated and self-regulated learners.

Lesson Contexts

K–2 EXAMPLE LESSON CONTEXTS FOR ASSESSING DEEP UNDERSTANDING

Grade	Subject	Topic	Assessment Questions
K–2	Language Arts	Reading comprehension	Make a cartoon drawing showing the most important events in *Charlotte's Web*. Be ready to explain why you chose them and why they are important.
		Dramatic interpretations	Think about what Jack and the Beanstalk's mother would have thought when Jack returned with only seeds for selling the family cow. Work with a classmate to create a dramatic re-enactment of the discussion between Jack and his mother regarding his trade. Try to give some reasons Jack might have had for his decision.
K–2	Mathematics	Number, operation, and quantitative reasoning	Show the relationship between addition and subtraction with blocks.
		Number, operation, and quantitative reasoning	Create a candy store price list and use pretend money to make several purchases. Show how to add up the value of different coins and how to determine and give proper change as well.
K–2	Science	Scientific processes	Take a walk in your neighborhood and identify several sources of air or water pollution. Draw pictures of the pollution problems and then create separate pictures showing ways to get rid of the problems.
		Scientific processes	Draw a picture of the nighttime sky and identify patterns among the stars. Try to find some well-known patterns such as the Big and Little Dipper. Use reference books to identify others.
K–2	Social Studies	Social Studies skills	Interview an older friend or relative and tell us about his or her experience with an historical event that occurred before you were born, such as World War II, the Vietnam War, the Depression, the Civil Rights movement, or the landing on the moon. Use photographs, pictures, or other props as visual aids.
		Geography/ Social Studies skills	Draw a map showing how to get from your house to the school. Try to keep things to scale and include important landmarks, such as street crossings, parks, streams, and commercial buildings.
K–2	Health	Health behaviors	Create several posters promoting bicycle safety. Be ready to explain why your tips are important.
		Health information	Demonstrate with a fellow classmate a simple first-aid treatment, such as washing, disinfecting and bandaging a cut, or stopping a nosebleed. Be prepared to explain the reasons behind your actions.

GRADES 3–5 EXAMPLE LESSON CONTEXTS FOR ASSESSING DEEP UNDERSTANDING

Grade	Subject	Topic	Assessment Questions
3–5	Language Arts	Reading comprehension	Design a book jacket for your outside reading project. (a) Create a front cover that captures the reader's attention. (b) Write a brief summary on the front inside flap that gets us interested without giving away the plot. (c) Tell us something about the author on the back inside flap. (d) Make up rave reviews on the back cover.
		Reading skills, decoding	Tutor a classmate having problems with reading. Teach him or her ways to sound out words, recognize sight words, and use the context to guess at the meaning of unknown words. Allow your teacher to observe you.
3–5	Mathematics	Geometry	Create a simple board game for primary students that reinforces identification of geometric shapes and their relationship to each other.
		Underlying processes and mathematical tools	Rework the measurements in several recipes to increase or decrease the number of servings. Be able to explain to the class the mathematical operations you went through to alter ingredient amounts. You may want to prepare one of the best tasting recipes to be a part of your class presentation.
3–5	Science	Scientific processes	Demonstrate the correct way to obtain water samples from streams and show how to perform some simple tests to determine degrees of pollution.
		Scientific concepts	Demonstrate your deep understanding of aerodynamics by building a paper airplane for our competition. Explain the design features that enhance its ability to perform. The plane that glides the longest will be awarded a prize.
3–5	Social Studies	History	Create a daily journal for a member of a wagon train going west. Include details that reflect your understanding of the historical hardships and challenges that faced these brave Americans.
		Government	Put your knowledge of the democratic process to work by becoming involved in an election first hand. You may run for a school or class office yourself, assist in the campaign of a classmate, or work in a local campaign. Make a presentation to the class of the realities of politics.
3–5	Health	Health behaviors	Demonstrate the effect of exercise and emotions on the heart rate by taking your own or a classmate's pulse under different situations. You might measure before and after running laps, and on a regular class day versus a test day.
		Personal/ interpersonal skills	Work with a small group of three to four classmates to create different scenarios demonstrating effective and noneffective refusal skills in unsafe situations, such as the temptation to use drugs, alcohol, or tobacco.

GRADES 6–8 EXAMPLE LESSON CONTEXTS FOR ASSESSING DEEP UNDERSTANDING

Grade	Subject	Topic	Assessment Questions
6–8	Language Arts	Sounds Devices	Demonstrate that the same sound devices that make poetry memorable, such as rhyme, alliteration, and assonance, also work in the marketplace. Clip advertisements from magazines, labels from products, and record or write down jingles from radio and television that utilize sound devices to sell their products. Explain the reason behind their effectiveness.
		Writing: Voice and style appropriate to audience	Write a sales pitch for a new midsize car for three different audiences—a young, fun-loving single professional, a soccer mom concerned with safety, and a company considering the purchase of a fleet of cars for pizza delivery. Choose your vocabulary, details, and persuasive emphasis to reflect these different audiences.
6–8	Mathematics	Measurement	Given that organic mulch should be three inches thick to retain soil moisture, that the school test garden is a plot ten by twenty-five feet in size, and that mulch sells for $1.99 for 2 cubic feet, how much will it cost the school to mulch the entire plot? Illustrate your calculations at the blackboard.
		Probability and statistics	Using your knowledge of probability and statistics, consult meteorological data to determine the best day for the class picnic. Consider both the likelihood of a sunny day and the optimal temperature range. Be prepared to justify your choice.
6–8	Science	Science concepts	Use readily available materials to demonstrate the use of a pulley. Explain how the relationship of force and motion underlies its function.
		Scientific process	Make a chart of several generations of family members tracing a genealogical trait such as eye or hair color. Explain the results according to principles of heredity.
6–8	Social Studies	Social Studies skills	Use newspapers, newscasts, and the Internet to study a local issue, such as various proposals to ease traffic congestion. Weigh and consider the alternate views and write a letter to the editor stating reasons for your support of one of the proposals.
		Economics	A very large amount of school funds are lost each year when students fail to return textbooks on loan to them. Study the situation at the local level by interviewing students and administrative personnel. Determine the underlying causes of this loss and propose a system to minimize it. Send a brief description of your solution to your school newspaper.
6–8	Health	Personal/ interpersonal skills	Design and implement a peer mediation project to resolve conflict among peers.
		Health behaviors	Create a problem-solving flow chart that incorporates decision strategies to deal with health emergencies.

TEMPLATE FOR YOUR LESSON CONTEXTS FOR ASSESSING DEEP UNDERSTANDING

Grade	Subject	Topic	Assessment Questions

10

Assessing Genuine Achievement: The Portfolio

We have woven a number of themes throughout the fabric of each chapter of this book. Some of these themes are

- Motivation for learning and doing well on tests occurs when assessments are learning experiences.
- Assessment must match what has been taught.
- The skills that learners demonstrate on assessments should be the skills that are practiced in class.
- Students become more engaged in learning when assessments represent challenging tasks encountered in the real world.
- A good assessment measures not only the products of learning but also the cognitive processes used to create them.

Performance assessment is an exercise that exemplifies all of these themes. As you will recall, performance assessment is a type of demonstration by which learners show their deep understanding of a particular area of learning. This demonstration is like a snapshot capturing what a learner has accomplished at a particular point in the year.

Another type of performance assessment provides more than a one-time picture or snapshot of what a learner has accomplished. Its principal purpose is to tell a story of a learner's growth in proficiency, long-term achievement, and significant accomplishments in a given area. It is called **portfolio assessment**. A measure of deep understanding like the performance demonstrations covered in chapter 9, the portfolio also shows growth in competence and understanding across a grading period, semester, or entire school year.

Portfolio assessment is based on the idea that a collection of a learner's work throughout the year is one of the best ways to show both final achievement and the effort put into getting there. You are already familiar with the idea of a portfolio. Painters, fashion designers, artisans, and journalists assemble portfolios that embody their best work. Television and radio announcers compile video- and audio-taped excerpts of their best performances and present these when interviewing for a job. A portfolio is their way of showing what they can really do. You may even develop a portfolio of lesson plans, assignments, and assessments and a video of your teaching for job interviews. This portfolio is your way of showing what you can really do.

Classroom portfolios serve a similar purpose. They show off a learner's best writing, art work, science projects, historical thinking, or mathematical achievements. They also show the steps the learner took to complete a project. Portfolios compile the learner's best work but also include works in progress: the early drafts, test runs, pilot studies, or preliminary trials. Thus, they are an ideal way to assess final mastery, effort, reflection, and growth in learning that tell the learner's "story" of achievement.

The idea of classroom portfolio assessment has gained considerable support and momentum. For example, Figure 10.1 represents an example portfolio assessment form intended for use by teachers in the state of Vermont as a cumulative record of their students' accomplishments over an extended course of study. Many school districts use portfolios and other types of exhibitions such as these to supplement classroom grades. Researchers (Stecher & Herman, 1997) point out that portfolios also have potential for supplementing the information that standardized tests, called **high-stakes assessments**, provide about learners. Nevertheless, some researchers express reservations about the reliability of portfolios for making important decisions about learners related to grade advancement or graduation.

The purpose of portfolio assessment is not to make high-stakes decisions about learners. Rather, it is to motivate effort and show achievement and growth in learning. Although the reliability and validity of a classroom teacher's judgments are always a matter of concern, they are less so when the teacher has multiple opportunities to interact with learners and numerous occasions to observe their work and confirm judgments about their capabilities.

Thus, the purpose of this chapter is to demonstrate the potential of portfolio assessment for accomplishing the learning goals you have for your students. We look first at a rationale for incorporating portfolio assessment into your classroom. Then, we discuss the validity of your portfolio assessments. Finally, we cover how to plan a portfolio assignment including: deciding on the purpose of the portfolio; the outcomes to be assessed; who will plan the portfolio; what products to include; the criteria for assessing the outcomes; the data that need to be collected to document progress, effort, and achievement; the logistics of where the products are kept; and finally, how feedback about the adequacy of the learner's portfolio will be communicated to the student.

Running throughout this chapter is the story of Keith Jefferson, an eighth-grade teacher who decides to incorporate portfolio assessment into his classroom. As you read about the components of portfolio assessment, you can follow his progress as he applies the principles of portfolio assessment to his own classroom.

	A1 Understanding of Task: SOURCES OF EVIDENCE • Explaining of task • Reasonableness of approach • Correctness of response	**A2 How—Quality of Approaches/Procedures** SOURCES OF EVIDENCE • Demonstrations • Descriptions (oral or written) • Drafts, scratch work, etc.	**A3 Why—Decisions Along the Way** SOURCES OF EVIDENCE • Revisions in approach • Explanations (oral or written) • Validation of final solution
Student: _Julia Coe_ Grade: _8_ Date: _4/16_ Rater: _Mrs Hartley_			
Entry 1 Title: _Photosynthesis_ D ⓘ A O Demonstration Investigation Application Other	4 Good oral presentation	2 Graphing procedures not uniform	2 Logical conclusions with supporting data
Entry 2 Title: _Game of chance_ D I Ⓐ O Demonstration Investigation Application Other	3 Practical example	2 Looks some sources from text	4 Shows careful thinking
Entry 3 Title: _____ D I A O Demonstration Investigation Application Other			
Entry 4 Title: _____ D I A O Demonstration Investigation Application Other			
Entry 5 Title: _____ D I A O Demonstration Investigation Application Other			
Overall Ratings ⬆	**A1 Understanding of Task** **Final Rating** ① Totally misunderstood ② Partially understood ③ Understood ④ Generalized, applied, extended	**A2 How—Quality of Approaches/Procedures** **Final Rating** ① Inappropriate or unworkable approach/procedure ② Appropriate approach/procedure some of the time ③ Workable approach/procedure ④ Efficient or sophisticated approach/procedure	**A3 Why—Decisions Along the Way** **Final Rating** ① No evidence of reasoned decision making ② Reasoned decision making possible ③ Reasoned decisions/adjustments inferred with certainty ④ Reasoned decisions/adjustments shown/explicated

Figure 10.1

Example of portfolio assessment form

Source: Adapted from *Looking Beyond "The Answer," the Vermont Mathematics Portfolio, 1992*, report of the Vermont Mathematics Portfolio Assessment Program, publication year 1990–91. Montpelier, VT: Vermont Department of Education.

Act I, Scene 1: Planning for Something New

Mr. Jefferson is about to start his seventh year of teaching eighth-grade honors English. It is August and the last day of a two-week continuing education program for teachers on classroom portfolios. The instructor, Maria Peron, is starting to wrap things up:

> **Ms. Peron:** So the important thing to remember is that you don't decide on Friday to do portfolio assessment and start it on Monday. Portfolio assessment is a philosophy of teaching and learning based on planning.

As Mr. Jefferson leaves the seminar and enters his empty classroom, he is apprehensive. He wants to do something different this year but doubts that he can pull it off. He has a system for teaching writing that took six years to develop and is working well. "If it's not broke, don't fix it," he says to himself. But, as Maria said, and as many teachers like him have done, why not just get started and work things out as they go along—but with a good plan at the start.

Act I, Scene 2: First Day of Class

During the first 15 minutes of class, Mr. Jefferson went over the general rules and routines that he expects his learners to follow. He's now explaining his goals and class requirements:

> **Mr. Jefferson:** My goal this year is to help you to be show-offs, to show you how to "strut your stuff." Ice skaters are show-offs . . . so are painters, track stars, and guitar players. Only in this class you're going to show off your writing. During this grading period, you're going to collect examples of your best stuff and show it off. But you're not showing it off for me. You'll be showing it off to someone else. It may be your parents, a magazine or newspaper editor, a writer you respect, a special high school you want to get into, an employer that you want to work for, or maybe a television producer for whom you want to develop a new program. But the most important purpose of this class is to collect a sample of your best writing that shows what you can do when you really try. We'll call this collection your portfolio. It will be your story, your one-person show, your exhibition of your best stuff.

> **Joan:** But how do we know what goes in it?

> **Mr. Jefferson:** That's mostly up to you to decide. I'll give you some basic requirements. I think it would be a good idea if people see not only your best work but also the effort behind it. So, you'll be putting first drafts and second drafts in your portfolio so that someone can see how much your writing improved.

> **Tyrone:** Like what kind of things do we put in it?

Mr. Jefferson: We'll be learning about a lot of different kinds of writing this year: poetry, essays, writing to persuade someone, criticism, autobiography, short fiction, dialog. You'll select among these types and decide which writing pieces you want to put in your portfolio.

Samantha: How will you grade us?

Mr. Jefferson: Both your parents and I want to know how clearly you write, how well you plan, how flexible you are when revising. My grades will tell how well you do. I'll be explaining how I assign the grades as you begin to design the portfolio. Any other questions? Okay. For the next 20 minutes we'll break into small groups and you'll discuss among yourselves what you want your portfolio to say about you, what you want in your portfolio, and who you want to see it. Each of you will write your personal choices on this form, bring it home tonight, show it to your parents, and discuss your portfolio with them. Return this on Thursday. I've also prepared a handout for you and your parents explaining exactly what a portfolio is and how you will build one.

(Mr. Jefferson quickly organizes the groups, gives them some directions for discussion, and hands out a form to plan the portfolio.)

This scenario illustrates the first steps in portfolio design: deciding (a) the purpose for which the portfolio will be used, (b) what cognitive skills the portfolio will assess, (c) who will plan the portfolio, and (d) what work will go in it. We will discuss each of these considerations in this chapter.

Rationale for Portfolio Assessment

The portfolio's greatest potential is for showing teachers, parents, and learners a richer array of what students know and can do outside of paper-and-pencil tests and other "snapshot" assessments. If designed properly, portfolios can show a learner's ability to think and problem solve, to use cognitive strategies and performance-type skills, and to organize knowledge. In addition, they also can tell something about a learner's persistence, effort, willingness to be flexible, skill in monitoring their own learning, and ability to be self-reflective or metacognitive. So, one purpose for a portfolio is to give a teacher information about a learner that no other measurement tool can provide.

There are still other reasons for using portfolios. They can alter the nature of classroom instruction by changing the relationship between teacher and learner. As was evident in the classroom scenario, Mr. Jefferson was not just making a commitment to teach writing. He was making a commitment to be a coach or mentor. Just as promising young musicians, ice skaters, swimmers, actors, or gymnasts seek to apprentice themselves to masters, likewise, Mr. Jefferson's learners will look to him to help tell their story. He is setting up his classroom to be a "cognitive apprenticeship" (Collins, Brown, & Newman, 1989). In other words, he is giving his students plenty of opportunities to practice and improve their thinking and performance skills, just as an on-the-job apprenticeship would.

Portfolios are also means to communicate to parents and other teachers the level of achievement a learner has reached. Report card grades give us some idea of this. Portfolios supplement grades by showing parents, teachers, and learners the supporting evidence.

Portfolios are not an alternative to objective tests, essay tests, or performance tests. Each of these tools possesses validity for a purpose not served by a different tool. If you want to assess a learner's factual knowledge base, then objective-type tests are appropriate. If you are interested in a snapshot assessment of how well a learner uses a cognitive strategy, a performance assessment might be appropriate. But if you want to assess both achievement and growth over time in an authentic context, portfolios are a tool that you should consider.

Finally, portfolios are a way to motivate learners to higher levels of effort. They provide a seamless link between classroom teaching and assessment in a way that is consistent with recent cognitive theories of learning and instruction. In this text we define portfolio to include the important elements just discussed. A **portfolio assessment** is a planned collection of learner achievement that documents what a student has accomplished and the steps taken to get there. The collection represents a collaborative effort among teacher, learner, and parent to decide on portfolio purpose, content, and evaluation criteria.

Ensuring Portfolio Assessment Validity

As Maria Peron pointed out, portfolio assessment takes planning; otherwise, teachers may end up with a drawer full of manila folders that students give little thought to until they get a grade. When properly designed, portfolios can accomplish many objectives. When carelessly designed, they can be misleading to parents, teachers, and students as to what was accomplished. Because improper planning and careless design reduce the validity of portfolio assessment, issues of validity should be among the first considered when planning a portfolio assessment system. Recall that validity asks the question, "Does your portfolio measure the behaviors you want it to?"

Let's say that one of the goals you have for the portfolio is to assess how well learners can communicate to a variety of audiences. However, you collect only samples of a writing type you would submit to a literary journal. You may want your math portfolio to assess growth in problem-solving ability; yet your evaluation criteria may place too heavy an emphasis on the final solution to the exclusion of the process used to get there. These are some of the pitfalls that can undermine the validity of the portfolio. In general, there are three challenges to validity that you need to address: representativeness, rubrics, and relevance. Let us consider each of these.

Representativeness

The best way to ensure representativeness is to be clear at the outset about the cognitive learning skills and dispositions that you want to assess and to require a variety of products that reflect these. You want to ensure that the samples of writing, stories read, scientific thinking, coloring, mathematical problem solving, or drawing reflect the higher order thinking skills, procedural skills, and dispositions you want the portfolio to measure.

Rubrics

You have already had practice at designing rubrics in the previous chapter. The same considerations for designing clear criteria to assess complex performances or demonstrations also apply to assessing portfolios. You will want criteria for assessing both individual entries and the portfolio as a whole.

Relevance

Assembling the portfolio should not demand abilities of the learner extraneous to the ones you want to assess. A second-grade geography portfolio whose purpose is to reflect skill in map reading and map making should not demand fine motor skills beyond what you would expect a seven-year-old to possess. Likewise, a seventh-grade science portfolio designed to reflect problem solving should not require the reading of scientific journals that are beyond the ability of a seventh grader to understand. Assessments often lack relevance because they require learner skills that are extraneous to those the instrument was built to measure.

Building a System for Portfolio Assessment

Now that we have given some consideration to validity, let's get started on designing a portfolio assessment system for your teaching area. The eight steps illustrated below take you through the process, from deciding on purposes to planning a final portfolio conference with each of your students.

Step 1. Decide on the Purposes

In our scenario Mr. Jefferson wants his learners to think about their purpose in assembling a portfolio. Having learners identify for themselves the purpose of the portfolio is one way to increase the authenticity and ownership of the task. We encourage you to use this as part of your teaching strategy. However, your learners' purposes for the portfolio (e.g., getting a job with the local news station) won't necessarily coincide with yours (e.g., evaluating their learning). Step 1 of the portfolio design process requires you be clear about your purposes at the outset.

Portfolios can achieve many classroom purposes, some of which are

- Monitoring student progress
- Communicating what has been learned to parents

- Passing on information to subsequent teachers
- Evaluating how well something was taught
- Showing off what has been accomplished
- Assigning a grade

There are three major types of portfolios: working portfolios, display or "show" portfolios, and assessment portfolios, parts of which may in practice overlap (Danielson & Abrutyn, 1997). Let us look at how each of them can tell a story of your learners' efforts, progress, and achievements.

Working Portfolios.   Working portfolios represent "works in progress." They serve as a depository for student accomplishments *on the way* to being selected and polished for a more permanent assessment or display portfolio. Working portfolios can be helpful to the teacher in diagnosing student needs by providing evidence of a student's strengths and weaknesses in achieving learning objectives. But the main audience for the working portfolio is the student, who, with guidance from the teacher, learns to focus and reflect on the quantity and quality of their work. This may also involve parents who see the student's progress and offer their own suggestions for additions or changes. From the working portfolio, the student is expected to revise and select their best work for a display and/or assessment portfolio.

Display Portfolio.   A display or show portfolio is where the student selects his or her best works from a working portfolio. From the display portfolio the student, with the aid of the teacher, learns to critically judge his or her works focusing on those qualities that make some works stand above others. These selections should demonstrate the highest level of achievement attained by the student, which can be the result of many prior drafts within the working portfolio. A display portfolio expands throughout the school year with new additions documenting the learner's growth. The display portfolio represents a sense of pride and self-esteem which the student shows off to classmates, friends, older siblings, and parents through a selection of real-world accomplishments, such as works of visual art, poems or stories, dramatic scripts, a list of books read, or experiments/investigations which may be presented in video, audio, digital or "hard copy" format. Display portfolios represent your learners' *best works* which they select.

Assessment Portfolios.   An assessment portfolio may contain all or some of the selections in a display portfolio as well as some of those that began in a working portfolio. Although the purpose of the working portfolio is to develop good products, and the display portfolio to show off, some of the contents of these are often used for the purpose of assessment. The purpose of an assessment portfolio is to document what a student has learned from the school curriculum, often going beyond it to apply and extend in novel ways the principles and concepts taught. The content of the curriculum therefore determines what will be selected from the display portfolio for the purpose of assessment. Although working and even show portfolios may, at the discretion of the teacher, include some accomplishments supplemental to the curriculum, the assessment portfolio has its selections rooted in the curriculum and, hence, provides a demonstration of the extent of mastery of a curricular area. The teacher, therefore, is the primary audience of the assessment portfolio. He will not only use the portfolio as a percentage of grade, but along with school administrators, may help in determining placement in special programs and advanced courses. With suggestions from the student, the teacher selects entries for the assessment portfolio, providing student input into the selection process.

Step 2. Identify Cognitive Skills and Dispositions

Portfolios, like performance assessments, are measures of deep understanding and genuine achievement. They can measure growth and development of competence in cognitive areas such as knowledge construction (e.g., knowledge organization), cognitive strategies (analysis, interpretation, planning, organizing, revising), procedural skills (clear communication, editing, drawing, speaking, building), and metacognition (self-monitoring, self-reflection). They can also provide evidence of certain dispositions—or habits of mind—such as flexibility, adaptability, acceptance of criticism, persistence, collaboration, and desire for mastery. Throughout this text you have had practice in specifying different types of cognitive learning, in identifying aspects of these learning outcomes, and in planning to assess them. Apply this same practice to specifying what you want to know about your learners from their portfolios. As part of your teaching strategy, you will want to discuss these outcomes with your learners. Wolf and Reardon (1996) described a classroom context in which the evaluation criteria were negotiated with students and made a part of the learning process by initiating activities fostering reflection on the criteria at different intervals of their work.

In Box 10.1 we asked Mr. Jefferson to indicate any cognitive strategies, procedural skills, metacognitive behaviors, and any habits of mind (such as flexibility, adaptability, acceptance of criticism, persistence, collaboration, and desire for mastery) he would like to encourage and develop as a result of his portfolio assignment. Using Mr. Jefferson's lesson as a guide, in Application 10.1 indicate the outcomes you would like your learners to acquire from a portfolio assignment.

Step 3. Decide Who Will Plan the Portfolio

The principal stakeholders in the use of the portfolio are you, your learners, and their parents. Therefore, it makes sense that all have a role in planning. Mr. Jefferson handled this issue by having learners identify their goals for the portfolio. He involved parents by sending home an explanation of portfolio assessment. In addition, he asked that parents and students discuss its goals and content.

When deciding who will plan the portfolio, consider what is involved in preparing gymnasts or skaters for a major tournament: The parent hires a coach and the coach, pupil, and parent plan together the routines, costumes, practice times, music, and so forth. They are a team whose sole purpose is to produce the best performance possible. The gymnast or skater wants to be the best that he can be. He also wants to please his parents and coach and meet their expectations. The atmosphere is charged with excitement, dedication, and commitment to genuine effort.

This is the atmosphere you are trying to create when using portfolios. You, the learner, and the parents are engaged in a team effort to help the student improve

---

BOX 10.1   Mr. Jefferson's Cognitive Strategies, Procedural Skills, Metacognitive Behaviors, and Habits of Mind

---

Cognitive Strategies:

I would like my students to acquire the cognitive strategies of being able to identify the appropriate criteria for judging the adequacy of their work and to analyze how much their product does or does not meet these criteria.

Procedural Skills:

I would like my students to learn how to edit their portfolio of work in a visually attractive manner exhibiting the improvements made across drafts of the same product and over time.

Metacognition:

I would like my students to acquire the skill of monitoring the quality of their work and reflecting on their initial drafts and tryouts to improve their writing.

Habits of Mind:

I would like my students to learn to persist in rewriting, even when early drafts are crude and unpolished versions of what the student would like to produce.

---

writing, math reasoning, or scientific thinking, and to assemble examples of this growing competence. Learners want to show what they can do and to verify the trust and confidence that you and their family have placed in them. The portfolio is their recital, their tournament, their competition.

Box 10.2 contains the letter that Mr. Jefferson mailed to the parents of his learners informing them of his plans for a portfolio and eliciting their cooperation. In Application 10.2, write your own letter to parents informing them of the portfolio project you have chosen and asking for their assistance. Tailor your letter to a specific request for help that would be crucial for enhancing the quality of your students' work.

Step 4. Choose Products and Number of Samples

In deciding which products to put in the portfolio, two key issues must be considered: ownership and the portfolio's link with instruction. Ownership refers to your learners' perception that the portfolio contains what they want. You have considered this issue in step 3. By involving learners and their parents in the planning process, you enhance their sense of ownership. You also do this by giving them a say in what goes into the portfolio. The task is to balance your desire to enhance ownership with your responsibilities to see that portfolio content measures the cognitive skills and dispositions identified in step 2. This relates to the second key consideration: the portfolio's link with instruction.

APPLICATION 10.1

Identify a topic for a portfolio assignment and give some examples of the behaviors you want your learners to acquire as a result of their work.

Your portfolio project:

The behaviors you will want your learners to acquire:

Cognitive strategies:

Procedural skills:

Metacognitive behaviors:

Dispositions (habits of mind):

Both learners and their parents need to see that your class instruction focuses on teaching the skills necessary to fashion the portfolio's content. You do not want to require products in math, science, or social studies that you did not prepare learners to create. For a writing portfolio, your instructional goals must include teaching skills in writing letters, essays, dialog, editorials, or whatever your curriculum specifies. The same holds for reading and writing, science, math, geography, or history portfolios. Thus, you will want included in your learners' portfolios only products that you have taught your learners to develop.

The best way to satisfy learner needs for ownership and your need to measure what you teach is to require certain categories of products matching your instructional purposes and cognitive outcomes, and then allow learners and parents to choose the samples within each category. For example, you may require that an eighth-grade math portfolio contains the following categories of math content (Lane, 1993):

1. *Number and operation* in which the learner demonstrates the understanding of the relative magnitude of numbers, the effects of operations on numbers, and the ability to perform those mathematical operations

2. *Estimation,* in which the learner demonstrates understanding of basic facts, place value and operations; mental computation; tolerance of error; and flexible use of strategies

3. *Predictions* in which learners demonstrate abilities to make predictions based on experimental probabilities; to systematically organize and describe data; to make conjectures based on data analyses; and to construct and interpret graphs, charts, and tables.

Learners and their parents can help choose which products to include in each of the categories. For each sample learners would include a brief statement about what the sample says about their development of mathematical thinking skills.

BOX 10.2   Mr. Jefferson's Letter Home

Hello Dear Parent,

I am your child's eighth-grade English teacher. I would like your help with an exciting project we are about to begin in our class. The project will be to have each student during the semester create a portfolio of their writing that they can show to you, me, and their classmates. The examples of writing they may choose to put in their portfolio can include letters, essays, writing to persuade someone, criticism, poetry, autobiography, fiction, and even dramatic scripts. Your son or daughter can choose from among the combinations of writing they would most like to place in their portfolios.

What I would like to ask of you is your assistance in helping your son or daughter revise and edit their writing so that they are the very best that they can be and in selecting which samples of writing are placed in their portfolio. I have found that one of the best ways to become a good writer is to have someone else read what is written and provide suggestions as to what to edit and revise. Your willingness to read what your child writes and to suggest improvements in spelling, grammar, and content would be invaluable in encouraging your child's best work. At the end of the semester we will display everyone's portfolio of writing in the classroom at which time you will be invited to see all of the children's portfolios.

May I ask you to initial each sample of writing that you read to indicate that your son or daughter has sought your assistance in improving their writing sample.

Thank you for your help and I look forward to seeing you at our exhibition of writing skills at the end of the semester.

> **APPLICATION 10.2**
>
> Write a letter to parents describing your plans for a portfolio project and elic-
> iting their cooperation. Be sure to include what you will expect of your learn-
> ers and in what ways you would like them to help.

For a writing portfolio, the teacher might require samples of the following categories of writing: narrative story, creative writing, autobiography, movie or theatrical dialog, and so forth. Learners would choose the writing samples for each
category. For each sample they would include an explanation of why the sample
was chosen for the portfolio.

You will also have to decide how many samples of each content category to include in the portfolio. For example, do you require two samples of a narrative story,
one autobiography, and three of dialog? About five products or tasks covering different topic areas will be needed to obtain a reliable estimate of performance from
portfolios. It would be best for you, rather than students and parents, to select the
appropriate numbers of samples.

Act II, Scene 1: Third Week of Class

Over the weekend Mr. Jefferson reviewed the portfolio plans of each of his learners from the response form he asked each of them to complete. He was pleased
with the results. He had learners and their parents choose 5 categories of writing
from the 10 that would be the focus of class instruction. He also listed on the form
the cognitive skills and dispositions he hoped to develop with the use of portfolios and asked that they identify some of the ways they would try to reach those
goals. He especially liked the reasons given for their choices of categories. Over
the past 2 weeks, his lessons have centered around the qualities of different types
of writing. He returned the forms that each student had completed along with
some suggestions for expanding or changing their individual selections. In Box
10.3, we asked Mr. Jefferson to share with us the portfolio response form he prepared for his students. In Application 10.3, construct a similar form for your portfolio assignment indicating the products and behaviors you want your learners to
acquire.

Here is how Mr. Jefferson followed up with his students:

Mr. Jefferson: On the forms I passed back, I asked you to indicate what you
want in your portfolio and what you want the portfolios to tell about you
as a writer. Joni, share with us some of the things you and your parents said.

BOX 10.3   Mr. Jefferson's Portfolio Response Form

Portfolio Response Form

From among those listed below, check five samples of writing you want to submit for your portfolio.

- ☐ letter to the editor
- ☐ poetry
- ☐ descriptive essay
- ☐ investigative report
- ☐ writing to persuade
- ☐ criticism
- ☐ advertisement
- ☐ autobiography
- ☐ short fiction
- ☐ theatrical or movie dialog

By completing samples of some of the types of writing I have listed above, I would like you to be able to:

1. Identify the correct criteria for judging the adequacy of your work and the degree to which your product meets these criteria.
2. Write increasingly improved drafts of your work.
3. Organize and display your portfolio in a visually attractive manner.

Explain briefly some of the ways you will accomplish these goals.

APPLICATION 10.3

Prepare a set of options to be discussed orally for your learners in the early grades or given as a questionnaire in the higher grades that would elicit their choices for the kinds of products they can include in their portfolios. Be sure to identify options that, while encouraging their engagement in the project, would also accomplish the goals of your curriculum.

Joni: Well, I think it would be cool to work for a newspaper, so I want some descriptive writing in my portfolio. I want the portfolio to show how I can make things interesting to read.

Mr. Jefferson asked several other students to describe their portfolios and then explained the day's lesson.

Mr. Jefferson: For the past two weeks we've been talking about what makes good writing. Now look at your notes and tell me what we said about a good short story. Tobie?

Tobie: Good word choice, imagery, metaphors, and a central idea.

Mr. Jefferson: Good. Today, I want you to get into your groups, take all the characteristics of good writing we have covered, and discuss how you would use these characteristics to judge a piece of writing. I'll be showing you how to put these characteristics in the form of a rating scale to help you judge the quality of your own writing.

Mr. Jefferson gave some examples of the criteria with which he wanted his students to construct their rating scales and started them on the task. It took several days, but by the end of the week each student had constructed a list of criteria for each category of writing selected for their portfolio. His plan was to have students take the criteria home, get their parent's input, and return them. Where needed, he would add to or revise the criteria to better meet the needs of each student and the goals of the curriculum.

Step 5. Determine the Scoring Rubrics

In step 2 you identified the major cognitive strategies, procedural skills, metacognitive behaviors, and dispositions that your portfolio will measure. In step 4 you specified the content categories that your portfolio will contain. Now, you must decide what good, average, and poor performance look like for each entry in the portfolio and the portfolio as a whole. Mr. Jefferson has decided to involve his learners in identifying the criteria by which each portfolio will be judged. He will take final responsibility for developing the criteria by revising or adding to student and parent criteria to best meet the goals of his writing class.

In chapters 8 and 9 you identified the important characteristics of problem-solving strategies and deep understanding that you wanted to teach and measure. You will follow the same process to develop your portfolio rubrics. For each type of sample to be placed into the portfolio, list the cognitive behaviors that are important for creating a good product. Next, construct a rating scale that describes the range of student performance that can occur for each behavior. Figures 10.2 and 10.3 show how Mr. Jefferson did this for the descriptive essay portfolio entry, which included the cognitive and metacognitive behaviors of reflection, use of writing conventions, organization, planning, and revision.

Figures 10.4 and 10.5 show examples from a math portfolio under the content category of problem solving. This teacher wants to measure behaviors pertaining to

Essay Portfolio Rating Form

Student's name: _____

Check one:
_____ First Draft
_____ Second Draft
_____ Final Draft

To be Completed by Student:

1. Date submitted:
2. Briefly explain what this essay says about you.

3. What do you like best about this piece of writing?

4. What do you want to improve on the next draft?

5. If this is your final draft, will you include it in your portfolio? Why or why not?

To be Completed by Teacher (*circle the appropriate rating*):

1. Quality of Reflection
   5   States very clearly what he/she likes most and least about the essay. Goes into much detail about how to improve the work.
   4   States clearly what he/she likes and dislikes about the essay. Gives detail about how to improve the work.
   3   States his/her likes and dislikes but could be clearer. Gives some detail about how the work will be improved.
   2   Is vague about likes and dislikes. Gives few details about how essay will be improved.
   1   No evidence of any reflection on the work.

2. Writing Conventions
   5   The use of writing conventions is very effective. No errors evident. These conventions are fluid and complex: spelling, punctuation, grammar usage, sentence structure.
   4   The use of writing conventions is effective. Only minor errors evident. These conventions are nearly all effective: spelling, punctuation, grammar usage, sentence structure.
   3   The use of writing conventions is somewhat effective. Errors don't interfere with meaning. These conventions are somewhat effective: spelling, punctuation, grammar usage, sentence structure.

(continued)

Figure 10.2
Essay portfolio rating form

> 2   Errors in the use of writing conventions interfere with meaning. These conventions are limited and uneven: spelling, punctuation, grammar usage, sentence structure.
> 1   Major errors in the use of writing conventions obscure meaning. Lacks understanding of spelling, punctuation, grammar usage, sentence structure.
>
> 3. Organization
>   5   Clearly makes sense.
>   4   Makes sense.
>   3   Makes sense for the most part.
>   2   Attempted but does not make sense.
>   1   Does not make sense.
>
> 4. Planning (1st draft only)
>   5   Has clear idea of audience. Goals are very clear and explicit. An overall essay plan is evident.
>   4   Has idea of audience. Goals are clear and explicit. Has a plan for the essay.
>   3   Somewhat clear about the essay's audience. Goals are stated but somewhat vague. Plan for whole essay somewhat clear.
>   2   Vague about who the essay is for. Goals are unclear. No clear plan evident.
>   1   Writing shows no evidence of planning.
>
> 5. Quality of Revision (2nd draft only)
>   5   Follows up on all suggestions for revision. Revisions are a definite improvement.
>   4   Follows up on most suggestions for revision. Revisions improve on the previous draft.
>   3   Addresses some but not all suggested revisions. Revisions are a slight improvement over earlier draft.
>   2   Ignores most suggestions for revision. Revisions made do not improve the earlier draft.
>   1   Made minimal or no attempt to revise.
>
> SUM OF RATINGS: _____   AVERAGE OF RATINGS: _____
> Comments:

Figure 10.2
(*continued*)

knowledge base, cognitive strategies, communication, and reflection. Once you design rubrics for each entry in the portfolio, you design scoring criteria for the portfolio as a whole product. Some traits to consider when developing a scoring mechanism for the entire portfolio are thoroughness, variety, growth or progress, overall quality, self-reflection, flexibility, organization, and appearance. You can choose among these traits and include others to build a rating scale for assessing the portfolio as a whole.

Essay Summative Rating Form

(Attach to each completed essay.)

Student's name: _____

Check one:
_____ Sample One
_____ Sample Two
_____ Final Sample

Draft 1		*Draft 2*		*Final Draft*	
Criteria	**Rating**	**Criteria**	**Rating**	**Criteria**	**Rating**
Reflection	3	Reflection	4	Reflection	3
Conventions	3	Conventions	4	Conventions	4
Organization	4	Organization	5	Organization	5
Planning	4	Revision	4	Revision	3
AVERAGE	3.5	AVERAGE	4.25	AVERAGE	3.75

Teacher comments on final essay development:

Student comments on final essay development:

Parent comments on final essay development:

Included in portfolio: _____ Yes _____ No

Figure 10.3
Essay summative rating form

In summary, to prepare the scoring rubrics, you must do the following:

1. Identify each behavior you want to assess (cognitive strategies, procedural skills, metacognitive behaviors, and dispositions) for each type of product to be placed in the portfolio.
2. Arrange these behaviors on a form that allows you to numerically rate early drafts and the final product.
3. Prepare a rating for the portfolio as a whole.

For Application 10.4, practice preparing a rubric for one of the products in your portfolio and another for rating the portfolio as a whole.

Step 6. Aggregate All Portfolio Ratings

For each content category you include in the portfolio, learners should receive a score for each draft and the final product. You will have to decide how to aggregate these scores into a final score or grade for each content area and, then, the portfo-

---

Math Problem Solving Portfolio Rating Form

Student's name: _____   *Check one:*
                                                  _____ Sample One
                                                  _____ Sample Two
                                                  _____ Final Sample

To Be Completed by Student:

1. Date submitted:
2. What does this problem say about you as a problem solver?

3. What do you like best about how you solved this problem?

4. How will you improve your problem-solving skill on the next problem?

To Be Completed by Teacher (*circle the appropriate rating*):

1. Quality of Reflection
   5   Has excellent insight into his/her problem-solving abilities and clear ideas
          of how to get better.
   4   Has good insight into his/her problem-solving abilities and some ideas of
          how to get better.
   3   Reflects somewhat on problem-solving strengths and needs. Has some
          idea of how to improve as a problem solver.
   2   Seldom reflects on problem-solving strengths and needs. Has little idea of
          how to improve as a problem solver.
   1   Has no concept of him/herself as a problem solver.

2. Mathematical Knowledge
   5   Shows deep understanding of the problems, math concepts, and princi-
          ples. Uses appropriate math terms, and all calculations are correct.
   4   Shows good understanding of math problems, concepts, and principles.
          Uses appropriate math terms most of the time. Few computational
          errors.
   3   Shows understanding of some of the problems, math concepts, and princi-
          ples. Uses some terms incorrectly. Contains some computation errors.
   2   Errors in the use of many problems. Many terms used incorrectly.
   1   Major errors in problems. Shows no understanding of math problems, con-
          cepts, and principles.
                                                          (*continued*)

Figure 10.4
Math problem solving portfolio rating form

3. Strategic Knowledge

    5   Identifies all the important elements of the problem. Reflects an appropriate and systematic strategy for solving the problem; gives clear evidence of a solution process.

    4   Identifies most of the important elements of the problem. Reflects an appropriate and systematic strategy for solving the problem and gives clear evidence of a solution process most of the time.

    3   Identifies some important elements of the problem. Gives some evidence of a strategy to solve the problems, but process is incomplete.

    2   Identifies few important elements of the problem. Gives little evidence of a strategy to solve the problems, and the process is unknown.

    1   Uses irrelevant outside information. Copies parts of the problem; no attempt at solution.

4. Communication

    5   Gives a complete response with a clear, unambiguous explanation; includes diagrams and charts when they help clarify explanation; presents strong arguments that are logically developed.

    4   Gives good response with fairly clear explanation, which includes some use of diagrams and charts; presents good arguments that are mostly but not always logically developed.

    3   Explanations and descriptions of problem solution are somewhat clear but incomplete; makes some use of diagrams and examples to clarify points, but arguments are incomplete.

    2   Explanations and descriptions of problem solution are weak; makes little, if any, use of diagrams and examples to clarify points; arguments are seriously flawed.

    1   Ineffective communication; diagrams misrepresent the problem; arguments have no sound premise.

SUM OF RATINGS: _____

AVERAGE OF RATINGS: _____

Comments:

Figure 10.4
(*continued*)

lio as a whole. Figures 10.3 and 10.5 were examples of a summative rating form in two content areas (essay and math). You should have a summative rating form for each portfolio submission identified in step 4. Thus, if you want a writing portfolio to include five areas of content (persuasive writing, dialog, autobiography, criticism, essay), you should have five summative rating forms, each of which rates drafts and final product.

In Figures 10.2 and 10.4, notice that the teacher averaged the ratings for the two preliminary drafts or problems and the final one. The next step is to develop a procedure for combining these three scores into an overall score. One procedure would

Math Problem Solving Summative Rating Form

(Attach to problem-solving entries.)

Student's name: _____

Check one:
_____ Sample One
_____ Sample Two
_____ Final Sample

Problem 1		*Problem 2*		*Final Problem*	
Criteria	Rating	Criteria	Rating	Criteria	Rating
Reflection	3	Reflection	4	Reflection	3
Knowledge	2	Knowledge	3	Knowledge	3
Strategies	2	Strategies	2	Strategies	2
Communication	2	Communication	2	Communication	2
AVERAGE	2.25	AVERAGE	2.75	AVERAGE	2.5

Teacher comments on problem-solving ability and improvement:

Student comments on problem-solving ability and improvement:

Parent comments on problem-solving ability and improvement:

Figure 10.5
Math problem solving summative rating form

APPLICATION 10.4

Complete a rubric for one of the products in your portfolio and another for the portfolio as a whole, by (a) choosing among a rating scale, checklist, or combination of the two, (b) selecting the number of numerical points (e.g., 3-, 5-, or 7-point scale) you will have on your scales, and (c) labeling the scale with descriptions that indicate the degrees of behavior that anchor each point on the scale.

Rubric for a product within the portfolio:

Rubric for the whole portfolio:

be to compute a simple average of three scores. This method gives equal importance in the final score to the drafts and final product.

Another procedure would be to assign greatest importance to the final product, lesser importance to the second draft, and least importance to the first draft. This procedure is called weighting. If and how you weight scores is up to you. You might seek input from learners and parents, but there are no hard and fast rules. Here are some simple guidelines to follow should you decide to assign different weights to the products in a content area:

1. Decide on the weight in terms of a percentage; for example, first draft counts 20 percent, second draft counts 30 percent, final draft counts 50 percent of final score. Make sure the percentages add up to 100 percent.

2. Take the average score for each product and multiply that by the weight. For the rating scale shown in Figure 10.3, this would involve the following calculations:

$$\begin{array}{lll} \text{Draft 1:} & 3.50 \times 0.20 = 0.7 \\ \text{Draft 2:} & 4.25 \times 0.30 = 1.3 \\ \text{Final:} & 3.75 \times 0.50 = 1.9 \end{array}$$

3. Add up these products (0.7 + 1.3 + 1.9) to an overall score (3.9) for the content area (essay writing). We will consider the meaning of this value shortly.

Follow this same procedure for each content area. If you have five content areas in the portfolio, each measured on a 5-point scale, you will have five scores. For example:

Content Area	Score
Essay	3.9
Dialog	4.0
Criticism	4.0
Autobiography	3.8
Persuasion	3.8

The next step is to decide how to aggregate these scores. Again, you can choose to weight or not to weight. You may decide to involve learners and their parents in this decision. For example, for the above areas the unweighted average is 3.9.

Finally, assign a rating to the portfolio as a whole. Let's say that the rating came out to be a 4.5. Now you must decide how to include this rating in the overall portfolio grade. If you take an unweighted average, you assign as much importance to that one rating as you did all the separate content ratings. That is probably not a good idea. Your average grade for the content areas taken separately is a more reliable rating than your one rating for the whole portfolio. So, we recommend that you assign more weight to the former score than the latter—perhaps 90 percent versus 10 percent.

$$3.9 \times 0.90 = 3.51$$

$$4.5 \times 0.10 = 0.45$$

$$\text{Final Grade} = 3.51 + 0.45 = 3.96$$

(versus 4.2 had you not weighted)

Now, let us consider what 3.96 (or 4.0 rounded) means in terms of the quality of the overall portfolio The value 4.0 is a measurement. It is a number that reflects the performance of the learner. But how good is a 4.0 in indicating the competence of the learner? Making this decision involves valuing.

Here is one way to assign meaning or add value to our measurement of 4.0. Schools usually assign the following values to grades:

Grading Schemes			Descriptors	
90–100	A	E	Outstanding	Excellent
80–89	B	S+	Above average	Satisfactory plus
70–79	C	S	Average	Satisfactory
60–69	D	S−	Below average	Satisfactory minus
Below 60	F	N	Unsatisfactory	Needs improvement

When using 5-point rating scales, 3 is considered as average, 1 as below standard, and 5 as outstanding. Similarly, with a 7-point scale, 3.5 is average, ratings between 1 and 2 are below standard, and ratings between 6 and 7 are above standard. So, one way to assign value to a 4.0 would be to link the traditional grading systems and their conventional meanings to scores on the rating scale. Pick a range of rating scale values corresponding to a letter or numerical grade in your school and link the two:

Average Rating	Grade	
1.0–1.9	F	50–59
2.0–2.5	D	60–69
2.6–3.6	C	70–79
3.6–4.3	B	80–89
4.4–5.0	A	90–100

If we use the above chart, a 4.0 would represent a grade of B, a numerical grade somewhere between 80 and 89, or a grade of Satisfactory plus (+). You may want to add pluses and minuses to your grading system, or you may decide that a B gets a grade of 85, B- gets a grade of 80, and B+ a grade of 89. Making these decisions before you begin grading the portfolios and evaluating each portfolio using the same criteria helps minimize subjectivity.

Now try your hand at planning a system for aggregating all your portfolio ratings in Application 10.5.

APPLICATION 10.5

Describe the procedure you will use to aggregate all portfolio ratings and to assign grades to the completed portfolio. Decide how you would weight (a) drafts, (b) content area products, and (c) the overall portfolio.

Drafts:

Content area products:

Overall portfolio:

Now, show how you will link the overall portfolio score with either a school's letter grade or numerical grading scheme.

Act III, Scene 1: Fifth Week of Class

During the past week Mr. Jefferson held individual conferences with each student and finalized the grading scheme. His plan for this week is to tie up some loose ends.

Mr. Jefferson: We have to decide when you turn in the work. Look at the class syllabus you got the first week of class and see the order in which you'll be learning the different writing styles. First is persuasive writing, which we already started, then editorials, and so forth. So let's take persuasive writing first, and let's write in the dates when the drafts and the final work are due.

Abebe: How do we know when we'll get them back so we can revise?

Mr. Jefferson: Good question. You'll get them back after three class days. Okay? You'll need to get the first draft of your first sample of persuasive writing in by October 21. Write this date down next to persuasive writing on the Portfolio Response Form you completed earlier. Any more questions?

Step 7. Determine the Logistics

Thus far, you have accomplished these aspects of portfolio design: (a) specified the purpose of the portfolio, (b) identified the cognitive and metacognitive behaviors it will reflect, (c) decided who will help plan it, (d) decided what and how many products go in it, (e) specified the rubrics by which to score it, and (f) developed a rating and grading scheme. Now is the time to work out a few logistical details.

What Are the Timelines?   Your learners and their parents need to know exact dates when assignments are due. It is helpful to link these dates with your syllabus, as Mr. Jefferson did and to point this out to your learners. This reinforces in your learners' minds the link between your teaching and what is required in the portfolio. Be prepared to revise some of your requirements. You may find that there is not enough hours in a week for you to read all the drafts and products and get them back to your learners in a timely fashion.

How Are Products Turned In and Returned?   Decide how you want your learners to turn in their products. At the start of class? Placed in an "In" basket? Secured in a folder or binder? You must also determine how you will return products. In an "Out" basket? How will late assignments be handled? How will absent learners submit and get back assignments? Will there be penalties for late assignments?

Where Are Final Products Kept?   Decide where the final products will be stored. Will it be the learner's responsibility to keep them safely at home? Do you want to store products so they can be assembled easily for a final parent conference and passed on to other teachers? Remember that the products may include video- or audiotapes, so a manila folder might not work. You may need boxes, filing cabinets, or closet space.

Who Has Access to the Portfolio?   Certainly you, the learner, and parents have a right to see what is in a portfolio. But do other students, current and future teachers, administrators? You might want learners (and their parents) to help make these decisions because it is their portfolio and their story.

How Will You Provide Feedback for Improvement to the Learner?   Although you have rated, scored, and given a grade to each student's portfolio, you should also communicate what the learner can do to improve her portfolio and learn from her mistakes. For example Wilson, Draney, and Kennedy (2001) suggested that you include with rubrics suggestions that provide explicit feedback to the learners as to how they can improve a given product. In one such example they rated each product as "Advanced," "Correct," "Incomplete," "Incorrect," and "Off Task" using a 4- to 0-point scale and then provided instruction for improvement specifically tailored to the numerical rating received, as shown in Figure 10.6.

Notice that each set of suggestions to improve provided in Figure 10.6 corresponds with the specific rating given, marked with an asterisk. To avoid having to write all your improvement suggestions by hand for each student and concept rated, you could create multiple copies of your suggestions and simply distribute the proper combination to individual students. Whether feedback is written or given orally to younger learners, your suggestions for improvement can be the most valuable asset your learners receive from this portfolio assignment.

Step 8. Plan a Conference

Plan to have a conference with individual learners and, if possible, with their parents, perhaps as part of a Parent–Teachers Night, to discuss the portfolio and what it says about your learner's development and final achievement. This final event can

Name: Brown, Amy

		To Improve Your Performance, You Can				
Designing and Conducting Investigations	❑ 4 Advanced ❑ 3 Correct ☑ 2 Incomplete ❑ 1 Incorrect ❑ 0 Off Task	Think about the limits of your investigations	Identify possible alternative procedures	Think of new data displays	Explain any unexpected results	Think about additional investigations you could do
Evidence and Tradeoffs	❑ 4 Advanced ❑ 3 Correct ❑ 2 Incomplete ❑ 1 Incorrect ☑ 0 Off Task	Be sure to include all major reasons for your choice	Make sure you find all of the important evidence	Make sure you've described at least two complete and accurate perspectives		
Understanding Concepts	❑ 4 Advanced ☑ 3 Correct ❑ 2 Incomplete ❑ 1 Incorrect ❑ 0 Off Task	Think about other ways you could use the scientific information	Think about other scientific information that might be helpful	Think about possible limitations of the scientific information provided		
Communicating Scientific Information	❑ 4 Advanced ☑ 3 Correct ❑ 2 Incomplete ❑ 1 Incorrect ❑ 0 Off Task	Think of creative things you could add to your work to make it stand out, such as extra charts or pictures that are not required, use of color in graphs and charts, special labels, and so on				

Figure 10.6

An example portfolio rubric with feedback to the learner

Source: Adapted from Wilson, M., Draney, K., and Kennedy, C. (2001). GradeMap [computer program]. Berkeley, CA: BEAR Center, University of California.

be a highly motivating force for your learners to produce an exemplary portfolio. Figure 10.7 is a checklist and summary that will help remind you of all of the important considerations for designing a portfolio project.

Portfolio Development Checklist

1. What purpose(s) will your portfolio serve? (*Check any that apply.*)
   - ❑ Prepare a sample of best work for future teachers to see
   - ❑ Communicate to parents what's been learned
   - ❑ Evaluate my teaching
   - ❑ Assign course grades
   - ❑ Create collections of favorite or best work
   - ❑ Document achievement for alternative credit
   - ❑ Submission to a college or employer
   - ❑ To show growth in skill and dispositions
   - ❑ Other (*specify*): _____

2. What cognitive skills will be assessed by the individual entries? (*Specify skills.*)
   - ❑ Cognitive strategies: _____
   - ❑ Deep understanding: _____
   - ❑ Communication: _____
   - ❑ Metacognition: _____
   - ❑ Procedural skills: _____
   - ❑ Knowledge construction: _____
   - ❑ Other (*specify*): _____

(continued)

Figure 10.7

Portfolio development checklist

3. What dispositions do you want the entries to reflect?
   - ❑ Flexibility
   - ❑ Persistence
   - ❑ Acceptance of feedback
   - ❑ Others (*specify*) _____
4. What criteria or rubrics will you use to judge the extent to which these skills and dispositions were achieved?

5. In rating the portfolio as a whole, what things will you look for?
   - ❑ Variety of entries
   - ❑ Organization
   - ❑ Presentation
   - ❑ Growth in reflection
   - ❑ Growth in skill or performance
6. What kind of scale will you construct to rate the overall portfolio?

7. How will you combine all your ratings into a final grade?

8. Who will be involved in the planning process?
   - ❑ Learners
   - ❑ Teacher
   - ❑ Parents
9. What content categories are included in the portfolio?

10. Will learners have choice over content categories?
    - ❑ Yes
    - ❑ No
11. Who decides what samples to include in each content area?
    - ❑ Learner
    - ❑ Teacher
    - ❑ Parents
12. How many samples will be included in each area?
    - ❑ One
    - ❑ Two
    - ❑ More than two
13. Have you specified deadlines for the entries?
    - ❑ Yes
    - ❑ No
14. Have you developed forms to rate and summarize ratings for all drafts and final products?
    - ❑ Yes (*specify*): _____
    - ❑ No
15. What are your instructions for how work gets turned in and returned?

16. Where will the portfolios be kept and who has access to them?
    - ❑ Where (*specify*): _____
    - ❑ Who (*specify*): _____
17. Who will plan, conduct, and attend the final conference?
    - ❑ Learner
    - ❑ Other teachers
    - ❑ Parents
    - ❑ Others (*specify*): _____

Figure 10.7
(*continued*)

Summary

Portfolios are a means of communicating to parents, learners, and other teachers the level of authentic learning and performance that a learner has achieved. By utilizing actual tasks—projects, scripts, essays, research reports, demonstrations, models, and so forth—the learner applies knowledge to exhibit the level of deep understanding that has been acquired from your instruction. Portfolio assessment is often the best method for gauging your learners' levels of deep understanding. But planning and designing a portfolio assessment must be as systematic and methodical as constructing an objective test or essay exam. Each cognitive skill and disposition, in each content area, must be identified and assigned a scoring rubric. This chapter showed you how to select the purpose of your portfolio, the cognitive and metacognitive behaviors and dispositions it will measure, the criteria by which you will judge degrees of proficiency, and the scoring rubrics by which you will rate and quantify your judgments.

Activities

Review the lesson contexts and examples at the end of this chapter. For this chapter these lesson contexts and examples illustrate learner portfolios. Review them as a guide for completing the activities below.

1. Identify three threats to the validity of a portfolio and indicate what you would do to minimize these threats.
2. Plan a real portfolio by answering each of the questions on the Portfolio Development Checklist (Figure 10.7). Check the boxes that apply and provide the necessary details where requested.
3. Develop a portfolio rating form and summative rating form for the entries in your portfolio, using Figures 10.2 and 10.3 as a guide. Be sure to include definitions for all the scale alternatives (e.g., 1 to 5), as illustrated in Figure 10.2.
4. Describe the procedure you will use to aggregate scores for all the portfolio ratings. By providing hypothetical ratings for the entries on your rating form, indicate with actual numbers and averages, how you will (a) calculate weights, (b) take the average score for each entry, (c) add up all the entries to get an overall score, and (d) assign a grade symbol (e.g., A–F) to the average score.
5. Using the lesson contexts and examples at the end of this chapter as a guide, create three portfolio projects of your own.

Suggested Readings

Danielson, D., & Abrutyn, L. (1997). *Introduction to using portfolios in the classroom.* Alexandria, VA: ASCD.

This practical guide provides a useful resource for educators who would like to begin using portfolios in the classroom. In a concise format, the authors examine the many uses of portfolios and offer guidance on strategies to increase the effectiveness of your portfolio assessment.

Marzano, R. J., Pickering, D., & McTighe, J. (1993). *Assessing student outcomes.* Alexandria, VA: ASCD.

This book provides an exceptionally thorough treatment of the dimensions of learning that portfolios can assess and presents numerous examples of scoring rubrics.

Lesson Contexts

K–2 EXAMPLE LESSON CONTEXTS FOR ASSESSING PORTFOLIOS

Grade	Subject	Topic	Assessment Questions
K–2	Language Arts	Reading comprehension	Look through the cartoons you have drawn to show the most important events in stories we have read or listened to this school year. Choose two from the beginning of the year, two from the middle of the year, and two from the end of the school year. Be able to tell what similarities there are in these events and what patterns you can see.
		Writing skills	Keep a handwriting sample from each month of the school year. In what ways has your handwriting or printing improved? What do you think you still need to work on? Talk with your parents to get their opinions, too.
K–2	Mathematics	Underlying processes	Once a week write down or draw a picture of a way you have used math in your everyday life. It might be counting money, dividing blocks or toys, or helping measure amounts for cooking, and so forth. Be able to tell what skills you have used.
		Number, operation, and quantitative reasoning	Keep samples of your homework papers from each week in school. Make corrections to your mistakes and create more practice problems like those you missed. Share your work with your parents; perhaps they may wish to help you if you get stuck.
K–2	Science	Science concepts	Complete a journal entry every time the class goes on a nature walk or field trip. Record your observations and draw pictures of what you have seen. How were these experiences different from learning in the classroom?
			Choose a favorite plant or animal. Draw or collect pictures of them. Maybe you want to collect the specimens themselves, such as leaves, flowers, or certain types of insects, and dry them or mount them. Write down (or dictate to your parent) all the similarities and differences you can see among your specimens.
K–2	Social Studies	History	Let your teacher help you to locate a pen pal in another state or country. Keep a copy of all the letters you exchange with each other. Try to find out as much as you can about them and where they live. Be able to tell us or write down what you have learned from each other.
		Geography	Keep samples of maps you have made from the beginning, middle, and end of the school year. In what ways have your maps improved? What is the hardest part of drawing a good map? What does a map tell you that oral or written description does not?
K–2	Health	Health behaviors	Keep a journal for one month and write down a health tip for each day. You may wish to make your own illustrations.
		Health behaviors	Keep a food diary of what you eat each day for several weeks. Talk to your parents about which foods are the most healthy choices and what better choices you can make for those that are not so good.

GRADES 3–5 EXAMPLE LESSON CONTEXTS FOR ASSESSING PORTFOLIOS

Grade	Subject	Topic	Assessment Questions
3–5	Language Arts	Writing skills	Assemble all of your daily warmups. Choose the best example from the beginning of the year, the middle of the year, and the end of the year. Edit and proofread for spelling and complete sentences. Improve vocabulary choices and copy over in your best writing. Put them in the front of the folder.
		Reading	Create a reading journal recording your daily silent reading material. Write down the author, the title of the book, chapter, or article, and the pages read. Include a three sentence summary for each entry.
3–5	Mathematics	Geometry	Choose a geometric shape, such as a circle, rectangle, or square. Clip pictures from magazines that show that shape in real life. What important traits does your geometric shape have that help make it useful?
		Number, operation, and quantitative reasoning	Clip advertisements that use decimals, fractions, or percentages. Draw a graph to represent each of these numbers.
3–5	Science	Scientific processes	Examine ten things with a microscope. Draw what your object looked like to the naked eye and under magnification. Describe the differences in a sentence or two.
		Scientific processes	Keep a notebook to record field trips and simple classroom experiments. Include important details and drawings.
3–5	Social Studies	Culture	Describe the special customs, food, and celebration for a favorite holiday. Ask an adult to explain the history behind these practices. Include drawings and recipes.
		History	Select a favorite period of history and pretend that you have been transported to it. Write a daily journal covering two weeks of your life. Be careful not to include anything that didn't exist back then. Or you can go forward in time and do the same thing.
3–5	Health	Health information	Take everything we have learned in our safety unit and create a manual for home and school. Illustrate with pictures and your own slogans.
		Health behaviors	Select a goal to improve your health, such as cutting down on sweets, or getting more exercise. Write down how you plan to achieve this goal and record your efforts and progress in a health diary for six weeks.

GRADES 6–8 EXAMPLE LESSON CONTEXTS FOR ASSESSING PORTFOLIOS

Grade	Subject	Topic	Assessment Questions
6–8	Language Arts	Vocabulary development	Create a personal dictionary portfolio. From your class or outline reading find five words a week that you do not know. (a) Write down the sentence that contains the *word*. (b) Make a guess definition by using the context and word structure. (c) Look up the word in the dictionary and write down the correct definition. (d) Write down the correct pronunciation as shown in the dictionary. Continue throughout the year.
		Writing process	Choose your favorite type of writing—poetry, essay, letter to the editor, or journal entry. Show us several examples throughout the year. Be sure to include brainstorming, drafts, and revisions, as well as the final products. How has your writing changed and improved throughout the year? What areas do you think still need to improve?
6–8	Mathematics	Mathematical thinking	Display several ways you can present data, selecting your most precise graphs, tables, charts, and equations. What are the advantages and shortcomings of each?
		Underlying processes and mathematical tools	Collect examples from other subject areas, such as art, science, or social studies, where you utilize mathematical skills or reasoning.
6–8	Science	Science concepts	Choose an area of interest in nature that changes seasonally, such as the climate, a plant, an animal, or the nighttime skies. Use a systematic method to observe, record, and measure changes regularly throughout the year.
		Science concepts	Choose a physical force, such as heat, cold, wind, water movement, or gravity. Make notations throughout a 6-week period of some common effects of this force. Can you find evidence of long-term as well as short-term effects?
6–8	Social Studies	History	Yesterday's events are tomorrow's history. Read the newspaper once a week and pick out a story that you think will have some impact on history. Clip it out and explain your reasoning in a sentence or two. At the end of the year, choose the top 10 events of the year.
		History	Choose an explorer we have studied this year. Take what you have learned about his or her life and adventures and create a diary he or she might have written during the most difficult period of his journey.
6–8	Health	Health information	Collect the labels from five similar food choices, such as breakfast cereals, frozen dinners, snack items, desserts, or beverages. Using your knowledge of healthy dietary guidelines, select the healthiest choices. Explain your reasoning as well as the problems with the less healthy choices.
		Influencing behaviors	Become a TV critic. Choose five popular television programs and evaluate them for 6 weeks in terms of the personal/interpersonal skills they model. For example, which ones demonstrate healthy ways to deal with stress, peer pressure, or family problems?

TEMPLATE OF YOUR LESSON CONTEXTS FOR ASSESSING PORTFOLIO ACHIEVEMENT

Grade	Subject	Topic	Assessment Questions

11

Understanding and Interpreting Standardized Assessments

In this chapter we explain what standardized tests are and how they can be used alongside classroom assessments to monitor student performance, guide instructional decisions, and identify learning problems. We will first explain how the data from standardized tests are interpreted. Then, we will present an approach for assessing learning which combines information from standardized tests with information from classroom assessments. We will show you how the information from standardized tests can be used with your classroom assessments to help guide the instructional decisions you must make. We conclude this chapter with some ways you can help your students perform better on standardized tests. Before we consider these issues, however, let us build on what we learned about standardized tests from chapter 3.

Standardized Tests and Standardized Test Data

You are already familiar with standardized tests because you have taken them throughout your academic career. The principal characteristics of standardized achievement tests are that they:

1. Typically focus on general skills and content that are part of the educational objectives of school districts across the country

2. Are ordinarily administered annually to large groups of students or on demand when learning problem referrals are made for individual students

3. Are administered according to strict guidelines so that there is no variation from examiner to examiner in how directions are given or questions are scored

4. Usually have strict time limits

5. Yield scores that are interpreted in a norm-referenced manner, that is, in comparison with other learners

When social psychologists use the term "norm," they refer to a group standard of conduct that governs how the members of the group behave. Group norms give people information about how they should speak and act in a multitude of group settings, for example, what they should wear, where they should sit at a wedding, how they should cut their hair.

When used in assessment, **norm-referenced** refers to comparison with the average group performance on a test. If the class average on a spelling test was 83, and you received a 92, a norm-referenced interpretation would be, "You scored above average." With this interpretation, you know little about how much you know or how expert you are in the subject on which you have been tested. But you do know that you did better than average.

Norm-referenced interpretations of learner performance occur routinely when standardized tests are used. A student who scores at the 56th percentile is someone who did better than 56 percent of those who took the test. We do not know the degree of mastery of math or reading achieved by a learner who scores at the 56th percentile. We know only that performance is slightly above average.

Although all standardized tests are norm referenced, not all norm-referenced tests are standardized. Teachers, for example, sometimes make norm-referenced interpretations from their own teacher-made tests which have not been linked to the performance of any larger group. They do this when they compute each student's score for a test, rank scores from highest to lowest, and assign a grade based on where a student ranks in the class. When a teacher assigns a grade of C to the middle 50 percent of the group, she is giving a norm-referenced interpretation of student performance. Students who receive norm-referenced grades know where they stand relative to others in the class but may not know how competent they are in solving algebra problems or writing essays. One result of norm-referenced grading practices is that they tend to foster a competitive orientation to school learning. They may also mask degrees of mastery or improvement of specific domains of knowledge, skills, and competencies, because they represent an *average* performance over many specific skills.

In chapter 3 (Figure 3.1) you saw a distribution of grades using a norm-referenced interpretation of learner performance which took the form of a bell-shaped curve. From that curve you learned that only so many students could attain an A, B, C, and so forth, and that there will be fewer As than Bs and fewer Bs than Cs. In a standardized test, such as that given by your school district at the end of the school year, items are purposely chosen and revised to produce this bell-shaped distribution of scores where students compete with each other for the highest scores. Standardization and norms, however, are what make this type of test different from a classroom test that is "graded on the curve."

Standardization involves administering the test to all persons in a defined group in the same way under the same conditions. The group of individuals upon whom the test is standardized is called the **norm group**. Although you may choose at times to grade students relative to how others in your class perform, you will not create a standardized test. You will, however, need to know what standardized test scores mean and how to interpret them to students and parents. The following will help you become knowledgeable about what a standardized test score can and cannot tell you about your learners' achievement.

Let us see how the concepts of standardization and norms apply to Jarad, a learner in the fourth grade. Jarad is not doing well in math computation for the first marking period. You ask your school psychologist to consult Jarad's scores on a standardized achievement test to see what the problem is. The school psychologist looks at Jarad's standardized test results at the end of the third grade as shown in Figure 11.1. The conversation goes something like this:

Teacher: Well, how did Jarad do?

Psychologist: He scored at the 72nd percentile on the math computation test.

Teacher: Is that good or bad?

Psychologist: Good.

Teacher: You mean he got 72 percent of the questions right?

Psychologist: No. It's not like a spelling test. A percentile only makes sense when you compare it with how others did. And his performance in math in comparison with others is good.

Teacher: How good?

Psychologist: 72 percent of all the learners who took the math computation test scored lower than Jarad. And, he scored at the 66th percentile for math concepts and estimation, at the 59th percentile for problem solving and data interpretation, and at the 59th percentile for math total.

Teacher: Who else took the test?

Psychologist: I compared his score with a national group of learners that was made up of learners like Jarad.

Teacher: How intelligent is Jarad?

Psychologist: I don't know. But his score on this test, which measures how much he has achieved in math through the third grade, indicates that he did as well or better than most learners at that grade.

Teacher: Is there cause for concern?

Psychologist: Not about what his standardized test scores tell us. You'll have to look elsewhere for an answer to his poor work in math.

From this conversation we see that norms, established during the standardization process, allowed the psychologist to compare Jared's score with the scores of others like him. To determine how well Jared did in math computation compared to others, the psychologist consulted the norms under **B** for the entry titled "Computation" in Figure 11.1. There you will find under the column titled NPR (for National Percentile Rank), Jarad's percentile rank of 72, telling us that 72 percent of the

PERFORMANCE PROFILE FOR JARAD NICOLES
Iowa Tests of Basic Skills® (ITBS®)

THE IOWA TESTS

Student ID: 0000157073
Form/Level: A/9
Test Date: 04/2002
Norms: Spring 2000
Order No.: 002-A7000028-0-002
Page: 1   Grade: 3

Student: Jarad Nicoles
Class/Group: Ness
Building: Longfellow
System: Dalen Community

In the upper left part of this report, scores are printed for the tests, totals, and, if available, the composite. Several types of scores are reported, including the national percentile rank (NPR), which is the percentage of students in the nation with a lower score on that test, total or composite.

The display to the right of the scores provides a visual display of the student's performance on each test relative to the other test areas. The NPRs for tests, totals and the Core Total, the Composite, or the Survey Total, are displayed as horizontal bars. The varying lengths of these bars permit identification of the student's stronger and weaker areas of achievement.

The lower part of the report provides detailed information about skills in each test. The number of items for each skill, the number attempted, the percentage correct for the student, and the percentage correct for students in the nation are reported. The difference between the student's percentage correct and the percentage correct for students in the nation is displayed as a horizontal bar. These bars permit identification of skills that stand out as high or low when compared with students in the nation.

SS = Standard Score   GE = Grade Equivalent   NPR = National Percentile Rank

* Math Computation not included in Totals or Composite

B / C

TESTS	SS	GE	NS	NCE	NPR	PERCENTILE RANK (Low 1 – 25 – 50 – 75 – High 99)
Vocabulary	172	3.0	4	40	31	
Reading Comprehension	198	4.6	6	62	71	
Reading Total	**185**	**3.8**	**5**	**50**	**50**	
Word Analysis	172	3.0	4	40	31	
Listening	196	4.6	6	62	71	
Spelling	183	3.6	5	49	48	
Capitalization	148	1.7	2	22	9	
Punctuation	184	3.7	5	51	52	
Usage & Expression	179	3.5	5	47	44	
Language Total	**173**	**3.1**	**4**	**39**	**30**	
Concepts & Estimation	176	4.3	4	42	66	
Problem Solving & Data Interp.	188	4.1	5	55	59	
*Computation	175	4.6	4	42	72	
Mathematics Total	**182**	**4.2**	**5**	**49**	**59**	
Social Studies	187	4.0	5	58	58	
Science	183	3.6	5	49	49	
Maps and Diagrams	192	4.2	6	59	67	
Reference Materials	191	4.1	6	57	63	
Sources of Information Total	192	4.2	6	58	65	
COMPOSITE	**184**	**3.7**	**5**	**50**	**50**	

Tests and Skills (E)

	Total Items	No. Att.	%C Stu.	%C Nat.	Diff.	Difference −20 / 0 / +20
Vocabulary						
Vocabulary	29	29	45	69	−24	
Reading Comprehension						
Factual Understanding	17	17	76	61	15	
Inference and Interpretation	12	12	83	61	22	
Analysis and Generalization	8	8	50	48	2	
Word Analysis						
Phono. Awareness and Decoding	11	11	82	71	11	
Identify & Analyze Word Parts	24	24	50	67	−17	
Listening						
Literal Comprehension	16	16	81	74	7	
Inferential Comprehension	15	15	80	65	15	
Spelling						
Root Words	21	21	62	67	−5	
Words with Affixes	3	3	100	55	45	
Correct Spelling	4	4	75	76	−1	
Capitalization						
Names and Titles	4	4	50	73	−23	
Dates and Holidays	4	4	25	62	−32	
Place Names	7	7	14	59	−45	
Writing Conventions	5	5	20	56	−36	
Overcapitalization/Correct Cap	4	4	25	60	−35	
Punctuation						
End Punctuation	12	12	75	64	9	
Commas	6	6	50	49	1	
Apostrophe/Quotes/Colon/Semi	3	3	33	55	−22	
Correct Punctuation	3	3	67	58	9	

Tests and Skills (D)

	Total Items	No. Att.	%C Stu.	%C Nat.	Diff.	Difference −20 / 0 / +20
Usage & Expression						
Nouns, Pronouns, and Modifiers	6	6	50	62	−12	
Verbs	8	3	62	60	2	
Conciseness and Clarity	3	3	67	68	−1	
Organization of Ideas	5	5	40	53	−13	
Appropriate Use	8	8	88	68	20	
Concepts & Estimation						
Number Properties & Operations	9	9	88	72	8	
Algebra	5	5	60	60	0	
Geometry	4	4	90	85	5	
Measurement	3	3	87	77	10	
Probability & Statistics	3	3	100	90	10	
Estimation	7	7	38	54	−16	
Prob. Solv. & Data Interp.						
Problem Solving	14	14	69	66	3	
Single-step	7	7	90	80	10	
Multiple-step	3	3	75	58	17	
Approaches and Procedures	4	4	50	49	1	
Data Interpretation	8	8	55	53	2	
Read Amounts	3	3	75	72	3	
Compare Quant./Relationships	5	5	60	58	2	
Computation						
Add with Whole Numbers	8	8	100	87	13	
Subtract with Whole Numbers	8	8	89	69	20	
Multiple/Divide Whole Numbers	9	9	63	57	6	

Tests and Skills

	Total Items	No. Att.	%C Stu.	%C Nat.	Diff.	Difference −20 / 0 / +20
Social Studies						
History	5	5	60	67	−7	
Geography	6	6	83	66	17	
Economics	7	7	57	61	−4	
Government and Society	12	12	67	61	6	
Science						
Scientific Inquiry	9	9	44	44	0	
Life Science	10	10	50	60	−10	
Earth and Space Science	8	8	62	62	0	
Physical Science	3	3	67	53	14	
Maps and Diagrams						
Locate/Process Information	12	12	75	74	1	
Interpret Information	9	9	78	54	24	
Analyze Information	3	3	33	41	−8	
Reference Materials						
Using Reference Materials	10	10	70	57	13	
Searching for Information	18	18	67	58	9	
Critical Thinking Skills						
Reading	20	20	70	56	14	
Language	17	17	53	59	−6	
Mathematics	12	12	46	56	−10	
Social Studies	12	12	58	59	−1	
Science	11	11	45	43	2	
Sources of Information	19	19	63	55	8	

*A plus (+) or minus (−) sign in the difference graph indicates that the bar extends beyond +/− 20.   No. Att.= Number Attempted   %C = Percent Correct

Figure 11.1

Adapted from Riverside 2003 Catalog. Copyright © 2000. Reprinted with the permission of the publisher, The Riverside Publishing Company, 425 Spring Lake Drive, Itasca, IL 60413 students who took the test in the norming sample scored below Jarad on math computation. Likewise, Jarad's percentile ranks for "Concepts & Estimation," "Problem Solving & Data Interpretation," and "Mathematics Total" were all average or above. Percentiles for these and all the other tests Jarad took across subject areas are conveniently summarized with the bar graphs in section **C**.

Recall from our dialog that a common misconception is that Jarad's percentile rank means that Jarad got 72 percent of the items correct. Percentage correct and percentile are different. A percentage compares the number of items Jarad got correct with the total number of items on the test. A percentile represents the percentage of students in the norming sample who received a score lower than Jarad's. Notice the values provided in section **D** under the columns labeled % C Stu. (for percentage of items this student got correct) and % C Nat. (for percentage of items students in the nation got correct). With these values from section **D** you can compare Jarad's percentage correct with the average percentage correct in the nation for each of the math skill tests listed under the headings "Concepts & Estimation," "Problems & Data Interpretation," and "Computation." The data are summarized with the bar graphs in section **E**. These bar graphs indicate the difference between the student's percentage correct and the percentage correct for students in the nation. They permit identification of skills that stand out as high or low when compared with students in the nation. The bar graphs indicate that Jarad is an average to above average student in almost all areas of math. The psychologist correctly concluded that Jarad's math achievement through the third grade is not the cause of his learning difficulty.

Figure 11.1 also contains norms in **grade-equivalent scores**. Look at section **B** again, this time under the column labeled GE (for Grade Equivalent), and you will find that Jarad's mathematics total score at the end of the third grade was equivalent to the math achievement of students who were in the second month of the fourth grade, expressed as 4.2. Above it you will find that Jarad's computation score was equivalent to the math achievement of students who were in the sixth month of the fourth grade, expressed as 4.6. These data also confirm that Jarad is performing at or above his grade level.

A common misperception in interpreting a norms table is that, even though a grade-equivalent score for an individual may suggest that the learner is performing above her grade level, it does not mean that the learner could satisfactorily complete work at that higher grade level. A parent whose child's grade-equivalent score is well above his current grade level may suggest to you that this child should be given texts and workbooks at that higher grade. But, even though a student may have scored well above his grade, it does not necessarily mean that the student can do the work at that advanced grade without the prerequisite content being taught at the present grade. All that Jarad's grade-equivalent scores measured was his ability to do third-grade math. Jarad did not take a test designed to measure math content taught in any higher grade, so we do not know how he would perform at that grade.

At times you may request your school psychologist to individually administer a standardized *ability* test to diagnose the source of a persistent learning problem. Ability tests usually provide another type of score, called age-equivalent scores. **Age-equivalent scores** indicate whether a learner's score is below, at, or above the average score of those at particular ages (instead of grades) in the norming sample. Otherwise grade- and age-equivalent scores are alike. If Jarad had taken a standardized ability test you might find that Jarad's raw score at age 9 years and 2 months (expressed as 9.2) is equivalent to a score typical of the average learner who is 10 years and 3 months old (10.3). In other words, Jarad's measured ability is about a year above what would be expected, given his chronological age.

Percentiles and grade- or age-equivalent scores can be a valuable asset in helping you determine how a learner performs compared to the norm. However, keep in mind the following cautions when using grade-equivalent and percentile scores to determine student progress or to identify a learning problem.

With respect to grade-equivalent scores:

1. Equal differences in scores do not necessarily reflect equal differences in achievement. For example, growth in reading comprehension from grade 2.6 to 3.6 may not mean the same degree or amount of growth as a change in reading comprehension from grade 7.6 to 8.6. It is likely that the one-year improvement is attributable to different factors in each case.

2. Grade equivalents are not meaningful unless a subject is taught across all grades. Why report a physics grade equivalent of 7.2 when physics is only taught during the eleventh grade? What does it mean to say your performance in physics is equivalent to that of a beginning seventh grader? For this reason, grade equivalents are usually more useful in the elementary and middle schools where they can be used to compare growth across a common core of subjects.

3. Grade equivalents are often misinterpreted as *standards* rather than as norms. That is, teachers often forget that grade equivalents are averages—about half the students will score above and half below grade placement, if your students are representative of the norming sample.

4. Grade equivalents may not be directly comparable across school subjects. A fifth grader who is one year behind grade placement in reading is not necessarily as far behind in reading as she may be in math, even though she is one year behind in math, too. This is because growth in different subjects occurs at different rates. Equal levels of growth or deficiency, as indicated by grade-equivalent scores, may mean quite different things.

With respect to percentile ranks:

Percentile ranks are an improvement over grade- and age-equivalent scores in that they do not have the limitations of the latter. Because comparisons are within-grade, it does not matter whether subjects are taught across grades, and because growth is only relative to others in the grade, the problem of growth being unequal at different grade levels is avoided. In addition, percentile ranks are less likely to be considered as standards for performance. However, percentile ranks do have two shortcomings:

1. As we saw in our dialog with Jarad, percentile ranks are often confused with *percentage correct*. In using percentile ranks, be sure you are communicating

that a percentile rank of 62, for example, is understood to mean that 62 percent of those taking the test received scores lower than this individual. Commonly, a score at the 62nd percentile is misinterpreted to mean the student answered only 62 percent of the items correct. A score at the 62nd *percentile* might be equivalent to a B or a C, whereas a score of *62 percent* would likely be an F.

2. Equal differences between percentile ranks do *not* necessarily indicate equal differences in achievement. In a class of 100 students, the difference in achievement between the 2nd percentile and the 5th percentile is substantial, whereas the difference between the 47th and the 50th is negligible—assuming a normal distribution of scores. Interpretation of percentile ranks must consider that units toward the tails of the distribution tend to be spread out like a rubber band, whereas units toward the center tend to be compressed.

As long as you keep these limitations in mind, grade equivalents and percentiles represent a useful means of interpreting your students' performance compared to the norm. In Application 11.1, test your understanding of percentile ranks and grade equivalents by writing a note to parents who would like a common sense interpretation of the meaning of their child's standardized test results.

APPLICATION 11.1

Joy, a student in your fifth-grade class, received a percentile rank of 19 in reading comprehension and a grade equivalent for this skill of 2.1 on the end-of-the-year standardized achievement test. Respond to a phone call from her concerned parents by writing a note to them explaining what each of these scores means for Joy's ability to read and for any suggestions of how Joy can improve her score next time.

Mark, a third-grade student, received a grade-equivalent score of 5.9 for math on a standardized achievement. Because all of Mark's percentiles and grade-equivalent scores are well above the third grade, Mark's parents asked if Mark could skip the fourth grade, because as they put it, "Mark has proved he can do fourth-grade work." Write a response to Mark's parents as to why his test results do not indicate that he necessarily can do fourth-grade work despite the fact that almost all of his grade-equivalent scores are at or beyond the fourth-grade level.

The Assessment Triangle and Standardized Tests

In chapter 1 we presented the Assessment Triangle comprising three essential sources of information—observation, interpretation, and cognition. In this section we will revisit this triangle to show how standardized test data can be used alongside classroom assessments to direct instructional decisions, monitor student performance, and identify learning problems.

Throughout this book we have stressed the importance of developing classroom assessments that inform you about how your learners are developing as good thinkers. To this end we suggested that you link the various assessment techniques to a model of cognition that includes your learners':

Declarative knowledge

Procedural knowledge

Cognitive strategies

Metacognitive strategies

Dispositions or habits of mind

In the previous chapters we presented specific assessment techniques that can provide information on how these components of thinking and reasoning are developing. We emphasized that these techniques are ideally suited to inform you about your learners' thinking because they are built from classroom-specific knowledge and processes. Who better to design an assessment system to provide data on your learners' declarative and procedural knowledge, cognitive and metacognitive strategies, and habits of mind than the teacher who taught them these behaviors and skills? Once you apply this cognitive model to your expectations for learners in a subject area like spelling, math computation, or writing, you can more easily and efficiently select and develop assessments that are sensitive to capturing what has been learned.

How can the data from standardized tests help enrich the interpretations you make from classroom assessments? In other words how can standardized tests help:

1. Give you a clear view of your learning goals, such as declarative and procedural knowledge, cognitive and metacognitive strategies, and habits of mind

2. Inform you about the present state of your learners with respect to these goals

3. Guide actions to close the gap

4. Help you evaluate if the gap is closed

Standardized tests can help accomplish these goals if they are used in a manner that follows the Assessment Triangle. In other words, your assessment system should use standardized tests that include tasks representing a model of your learners' cognition, provide observable data representing that cognition, and provide an interpretation of what the data mean for you and your students. Whether or not you use standardized achievement tests to measure your students' knowledge of reading, spelling, mathematics, social studies, or science, these formal measures can complement your classroom assessment system if they:

1. Measure worthwhile cognitive learning goals
2. Define the instructional needs of individual students
3. Provide feedback to learners and parents
4. Help evaluate your classroom instruction
5. Promote and assess transfer of knowledge to new areas
6. Identify learning problems

Let us look at how a standardized test of your learners' achievement can help with each of these goals.

Setting Worthwhile Goals

Standardized tests, when constructed from a cognitive theory of how children develop into good thinkers in a specific subject area, can help focus instruction on important areas of learning. But, not all standardized tests have been built on a cognitive theory of learning in a domain-specific area. Some of these tests are more task focused than process focused.

Task-focused tests are ones that have been constructed to provide information about the facts or concepts that learners know but say little about the cognitive processes learners use while taking these tests. In addition, decisions about what content to include on these tests may be made from a broad sampling of national school curricula rather than from research on the critical declarative and procedural knowledge that children must have to become expert thinkers in domain-specific areas like reading, science, spelling, math computation, or expository writing.

Process-focused tests are constructed differently. These tests are built on a theory of how novice thinkers develop into expert thinkers in specific content domains. Consequently, they include tasks that provide information to test users about the critical knowledge and processes that learners use in specific subject domains important for good thinking. You have already seen examples of two such tests: the Diagnostic Math Assessment shown in chapter 3 (Figure 3.2) and the Subtraction Bugs Assessment in chapter 7 (Table 7.1). Both assessments were developed to reveal how learners must think and process information while completing a math problem in order to detect processing problems and what the classroom teacher can do to remediate them.

More and more standardized achievement tests are being constructed on a process- rather than task-focused model of subject matter learning. When process-focused, they provide direction for classroom learning goals not only at the state and school district level, but also at the classroom level. These goals will be subject-related goals such as "can mentally represent the number line" in first-grade math computation, or "can compensate for an adjustment by making an equal and opposite adjustment" in seventh-grade science. Thus, standardized tests play a critical role in providing direction to domain-specific learning, whereas your classroom assessments play an equally critical role in guiding day-to-day decisions about lesson content.

For example, let us assume a summary of the standardized math results has been requested by your school district for individual classrooms. Publishers commonly provide specific class averages by teacher for each skill area, such as those listed in Figure 11.1, in addition to individual student reports. From this type of classroom profile, Mr. Watts may learn that his third-grade students scored below the 50th percentile in number concepts related to measurement (38th percentile), probability and statistics (43rd percentile), and multiple-step problems (35th percentile). Mr. Watts shares these results with Ms. McGinn, who shortly will begin teaching fourth grade to these same students. This information will be of value to Ms. McGinn in trying to meet her school's goal of raising the average math achievement level to at least the 50th percentile. In order to achieve this goal she plans to meet with Mr. Watts to learn what his classroom assessments told him about his students' declarative knowledge involving number concepts, probability, and statistics and any gaps that the standardized math skill tests did not reveal. Similarly, she will want to know something about the procedural knowledge of Mr. Watts's students with respect to multiple-step problem solving. This will help her design assessments to strengthen the problem-solving skills of her fourth graders. Thus, we see how standardized test results can help establish worthwhile learning goals for Ms. McGinn's classroom, whereas Mr. Watts's classroom assessments can provide information to guide decisions about what specific declarative and procedural knowledge to focus on at the beginning of the fourth grade.

Defining the Instructional Needs of Individual Students

Defining areas of instructional need for individual students is another goal for which standardized test results can be helpful to the classroom teacher. Recall that standardized test profiles like that shown in Figure 11.1 report both absolute (percentage of items correct) and comparative (percentile and grade-equivalent) information about the level of declarative or procedural knowledge that a learner possesses in specific subject areas. Ms. McGinn used this information at the beginning of the school year to plan her lessons and anticipate the problems her class could be expected to have. These same data could direct her attention to the learning problems of individual learners and subgroups of learners.

For example, the results of your learners' standardized scores in comprehension might inform you that some of them may lack skills in deriving meaning from text. Researchers agree that automatic decoding of short vowel sounds or vowel combinations is essential for learners to derive meaning from what they read. As a result you might construct a classroom assessment to determine if in fact some of your students lack the ability to automatically decode short vowel sounds or vowel combinations. If so, a major area of instructional need would be to teach procedural knowledge involving sound processing and the encoding of these processes in long-term memory.

Likewise, your students' standardized skill scores in science may indicate that some of them may lack a deep understanding of Maps and Diagrams that is prerequisite knowledge for future lessons. As we saw in chapter 7 misconceptions can interfere with the learning of new knowledge in domain-specific areas such as math, science, or social studies. As a result you might construct a classroom assessment to determine what "bugs" or misconceptions some of your learners may have. Thus, a standardized test, in combination with your classroom assessments can provide domain-specific declarative knowledge in math, science, social studies, or spelling that can help direct the instructional needs of individual students and subgroups of students.

Providing Feedback

Theories of self-regulated learning assign feedback a crucial role in becoming an expert learner and thinker. Standardized tests can perform this important feedback in two ways.

First, reports like Jarad's in Figure 11.1 will inform his parents how he is doing in comparison to other children in his grade. These results, if shared with Jarad in a constructive manner, may not only inform him of his progress but also over the course of a year motivate him to higher levels of effort. The manner in which the standardized test results are shared with learners will determine their understanding of the results and their motivation to improve. When the results of standardized assessments are meaningfully integrated with student performance on classroom assessments, your feedback can inspire students to higher levels of effort by providing a balanced and more comprehensive profile of performance to both learner and parents. If, on the other hand, your students' standardized tests are communicated in the absence of feedback about their everyday classroom performance, the results can easily be taken out of context, precluding a more balanced and accurate profile of a student's achievements.

Reports of standardized results also provide feedback to administrators and teachers on the success of their efforts to improve instruction. This feedback can work to motivate school personnel to continue present efforts or initiate new efforts to move learners to higher levels of learning. Without standardized assessments your school district and state would lose its ability to differentiate the performance of schools and school districts by way of a common benchmark. They will have lost a reliable index of how classrooms, schools, and school districts perform relative to a norm group that can direct educational reform and resources at the district, state, and national level where they may be most needed. While standardized tests will not be as diagnostically useful as your content-specific classroom assessments in all the varied formats presented in the previous chapters, they do provide an objective way to allocate material resources, staff training, and administrative leadership to correct undesirable trends in school performance and to provide examples of higher performing schools.

Evaluating Classroom Instruction

Your carefully crafted and tailored classroom assessments will help you make day-to-day and week-to-week decisions about what to teach. If constructed with a model of cognitive learning in mind, they will allow you to efficiently assess the effectiveness of your day-to-day lessons. In contrast to this formative assessment of your instruction, standardized tests provide summative assessments of your learners' achievement and your teaching. From Mr. Watts's third-grade classroom results and Ms. McGinn's follow-up planning, you saw how class averages by teacher for each skill can play an important role in initiating a dialog between teachers of successive grades. Using Mr. Watts's math results, Ms. McGinn not only set some learning goals for the coming year but also decided on some ways to achieve them involving new instructional techniques as well as alternative approaches to classroom assessment. If the classroom report at the end of the fourth grade shows an improvement in national percentile rankings and more learners are at or beyond grade level compared to the third grade, Ms. McGinn has good reason to consider her instructional efforts successful.

Assessing Transfer

As we pointed out in chapter 1, you teach not just for immediate learning but also for the longer term use of knowledge and skills in new contexts. Standardized tests present learners with questions which assess their declarative and procedural knowledge in contexts that may be novel or different from your classroom assessments. Hence, the results of these tests, particularly for individual learners like Jarad, may allow the teacher to make tentative judgments about a learners' ability to transfer what they have learned.

In Jarad's case, we can see from his math concepts and estimation skill profile in Figure 11.1 that he scored low in estimation. If on the other hand his classroom assessments show that Jarad has mastered these skills, the problem may be one of transfer. In other words, estimation skills may have been assessed in class using only one type of example or one type of problem context and tested on the standardized test in another context. If so, you would want to alter your examples to include a variety of problem contexts to enhance its transfer to standardized test formats as well as to real-world applications.

In Application 11.2, put your understanding of transfer to work by indicating how you would assess for the transfer of learning to different, new, or real-world applications for a lesson you would like to teach.

Diagnosing Learning Problems

The memory system is a principal focus of interest when trying to understand how children develop as good thinkers. As we saw in chapter 1, research into the memory system suggests that you should view your learners' memories as a set of fluid, interrelated processes over which your learners and your instruction have some

APPLICATION 11.2

Think of a lesson topic that you would like to teach at your grade level or in your subject area. Describe what you would teach and how you would assess the lesson to be certain that your learners would be able to transfer what they had learned to a context outside of your classroom, for example, in a subsequent grade or in the real world.

Your lesson topic:

Method of presentation:

Assessment for transfer:

control rather than as a static and unchangeable storehouse. Consequently, we have referred to problems of cognition that are related to the memory system as "processing problems." Basically a processing problem occurs when one or more of the networks processing different types of information coming from the senses (auditory, visual, kinesthetic, etc.) do not function efficiently or do not transmit information errorlessly.

Saying that someone has a processing problem that underlies an inability to master reading skills or math computation, or science problem solving skills should not be taken lightly. Data that need to be examined and interpreted to draw such a conclusion are varied and include standardized tests and classroom assessments as well as your learners' developmental and school history. In other words, there are several principal and equally important types of information that need to be examined before concluding that there is a processing problem underlying an inability to learn a particular skill or competency. Let us look at some of these types of information.

Developmental History.   Learners with processing problems show particular symptoms between the ages of two to six. Such early precursors of auditory processing problems may be difficulty hearing rhymes, poor language fluency, difficulty finding the right words to say something, or slow speech. Thus, before diagnosing a child with a processing disorder, ask your school district psychologist to talk with parents and check records for signs that the learner has exhibited certain symptoms of the disorder during early childhood years. A learner's developmental history of learning problems whether in spelling, reading, writing, or math computation, when combined with other signs, can provide important information in correctly diagnosing a processing problem.

School History. Processing problems related to memory, reading, math calculation, or spatial orientation become evident as soon as a child begins to receive formal instruction. You or your school psychologist can consult standardized achievement records to look for early signs of learning problems before a diagnosis of a processing problem is made. Positive findings support the inference of a processing problem, but, it cannot confirm it without classroom assessments.

Classroom Assessments. If a learner has a processing problem related to reading, math, writing, spelling, or problem-solving, it will be evident in the kinds of things you ask your learners to do: homework, class assignments, classroom tests, projects, oral recitation, discussion, and so forth. Teachers who suspect a processing problem should collect a varied sample of classroom assessments that indicate symptoms of the problems related to various types of learning disorders.

Standardized Test Results. Finally, professionals responsible for diagnosing processing problems will consult standardized test scores to look for patterns of scores suggesting problems in the information processing system (e.g., auditory, visual, etc.). Particularly helpful will be the standardized test results regarding a learner's thinking skills. Notice from Figure 11.1 that Jarad's standardized test results include information about thinking skills, including his ability to focus and gather information, remember, organize, analyze, generate information, and to integrate and evaluate. Jarad's percentage of items correct for these cognitive strategies can provide an indication as to why a learning problem may be present, suggested by a pattern of below average performance across a number of content-related areas. When standardized test score interpretations such as these are consistent with results from your classroom assessments and supported by a learner's developmental and school history, a specific learning problem may have been identified. With the aid of standardized tests, your school psychologist can make the proper interpretations and provide help in locating the instructional resources needed to address the learning problem. Therefore, a system of multiple and independent sources of information should converge to provide evidence of a learning problem. Standardized test results together with your classroom assessments will be among the most important contributions to making this determination.

Helping Students Prepare for Standardized Tests

We end this chapter with a word about how you can empower your learners to do their best on the standardized tests they will be required to take. Standardized tests are often called "high-stakes" tests because they can be used to determine whether a student receives access to advanced placement and honors courses, is promoted to the next grade, or even graduate from high school. Likewise they are high stakes for principals and teachers when they receive recognition or reprimands depending on their outcome. Regardless of how you personally may feel about these tests, they are used in all 50 states and are likely to be around for some time to come. So, here are some suggestions from Kubiszyn and Borich (2003) concerning how you can do something about the frustration you and your learners may sometimes feel about standardized tests, and how you can help your students improve their performance on them.

Focus on the Task, Not Your Feelings About It

Because your students' grade promotion and your teaching can be affected by your state's standardized assessment program, it makes sense to focus less on your feelings about the test and more on the demands of the task before you. So, it will be critical that you obtain your state's academic standards at your grade or subject which are usually available from the Web site for your state education agency. Ensuring that you target your state standards in your classroom is the single most important thing you can do to prepare your students to perform well on these tests. For this you may have to modify your instructional methods to better match the content and processes identified in the state standards.

Inform Students and Parents About the Importance of the Test

Although some students will already understand the purpose and relevance of the test, there will be some who do not. To get students to try their best, some advocate warning students or issuing rewards. Others say such strategies send the wrong message and only increase the stress and pressure that can impair student performance. Neither of these approaches will be as effective as taking the time to explain to your students the reason the test is being administered, how the results will be used, and how the test is relevant to their learning. In this manner you are more likely to engage and motivate your students to do well and to take the test seriously and carefully. And, instead of presenting a lecture on the pros or cons of tests, keep it simple: Let your students know they have learned what will be necessary to do well on the test, and that you expect them to do well.

Teach Test-Taking Skills from the First Day of School

Some students seem to perform better on tests than other students. This may seem to be because of luck, aptitude, confidence, or some other factor. However, there is also an element of skill in test taking that affects student performance. If all students in your class are aware of various test-taking skills, their overall performance will increase. For example, you can teach your students to:

1. *Follow directions carefully.* Some students, especially those who may be impulsive or who have difficulty reading, may neglect to read directions carefully or read them at all. You can address this critical point frequently during your daily classroom routine and remind students about it during your regular classroom tests.

2. *Read test items, passages, and related information carefully.* Who hasn't rushed through a test item only to find that you missed or misread a word and lost credit as a result? You can reduce the likelihood that your learners will do this by providing practice during in-class and homework assignments and during your regular tests by highlighting key words, re-reading items, and double-checking answers. For multiple-choice questions, remind students to read each option before selecting their answer. This may be especially important for learners who have come from cultures where standardized tests are not used or used as much as they are in the United States.

3. *Manage test-taking time.* Although students must work quickly to complete standardized tests, they must also work accurately. This skill, too, can be improved with practice in the classroom. Instead of giving students "as much time as they need" to answer questions on a classroom test, impose a time limit. For lengthy tests have students plan out the number of minutes they will spend on each phase of the test.

4. *Attempt easier items first.* Many teacher-made tests begin with easy items and then end with the most difficult items. But, standardized tests typically have a more random order to their difficulty level. Unprepared students may encounter a difficult question early in the test and spend an inordinate amount of time on a question that even many of the best students may miss. When you administer your classroom tests encourage students to answer as many items as they know the answer to, before they attempt the more difficult items.

5. *Eliminate options before answering.* Testwise students know that they can increase their chances of answering correctly if they can eliminate one or two multiple-choice or matching options before attempting to choose the correct one. Have your students practice this in class and remind them during your objective tests to follow this strategy.

6. *Teach students to check their answers after completing the test.* Some students have such an aversion to tests, or take them so lightly, that they do not check their answers after they finish a test—even if time remains. You can practice this by reminding your students to use the full testing time to go over their answers when giving your classroom tests.

As the Standardized Test Day Approaches Respond to Student Questions Openly and Directly

Before a standardized test you can expect that some children will begin to wonder or worry about the test (e.g., What will it look like? Will I be the last one finished?

What if I get a bad grade? What can I do if I have a question during the test?, etc.). This sense of uncertainty is a common cause of anxiety, too much of which will interfere with your students' test performance. To prevent this before the test day, provide your learners with as much information about the test's format and administration procedures as you have. This can include basic information such as test days and times and the subjects, format, or style of responding and how their questions may be addressed. You may also want to role play various scenarios with the class to ensure they are clear on the procedures.

Take Advantage of Whatever Preparation Materials Are Available

In many states your state education agency or school district will provide for you some helpful practice tests and exercises designed to familiarize students with the style, format, and subject matter of the test. Although these exercises take classroom time, they will help test-taking efficiency and manage your students' stress by minimizing their uncertainties and increasing the time they spend focusing on the test items rather than wondering how they fill in the answer sheets. Take full advantage of the preparation materials that are provided and supplement them with others of your own, when available.

Summary

This chapter has helped you understand and interpret standardized tests. Although sometimes frustrating for the teacher and almost always anxiety provoking for the learner, standardized tests, as do all tests, have their advantages as well as disadvantages. This chapter has shown how standardized tests, although not as sensitive to your day-to-day objectives as classroom assessments, can help you become aware of individual learning problems in your classroom, better monitor your students progress over time, and direct some of the instructional decisions you will need to make. Most important, this chapter has shown you how your classroom assessments can be a valuable adjunct for interpreting the results of standardized tests and using them to confirm and enhance decisions you will make about individual learners and your instructional methods.

Activities

1. In your own words, describe the differences among a percentage, percentile, grade-equivalent score, and age-equivalent score.

2. Why is the manner in which the norming sample is selected so important for interpretation of a standardized test score? What would likely be the effect of local norms versus national norms for an elementary or secondary school?
3. Provide an example of how a standardized test result might influence how you would change your teaching approach or method.
4. List all the things you can think of that might help your learners improve their performance on a standardized achievement test.

Suggested Readings

Harris, J., & Turkington, C. (2000). *Get ready for standardized tests.* New York: McGraw-Hill. (Separate volumes for Grades 2, 3, 4, 5, and 6.)
   These grade-specific standardized test preparation guides are filled with empowering information for both teacher and learner that can optimize the performance of test-anxious learners and help them improve in specific skill areas.

Kubiszyn, T., and Borich, G. (2003). *Educational testing and measurement, seventh edition.* New York: Wiley.
   Chapters 18 and 19 will extend your knowledge of standardized tests and provide additional information on the influence of language, sociocultural factors, age, gender, development, motivation, and learning disabilities on the interpretation of standardized achievement and ability tests.

12

Developing a Worthwhile Grading Plan

Consider these comments made about grading by some first-year teachers:

> Of all the paperwork, grading is the nitty-gritty of teaching for me. Students take their grade as the bottom line of your class. It is the end-all and be-all of the class. To me, a grade for a class is, or at least should be, a combination of ability, attitude, and effort. Put bluntly: How do you nail a kid who really tried with an F? Or how do you reward a lazy, snotty punk with an A? (Ryan, 1992, p. 4)

> I have been amazed at the comments they make about grades. Those with A's ask if they are flunking; others who rarely hand in assignments ask if they'll get a B. They make no connection between their own efforts and the grade they receive. . . . Of course, there is some truth in their view of the arbitrariness of grading. But I don't like the powerlessness it implies. "I don't give you your grade," I tell them. "You do!" (Ryan, 1992, p. 96)

> Grading is still kind of a problem with me . . . I try not to play favorites (even though I have them)—I don't like S's personality . . . I do like J's, isn't it unfair? You want to be easier on someone you like. Or harder on someone you don't. . . . I wouldn't mind taking a class on grading. I think grading could be hit much harder in college . . . I just don't know what to do, kind of. (Bullough, 1989, p. 66)

Confusion, uncertainty, even fear can surround the practice of grading for beginning teachers for several reasons. First, there is little research supporting the value of one grading practice over another (Thorndike et al., 1997). Teachers' choices of grading systems generally reflect their own values, past experiences with grades, and the norms and traditions of the school in which they teach. Second, grades become part of a learner's permanent record and have important consequences both at the time the grade is given and in the future. Teachers, therefore, are naturally cautious about how they assign grades and conscientious when they do so.

The goal of this chapter is to prepare you to develop and defend a grading plan. We highlight significant decisions you will have to make in developing a grading plan and describe specific methods of calculating and assigning grades. Rather than describing a "best" method, we provide a menu of grading methods and some recommendations about effective grading practices. These recommendations will help you select the approach that makes sense to you and that you can explain and defend to learners and parents.

Why Assign Grades?

Why you assign grades to learners is one of the most important questions that you must answer. If you clearly articulate the purpose of your grades before deciding on how to assign them, you can resolve many potential problems.

Often the most important reason for assigning a grade is to communicate the extent to which learners achieve classroom goals. This reason is so obvious you may say that it is not worth mentioning. But if it is obvious, why is it often ignored? When a teacher lowers a grade because a particular student shows "poor attitude," the grade no longer communicates just what the learner achieved. Which part of the grade represents achievement and which attitude? Some teachers decide to add points to a grade because the learner "tried hard," or they raise a grade because the student made a lot of progress. Which part of the grade represents achievement and which progress or effort? How would next year's teacher interpret a D grade assigned to reflect some achievement and a lot of progress compared to another learner's F grade assigned to reflect only achievement?

The principle that grades should be assigned to communicate what a student learned, although obvious, is often ignored in practice. Letter and number grades may communicate many things: achievement, effort, attitude, progress, the teacher's personal feelings about the learner, and more. If you want your grades to tell learners, parents, and other teachers how well a learner has mastered your objectives, then your grades should communicate your students' achievement.

In Application 12.1, explain the purpose of a grade in your classroom in a manner that could be understood by parents at the first back-to-school night. You will have an opportunity to refine and focus your purpose later in the chapter.

APPLICATION 12.1

Think about what your most important purpose for assigning a grade might be. Then write your purpose out as though you were explaining it to a parent.

Cultivating a Grading Philosophy

You will face many decisions on the way to developing a grading plan. In this section we highlight some of the questions you should consider before assigning grades and, afterward, provide you with the tools to answer them.

1. *What Meaning Should Each Report Card Grade Convey?*   The choices are many: Should Marva's grade of 85 in eighth-grade science tell how much information she has acquired, how much she has learned relative to her classmates, how much effort she put into the class, her class attendance and punctuality, how much progress she made from the start of the year, how much she contributed to class discussions, her appreciation for science, or how well she got along with her peers and the teacher? An 85 cannot tell all of these things. What will it tell learners, parents, and future teachers?

2. *How Should Class Grades Be Distributed?*   It is rare to find a school district with a written policy on how many students can receive a given grade. So you must make your own decision about what percentage of your learners get As, Bs, Cs, and so forth. Is it okay for 90 percent of your learners to get As? Should some students fail? Should your average grade be a B or a C? Were you to graph the distribution of grades, would it resemble the bell curve, as you saw in chapter 3?

3. *What Components Go into a Final Grade?*   Students are asked to do many things in a classroom: complete classwork, homework, and projects; turn in rough drafts; keep a notebook or journal; take tests and pop quizzes; and make oral presentations. Do all these go into a final grade? Is there a minimum or maximum number of grade components?

4. *How Do You Establish the Importance of Each Component in the Final Grade?*   Should all of the components identified carry equal weight in your final grade? Are some more important than others? Should the pop quizzes count as much as a chapter test? What percentage of the grade should depend on homework? How do you decide which should be more important, and how should this be reflected in the final grade?

5. *How Should You Assign the Grades?*   Once you have combined the grade components into a final score based on the decisions made thus far, you must specify a final grade for each learner. How you do this depends on the conclusions you draw about the meaning of a grade. If you decide that grades should tell what a student has learned in an absolute and not relative (comparison with other learners) sense, then you should not be concerned with how many learners get what grade. But there are several methods of assigning absolute grades. Which should you use?

6. *Should Students Be Given Extra Opportunities to Raise Their Grades?*   What teacher hasn't had a student ask for special consideration regarding a grade? Sometimes just a few points affect whether a student goes to summer school, receives an award, passes the course, or earns a scholarship. What should you do in such cases? Should you give an extra assignment, have the student take a makeup test, or be a nice person and just give the extra points?

APPLICATION 12.2

Each of the following questions is a step to developing a comprehensive grading plan. Read each question and write down some preliminary decisions about how you would answer each question.

1. What will be my purpose for giving a report card grade?

2. How will I distribute As, Bs, Cs, and so forth, across the class?

3. What different components of performance will I consider for the final grade?

4. How will I weigh the importance of each component of the final grade?

5. Will my grades be absolute or relative measures of achievement—or both?

6. Will I give extra opportunities for student's to raise their grade? If so, how?

In Application 12.2, make some preliminary decisions regarding each of these six steps to develop a grading philosophy. We will ask you to reflect on these decisions later in the chapter.

Constructing a Grading Plan

Here are some important steps to follow when constructing a grading plan. They are numbered sequentially, but you can anticipate having to revise an earlier decision after resolving a later one. Developing a grading plan is more like making Texas chili than baking a cake. Your final outcome will reflect some adherence to procedure but also a lot of judgment, insight, and experience. Now, let us consider some steps that can help you answer these questions.

Step 1. Check School District Policy

Every school district and most schools will have a policy regarding grades. The policies will likely indicate the grade symbols that you can use (A–F, 60–100), whether a final exam is required, what percentage of the final grade can be based on the final exam, and so forth. Although the policy may include detailed rules, it more likely consists of general statements closer to a philosophy than a rubric, as shown in Figure 12.1.

You are bound to follow the district grading system. When conflicts arise between your approach and the district's or school's, discuss this with your principal or department head. Even if there is no obvious inconsistency between how you choose to assign grades and district guidelines, it is always helpful to discuss your grading approach with other teachers. This will help you identify the grading norms that exist in your school and prevent some potentially awkward situations.

Step 2. Decide What Each Grade Symbol Will Mean

The two basic classifications of symbols used in most schools are letter symbols and number symbols.

Letter Symbols.   Grades A through F are the most widely used of the letter symbol systems. When plus and minus designations are added, the A through F system allows the teacher to judge 13 degrees of learning: A+, A, A-, B+, B, B-, C+, C, C-, D+, D, D-, F. But, you may have some difficulty discriminating 13 levels of learning, as we will discuss shortly.

Many elementary and middle schools use E (excellent), S+ (above expectations), S (satisfactory), S- (below expectations), and N (needs improvement). This five-level grading system often includes another symbol that indicates whether the learner is working below (1), at (2), or above (3) grade level. This second symbol may also be influenced by the teacher's appraisal of a learner's self-regulation as discussed in chapters 1 and 9. If so, it should be a conscious goal of your grading system and measured objectively. Thus, a grade of S-3 indicates that the child is doing above grade level work at a satisfactory level and may have the intrinsic motivation to be self-determined and self-regulated.

Teachers who judge that the special content of their class objectives requires a pass/fail grading system use P/F or M/NI (mastery, needs improvement) letter systems. These alternatives are most often applied to objectives that expect the learner to attain procedural knowledge (know how to perform an action or behavior) to some established standard. This might include the safe and effective execution of laboratory skills in science, gymnastics on the playground, computer literacy, or

---

Sample District Grading Policy

Assessments

- Should measure student knowledge and skills
- Should be used to improve instruction
- Should be valid, reliable, practical, and credible

Communication

- Standards and criteria for student performance should be communicated in advance and actual student performance reported in detail following assessment.
- The reporting system should be clear and user-friendly. All parties interested in the grading should know what the grade means and represents.
- The elements of the reporting system—grades, scores, and comments—are the primary means of communication from the teacher to the students and parents.
- Communication of scores and grades needs to be regular and frequent enough so as to be motivating and encouraging.

The Purpose of Grades and What Grades Represent

- The purpose of grades is to report student achievement related to clearly defined content standards.
- There will be separate reports on growth, effort, group work, participation, and so forth.
- The grades will be consistent from class to class with respect to what the grade is measuring.

Reporting System

- A reporting system should include, in addition to grades, progress/improvement, effort, attitude factors, and relative achievement.
- A reporting system should be fair, accurate, consistent, and honest.

Specific Guidelines

- The course grade is based on student achievement.
- The course grade will be reported in an A–F format.
- No single assessment can count more than 20 percent of a course grade.
- Student performance on key performance factors will be reported to students and parents separately using an *O*utstanding, *S*atisfactory, and *U*nsatisfactory scale.
- These performance factors will be identified and communicated to students and parents at the beginning of each grading period.
- These factors may include the following: attendance, completion of work, cooperative behavior, effort, quality work, self-directed learning, collaborative work, community contributions, complex thinking, and quality production.
- Academic grades will not be affected by performance on developmental or practice tasks, homework used as practice, or performance in other areas, such as discipline, attitude, and/or attendance.

Figure 12.1
Sample district grading policy

successfully reading at grade level. In each case the criterion for passing from "needs improvement" to "mastery" is clearly established and assessed in an authentic, real-world context.

Numerical Symbols.   The two numerical systems are the 0 to 100 scale and the grade point average. With the former the teacher assigns scores between 0 and 100 to all components of the grading system: tests, projects, quizzes, notebooks, homework and classwork assignments, and so forth. These scores are averaged at the end of the grading period, and this average is the grade reported on the report card. Although the teacher can record a grade anywhere in the 0 to 100 range, some school grading programs treat all grades below 60 as a 60. So, in effect, the 0 to 100 system is a 60 to 100 system.

Grade point average (GPA) systems assign a numerical rating to the letter grades that are reported by the teacher. Thus, an A = 4, B = 3, C = 2, D = 1, and F = 0. These numbers are averaged for all subjects, and this GPA represents the student's overall grade. Example report cards using numerical and letter symbols appear in Figures 12.2a, and 12.2b.

Limitations of the Symbol Systems.   The principal limitation of any grading system requiring the teacher to assign one number or letter to represent course learning is that one symbol can convey only one meaning. But how can one symbol fully represent all that a student learns in a classroom? In the typical subject students acquire declarative and procedural knowledge, cognitive and metacognitive strategies, and dispositions about learning. One symbol cannot do justice to the different degrees of learning a student acquires across all learning outcomes. This limitation is an inherent feature of any symbol system.

Another limitation of the various symbol systems is that they may require teachers to make either too few or too many judgments about levels of learning. For example, the 13-level A through F (plus/minus) system assumes that a teacher can detect that many degrees of performance. Point systems of 100(0–100) or even 40 (60–100) points put nearly impossible demands on a teacher's ability to distinguish different levels of learning. At the other extreme, P/F or M/NI symbols may fail to reflect the varying degrees of learning occurring in a classroom. Most measurement specialists recommend that a grading system include no fewer than five and no more than ten degrees of quality.

Assigning Meaning to the Symbols.   Grade symbols typically represent one or more of the following standards and assessment methods:

1. Achievement in comparison to a relative or absolute standard

2. Effort a learner puts into the class, for example, self-regulation

3. Growth in achievement over the grading period or semester

Achievement in comparison to a relative or absolute standard.   Grades that make *relative* comparisons show how a student performs in comparison to other learners in the class. For example, a grade of C is given to learners who achieve

Teacher: _____

Principal: _____

Student: _____

School: _____

First Grade Report Card

Year: _____ to _____

INSTRUCTIONAL LEVEL CODES

Levels noted for Reading, Language, and Mathematics indicate how instruction is being delivered.

O – On Level
B – Below Level
ESL – English as a Second Language

With ARD Committee requirements for:
IMO – Instructional Modifications On-Level
IMB – Instructional Modifications Below-Level
IEP – Individual Educational Plan

END-OF-YEAR PLACEMENT

Students may be advanced to the next grade level by meeting promotion or placement standards. To be promoted, a student must be working on-level and earn an end-of-year performance grade of Satisfactory in Reading, Language, and Mathematics. Students who do not meet full promotion standards because of instructional level or end-of-year performance may be placed in next grade or retained in first grade, depending on the extent/severity of the academic deficits

☐ Promoted to Grade 2   ☐ Placed in Grade 2
☐ IEP   ☐ Retained in Grade 1

SUMMER SCHOOL RECOMMENDED
☐ Yes ☐ No

GRADING CODES

LANGUAGE ARTS & MATHEMATICS*
E – Excellent (Exceeds Expectations)
S – Satisfactory
N – Needs Improvement
*Areas not assessed are shaded.

ALL OTHER AREAS*
✓ – Satisfactory
– – Needs Improvement

PHYSICAL EDUCATION (✓,–)

	1st	2nd	3rd	4th	5th	6th
Is acquiring skills for life-long physical fitness						
General Conduct						

ART (✓,–)

	1st	2nd	3rd	4th	5th	6th
Expresses ideas creatively						
General Conduct						

MUSIC & THEATRE ARTS (✓,–)

	1st	2nd	3rd	4th	5th	6th
Expresses self through music and movement						
General Conduct						

SPECIAL PROGRAMS (☒)

Reporting Period

	1st	2nd	3rd	4th	5th	6th
Alternative Educational Program (AEP)						
Bilingual						
ESL						
Gifted/Talented						
Reading Enrichment						
Reading Recovery						
Special Education						
Speech						
Tutorials						
Additional Classroom Support						

ATTENDANCE

Reporting Period

	1st	2nd	3rd	4th	5th	6th
NUMBER DAYS PRESENT						
ABSENT						
TARDIES						

Regular attendance is important. A circled number indicates that absences and/or tardies have affected performance.

READING (Overall Performance)

Reporting Period

	1st	2nd	3rd	4th	5th	6th	End-of-Year Performance
Instructional Level							
Reading Comprehension							
Reading Fluency							
Phonics							
Reading Strategies							
Reading Vocabulary							

-PARENT CONFERENCE-

LANGUAGE (Overall Performance)

	1st	2nd	3rd	4th	5th	6th	End-of-Year Performance
Instructional Level							
Writing Composition							
Spelling							
Handwriting							
Capitalization & Punctuation							
Listening & Speaking							

-PARENT CONFERENCE-

MATHEMATICS (Overall Performance)

	1st	2nd	3rd	4th	5th	6th	End-of-Year Performance
Instructional Level							
Number Concepts							
Number Operations							
Problem Solving							
Patterns & Relationships							
Measurement/Geometry/Statistics							

-PARENT CONFERENCE-

SCIENCE (✓,–)

Uses senses & scientific tools to acquire data and classify objects/events. Applies scientific method to investigate and solve problems.

	1st	2nd	3rd	4th	5th	6th

SOCIAL STUDIES (✓,–)

Uses & demonstrates an understanding of maps/globes/pictures/charts/community symbols.
Recognizes similarities/differences among people.

	1st	2nd	3rd	4th	5th	6th

-PARENT CONFERENCE-

HEALTH

Texas Essential Knowledge and Skills are included in Science, Social Studies, and Physical Education.

CONDUCT & WORK HABITS (✓,–)

Reporting Period

	1st	2nd	3rd	4th	5th	6th
Follows directions and rules						
Uses self-discipline						
Talks at appropriate times						
Works & plays well with others						
Cooperates with adults						
Accepts responsibility for own actions						
Attempts to solve problems independently						
Stays focused and on task						
Completes work on time						
Puts forth best effort						
Completes homework						

Figure 12.2a

A comprehensive report card for kindergarten and first grade

Grades 1 - 6 Report Card Year: _____

Student: _____
Homeroom: _____   Conference _____
Teacher: _____   Time _____
School: _____   Grade _____

Attendance	1	2	3	4	TOTAL
Days Absent					
Days Present					

EVALUATION KEY
Please note your child's grade in READING and MATH. If your child is working significantly below grade level, RETENTION MAY BE CONSIDERED.

Explanation of Grades

Excellent	Good	Fair
A+ (E+) 97 - 100	B+ (S+) 87 - 89	C+ (N+) 78 - 79
A (E) 93 - 96	B (S) 83 - 86	C (N) 75 - 77
A- (E-) 90 - 92	B- (S-) 80 - 82	

Danger Of Failing	Failing
D+ 73 - 74	F (U) 0 - 69
D 71 - 72	
D- 70	

The school communicates student progress to parents in many ways.
1) Classroom evaluation
2) Written communication
3) Phone conferences
4) Report cards
5) School conferences

Both parents and teachers should take the initiative in scheduling teacher conferences as needed. All teachers have specific conference periods scheduled during the day. Parents may write the teacher a note or call the school office to request a conference time.

TAAS PROGRESS
1 = Ongoing TAAS evaluation shows your child is progressing at a rate that he/she is likely to pass the TAAS with regular classroom instruction.
2 = Ongoing TAAS evaluation shows that your child needs additional help to be prepared for TAAS.
3 = Ongoing TAAS evaluation shows that your child may have difficulty passing TAAS.

GRADING PERIOD	1	2	3	4	TOTAL
LANGUAGE ARTS / READING					
READING GRADE					
READING TAAS PROGRESS					
LANGUAGE GRADE					
WRITING TAAS PROGRESS					
GRAMMAR TAAS PROGRESS					
SPELLING GRADE					
MATH					
MATH GRADE					
MATH TAAS PROGRESS					
SCIENCE / HEALTH					
SOCIAL STUDIES					
PHYSICAL EDUCATION					
MUSIC / BAND					
ART					
THEATER ARTS					

PERSONAL DEVELOPMENT
E = Excellent S = Satisfactory N = Needing Improvement & U = Unsatisfactory

GRADING PERIOD	1	2	3	4	TOTAL
PAYS ATTENTION IN CLASS					
WORKS WITHOUT DISTURBING OTHERS					
WORKS COOPERATIVELY IN GROUPS					
FOLLOWS DIRECTIONS					
USES TIME WISELY					
COMPLETES ASSIGNED TASKS					
BRINGS MATERIALS TO CLASS					
COMPLETES WRITTEN WORK NEATLY / HANDWRITING					
COMPLETES HOMEWORK					
BEHAVIOR OUTSIDE THE CLASSROOM					
CONDUCT					
PHYSICAL EDUCATION					
MUSIC / BAND					
ART					
THEATER ARTS					

ADDITIONAL COMMENTS
First Reporting Period

Second Reporting Period

Third Reporting Period

Fourth Reporting Period

Your Child is receiving service in the following special areas:
- Reading Intervention
- Bilingual
- ESL
- Dyslexia
- Content Mastery
- Artist Tutoring/Volunteers
- Working on Grade Level
- Tutorials
- Modified Assignments
- Reduced Class
- Special Education
- Gifted/talented
- Working below grade level
- *Special Education

Local school board policy requires any student to attend before or after school tutorials if the student is not making adequate TAAS progress. All students are encouraged to attend tutorials as needed.
*Tutorials required _____

PROMOTION / RETENTION PLACEMENT
PROMOTED TO GRADE:
PLACE TO GRADE:
RETAIN IN GRADE:

Figure 12.2b
A numerical and letter symbol report card for grades 1 through 6

scores similar to most students on tests, papers, and other aspects of the class grading system. Learners whose class performance is well above the performance of most other learners receive A grades. In this system the majority of class members must receive Cs. We referred to this grading system as norm-reference in chapters 3 and 11, because the performance of an individual learner is graded relative to the performance of others.

Grades that make *absolute* comparisons are based on the degree to which a learner meets a certain predetermined standard of performance. For example, a grade of C would be given to learners who achieve scores between 70 and 80 on all tests and ratings of 3 (on a 1–5 rating scale) on papers and projects. Learners who earn 90 or better on all tests and scores of 5 on papers and projects would receive a grade of A. This system does not restrict or in any way determine the number of students who may receive a given grade. We referred to this grading system as criterion-referenced in chapter 3, because it compares the performance of an individual learner with a specific criterion of mastery for a particular area of content. Table 12.1 compares two grading systems that assign relative and absolute meanings to A through F symbols.

Whether you choose an absolute or relative standard for your grades will affect the type of tests you construct or select as well as how you teach. Choosing grade symbols reflecting absolute standards require that you use measurement tools that are performance, mastery, or criterion-referenced. Giving grades based on how others performed requires that you use norm-referenced measurement tools and scoring systems that distribute grades in the form of a bell curve.

Table 12.1
Absolute and Relative Grading Plans

Grade	Absolute Scale	Relative Scale
A	Test scores average 90% Papers, projects, etc., average to an A grade Command of knowledge is extensive	10% of class
B	Test scores average 80% Papers, projects, etc., average to a B grade Command of knowledge well beyond minimum	20% of class
C	Test scores average 70% Papers, projects, etc., average to a C grade Has command of basic knowledge	40% of class
D	Test scores average 60% Papers, projects, etc., average to a D grade Lacks some basic knowledge	20% of class
F	Test scores average below 60% Papers, projects, etc., average below a D grade Has not learned most basic concepts and principles	10% of class

Effort a learner puts into the class. Teachers often choose to have a grade describe not only what the learner achieved but also the extent of the learner's effort. They do this by assigning a certain number of points (if using a 0–100 grading system) or parts of letter grades (raising a B grade to a B+ or lowering an A grade to an A−) based on their perception of how hard the student tried. Ideally, ratings of effort and ratings of achievement should be separated on the report card. Otherwise, a parent or future teacher will be unable to accurately interpret what the single grade means. One important indication of effort is self-regulation. In earlier chapters we identified a number of important signs of learner self-regulation, such as flexibility, adaptability, acceptance of criticism, persistence, collaboration, and desire for mastery. These can be selected for their relevance to your specific classroom goals and assignments, such as group work and portfolios, and conveniently placed in the form of a checklist, as shown in chapter 9. We would suggest, however, that grades for student effort, such as might be recorded with a self-regulation checklist, not be merged with a single score representing a student's achievement. Rather, indications of student effort, if objectively recorded with a self-regulation checklist, provide useful feedback to parents as to *why* their child may have received the letter grade they did. It also can be a significant reminder to students as to what behaviors need to change for better grades to be forthcoming.

Growth in achievement over the grading period or semester. Finally, some grading systems incorporate measures of growth or progress in addition to achievement and effort. A distinction can be made between how much a student learned over time and level of learning attained at the end of the class. But, there are problems associated with basing an achievement grade's meaning solely on growth. An obvious one is that learners who enter the class with a high degree of skill have less room to improve than those who enter with low skill levels.

Generally, grades should reflect the student's level of achievement at the end of the course and not the progress made across the term. Whereas parents and their children are concerned about progress and growth, of more importance to them is the level of learning represented by the grade and whether this level is sufficient to allow the student to succeed in the next learning experience. With that said, a learner's change or growth over the course of a grading period is an important index to both parents and students who should take note of it. Upward and downward swings provide reasons for words of encouragement or for caution that can help a child become more self-regulated and work harder. Along with a measure of self-regulation, information about a student's growth can be a significant adjunct to explaining why a student received the grade that he did and what needs to be done about it.

In summary, you should plan to have one meaning (e.g., achievement of course objectives) for one grade. Indications of effort and growth, if objectively recorded, often provide meaningful complementary information as to why a particular grade was obtained. We also recommend that once you determine the meaning you wish to assign to a grade that you reflect on whether the meaning is consistent with your approach to teaching and assessment. For example, an obvious inconsistency would be if a teacher assigns grades with the intention of communicating absolute (mastery) achievement but uses a bell-shaped distribution of grades, does not allow learners multiple opportunities to improve performance, and emphasizes competition, comparison, and ability over subject mastery.

Step 3. Distinguish Reporting and Grading Factors

You may feel uneasy about the "one symbol, one meaning" suggestion proposed in step 2. Although incorporating behaviors such as growth, effort, attitude, conduct, and attendance into a grade hampers the interpretation of achievement, these factors, nevertheless, are important aspects of a learner's overall classroom behavior. So, how do teachers communicate their judgments of these other behavioral components of a learner's classroom performance?

Teachers acquire a lot of information about the learning habits of their students during the course of a school year or semester: interests, conduct, motivation, study skills, social skills, effort, and persistence, just to name a few. These behaviors represent **qualitative information** that you will want to communicate about student performance in the classroom to parents, learners, school psychologists, and future teachers. Other behaviors, using an A through F or 60 to 100 scale, will consist of **quantitative information**, scored on the basis of objective criteria and used to assign a grade. One important planning step for communicating qualitative components of learning is to distinguish at the start of the school term the qualitative information (e.g., narrative statements) you want to report to learners, parents, and other teachers from the quantitative information (e.g., numerical test, homework, and portfolio scores) you want to use in composing a final grade.

As a teacher, you have a variety of ways to communicate a student's conduct, persistence, study and social skills, and effort, such as comments on report cards, narrative statements, conferences with parents, and letters of reference. But when it comes to grading achievement, you will have to use the grading symbols required by your school district. As you work out your grading plan, identify the qualitative information you want to report to learners, parents, and future teachers to indicate study and social skills, effort, conduct, and so forth, along with the quantitative information you will use as a basis for your numerical or letter grades.

How do you hold students accountable for attendance or effort if the grading system does not allow for these? Behaviors related to attendance, cheating, and punctuality are often addressed by the school's disciplinary policy. There are usually consequences for unexcused absences, academic dishonesty, and tardiness identified in your school's disciplinary policy. With respect to assessing effort and social skills, we have suggested a number of behaviors in chapter 9 which can be conveniently placed in the form of a checklist or rating scale that can be shared with parents and learners. Another suggestion comes from an experienced middle-school teacher. On the first day of class she goes over her grading plan and identifies a list of privileges. She makes it clear that these privileges are only for those learners who demonstrate both excellent learning and good conduct and effort. Her learners get the message that all their actions in class have consequences. Some of these consequences are delivered in the form of grades; others are not.

Step 4. Identify the Components of Your Grade

When you complete the previous two steps, you will have made two important decisions. Let us assume that you choose to make your grade symbols indicate achievement of your learning objectives and that you have identified the information you want to either qualitatively report to students and parents or use in determining a final numerical grade.

Your set of reporting variables can include practice tests, rough drafts, daily homework assignments, in-class work, and written answers to oral questions. Some of these variables may be assessed by more subjective criteria (effort, progress, creativity) measured on a checklist or scale from low to high. They may be reported to students and parents but not included in the final grade. The final grade indicating mastery of course objectives represents those components that indicate achievement at the end of a unit of instruction: final drafts of portfolios, performance tests, knowledge tests, projects, completed reports, and so forth that are assessed by set criteria (right/wrong, percentage achieved) measured on a scale of A through F or 0 to 100.

How many examples (e.g., assignments, reports, tests) of each component to include in your grade will depend on the length of the grading period. One or two assessments in a 6- or 9-week grading period is too little on which to base a grade. In general, the more information you have, the more likely your grades will represent your learners' true achievement levels.

Step 5. Decide the Weight of Components in the Final Grade

Figure 12.3 shows six grade components and the weight (expressed as a percentage) of each component in determining the final grade.

This teacher has decided that certain aspects of her grading plan will be more important for determining the final grade than others. How did she go about making this decision? There are three considerations: (a) the importance of the component as indicated by the number or extent of class goals and objectives that it

Figure 12.3
Six grading components and weights for determining a final grade

Component	Weight
Homework	15%
Objective tests	20%
Performance tests	25%
Portfolio	20%
Classwork	10%
Notebook	10%

measures, (b) the uniqueness of the objectives or goals measured by different components, and (c) the reliability of the scores.

The most important consideration in determining the weight of a component is the number of learning goals and objectives it covers. For example, let us say that when you plan your seventh-grade science class you identify a total of eight learning objectives you are working toward: Two refer to developing declarative and procedural knowledge, two relate to deep understanding, three refer to problem-solving strategies, and one deals with collaborative skills. You might decide that measures of deep understanding and problem solving together should carry the most weight and collaborative skills should carry the least weight. Table 12.2 provides an illustration of an assessment blueprint for a seventh-grade science unit that covers the eight objectives.

Depending on the age of your learners, you may want to use both notebook assignments and objective tests to assess the knowledge base but performance assessments and a portfolio assignment to measure deep understanding and problem solving. If your classroom objectives focus more on higher order outcomes than on the knowledge base, be sure that the combination of the former objectives are weighted more than the latter.

Step 6. Determine How to Combine Components into a Final Grade

How many points should a test, quiz, homework assignment, portfolio, performance test, and class worksheet be worth when combining all component scores into a single score or grade? One approach is to score everything on a 100-point scale, average the scores for each component (e.g., average the scores of three objective tests), multiply each component average by the weight assigned, and add up the weighted component points to arrive at the final grade. Figure 12.4 shows this process.

Table 12.2
Assessment Blueprint for a Seventh-Grade Science Unit

	Objectives				
Content	Knowledge	Deep Understanding	Problem-Solving	Collaborative Skills	Totals
Sources of pollution	Objective test (10%)			Classwork (5%)	15%
Environmental laws		Performance essay (10%)			10%
Resource management	Objective test (10%)		Homework (15%)		25%
Ecological principles	Notebook (10%)	Performance application (15%)		Classwork (5%)	30%
Ecological solutions			Portfolio (20%)		20%
Totals	30%	25%	35%	10%	100%

Component	Weight
Homework	15%
Objective tests	20%
Performance tests	25%
Portfolio	20%
Classwork	10%
Notebook	10%

Homework Scores: 85, 79, 90, 80, 70; Average = 80.8 × .15 (weight) = 12.1 pts
Objective Test Scores: 85, 77, 93; Average = 85 × .20 = 17 pts
Performance Test Scores: 90, 100, 60, 80; Average = 82.5 × .25 = 20.6 pts
Portfolio Scores: 75, 90; Average = 82.5 × .20 = 16.5 pts
Classwork Scores: 78, 82, 90; Average = 83.3 × .10 = 8.3 pts
Notebook Scores: 86, 90, 80; Average = 85.3 × .10 = 8.5 pts

Final Grade = 12.1 + 17 + 20.6 + 16.5 + 8.3 + 8.5 = 83.0

Figure 12.4
Combining components into a final grade

This is the most commonly used procedure for combining the various subcomponent and component scores into a final grade. The principal problem with this procedure, however, is that it requires you to score every grading variable on a 0 to 100 point scale. For objective tests with 50 items and 2 points to each item, or 25 items and 4 points per item, this does not present a problem. But consider a five-question pop quiz. To grade such a quiz on a 100-point basis by assigning 20 points to each question, you would have to make minute distinctions between scores—say, a 19 from a 20, or an 8 from a 9.

How do you assign 100 points to a homework assignment that asks the student to answer three essay questions at the end of a chapter? How do you reliably distinguish 50 degrees of quality in the answers of a two-question essay test? Grading a book report on the basis of 100 points assumes that you can reliably distinguish an 85 from an 86 or a 94 from a 95. Everything we know about a scorer's ability to detect degrees of quality in a performance suggests that, at best, only 7 to 10 degrees of quality can be discriminated reliably.

Thus, the question "How many points should a grading variable be worth?" is best answered by, "As many points as can be reliably distinguished." Grade combination systems based on 100 points would tax the ability of any teacher to reliably discriminate 100 degrees of communication skill, problem-solving skill, depth of understanding, or knowledge.

The solution is to use a "percentage of total points system." Percentage of total points systems involve four steps:

1. Decide the components of your grading plan and assign each component a weight. A weight is the percentage of total points a particular component carries (see Figure 12.4).

Component:	Homework	Objective Tests	Performance Tests	Port-folio	Classwork	Note-book
Dates	8/20 9/7 9/14 9/20 9/28 10/6 TOTAL	9/17 10/7 TOTAL	9/23 10/8 TOTAL	10/7	9/2 9/6 9/14 9/23 10/5 TOTAL	10/8
Marvin	10/10 8/10 14/15 10/10 8/15 0/10 50/70	20/30 25/30 45/60	15/20 18/20 33/40	18/20	9/10 7/15 10/10 9/10 4/5 39/50	5/10
Darnell	10/10 5/10 12/15 8/10 12/15 8/10 55/70	15/30 20/30 35/60	20/20 19/20 39/40	15/20	8/10 14/15 0/10 10/10 5/5 37/50	8/10

Figure 12.5
Sample grade recording sheet, first marking period

2. Record the actual points each student earned out of the number of points possible. Leave a column for totals. (See the sample grade record in Figure 12.5.) Each component and each separate assignment has varying numbers of possible points that can be earned. Assign points to each component based on the complexity of the required performance, the length of the assignment, and your perception of your ability to assign reliable ratings.

3. Total the actual points earned for each component and divide by the maximum points possible. The results represent the percentage of points earned for each particular component. Thus, in our example from Figure 12.5, Marvin and Darnell earned the following points and totals:

	Marvin	**Darnell**
Homework	50/70 = 71%	55/70 = 79%
Objective tests	45/60 = 75%	35/60 = 58%
Performance tests	33/40 = 83%	39/40 = 98%
Portfolio	18/20 = 90%	15/20 = 75%
Classwork	39/50 = 78%	37/50 = 74%
Notebook	5/10 = 50%	8/10 = 80%

4. Multiply each of these percentages by the weights assigned, as shown below:

	Marvin	**Darnell**
Homework	71 × 0.15 = 10.6	79 × 0.15 = 11.8
Objective tests	75 × 0.20 = 15	58 × 0.20 = 11.6
Performance tests	83 × 0.25 = 20.7	98 × 0.20 = 24.5
Portfolio	90 × 0.20 = 18	75 × 0.20 = 15
Classwork	78 × 0.10 = 7.8	74 × 0.10 = 7.4
Notebook	50 × 0.10 = 5	80 × 0.10 = 8
TOTALS	77.1	78.3

5. Record the grade either as a letter grade (A = 90–100 percent, etc.) or as the percentage itself, depending on your school's grading system.

Step 7. Choose a Method for Assigning Grades

Once you have computed the total number of points that a learner has accumulated across the various grading variables or components, you then must assign the grade that appears on the report card. If the report card is one where number grades are recorded, then the learner's grade for a subject area is the number you recorded in step 6. It is more likely, however, that you will have to associate this number with a letter grade (A–F or excellent, satisfactory, or needs improvement).

There are several relative and absolute grading methods of assigning letter grades. The former approaches include the grading-on-the-curve method or norm-referenced approach (Frisbie & Waltman, 1992) discussed earlier. The following are two absolute grading methods for communicating the results of your assessments.

Fixed-Percentage Method.   Teachers who use this method establish fixed ranges of cumulative grade scores (step 6) as the basis for assigning the final letter grades. For example, a common set of ranges is: A+ = 95 to 100, A = 90 to 94, B+ = 85 to 89, B = 80 to 84, and so forth. These ranges are established at the start of the term. Thus, a learner whose cumulative point score from step 6 is an 84 would receive a grade of B on his report card.

This is called an "absolute" method of assigning grades because the results of step 6 determine the letter grade and nothing else. There are no limits set on how many As, Bs, or Fs the class can receive. Theoretically, every learner could receive an A or F, although this would be unlikely.

The principal drawback to this method of assigning grades is that the teacher does not know ahead of time how difficult or easy her assessment tasks are going to be. Consequently, in the case of difficult tests, no learner would receive an A grade. When a teacher notices that all or most of his learners are earning no higher than B grades, he may adjust his ranges or add points to everyone's scores to get more A grades. This process diminishes the interpretability of the grade.

Another problem with fixed-percentage approaches is the arbitrary nature of the cutoff scores. There is no logical reason why an 89 is a B+ and a 90 is an A. Although only 1 point separates the A and B+ student, these two grades have vastly different culturally derived meanings for learners, parents, and future teachers. Thus, the grades themselves and the ranges of points that they encompass may have little meaning in terms of mastery of course content.

Total-Point Method.   Some teachers, rather than decide ahead of time the score ranges for a letter grade, accumulate points earned by their learners on all grade components and assign grades to the point total at the end of the grading period. Advance planning is needed for this method of assigning grades. First, the teacher must decide which components go into the final grade, how many scores for each component there will be, and the maximum number of points that each component and subcomponent represents. This is decided before tests, papers, projects, or portfolios are developed and before the scoring criteria for the performance assessments have been established.

For example, a teacher may decide to use three tests of 20 points each (60 points), five quizzes of 5 points each (25 points), one project worth 25 points, a portfolio worth 40 points, a notebook worth 10 points, and six weekly assignments worth 10 points each (60 points). Thus, the total number of points that can be earned is 220 points.

Next the teacher decides that he will assign A grades to learners who earn 90 percent of the total points, B grades to those earning 80 percent of points, and so forth. This produces score ranges of A = 198 to 220, B = 176 to 197, C = 154 to 175, D = 132 to 174, and F = 110 to 131. The cutoff points are arbitrary as were those in the fixed-percentage method.

As with the fixed-percentage method, unknown task difficulty levels also limit this system. Some teachers avoid this limitation by using the average of the point totals earned by the top three students as the grade reference point. For example, if the top three learners earned total point scores of 200, 210, and 190, the teacher would average these (200) and use this total to set the ranges. Thus, 90 percent of 200 would set up a 180 to 220 range for A, 80 percent of 200 establishes a 160 to 179 range for B, and so forth. This procedure controls somewhat for difficulty level but makes the interpretation of an A grade more difficult in terms of absolute learning criteria.

Another aspect to this system is that the teacher must decide ahead of time how many points all tests are worth. For example, he decides that a unit test will be worth 20 points. As he starts building the test, he wants to ask 12 objective-type questions worth 2 points each and three short essays worth 5 points each. But this exceeds the allowable point total by 9 points. So he takes out two objective-type questions and one essay to get the correct point total. In doing this, he must be careful not to delete questions that are the most important for assessing specific content objectives. Regardless of which method of assigning grades you select, or which method your school system requires that you adopt, you will not eliminate problems of subjectivity and interpretability, particularly when the report card requires that one symbol be assigned to summarize course achievement. The important point is to recognize the limitations of whatever grading system you develop.

Step 8. Decide What to Do About Borderline Scores

Expect to have learners whose point totals are one or two points away from the next higher grade category. Thus, a few points will make a difference between passing and failing a course, getting an A or B grade, or getting a particular award. There is a tendency to give learners extra credit work to make up the few points that they need, or even to give them the extra points to raise the grade.

Here are some questions to consider in advance when deciding how to deal with borderline cases:

1. How many points below a grade cut off must a student be to be considered borderline?

2. Will every borderline learner be given the opportunity to raise his score or just those assertive or motivated enough to ask you to do so?

3. If you give extra-credit work, how closely will this be related to the objectives or goals that the learner failed to master on your tests, projects, or portfolios?

The grading plan checklist in Figure 12.6 will help you develop your grading plan.

Grading Plan Checklist

Check any that apply.

1. Have I checked my school district's school or department policy on grading?
   ☐ If yes, specify where: _____

2. What symbol system does my school or school district use?
   ☐ A–F   ☐ 0–100
   ☐ E, S+, S, S–, N (needs improvement) ☐ Other (*specify*):_____
   ☐ M (mastery), I (incomplete)

3. What behaviors will I assign a grade?
   ☐ Achievement   ☐ Effort
   ☐ Growth   ☐ Other (*specify*):_____

4. How will I separate effort and growth from achievement in my grading plan?

5. What type of comparisons do I want my grades to represent?
   ☐ Criterion-referenced (absolute comparisons)
   ☐ Norm-referenced (relative comparisons)

6. Is the type of comparison I have chosen consistent with my approach to teaching? (*explain why*)

7. What behaviors have I decided to report but not grade?
   ☐ Growth   ☐ Attendance
   ☐ Effort/persistence   ☐ Group effort
   ☐ Preparation   ☐ Others (*specify*):
   ☐ Conduct

8. For those behaviors that I will not grade, how will I report and reward them? (*specify*)

                                                                                  (*continued*)

Figure 12.6
Grading plan checklist

9. What will be the components of my grading plan, their weights, and number of scores for each?

Components	Weight	No. of Scores
☐ Quizzes	——— %	———
☐ Major tests	——— %	———
☐ Homework	——— %	———
☐ Portfolios	——— %	———
☐ Performance tests	——— %	———
☐ Classwork	——— %	———
☐ Note/lab books	——— %	———
☐ Other	——— %	———

10. What method have I chosen for combining the components to form a final grade?
   ☐ 100-point scale
   ☐ Percentage-of-total-points system
   ☐ Other (*specify*):————————————

11. What method have I chosen for assigning final grades?
   ☐ Fixed-percentage method
   ☐ Total-point method
   ☐ Other (*specify*):————————————

12. How will I handle borderline cases?

Figure 12.6
(*continued*)

After completing the checklist in Figure 12.6, use Application 12.3 to extend and clarify the decisions you made in Applications 12.1 and 12.2 regarding your purpose for a grade. This time prepare some talking points for a back-to-school night presentation to your parents on how you will grade that includes: how you will distribute grades, what components of performance will be assessed, how or if you will weight them, whether absolute or relative—or both—measures of achievement will be used, and whether you will give opportunities for extra credit.

Summary

The more you teach and discuss grades with learners and their parents, the more your grading practices will change. Expect to revise your approach to grading many times in the course of your teaching career. What should not change, however, is the

APPLICATION 12.3

Each of the following questions is a step to developing a comprehensive grading plan that you completed for Application 12.2. Now that you have read the rest of this chapter, read what you wrote for Application 12.2 and write below any changes or additions you would like to make to any of the six steps.

1. What will be my purpose for giving a report card grade?

2. How will I distribute As, Bs, Cs, and so forth, across the class?

3. What different components of performance will I consider for the final grade?

4. How will I weigh the importance of each component of the final grade?

5. Will my grades be absolute or relative measures of achievement—or both?

6. Will I give extra opportunities for student's to raise their grade? If so, how?

systematic and thoughtful nature of how you go about developing a grading plan. If you follow the steps outlined in this chapter and summarized in the checklist in Figure 12.6, you may not have a perfect grading plan, but you will have one that makes sense to you and one you can explain and justify to learners and parents. You will have also learned a lot about assessment and grading to serve you, your learners, and their parents throughout your teaching career.

Activities

1. Complete the grading plan checklist, Figure 12.6, by checking the appropriate boxes and providing the information requested.
2. Using the information you have provided on the grading plan checklist, devise a final grade from combining scores for homework, objective tests, performance tests, portfolio, classwork, and notebooks. Indicate whether you have chosen a 100-point scale or percentage of total points system for combining components and whether you have chosen the fixed-percentage or total-point method for assigning the final grade.
3. Prepare a written response to a concerned parent justifying why you chose a lesser weight on your grading plan checklist for "objective tests" that measure recall and recognition than you did for portfolio and performance assessments that measure higher thought processes.
4. A parent asks you at parent–teachers night to justify why her son got a B when he missed an A by only 1 point. She explains how hard her son has worked in your class and offers to have him do an assignment for extra credit, if you would change his grade to an A. Prepare a response.

Suggested Reading

Stiggins, R. J., Frisbie, D. A., & Griswold, P. A. (1989). Inside high school grading practices: Building a research agenda. *Educational Measurement: Issues and Practice, 8,* 5–14. *This text concisely and clearly highlights the critical issues any teacher must grapple with when designing a grading plan.*

Glossary of Key Concepts

Age-Equivalent scores A learner's score on a test relative to the average performance of the norm group at the same age.

Assessment Blueprint A guide to developing a test used to identify the behaviors and content to be tested and content that has been taught.

Assessment Triangle The processes of cognition, observation, and interpretation representing the three key elements underlying any assessment.

Authentic Learning Assessment A type of assessment determining if a learner has not only deep understanding by challenging the learner with real-world tasks that not only require the recall of information but also knowledge construction or organization to solve problems requiring higher order thinking and metacognition. Also called performance assessment.

Cognition Cognition refers to a model, a set of assumptions or beliefs about how learners learn and become competent in various subject areas.

Cognitive Strategies A variety of thinking skills that include learning-to-learn skills, general thinking skills, reasoning skills, and problem-solving skills.

Consequence Validity The degree to which the assessment informs the teacher's behavior and changes the student's behavior.

Construct Relevancy An aspect of construct validity in which the behavior being measured, such as factual knowledge, not only correlates with other valid measures of the same construct but also does not correlate with other behaviors irrelevant to what is being measured, such as the reading level of the learner.

Construct Validity The degree to which the behaviors you decide to observe and measure correlate with the results of other well-established, measures of the same construct.

Constructivism An approach to teaching and learning in which learners are provided the opportunity to construct their own sense of what is being learned by building internal connections or relationships among the ideas and facts being taught.

Criterion-Referenced Assessment Comparison of the performance of an individual learner to a specific criterion of mastery for a particular area of content.

Declarative Knowledge Knowledge representing facts, concepts, rules, and generalizations; how they are related to one another and how their relationship changes over time.

Deep Understanding A level of understanding enabling the learner to organize new knowledge into concepts and generalizations, to see relationships and patterns, and to apply this understanding to novel problems.

Domain-General Strategies Routines or sequences of actions that are useful in any subject matter domain, including learning-to-learn or metacognitive skills.

Domain-Specific Basic Skills Procedural knowledge that is specific to a knowledge domain that requires the learner to spontaneously execute a sequence of actions smoothly, efficiently, and automatically, for example, focusing a microscope.

Domain-Specific Knowledge   Knowledge that contains the facts, concepts, rules, and generalizations pertaining to a specific subject matter area, or domain.

Domain-Specific Strategies   Procedural knowledge that is specific to a subject-matter domain requiring conscious, controlled, deliberate actions by the learner, for example, writing an essay.

Extended-Response Essay Question   An essay question that allows the student to determine the length and complexity of an answer. This type of question is most useful for assessing behaviors at the analysis, synthesis, and evaluation levels of the cognitive domain and for assessing deep understanding.

Formative Assessment   Assessment conducted to help diagnose classroom learning problems and to suggest ways to overcome them.

Frame of Reference for Assessment   Lenses through which the teacher collects and interprets information about learners, which include the norm-, criterion-, and growth-referenced approaches to assessment.

Grade-Equivalent Scores   A learner's score on a test relative to the average performance of the norm group at the same grade.

Growth-Referenced Assessment   Comparison of the performance of an individual learner at the end of instruction with that learner's performance before instruction.

High-Stakes Assessment   Assessments that make decisions about learners related to promotion, graduation, and future opportunities.

Index of Item Difficulty   The proportion of individuals taking a multiple-choice test who answered a particular item correctly.

Index of Item Discrimination   A statistic determining whether each item on a multiple-choice test reflects the overall trait or ability that the test is presumed to measure.

Instructional Validity of a Test   The degree to which learners are asked to do what was taught during their lessons and with the same degree of emphasis.

Interpretation   The way the teacher makes sense of assessment information in order to make judgments about learners' and decisions about what to do next.

Knowledge Base   Everything we know about a topic and the connections among its parts. Knowledge bases are dynamic and ever changing and become increasingly organized as the learner acquires more information.

Learning Hierarchies   A system whereby behaviors and their underlying thought processes are organized into categories from least to most complex.

Metacognition or Metacognitive Strategies   Conscious recognition of and control by the learner of the cognitive strategies being used.

Natural Assessment Setting   A setting in which an assessment occurs without the observer intervening or interrupting the normal flow of events, often accomplished by embedding the assessment in the context of a lesson.

Norm Group   The group of individuals upon whom the test is standardized and serves as the reference group.

Norm-Referenced Assessment   Comparison of the performance of an individual learner on a test with the average performance of the group to which he or she belongs.

Observation   The variety of tools that teachers use to gather information about their learners.

Performance Assessment   A type of assessment determining if a learner has deep understanding by challenging the learner with real-world tasks that require not only the recall of information but also the knowledge construction or organization to solve problems requiring higher order thinking and metacognition. Also called authentic assessment.

Portfolio Assessment   The systematic accumulation of student products that tell a story of a learner's growth in proficiency, long-term achievement, and significant accomplishments in a given area.

Procedural or "Know-How" Knowledge   Knowledge telling learners how to perform a sequence of actions leading to a process, for example, focusing a microscope or writing a composition.

Proceduralist View of Memory   A model of memory in contrast to the structuralist view that emphasizes the fluid processes involved in continually creating and re-creating new memories. The proceduralist view says that our memories are constantly changing, being recreated and growing richer with new experiences.

Qualitative Information   Student information that may be derived subjectively, for example, persistence, motivation, interests, social skills, effort, and so forth, and used by the teacher to communicate student behavior to parents, learners, and, future teachers that may help explain student grades.

Quality Assurance   The process of building validity and reliability into an assessment system.

Quantitative Information   Student information that may be derived objectively, for example, from numerical test, homework, and portfolio scores, and used by the teacher to assign a grade.

Recall   Simple factual knowledge assessed by tasks that ask learners to fill in blanks, list things in order, write down words, outline, or recite facts, names, or dates, and so forth.

Recognition   Simple factual knowledge assessed by tasks that ask learners to choose, select, or match.

Reliability   The degree to which a test is dependable, that is, produces the same results on repeated administrations.

Restricted-Response Essay Question   A question that poses a specific problem for which the student must recall proper information, organize it in a suitable manner, derive a defensible conclusion, and express it according to specific criteria.

Rightstart Math Program   An innovative program for kindergarten and first-grade students that teaches them learning strategies making them successful at basic computation and teaches them to avoid the arithmetic errors commonly made by children of this age.

Rubrics   Checklists, rating scales, and holistic scoring guides in which each level of behavior assessed is carefully defined to help provide an objective basis for judging the quality of a learners' response to a task.

Self-Efficacy Motivational Theory   A motivational theory that stresses the importance of learners' beliefs that they can succeed at school tasks, especially when they begin, persist at, and master tasks they think they are good at.

Self-Judgment   Self-judgment is a mental process self-regulated learners use to learn.

Self-Observation   Self-observation is a mental process self-regulated learners use to be informed about their achievement of personal goals.

Self-Reaction   A state in which self-regulated learners feel good about their progress and work and study harder as a result of feeling that they are the principal agents of their own learning.

Simple Factual Knowledge   Knowledge referring to the facts, dates, names, expressions, or labels a person knows without concern for depth of understanding or the ability to use this information.

Simulated Assessment Setting   A setting in which the assessment is conducted in a controlled but authentic environment, usually necessary when the procedure being taught is one that naturally occurs outside a classroom context, such as job interviewing, speaking before the school board, or ordering food in a restaurant.

Social Cognitive Theory   A theory about learning that starts from the fact that most learning, and especially classroom learning, occurs around other learners, that is, in a social context. In social settings, learners observe what others say and do and make comparisons to what they themselves say and do.

Standardization   Statistical standards allowing the comparison of a learner's score with those of a defined reference group. Also, an assessment instrument that is administered in the same manner at all times to all learners according to explicit instructions.

Structural View of Memory   A model of memory in contrast to the proceduralist view that considers memories to be static, representing information that has a particular location in the brain where they reside relatively permanently in their original form.

Structured Assessment Setting   A setting in which an assessment is scheduled to occur in a particular place and at a certain time, as opposed to occurring naturally in the context of a lesson or ongoing performance. The teacher asks the learner to execute a behavior rather than wait for it to occur.

Summative Assessment   Assessment conducted for the purpose of assigning a grade or rank to classroom learners.

Taxonomies of Educational Objectives   Systems for helping teachers identify the types of cognitive, affective, and psychomotor behavior they expect their students to learn.

Validity   The degree to which a test measures what it is intended to measure.

References

AERA, APA, NCME (1999). *Standards for educational and psychological testing*. Washington, DC: American Educational Research Association.

Alleman, J., & Brophy, J. (1997). Elementary social studies: Instruments, activities and standards. In G. D. Phye (Ed.), *Handbook of classroom assessment: Learning, adjustment and achievement* (pp. 321-359). San Diego: Academic Press.

Anderman, E. M., & Maehr, M. L. (1994). Motivation and schooling in the middle grades. *Review of Educational Research, 64,* 287-310.

Anderson, J. P. (1983). The architecture of cognition. Cambridge, MA: Harvard University Press.

Baddely, A. D. (1986). *Working memory*. New York: Oxford University Press.

Baddely, A. D. (1998). *Your memory: A user's guide*. London: Prion.

Baker, E. (1994). Making performance assessment work: The road ahead. *Educational Leadership, 51*(6), 58-62.

Bandura, A. (1986). *Social foundations of thought and action: A social cognitive theory*. Upper Saddle River, NJ: Prentice Hall.

Bandura, A. (1977). Self-efficacy: Toward a unified theory of behavioral change. *Psychological Review, 84,* 191-215.

Bloom, B., Engelhart, M., Furst, E., Hill, W., & Krathwohl, D. (1984). *Taxonomy of educational objectives. Handbook I: Cognitive domain.* New York: Longman.

Borich, G. (2003). *Observation skills for effective teaching* (4th ed.). Upper Saddle River, NJ: Merrill/Prentice Hall.

Borich, G., & Tombari, M. (1997). *Educational psychology: A contemporary approach* (2nd ed.). New York: Longman.

Bransford, J., Brown, A., & Cocking R. (1999). *How people learn: Brain, mind, experience, and school.* Washington, DC: The National Academy of Sciences.

Brown, J. S., & Burton, R. R. (1978). Diagnostic models for procedural bugs in basic mathematical skills. *Cognitive Science, 2,* 155-192.

Brown, J. S., & VanLehn, K. (1980). Repair theory: A generative theory of bugs in procedural skills. *Cognitive Science, 4*(4), 379-426.

Bruer, J. T. (1993). *Schools for thought: A science of learning in the classroom.* Cambridge, MA: MIT Press.

Bullough, R. V. (1989). *First-year teacher: A case study.* New York: Teachers College Press.

Ceci, S. J., & Liker, S. R. (1986). A day at the races: A study of IQ, expertise, and cognitive complexity. *Journal of Experimental Psychology, General, 115*(3), 255-266.

Champagne, A. B., Klopfer, L. E., Desta, A. T., & Squires, D. A. (1988). Structural representations of students' knowledge before and after science instruction. *Journal of Research in Science Teaching, 18,* 97-111.

Cizek, G. J. (1997). Learning, achievement and assessment: Constructs at a crossroads. In G. D. Phye (Ed.), *Handbook of classroom assessment: Learning, adjustment and achievement* (pp. 2-32). San Diego: Academic Press.

Cole, N. S. (1981). Bias in testing. *American Psychologist, 36*(10), 1067-1077.

Collins, A., Brown, J. S., & Newman, S. E. (1989). Cognitive apprenticeship: Teaching the crafts of reading, writing, and mathematics. In L. B. Resnick (Ed.), *Knowing, learning, and instruction: Essays in honor of Robert Glaser* (pp. 453–494). Hillsdale, NJ: Erlbaum.

Crowl, T. K., Kaminsky, S., & Podell, D. M. (1997). *Educational psychology: Windows on teaching.* Dubuque, IA: Brown and Benchmark.

Danielson, D., & Abrutyn, L. (1997) *Introduction to using portfolios in the classroom.* Alexandria, VA: ASCD.

Dansereau, D. F. (1988). Cooperative learning strategies. In C. E. Weinstein, E. T. Goetz, & P. A. Alexander (Eds.), *Learning and study strategies: Issues in assessment, instruction, and evaluation* (pp. 103–120). San Diego: Academic Press.

Deci, E. L., Vallerand, R. J., Pelletier, L. G., & Ryan, R. M. (1991). Motivation and education: The self-determination perspective. *Educational Psychologist, 26,* 325–346.

DiSessa, A., & Minstrell, J. (1998). Cultivating conceptual change with benchmark lessons. In J. G. Greeno and S. Goldman (Eds.), *Thinking practices in learning and teaching science and mathematics.* Mahwah, NJ: Lawrence Erlbaum Associates.

Edmondson, K. (2000). Assessing science understanding through concept maps. In J. Mintzes, J. H. Wandersee, & J. D. Novak (Eds.), *Assessing science understanding: A human constructivist view* (pp. 15–40). San Diego: Academic Press.

Elliot, S. N., & Shapiro, E. S. (1990). Intervention techniques and programs for academic performance problems. In T. B. Gutkin & C. R. Reynolds (Eds.), *The handbook of school psychology* (2nd ed., pp. 637–662). New York: Wiley.

Frisbie, D. A., & Waltman, K. K. (1992, Fall). Developing a personal grading plan. *Educational Measurement: Issues and Practice, 11,* 35–42.

Gagné, E. D., Yekovich, C. W., & Yekovich, F. R. (1993). *The cognitive psychology of school learning* (2nd ed.). New York: HarperCollins.

Gagné, R. M. (1985). *Conditions of learning* (4th ed.). New York: Holt.

Gardner, H. (1993). *Multiple intelligences: The theory in practice.* New York: Basic Books.

Gipps, C. V. (1995). *Beyond testing: Towards a theory of educational assessment.* Washington, DC: Falmer Press.

Glaser, R., Lesgold, A., & Lajoie, S. (1987). Toward a cognitive theory for the measurement of achievement. In R. R. Ronning, J. Glover, J. C. Conoley, & J. C. Witt (Eds.), *The influence of cognitive psychology on testing and measurement* (pp. 289–313). Hillsdale, NJ: Erlbaum.

Goetz, E. T., Alexander, P. A., & Ash, M. J. (1992). *Educational psychology: A classroom perspective.* Upper Saddle River, NJ: Merrill/Prentice Hall.

Griffin, S., & Case, R. (1975). *Rightstart: An early intervention program for insuring that children's first formal learning of arithmetic is grounded in their intuitive knowledge of number.* Year 2 report submitted to the James S. McDonnell Foundation.

Gronlund, N. E. (1993). *How to make achievement tests and assessments* (5th ed.). Boston: Allyn & Bacon.

Hall, V. C., & Edmondson, B. (1992). Relative importance of aptitude and prior domain knowledge on immediate and delayed posttests. *Journal of Educational Psychology, 84,* 219–223.

Haney, W. (1981). Validity, vaudeville and values: A short history of social concerns over standardized testing. *American Psychologist, 36*(10), 1021–1034.

Harrow, A. (1972). *A taxonomy of the psychomotor domain: A guide for developing behavioral objectives.* New York: David McKay.

Hoy, L., & Gregg, M. (1994). *Assessment in special education.* Pacific Grove, CA: Brooks/Cole.

Hunt, E., & Minstrell, J. (1994). A cognitive approach to the teaching of physics. In K. McGilly (Ed.), *Classroom lessons: Integrating cognitive theory* (pp. 51–74). Cambridge, MA: MIT Press.

Jensen, A. (1998). *The "g" factor: The science of mental ability.* Westport, CT: Praeger.

Johnson, D., & Johnson, R. (1991). *Learning together and alone* (3rd ed.). Upper Saddle River, NJ: Prentice Hall.

Kandel, E. R. (1991). Cellular mechanisms of learning and the biological basis of individuality. In E. R. Kandel, J. H. Schwartz, & J. M. Jessell (Eds.), *Principles of neural science.* New York: McGraw-Hill.

Kandel, E. R. (1999). *Principles of neuroscience.* New York: McGraw-Hill.

Kosslyn, S. M., & Koenig, O. (1992). *Wet-mind: The new cognitive neuroscience.* New York: Free Press.

Kubiszyn, T., & Borich, G. (2003). *Educational testing and measurement: Classroom applications and practice* (7th ed.). New York: Wiley.

Landuaer, T. K. (1998). Learning and representing verbal meaning: The latent semantic analysis theory.

Current Directions in Psychological Science, 7(5), 161–164.

Landuaer, T. K., Foltz, P. W., & Laham, D. (1998). An introduction to latent semantic analysis. *Discourse Processes*, 25(2–3), 259–284.

Lane, S. (1993, Summer). The conceptual framework for the development of a mathematics performance assessment instrument. *Educational Measurement: Issues and Practice*, 16–23.

Lieberman, D. A. (1992). *Learning: Behavior and cognition* (2nd ed.). Pacific Grove, CA: Brooks/Cole.

Macintosh, N. (1998). *IQ and human intelligence*. Oxford, UK: Oxford University Press.

Mayer, R. E. (1987). *Educational psychology: A cognitive approach*. Boston: Little, Brown.

McGilly, K. (1994). *Classroom lessons: Integrating cognitive theory*. Cambridge, MA: MIT Press.

McKeown, M. G., & Beck, I. L. (1990). The assessment and characterization of young learners' knowledge of a topic in history. *American Educational Research Journal*, 27, 688–726.

Mertler, C. (2001). Designing scoring rubrics for your classroom. *Practical Assessment, Research, & Evaluation*, 7(25). Available online: http://ericae.net/pare/getvn.asp? V =7&n=25.

Messick, S. (1989). Validity. In R. L. Linn (Ed.), *Educational measurement* (3rd ed., pp. 13–104). New York: Macmillan.

Minstrell, J. (2000). Student thinking and related assessment: Creating a facet-based learning environment. In N. S. Raju, J. W. Pellegrino, M. W. Bertenthal, K. J. Mitchell, and L. R. Jones (Eds.). *Grading the nation's report card: Research from the evaluation of NAEP* (pp. 44–73). Washington, DC: National Academy Press.

Mintzes, J., Wandersee, J. H., & Novak, J. (Eds.). (2000). *Assessing science understanding: A human constructivist view*. San Diego: Academic Press.

Mislevy, R., Steinberg, L., Almond, R., Haertel, G., & Penuel, W. (2000). Leverage points for improving educational assessment. Paper prepared for the Technology Design Workshop, Standford Research Institute, Menlo Park, CA, February 25–26.

National Commission on Excellence in Education (1983). *A nation at risk: The imperative for education reform*. Washington, DC: U.S. Department of Education.

National Research Council (2001). *Knowing what students know: The science and design of educational assessment*. Washington, DC: National Academy Press.

Neath, I. (1998). *Human memory: An introduction to research, data, and theory*. Pacific Grove, CA: Brooks/Cole.

Newman, F. M. (1997). Authentic assessment in social studies: Standards and examples. In G. D. Phye (Ed.), *Handbook of classroom assessment: Learning, adjustment and achievement* (pp. 360–380). San Diego: Academic Press.

O'Neil, H. F., & Klein, D. C. (1997). Feasibility of machine scoring of concept maps (CSE Technical Report 460). Los Angeles, CA: Center for Research on Evaluation Standards and Student Testing, University of California.

Oosterhof, A. (1996). *Developing and using classroom assessments*. Upper Saddle River, NJ: Merrill/Prentice Hall.

Orfield, G., & Kornhaber, M. (Eds.) (2001). *Raising standards or raising barriers?: Inequality and high stakes testing in public education*. New York: The Century Foundation.

Pressley, M. (1995). *Advanced educational psychology for educators, researchers, and policymakers*. New York: Harper Collins.

Pressley, M., Borkowski, J. G., & O'Sullivan, J. T. (1984). Memory strategy instruction is made of this: Metamemory and durable strategy use. *Educational Psychologist*, 19, 94–107.

Pressley, M., Borkowski, J. G., & O'Sullivan, J. T. (1985). Children's metamemory and the teaching of memory strategies. In D. L. Forrest-Pressley, G. E. MacKinnon, & T. G. Waller (Eds.), *Metacognition, cognition, and human performance* (pp. 111–153). New York: Academic Press.

Quellmalz, E. S. (1987). Developing reasoning skills. In J. R. Baron & R. J. Sternberg (Eds.), *Teaching thinking skills: Theory and practice*. New York: Freeman.

Quellmalz, E. S. (1991). Developing criteria for performance assessments: The missing link. *Applied Measurement in Education*, 4(4), 319–332.

Quellmalz, E. S., & Hoskyn, J. (1997). Classroom assessment of reasoning strategies. In G. D. Phye (Ed.), *Handbook of classroom assessment: Learning, adjustment and achievement* (pp. 103–130). San Diego: Academic Press.

Reber, A., Walkenfeld, F., & Hernstadt, R. (1991). Implicit and explicit learning: Individual differences and IQ.

Journal of Experimental Psychology: Learning, Memory, and Cognition, 17, 888-896.

Reschly, D. J. (1981). Psychological testing in educational classification and placement. *American Psychologist, 36*(10), 1094-1102.

Resnick, L. (1976). Learning in school and out. *Educational Researcher, 8*(3), 13-20.

Resnick, L. B., Nesher, P., Leonard, F., Magone, M., Omanson, S., & Peled, I. (1989). Conceptual bases of arithmetic errors: The case of decimal fractions. *Journal for Research in Mathematics Education, 204*(1), 8-27.

Ryan, K. (Ed.). (1992). *The rollercoaster year: Essays by and for beginning teachers.* New York: Harper-Collins.

Scardamalia, M., & Bereiter, C. (1986). Research on written composition. In M. C. Wittrock (Ed.), *Handbook of research on teaching* (3rd ed., pp. 778-803). New York: Macmillan.

Schacter, D. L. (1996). *Searching for memory: The brain, the mind, and the past.* New York: Basic Books.

Schacter, D. L. (2001). *The seven sins of memory: How the mind forgets and remembers.* Boston: Houghton Mifflin.

Schneider, W., Korkel, J., & Weinert, F. E. (1989). Domain-specific knowledge and memory performance: A comparison of high- and low-aptitude children. *Journal of Educational Psychology, 81,* 306-312.

Schunk, D. H. (2001). Social cognitive theory and self-regulated learning. In B. J. Zimmerman & D. H. Schunk (Eds.), *Self-regulated learning and academic achievement: Theoretical perspectives* (pp.125-152) Mahwah, NJ: Erlbaum.

Shavelson, R. J., & Baxter, G. (1992). What we've learned about assessing hands-on science. *Educational Leadership, 49*(8), 20-25.

Shavelson, R. J., & Ruiz-Primo, M. A. (2000). On the psychometrics of assessing science understanding. In J. Mintzes, J. Wandersee, & J. Novak (Eds.). *Assessing science understanding: A human constructivist view* (pp. 303-341). San Diego: Academic Press.

Slavin, R. (1987). Ability grouping and student achievement in elementary schools: A best evidence synthesis. *Review of Educational Research, 57,* 273-336.

Smith, C. (1990). *Cognitive studies for educational practice.* Paper presented at the McDonnell Foundation program meeting, Carnegie Mellon University.

Squire, L., & Kandel, E. (1999). *Memory: From mind to molecules.* New York: Scientific American Library.

Stecher, B. M., & Herman, J. L. (1997). Using portfolios for large scale assessment. In G. D. Phye (Ed.), *Handbook of classroom assessment: Learning, adjustment and achievement.* San Diego: Academic Press.

Sternberg, R. (1989). *The triarchic mind.* New York: Viking.

Sternberg, R. (1996). *Successful intelligence: How practical and creative intelligence determine success in life.* New York: Simon & Schuster.

Stiggens, R. (1994). *Student-centered classroom assessment.* Upper Saddle River, NJ: Prentice Hall.

Sulzer-Azaroff, B., Drabman, R. M., Greer, R. D., Hall, R. V., Iwata, B. A., & O'Leary, S. G. (1988). *Behavior analysis in education, 1968-1987.* Lawrence, KS: Society for the Experimental Analysis of Behavior.

Thorndike, R. L., Cunningham, G. K., Thorndike, R. L., & Hagen, E. P. (1997). *Measurement and evaluation in psychology and education* (7th ed.). Upper Saddle River, NJ: Merrill/Prentice Hall.

Tuckman, B. W. (1988). *Testing for teachers.* San Diego: Harcourt Brace Jovanovich.

Walker, C. H. (1987). Relative importance of domain knowledge and overall aptitude on acquisition of domain-related information. *Cognition and Instruction, 4,* 25-42.

Wechsler, D. B. (1963). Engrams, memory storage, and mnemonic coding. *American Psychologist, 18,* 149-153.

Wertheimer, R. (1990). The geometry proof tutor: An "intelligent" computer-based tutor in the classroom. *Mathematics Teacher, 33,* 308-317.

White, B. Y., & Frederickson, J. R. (1998). Inquiry, modeling and metacognition: Making science accessible to all students. *Cognition and Instruction 16*(1), 3-117.

White, B. Y., & Frederiksen, J. R. (2000). Metacognitive facilitation: An approach to making scientific inquiry accessible to all. In J. Minstrell and E. van Zee (Eds.), *Inquiring into inquiry learning and teaching in science* (pp. 330-370). Washington, DC: American Association for the Advancement of Science.

White, B. Y., & Horwitz, P. (1988). Computer microworlds and conceptual change: A new approach to science education. In P. Ramsden (Ed.), *Improving learning: New perspectives* (pp. 63-98). New York: Kogan Page.

Wiggins, G. (1993). *Assessing student performance.* San Francisco: Jossey-Bass.

Wiggins, G. (1998). *Educative assessment.* Upper Saddle River, NJ: Prentice Hall.

Wiggins, G., & McTighe, J. (1998). *Understanding by design*. Alexandria, VA: ASCD.

Wiggins, G., & McTighe, J. (1998). *Understanding by design*. Upper Saddle River, NJ: Prentice Hall.

Wilson, M., Draney, K., & Kennedy, C. (2001). *GradeMap*. In Knowing what students know. Washington, DC: National Research Council (p. 9).

Wilson, M., Draney, K., & Kennedy, C. (2001). *GradeMap*. Berkeley, CA: BEAR Center, University of California.

Wineburg, S. (1998). Reading Abraham Lincoln: An expert-expert study in the interpretation of historical texts. *Cognitive Science 22*, 319-346.

Wolf, D., & Reardon, S. (1996). Access to excellence through new forms of student assessment. In J. B. Baron & D. P. Wolf (Eds.), *Performance-based student assessment: Challenges and possibilities* (pp 1-3). Chicago: University of Chicago Press.

Ysseldyke, J. E., & Marston, D. (1990). The use of assessment information to plan instructional interventions: A review of the research. In T. B. Gutkin & R. Reynolds (Eds.), *The handbook of school psychology* (2nd ed., pp. 663-684). New York: Wiley.

Zimmerman, B. J., & Schunk, D. H. (2001). *Self-regulated learning and academic achievement: Theoretical perspectives*. Mahwah, NJ: Erlbaum.

Author Index

Subject Index

Absolute grading. *See* Fixed-percentage (absolute) grading
Affective domain, 53
  characterization level in, 50–51
  organization level in, 50
  receiving level in, 49–50
  responding level in, 50
  valuing level in, 50
Age-equivalent scores, 266–267, 302
Aptitude tests, 13
Assessment. *See also* Science, learning and assessment
  authentic learning, 31–32, 302
  authentic performance, 200–202
  collaborative, 16, 205
  computer, 115, 121
  formative vs. summative, 1
  good thinking, 7, 16
  link, teaching and, 29–32, 234
  memory, 12–13
  metacognition, 16
  novice-expert studies and, 13, 162
  online, 186–188
  performance changes and, 31
  purpose of, 1, 34
  Rightstart Program and, 30
  self-regulated, 17
  teacher activities and, 20
  ThinkerTools program and, 31, 186–188
  tracking, 29
Assessment blueprints, 68–69, 293, 302
Assessment framework development. *See also specific categories*

evaluating systems of, 56–57
frames of reference category of, 34–43
outcome determination category of, 46–59
purpose formulation category of, 43–46
teacher activities for, 59–60
Assessment triangle, 302
  cognition and, 3, 302
  development of, 2–3
  interpretation and, 3, 303
  observation and, 3, 303
  standardized tests and, 269–276
Authentic learning assessment, 302
  steps in, 31–32
Authentic performance assessment. *See also* Performance assessment
  authenticity in, 202
  communication in, 202
  developing, 200–201
  knowledge construction in, 201
  strategic thinking in, 201–202

Behavior, 291–292

Calculators, assessment checklist for, 149
Classroom instruction
  evaluation of, 273
  good thinking development and, 15
  knowledge construction role of, 15
  test settings and, 143
Cognition component, assessment triangle, 3, 302
Cognition model components, 269
Cognitive apprenticeship, 233

313